ARTIFACTS
FROM NINETEENTH-CENTURY AMERICA

ARTIFACTS
FROM NINETEENTH-CENTURY AMERICA

Elizabeth B. Greene

Daily Life through Artifacts

GREENWOOD

An Imprint of ABC-CLIO, LLC

Santa Barbara, California • Denver, Colorado

Library of Congress Cataloging-in-Publication Data

Names: Greene, Elizabeth B., author.
Title: Artifacts from nineteenth-century America / Elizabeth B. Greene.
Description: First edition. | Santa Barbara : Greenwood, 2022. | Series: Daily life through artifacts | Includes bibliographical references and index.
Identifiers: LCCN 2022030980 (print) | LCCN 2022030981 (ebook) | ISBN 9781440871863 (hardback) | ISBN 9781440871870 (ebook)
Subjects: LCSH: Material culture—United States—History—19th century. | United States—Social life and customs—History—19th century. | United States—Antiquities. | Americana.
Classification: LCC E161 .G747 2022 (print) | LCC E161 (ebook) | DDC 973.5—dc23/eng/20220727
LC record available at https://lccn.loc.gov/2022030980
LC ebook record available at https://lccn.loc.gov/2022030981

ISBN: 978-1-4408-7186-3 (print)
      978-1-4408-7187-0 (ebook)

27 26 25 24 23   1 2 3 4 5

This book is also available as an eBook.

Greenwood
An Imprint of ABC-CLIO, LLC

ABC-CLIO, LLC
147 Castilian Drive
Santa Barbara, California 93117
www.abc-clio.com

This book is printed on acid-free paper ∞
Manufactured in the United States of America

CONTENTS

RELIGIOUS LIFE

SLAVERY AND SERVITUDE

TOOLS AND WEAPONS

TRANSPORTATION AND TRAVEL

WORK AND EDUCATION

PREFACE

It may be a cliché to say that during the 19th century American society was transformed, but of course it was. Consider this—what was the daily life like for a farmer in Pennsylvania in 1800, as compared to a New York City office worker in 1900? What tools were available in 1900 that made life easier? By that year, a middle-class New York City resident had access to central heat, running water, telephone, electric light and electric appliances, long-distance trains and short-distance trolleys, safety bicycles, and typewriters. The farmer in Pennsylvania in 1800 still toiled with simple tools like the butter churn, and without the time-saving help of the mechanical reaper. The population of the United States in 1800 was 5,308,000 (of which 893,600 were enslaved) according to the U.S. Census. In 1900, it had grown to 76,212,000. In 1800, only sixteen states comprised the United States; by 1900, there were forty-five, stretching from the Atlantic to the Pacific and fulfilling the goal of Manifest Destiny. The California Gold Rush in 1848 enticed approximately 300,000 eager prospectors to take the long, treacherous trek across the country to search for gold, setting the stage for California to become the first Pacific state to join the union in 1850. In 1800, slaves were still being imported from Africa through the transatlantic slave trade. And with the invention of the cotton gin in the early 19th century, more slaves were demanded for the harvest of the lucrative cotton crops in the Deep South. By 1900, slaves had been officially emancipated for thirty-five years, and Reconstruction had introduced civil rights to African Americans. However, by the turn of the 20th century, the reaction against civil rights had begun and the racist Jim Crow laws were already entrenched.

The artifacts in this book illuminate the transformation that took place in the United States during the 19th century by examining objects in a broad swath of classifications. This volume is organized into twelve categories, and within those categories are the artifacts themselves, which are listed alphabetically. The categories are the following:

Communications
Cooking and Food
Entertainment
Grooming, Clothing, and Accessories
Health and Medicines
Household Items
Political and Civic Life
Religious Life
Slavery and Servitude
Tools and Weapons
Transportation and Travel
Work and Education

Within each of the categories is a selection of objects that tell a story about what was happening in the lives of Americans at that particular time. Some of the artifacts are transformational to society, like the telephone, telegraph, or transcontinental railroad. Some of the artifacts are deeply personal objects that explain something about the life of the user, like a corset or a shaving mug. A humble item like a corset can make a statement about the woman who wore it and what her life must have been like. Some artifacts, like the slave shackles included here, can explain a little bit about the horrors of slavery. The crude surgical instruments of a Civil War doctor explain a lot about the state of medical care at the time, though we ascertain through further research how the wide-ranging experience gained by the surgeons during the war was able to transform the medical profession. A simple piece of mourning jewelry explains how death was accepted and embraced in the 19th century, something that may be difficult to appreciate in today's death-phobic society. All these carefully chosen artifacts tell us something significant about the person who used them, or the person who invented them, or the person who made them. In this book we examine each artifact by describing it in detail and then broadening the examination to include its significance and its historical context.

INTRODUCTION

At the dawn of the 19th century, the United States was a fledgling nation, a rural expanse with a small population scattered along the East Coast. It was weak militarily and economically dependent on Europe for its manufactured goods. The United States was still seen in Europe as a fruitful source of raw materials, as it had been for centuries. The Industrial Revolution was underway in Britain, and the United States was lagging behind. But by the end of the century, the United States had become the leader of the world in manufacturing output, surpassing Britain for the first time. A technological revolution was taking place at the end of the century that modernized all aspects of American society. The concept of Manifest Destiny emboldened the young country to surge inexorably westward in a feat of expansionism that was believed to be both justified and preordained. The 19th century was an indisputably transformative period in the history of the United States, and in this volume we will examine a selection of artifacts that can help explain what was taking place in this dynamic new society.

The relentless industrialization of the country during the 19th century was sparked by a number of crucial inventions that had a momentous influence on American society. A transportation revolution was underway beginning with the invention of the steamboat by Robert Fulton, which allowed for transportation of goods up the Mississippi River and stimulated the development of the Midwest. Even more significant was the completion of the transcontinental railroad in 1869, which knit together the disparate regions of the now-massive expanse that made up the United States by the second half of the 19th century. Nearly forgotten today is the importance of the introduction of the safety bicycle in the 1880s that transformed personal travel, demanded better roads, and presaged the development of the automobile. A revolution in long-distance communications took place with the introduction of the telegraph in the 1840s. The invention of the telephone in 1876 was the next critical step in the communications revolution. On another front, over the span of the century, the nature of work was transformed. A once-rural and agricultural economy metamorphosed into an industrial and corporate one. Homely butter churns, and other tools of the early 19th century farm economy, were eventually succeeded by new inventions like cotton gins and mechanical reapers that revolutionized the farmers' lives. Farm families in Lowell, Massachusetts, took advantage of the area's industrialization by sending their young daughters to the textile mills where they worked and were able to send home money and enjoy the opportunity to contribute to the literary magazine *The Lowell Offering*. The burgeoning whaling industry attracted all types of men to volunteer for a long, arduous, and risky journey out to sea in search of the multiple varieties of whales that were crucial for use in the expanding industrial economy as well as for home lighting. The invention of the typewriter in the 1870s changed the nature of office work as more and more women were newly hired in the position of typist. Households were transformed by new inventions in the 19th century as well. The cookstove forever alleviated the drudgery of the home cook who had been toiling at the open hearth for centuries. The introduction of the home sewing machine created a new industry of home sewers, many of whom made money for the family through sewing piecework. Of course, the most transformative invention in both the household and in industry was Thomas Edison's usable version of the light bulb that lit up the nation and spawned the electrical transmission industry.

To some extent as a reaction to the escalation of industrialization in mid-19th century America, a movement called the Second Great Awakening emerged. With their lives changing so quickly, many Americans felt insecure and uncertain about their place in society. Not surprisingly, they turned to religion for comfort and solace. There was a rejection of rationalism and an upsurge in Protestant sects that were heavily reliant on the emotional appeal of the religious revival meeting. One of the longest lasting and influential sects was the Shakers, a celibate and communal group that was pacifist and believed in sexual equality. Their simple and efficient design innovations continue to be enjoyed today. The ubiquitous publications of the Sunday School Society were another manifestation of religion's influence in 19th-century society. Germans were an influential immigrant group in the early-mid-19th century, and their magnificent illustrations of fraktur art, observing life's milestones like baptisms and weddings, are celebrated today as prime examples of American folk art. The influence of religion was also evident in the Victorian "cult of death" that was an endemic component of 19th-century American culture. The specter of death was everywhere, as between 30 and 40 percent of all American children died before their fifth birthday. Families coped with this loss by compiling scrapbooks that commemorated the deceased or creating "hairwork," jewelry, or other trinkets made from the actual hair of the loved one. Another tradition that often contained religious overtones was the embroidery of a sampler by the family's young daughters. This venerable practice had multiple aims, which included teaching the alphabet and numbers, the art of sewing, and the inculcation of religious beliefs. Though surprisingly not specifically religious in intent, the celebration of the birth of Christ, Christmas, ballooned in popularity by the end of the 19th century. Elite members of New York City society encouraged a new type of Christmas celebration based on wholesome family gatherings in contrast to the drunken bacchanalia practiced by many hooligans in the cities. This novel Christmas celebration was influenced by Queen Victoria's introduction of the Christmas tree into her home and has become the quintessential American celebration, more cultural than religious.

The desire to bring democracy and American exceptionalism throughout the continent drove the relentless expansion to the West and later to a short-lived campaign for American expansion throughout the world. Before the completion of the transcontinental railroad, the western settlers made the arduous trek in wagon trains, often trudging along beside a Prairie Schooner or Conestoga wagon. In 1848, gold was discovered in California, and the Gold Rush was on, inspiring hundreds of thousands to attempt the grueling slog, either overland, through the Rockies, or by sea, around South America. The surge westward, fueled by a relentless flood of eager immigrants, meant that Native American tribes were pushed westward as well. The tribes suffered loss of life, loss of land, and later, loss of culture and language when their children were forced into residential schools miles away from their families. At the end of the 19th century, the United States had a brief encounter with imperialism, as a suddenly rich and powerful nation attempted to push its weight around on the international stage. The yellow journalism practiced by certain influential newspaper magnates encouraged the American public to support a war with Spain after exaggerating the atrocities that had supposedly taken place in Cuba. Many Americans favored the idea of taking on colonies, and in 1898, the United States took over Puerto Rico, Guam, the Philippines, Hawaii, and, temporarily, Cuba.

Slavery has been called America's original sin, and in the 19th century, it led to the nation's rupture. Many artifacts can be studied to learn lessons about the unspeakable practice. Slave shackles were used for centuries to transport or punish. Former slaves like Frederick Douglass eloquently enlightened the white American public about the lives of slaves. Abolitionists like Harriet Beecher Stowe also tried, through her immensely popular book *Uncle Tom's Cabin*, to call attention to the horrors of slavery. When the Civil War broke out, the Confederacy adopted a distinctive battle flag that would soon come to symbolize the South and its racist propensities. The Civil War, with its overwhelming number of casualties, provided an opportunity for undereducated surgeons to hone their skills on the battlefield with their primitive medical instruments. With the number of casualties rising, the Union was forced to institute a draft, which resulted in racially charged riots in New York City. The significance of the issue of slavery in the history of the United States obscures the fact that many white immigrants and citizens were also forced into indentured servitude, as we can see in the 1804 indenture document. The crucial difference, of course, was that the indenture had a time limit, and the family of the indentured servant was not enslaved.

During the 19th century, the population of the United States grew exponentially, and so did its wealth. Although the gap in income between the superrich and the poor became a yawning gulf, a pool of educated workers was forming a new middle class. This cohort, relocating from the farms to the cities, found jobs in newly constructed skyscrapers, doing office work for the huge corporations that gained power during the second half of the century. For the first time in the history of this hardworking country, the majority of Americans had disposable income and free time. This is when the entertainment industry emerged. Home entertainments, performed on the popular upright piano, were all the rage. Shows like the *Buffalo Bill Wild West* show and professional sports like baseball were another outlet for the working man and his family. Exhibitions like the Centennial Exhibition in 1876 and the World Columbian Exposition in 1893 drew crowds from all around the country. Women, saddled with the responsibility of running the household, enjoyed popular and influential magazines like *Godey's Lady's Book*. Science and pseudoscience also had influence on popular culture. The now discredited pseudoscience of phrenology focused on the head. It claimed to predict intelligence and character traits by examining the shape and the bumps on a person's head. Other scientific innovations of the 19th century included the treatment of the mentally ill. Thomas Kirkbride devised a novel treatment plan that he dubbed "Moral Treatment." His ideas were based on the humanitarian beliefs of the Quakers and were rooted in kindness and respect. However, his designs for large asylums were inevitably transformed into horrific warehouses for the mentally ill. Women, relegated to the sphere of the home, began to agitate for voting rights during the 19th century. It was a long slog, however, for it would be twenty years into the 20th century before women were able to attain that right. Public education did expand for both girls and boys in the 19th century, and by 1900, three quarters of American children were enrolled in common, that is, public schools, thanks to advocates for public education like Calvin Stowe and Horace Mann. The United States by 1900 was a literate, middle-class nation, powerful militarily and rich economically, and in this book, we examine some of the artifacts that help to explain how it got there.

HOW TO EVALUATE ARTIFACTS

A new field of research that has emerged in the second half of the 20th century is called "material culture." The study of material culture is defined in the Sociology Dictionary as "The physical objects or 'things' that belong to, represent, or were created by a group of people within a particular culture." All things that can be touched and felt, for example, objects, architecture, artwork, books, and written music, all made by and for humans, are examples of material culture. The inverse of material culture is called nonmaterial culture, which is nonphysical and refers to the abstract ideas, belief systems, and values that make up a culture. The field of material culture is interdisciplinary and broad and was developed in some part as a reaction to the traditional emphasis that focused on documents, artwork, and objects that were produced by the elite. This privileged, almost exclusively male cohort wrote the books, created the documents, made the artwork, and produced the decorative arts that were studied and celebrated as part of traditional historical research and teaching. On a personal note, as a student of art history in the 1970s, I was given a traditional university education that concentrated on what was considered to be the greatest pieces of artwork, the finest buildings by the most celebrated architects, and the most superlative examples of various styles of the decorative arts. I was fascinated by these wonderful works and the way the professors incorporated their historical contexts. But I was nonetheless left with an empty feeling in my gut: What about these charming antique chairs that were handed down in my family? How can I explain their style? What about the old houses on my block—what style were they, who built them, and why? There was little that I knew or appreciated that seemed to belong in these textbooks. What about all the people in the past who used or created these items? The history of these so-called vernacular-style objects was not part of the traditional curriculum until the new field of material culture emerged. This new field was influenced by the work of archeologists, who habitually utilized artifacts from everyday life to explain the lives of ancient peoples and cultures. The field of social history also influenced the study of material culture. In order to explain the lives of the non-elites of the past, objects and artifacts that they created and/or used were important tools.

Scholars in the field of material culture have proposed a number of procedures to analyze objects methodically. Pioneers in the field like E. McClung Fleming, Jules David Prown, and Kenneth L. Ames in the 1970s and 1980s all contributed to the introduction of the standard methodology utilized in artifact analysis. Ames described material culture as a "centrifugal" study, one that originates with a discrete object, and then expands "outward from small issues to larger, more encompassing, and more fundamental concerns" (Sheumaker and Wajda 2008: xii). Prown's artifact analysis methodology recommended performing three actions: description of the object; deduction about the object, from touching it or experiencing it, and; speculation about the object by formulating hypotheses about the object. Another scholar, Karen Harvey, has simplified the method in more recent research, into three related steps: First, provide a physical description of the object, that is: What is it made of? How was it made? When was it made? What is its size, weight, materials, design, and style? Second, place the object into its historical context by asking the following questions: Who owned it? When was it owned? How did they use it? And third, ask the following broader questions: What did the object mean in its sociocultural historical context? (Shrum 2019).

As an example of this method of artifact analysis, let's use an artifact that is familiar to many Americans—the American flag that inspired Francis Scott Key to write what would become the United States' national anthem, the "Star-Spangled Banner." This flag was flown at Fort McHenry in Baltimore, Maryland, at the Battle of Baltimore during the War of 1812, the first war fought by the young nation. Let's go through the artifact analysis guidelines as proposed by Karen Harvey, starting with the physical description. First, what is it? It is an American flag. The first American flag is believed to have been sewn by Betsy Ross. The design of the original American flag was approved by Congress on June 14, 1777, consisting of thirteen red and white stripes and thirteen white stars on a blue field. The thirteen stars and stripes represent the thirteen original colonies. The three colors on the flag represent the following: red—hardiness and valor; white—purity and innocence; and blue—vigilance, perseverance, and justice. What is the physical description of this American flag? The American flag flown at Fort McHenry is huge, measuring 30 by 34 feet, nearly three stories high. It weighs about 150 pounds. It has fifteen stars (one of which has been cut out) and fifteen stripes. The original flag was even bigger—30 by 42 feet, a typical size for a flag flown at a 19th-century garrison, on a 90-foot-high flagpole. It is made of dyed English wool bunting for the blue field and the stripes and white cotton for the stars. The flag was made by Mary Pickersgill, a Baltimore flag maker. She was commissioned by Major George Armistead, commander of Fort McHenry, in 1813 to sew two flags, the large garrison flag, and a smaller storm flag, which was 17 by 25 feet. Mary Pickersgill had a contract with the U.S. government to make these flags, and she was assisted in the project by her daughter, two nieces, and an indentured African American girl. The cost of the garrison flag was $405.90, and the cost of the smaller storm flag was $168.54.

The second step in the analysis of this artifact is to ask the following questions: Who owned it? When was it owned? How was it used? The owner of the garrison flag was Lt. Col. George Armistead. Though there is no documented evidence as to how the flag came into his personal possession, it is assumed that he retained it as a memento of the Battle of Baltimore. The flag remained in the Armistead family for many years. In 1861, when Col. Armistead's widow passed away, it was bequeathed to their daughter Georgiana Armistead Appleton. She recognized the symbolic value of the artifact and lent it out for several exhibitions including the 1876 Centennial Exhibition in Philadelphia. The flag was subsequently passed down to Armistead's grandson, Eben Appleton, in 1878. Understanding that the flag was a national treasure, he decided to lend it to the Smithsonian Institution in 1907, making it a permanent gift to the nation in 1912.

The third step in the artifact analysis process is to examine the significance of the object in its broader historical context. This object has so much history to tell. First, it was a beloved flag flown above the fort in a crucial battle that turned the tide in the nation's first war, the War of 1812. It provided inspiration for Francis Scott Key, a lawyer who was briefly detained on a British ship in the Baltimore harbor after securing the release of a civilian prisoner. Because of his detainment, Key was an eyewitness to the British bombardment of Fort McHenry. The war wasn't going well for the Americans prior to this point. The British had recently invaded Washington, DC, and set fire to the Capitol, the White House, and other government buildings. The fierce shelling of the fort in Baltimore took place on September 13, 1814, all day and throughout the night. The weather was rainy, and the smaller storm flag was flown above the fort. Francis Scott Key, anxiously awaiting the end of the battle, jubilantly noted the triumphant raising of the huge garrison flag "by the dawn's early light." The Americans had held the fort. Key began writing a poem to celebrate the victory, eventually completing four verses. With the encouragement of his wife's brother-in-law, Key had it printed and suggested a tune for it to be sung, an 18th-century British melody called "Anacreon in Heaven." It was first performed in October 1814 and soon became a beloved patriotic anthem. The song became the national anthem on March 3, 1931, after Congress passed the legislation and President Herbert Hoover signed it into law. The saga of the flag that inspired Francis Scott Key to write the "Star-Spangled Banner" has continued. Because of its extremely delicate condition, the flag required careful restoration, which began in 1999, and it is now on display at the National Museum of American History.

As suggested by material culture scholar Kenneth L. Ames, thinking about this artifact in a centrifugal way, let's consider even broader significance of the "Star-Spangled Banner" flag. Since the triumphant raising of the huge garrison flag at Fort McHenry in 1814 and the subsequent popularization of the "Star-Spangled Banner" poem and song, the American flag has become a potent symbol of American patriotism. This leads us to a larger, thornier issue about the flag. What did the flag mean to Americans in early 19th-century America? What did it mean to the population in the South that attempted to secede from the United States forming what they called the Confederate States of America? During the battles of the Civil War, the Confederates were forced to design a new flag, the Confederate battle flag, in order to easily differentiate the two opposing sides in the confusing fog of war. The Confederate battle flag still remains a potent and controversial symbol today. The American flag itself, as a symbol of American patriotism, has been co-opted by certain political groups who claim that it represents only their concept of American patriotism. In this highly polarized political climate, does the American flag symbolize patriotism, freedom, and American values, or does it represent only one political point of view? Has it become a symbol of e pluribus unum, out of many, one, or is it a symbol of political divisiveness? This type of broader analysis is what can be part of the artifact analysis process proposed by scholars in material culture. The artifacts in this book have all been examined with a similar method of analysis, describing the object itself and then asking the how, what, and why questions in the broader historical context.

FURTHER INFORMATION

Bell, Kenton, ed. 2013. "Material Culture." In Open Education Sociology Dictionary. Accessed November 30, 2021. https://sociologydictionary.org/material-culture/.

Fleming, E. McClung. 1974. "Artifact Study: A Proposed Model." *Winterthur Portfolio*, 9: 153–173.

Harvey, Karen. 2017. *History and Material Culture: A Student's Guide to Approaching Alternative Sources*. New York: Routledge.

Kurin, Richard. 2013. *The Smithsonian's History of America in 101 Objects*. New York: Penguin Books.

Prown, Jules D. Spring 1982. "Mind in Matter: An Introduction to Material Culture Theory and Method." *Winterthur Portfolio*, 17(1): 1–19.

Sheumaker, Helen, and Shirley Teresa Wajda, eds. 2008. *Material Culture in America*. Santa Barbara, CA: ABC-CLIO.

Shrum, Rebecca. 2019. "Material Culture." The Inclusive Historian's Handbook. June 3. Accessed November 23, 2021. https://inclusivehistorian.com/material-culture/#_edn6.

"Smithsonian's Star-Spangled Banner Conservation Laboratory and Exhibition Open at National Museum of American History." 1999. National Museum of American History. May 26. Accessed November 23, 2021. https://americanhistory.si.edu/press/releases/smithsonians-star-spangled-banner-conservation-laboratory-and-exhibition-open.

"Star-Spangled Banner." 2008. National Museum of American History. Star-Spangled Banner Project. Accessed November 29, 2021. https://www.si.edu/spotlight/flag-day/banner-facts.

CHRONOLOGY OF EVENTS

1800 Thomas Jefferson is elected President

1804 John Adams Mann becomes legally indentured to his master, David Parker Jr., in the town of Reading, Massachusetts

1804 Lewis and Clark begin their journey across the country

1807 Eli Whitney obtains a patent for the cotton gin

1807 Maiden voyage of Robert Fulton's steamboat *The Clermont* begins

1812 War of 1812 begins with England

1819 Sophia Dyer from Portland, Maine, at the age of fourteen, creates a sampler using silk thread on linen

1820 *The Missouri Compromise* is passed under President Monroe

1820 Peak of the popularity of the German folk art style called "fraktur"

1824 Founding of the American Sunday School Union, an organization that became influential in teaching Protestant values and American nationalism to children both in American cities and on the frontier

1825 The Erie Canal opens, providing the first waterway connecting the Atlantic Ocean and the Great Lakes

1828 Andrew Jackson is elected president

1830 The Indian Removal Act is passed

1830 South Carolina politician John C. Calhoun euphemistically calls slavery America's "peculiar institution"

1832 Beaver fur top hat produced by Peck and Co., a prominent Boston hat maker

1834 Cyrus McCormick obtains a patent for his mechanical reaper

1835 Alexis De Tocqueville publishes *Democracy in America*

1836 The Astor House Hotel in New York opens, with toilets and bathrooms on each floor

1837   Sarah Josepha Hale teams with Louis Antoine Godey to produce *Godey's Lady's Book*, a publishing powerhouse of the mid-late 19th century for the American middle-class housewife

1838   The eviction of the Cherokee Nation from the southeastern United States leads to the Trail of Tears

1839   John L. O'Sullivan coins the phrase "Manifest Destiny"

1840   Lowell mill workers, dubbed the "Lowell Girls," publish a literary magazine called *The Lowell Offering*

1840   Sending printed Valentines cards becomes all the rage, ushering in the American greeting card era

1844   First telegraph message sent from the Supreme Court in Washington, DC, to Baltimore, Maryland, with the Bible verse: "What hath God wrought!"

1848   First women's rights convention is held in Seneca Falls, New York

1848   The Mexican-American War ends with the Treaty of Guadalupe-Hidalgo

1849   The California Gold Rush begins

1850   Sarah Josepha Hale publishes an engraving depicting a family gathered around a Christmas tree in her magazine *Godey's Lady's Book*, igniting an American tradition

1851   Dorothea Dix convinces Congress to pass a law to federally fund mental hospitals. President Franklin Pierce vetoes it, sending the responsibility back to the states

1851   Isaac Merritt Singer receives a patent for a sewing machine, soon to be dubbed "the Queen of Inventions" by the influential and ubiquitous magazine *Godey's Lady's Book*

1852   Education made compulsory in Massachusetts after a law was passed by Horace Mann, the first Massachusetts secretary of the Board of Education

1852   First edition of Harriet Beecher Stowe's groundbreaking book *Uncle Tom's Cabin* is published

1853   The United States purchases a strip of land between Texas, California, and Mexico for $10 million in the *Gadsden Purchase*

1855   Quirky massive sideboards adorned with carved depictions of dead animals make a short-lived appearance in American middle-class dining rooms

1855   Second autobiography of Frederick Douglass is published, called *My Bondage and My Freedom*

1857   Central Park in New York City opens

1859   Discovery of petroleum in Titusville, Pennsylvania, prompts the long decline of America's powerful whaling industry

1860   Abraham Lincoln grows his beard after an eleven-year-old girl suggests to him that it would improve his appearance in photographs

1861   Civil War begins

1861   Abraham Lincoln exempts male members of the Shaker sect from serving in the military, making them the first official American conscientious objectors

1861   Confederate Battle Flag is designed, for use in battles as a replacement for the "Stars and Bars" flag that was dangerously similar to the Union's "Stars and Stripes"

1861   Based on its British progenitor, Congress creates the U.S. Sanitary Commission, which helped prevent thousands of deaths due to disease during the Civil War

1862   Charm made from the hair of Major William B. Hubbs, who died in the Civil War, is created as an example of the popular trend of "mourning jewelry"

1862   The Gatling gun is invented by Richard Gatling

1863   Abraham Lincoln issues the Emancipation Proclamation freeing slaves in the Confederate states

1863   A National Conscription Act is passed to increase troop levels for the Union, leading to brutal violence breaking out in New York City, mostly by Irish immigrants against African Americans

1865   Civil War ends

1865   Abraham Lincoln is assassinated by John Wilkes Booth

1866   The American Institute of Phrenology is incorporated as an educational institution

1869   The first continental railroad is completed at Promontory Point, Utah

1871   The Great Chicago Fire burns down much of the city of Chicago

1873   First commercially produced typewriter using the QWERTY keyboard is sold

1873   George A. Shastey's innovative reclining chair is patented

1876   Alexander Graham Bell demonstrates his new invention, the telephone, at the Centennial Exhibition in Philadelphia

1879   Eighty-two Indigenous children are sent to Carlisle, Pennsylvania, as the first class in what would become the Indian residential school system

1879   Thomas Edison invents the first commercially practical light bulb

1881   Helen Hunt Jackson publishes *A Century of Dishonor*, in which she documents the mistreatment of Native Americans by the U.S. government

1881   High-end porcelain oyster plate is produced by Tiffany and Co.

1882   The Chinese Exclusion Act is enacted

1883   Buffalo Bill's phenomenally successful *Wild West* show is inaugurated, establishing the enduring myth of Wild West

1884   First "safety bicycle" is invented by John Kemp Starling

1885   Ball's so-called healthful corset is introduced

1885   "Cocaine Toothache Drops" are advertised and sold to alleviate toothaches in children and adults

1886   Musical training is, increasingly, becoming a feature of proper preparation for entry into the American middle class

1887   John Montgomery Ward baseball card is produced by Allen & Gintner Tobacco Co.

1890   The Wounded Knee Massacre in South Dakota was the last battle in the American Indian Wars

1893   Panic of 1893 takes place

1893   World's Columbian Exposition takes place in Chicago

1896   Advertising card for Sterling Stove shows stacks of bread loaves produced by this marvelous new kitchen appliance

1896   Supreme Court rules on *Plessy vs. Ferguson* that "separate but equal" facilities are legal

1898   Battle between Joseph Pulitzer and William Randolph Hearst for newspaper circulation takes place in the run-up to the Spanish-American War

1898   The United States gains control of Cuba, Puerto Rico, and the Philippines after the Spanish-American War

Communications

Cartoon on Yellow Journalism

Telegraph Key

Telephone

Valentine's Day Card

1 Cartoon on Yellow Journalism

INTRODUCTION

Cries of "fake news" echo through the Twittersphere, while certain media outlets are justly accused of misrepresenting the facts and even of outright falsehoods. New forms of journalism and social media grab opportunities to target ever more partisan audiences. Media outlets are blamed for echoing government propaganda or credulously parroting false claims made by the military. All types of media drearily depend on the advertising revenue and on ratings, viewers, and sales. This situation sadly but accurately describes what's in the media landscape of the 21st century. But, alas, it's nothing new. This was also the state of affairs in a vastly different era, at the very end of the 19th century, when the blight of so-called yellow journalism marred the newspaper publishing industry, and the era of the political cartoon was at its peak.

DESCRIPTION

Innovations were accompanying new technologies in the newspaper field, and more newspapers were printed, more cartoonists were hired, and the cartoon reigned supreme, often placed prominently on the front page. The cartoonists became celebrities in themselves as their popularity helped the newspapers rocket to the top of the circulation wars. The cartoon shown here is an influential and famous cartoon of the era. Printed on June 29, 1898, in the magazine *Vim* and drawn by Leon Barritt (1852–1938), the cartoon humorously portrays the battle between Joseph Pulitzer and William Randolph Hearst for circulation in the run-up to the Spanish-American War. Two figures are portrayed, both in the signature yellow nightgown of the Yellow Kid, a popular figure in the Hogan's Alley cartoons by Richard Outcault. The two "kids" have the heads of Joseph Pulitzer and William Randolph Hearst and are pushing against opposite sides of a tower of three giant building blocks, spelling the word "WAR." Written on the nightgown of the Pulitzer figure on the left is the following text (parodying a German accent): "Say Young feller. Vatch de Tome. I'm de Tome—You Gant Buy

3

Id. I'm a Goot Ting Put Don't Push Me—See! Pulitzer." On the right is the figure of Hearst with the text: "Say—This is My War. I Bought and Paid for It and If You Don't Stop Bothering Me About It I'll Have You Put Off the Earth—See! P.S. My Name is Hearst." The cartoon is a satire of the tabloids' roles in ginning up American thirst for war with Spain in 1898.

It was the height of the Gilded Age, the last decade of the 19th century, and American society was changing. Immigrants from different regions of Europe, poorer ones, were flooding into the country. The cities, desperate for workers to populate the factories that manufactured thousands of new products, were crowded with new Americans who spoke poor English and had funny-sounding names. At the same time, technology had transformed the newspaper industry, with improvements in printing presses and reduction in the price of paper stock, allowing for bigger newspapers at cheaper prices. Telegraphs and railroad lines that crisscrossed the country by the end of the century made it easier to transmit breaking news and distribute newspapers throughout the region. This made for a changed media landscape. Newspapers had primarily been printed by political parties in the early part of the 19th century, but as the country grew, newspapers became purely independent commercial enterprises, dependent on sales and advertising and driven by the profit motive. And there were suddenly new and eager audiences for breaking news in the teeming immigrant neighborhoods of the nation's burgeoning cities. In the early days of the republic, newspapers were read primarily by the educated upper class. But by the end of the 19th century, a new cohort of literate but working-class Americans enthusiastically clamored for updates on current events. Some of these immigrants were not English-speaking, and they sought local newspapers in their native tongue. Others spoke English well enough to link up with the English-speaking working class, who were also hungering for a steady source of information. The newspaper industry was booming. By 1900, there were 2,200 daily newspapers published in the country and 11,000 weeklies. But this industry was also extremely competitive, with all these newspapers jousting for a bigger audience, using any means necessary. The table was set for the new era of "yellow journalism."

The term "yellow journalism" was derived from a popular cartoon strip published in Joseph Pulitzer's *New York World*. The strip was called Hogan's Alley, drawn by Richard F. Outcault, and it depicted life in the slums of New York City. It was published in color, and it featured a character called "the Yellow Kid." The *World* benefited from this cartoon strip, as it was extremely popular, so much so that Pulitzer's rival William Randolph Hearst, publisher of the *New York Journal*, hired him away from the *World* in 1896 after a bidding war. Pulitzer, never willing to give in to a fight with his competitor, hired another cartoonist to continue drawing the cartoon for the *World*. These two newspapers were the tabloids of the day, publishing lurid, sensational stories that attracted huge audiences. These articles, some true, some exaggerated, some totally made up, often used large cartoons on the front page to attract readers. They were aimed at the large working-class readership that made up much of New York City's growing population, in the city that formed the epicenter of the country's publishing industry. The two rivals for the hearts of the public were two men whose names and legacies have endured up until today: Joseph Pulitzer and William Randolph Hearst.

Pulitzer was an immigrant himself, from Hungary, an educated son of a Jewish grain broker. After his parents died, he attempted to join the Austro-Hungarian army but was rejected due to his skinny, gangly frame and poor eyesight. Still anxious to enlist, he took advantage of an opportunity to enlist in the American Union army when a recruiter came to town searching for replacements to fight in the Civil War. Pulitzer was accepted into the Union army into all-German unit in 1864. After surviving the war, Pulitzer moved to New York in 1865 but was unsuccessful in finding employment, and he decided to relocate to St. Louis, where there were many German speakers. At the library where he studied at night, eager to learn the law and the English language, Pulitzer met some influential German Americans and was hired by one as a reporter for a German-language newspaper. His intelligence and work ethic impressed his bosses, and he was offered controlling interest in the paper, which he parlayed into a number of other deals. Eventually he was able to purchase the *St. Louis Post-Dispatch*, the best-known and most respected newspaper in the city in 1878. Pulitzer worked indefatigably at the *Post-Dispatch*. Joseph Pulitzer was known to be intellectually curious and was a tireless advocate for the working class of the city. His newspaper relentlessly attacked government corruption and exposed the unsavory habits of the city's upper class. The wealthy did not appreciate the coverage, and Pulitzer's popularity among the upper class of the city seriously deteriorated. But the circulation shot up, and profits soared. In 1882, after an unfortunate incident involving an aggrieved attorney who was murdered in the paper's headquarters by the managing editor, Pulitzer opted to leave town and spend an extended holiday in Europe. But when he stopped in New York, he discovered that a newspaper, the *New York World*, was for sale. The newspaper was owned by Jay Gould, the railroad tycoon, who had obtained it in a prior sale. It had not been successful, and Gould wanted to offload it. Pulitzer offered Gould $346,000 for the newspaper, a small amount for such a big-city daily. The *World* was a blank slate for Pulitzer, who was anxious to remake it in the image of the *St. Louis Post-Dispatch*, infusing his new style of journalism, with sensational and juicy stories. Covering all sorts of corruption, the most heinous murders, and wicked examples of vice, populist politics and, of course, a staunch defense of the working class were all hallmarks of this new style. Pulitzer reduced the price of the newspaper to two cents, under-cutting his rival the *New York Herald*, and soon the newspaper's circulation grew and the profits rolled in.

Pulitzer made the *New York World* a dominant force in the New York City newspaper publishing world. In 1895, William Randolph Hearst, Pulit-zer's ultimate rival, came to town looking to buy a newspaper. Hearst was from San Francisco, the son of a mining magnate. Hearst had been brought up in a very wealthy household, though with the ups and downs of the mar-ket his father did suffer losses which affected the family during his child-hood. Hearst pledged to never feel financially insecure again. His father owned a failing newspaper in San Francisco, the *San Francisco Examiner*. William, a young man searching for a career, asked his father if he could run the newspaper. William began serving as the publisher of the *Examiner* in 1887. He worked hard to make the venture work, attempting to bring the paper into profitable status. He tried a variety of techniques that could add to its circulation—he used attention-getting headlines, cartoons, and sensa-tionalism. However, Hearst had bigger ambitions, and after his father died, he asked his mother to help him purchase a struggling New York newspa-per, the *Morning Journal*, for $150,000 in 1895. Hearst changed the name to the *New York Journal* and imported the punchy, aggressive reporting style that he had established at the *San Francisco Examiner*. The *Journal* soon became known for its splashy headlines, such as "He Hiccoughed for Five Days" and "White Woman among Cannibals" (Lind 2010: 2).

Hearst was a ruthless competitor, and he focused on Joseph Pulitzer's popular *World* newspaper as his target. He undercut the *World* by reducing the price of the *Journal* to a penny as opposed to the *World*'s two cents. The next four years saw the merciless tabloid war between the *Journal* and the *World*, a war that would usher in the era of yellow journalism. With both dailies competing for the same reading public, standards plummeted as the outrageousness ballooned. Bigger and bigger circulation numbers were the targets of both publishers' desires. And they were ready, will-ing and able to allocate all resources to the task. This set the stage for the high point of the tabloid wars. It was 1898, and the United States was on the lookout for strategic assets that could augment its empire. The fron-tier, as famously defined by historian Frederick Jackson Turner in 1893, was officially closed, and it forced the country to consider lands located off the mainland in order to expand the nation's boundaries and markets. The island of Cuba, one of Spain's last colonial possessions at the time, was in the sights of certain expansionist politicians, and the city of New York was home to a number of Cuban exiles. Spain had been cracking down on a violent rebellion by Cubans against Spanish rule. Taking aim at the Spanish, the Cuban exiles encouraged the tabloids to shed light on atrocities purportedly carried out by Spanish troops. Both the *Journal* and the *World* expended miles of printers' ink on articles regarding the brutality of the Spanish in Cuba. While the crackdown by the Spanish was violent, many of the stories coming out of Cuba and published by the *Journal* and the *World* were highly exaggerated or even totally fabricated. Joseph Pulitzer, who had previously been committed to publishing accurate, if sensational, stories, let his standards slip in his coverage of the Cuban situation. On February 15, 1898, the warship *Maine* sailed down to the Cuban harbor on a friendly visit when it exploded, most likely by an accidental coal fire inside the ship, killing over two hundred American sailors. The New York tabloids, however, jumped on the story. The *Journal*'s headline screamed, "Destruction of the War Ship Maine Was the Work of an Enemy," while the *World* questioned, "Maine Explosion Caused by Bomb or Torpedo?" Stirring up anti-Spain wrath among its readers, the tabloids were successful in also provoking fury in the government in Washington, DC. On April 11, 1898, President William McKinley submitted a war resolution, formally going to war with Spain.

SIGNIFICANCE

An anecdote that has been repeated countless times in the last century, but has now been debunked, contends that William Randolph Hearst sent a telegram to his photographer in Havana, stating, "You furnish the pictures, and I'll furnish the war." Though this direct evidence of the responsibility for the start of the war is untrue, what is true is that the highly influential tabloids of turn-of-the-20th-century New York were successful in stirring up a visceral anger against Spain among Americans, which resulted in the United States declaring war on Spain in Cuba in 1898. There were other factors involved in the desire for war shown by the U.S. government. Theodore Roosevelt, Henry Cabot Lodge, and other expansionist politicians entertained fantasies of enlarging the footprint of the United States outside the continental borders. They benefited from the biased, often misleading, and even false reporting coming out of the New York tabloids. As the war progressed, the tabloids continued to portray a favorable bias toward the government's role in the conflict. Roosevelt quit his job in the Naval Department to lead a unit of soldiers in Cuba that he dubbed the "Rough Riders." The war ended with Cuba gaining independence but with an amendment granting power to the United States to intervene at the discretion of the U.S. government at any time. The United States also inherited Puerto Rico, Guam, and the Philippines from the Spanish, which gave the nation an expanding empire and a source for new markets for American goods. The Philippines, however, did not have a happy outcome and suffered as the U.S. government brutally put down a rebellion that began in 1899 in a three-year conflict that resulted in seven thousand American casualties and a horrifying loss of more than two hundred thousand Filipinos.

The two dailies, the *New York Journal* and the *New York World*, were influential in many ways that are still felt today. The use of short, punchy headlines was a new concept in the 19th century, as was the idea that a newspaper's front page could handle a number of different stories and illustrations on the front page. The extensive use of cartoons was an innovation of the period, as was the perennially popular use of graphics. The owners of the *World* and the *Journal* launched the practice of covering all types of news, including local, national, and world news, and of using color to attract more readers in Sunday supplements. One of the beneficial influences of the tabloids of the 1890s was the innovation of muckraking journalism, which was born in the Progressive era and concentrated on rooting out corruption in business and government. In addition, for once the working class became a viable focus for a large newspaper. However, there were multiple after-effects of the tabloid wars and the yellow journalism period that have been felt in subsequent eras and were not so beneficial. The focus on ratings and advertising revenue, the attraction to lurid stories and crime, and the uncritical parroting of government propaganda have been issues felt by all types of media and continue today.

Hearst and Pulitzer ended their war after the government ended theirs, after 1898. Joseph Pulitzer regretted his regression into the tabloid circus and sought to regain the reputation he previously protected of ethical, accurate journalism. He later founded the school of journalism at Columbia University and endowed the renowned Pulitzer Prizes. William Randolph Hearst also continued his long and storied life, entering politics and eventually moving back to California where he built the estate at San Simeon. His media empire grew, and Hearst Magazines is still in existence. His life story was recounted in Orson Welles' movie *Citizen Kane*, considered one of the greatest films of all time.

FURTHER INFORMATION

Campbell, W. J. 2000. "Not Likely Sent: The Remington-Hearst 'Telegrams.'" *Journalism and Mass Communication Quarterly*, 77(2): 405–422.

Griffin, Brett. 2019. *Yellow Journalism, Sensationalism, and Circulation Wars*. New York: Cavendish Square.

Hess, Stephen, and Sandy Northrop. 1996. *Drawn & Quartered: The History of American Political Cartoons*. Montgomery, AL: Elliott & Clark Publishing.

Lind, Michael. 2010. "The Yellow Peril: Looking Back at the World the Press Lords Made." Bookforum. April.

Nasaw, David. 2000. *The Chief: The Life of William Randolph Hearst*. New York: Houghton Mifflin Harcourt.

Division of Medicine and Science, National Museum of American History, Smithsonian Institution

2 Telegraph Key

INTRODUCTION

Everyone reading this book is familiar with various types of instantaneous communication. There's the old-fashioned landline telephone, the newfangled cell phone, the internet, and email. Of course, there is the now ubiquitous option of text messaging on the cell phone. Sending text messages in real time is an accepted reality in today's world. However, imagine living in a society where the limits of communication depended on the physical speed of a human being or an animal. Letters could be written, newspapers and books could be printed, but the news and information could not travel any faster than the person or the horse that was carrying it. Humans were itching to invent a faster method of communicating urgent messages, but the technology just wasn't there. Over many centuries, clever systems of communicating were devised that were faster than the horse or the human. These methods were dubbed "telegraphy" from the French *telegraphe*, originating from the Greek, meaning "that which writes at a distance." The first method of sending messages was known as "optical telegraphy," relying on the actual visual sighting of the messages. Methods like smoke signals, originally utilized by the ancient Chinese, were further enhanced by the Greeks and also used by Native Americans. The length and complexity of the messages that could be sent were extremely limited, however. The semaphore system, another form of optical telegraphy, was developed in France during the French Revolution. A code was developed, using either lights or flags to send messages over long distances. The messages had to be transmitted using relay towers located about 20 miles apart. Messages could be relayed at the speed of about two words per minute. This method, perfected in the early 19th century and used by the British as well as the French, was expensive and cumbersome and was utilized primarily for military purposes. The concept of optical telegraphy had reached its limit of usefullness. The world was ready to embrace a transformative technological innovation in communication, and this innovation would be the electrical telegraph.

DESCRIPTION

The image shown here is believed to be a telegraph key, manufactured by Samuel Morse's assistant Alfred Vail, for the first Baltimore-Washington telegraph line. It dates from 1844. It was built in Morristown, New Jersey, at the Speedwell Iron Works, the plant owned by Alfred Vail's father. The telegraph key measures 3 inches wide by 6 ¾ inches long by 2 inches high. It is made of wood and brass. The artifact is owned by the Smithsonian National Museum of American History. The telegraph key operated when the switch was depressed, completing an electrical circuit that allowed the electrical pulse to pass along the wires to the receiving location, where the message would be interpreted, either by reading a recorded paper message or by listening to the message and interpreting the code, which came to be known as Morse code.

Samuel Finley Breese Morse was born in Charlestown, Massachusetts, on April 27, 1791. He was the son of Jedidiah Morse, a prominent Congregationalist preacher and published geographer. Jedidiah Morse sent his son Samuel to Phillips Academy in Andover, Massachusetts, and later to Yale University in New Haven, Connecticut. The ambitious Samuel demonstrated interest in the new study of electricity while at Yale but did not pursue it at the time, preferring to enter the field of oil painting. Morse traveled to England to study painting with two American artists, Benjamin West and Washington Allston. He displayed talent and was exhibited at the Royal Academy in London. Morse became a successful painter after returning to the United States, receiving several commissions for portraits including ones for President Monroe and Marquis de Lafayette. He is also credited with helping to found the National Academy of Design. However, Morse remained a "starving artist," as his painting commissions did not provide much in remuneration. He was anxious to supplement his income and developed a persistent fascination with becoming an inventor, a pursuit that his brother had attempted unsuccessfully. Morse had been devastated when his first wife and one of his children passed away in 1825 while he was in Washington, DC, working on a portrait of Lafayette. The news of her illness had taken so long to reach him that she was already buried by the time he returned home. This sad incident sparked an interest in improving methods of communications for Samuel Morse, an interest that would soon flower into a lucrative and transformative invention.

In 1832, Samuel Morse was heading back to the United States after another extended trip to Europe on the packet ship called the *Sully*. He entered into a conversation with a group of passengers who were discussing electricity and the experiments of the French mathematician and physicist Andre-Marie Ampere involving electromagnetism. One of the passengers remarked that electricity passes over any length of wire. Morse immediately responded that intelligence can also travel over the length of a wire. With a spark of imagination bordering on brilliance, Morse immediately drew a sketch, which is a recognizable image of an electrical telegraph. Though not a scientist, Morse was an inveterate entrepreneur, and he pursued his idea of the electrical telegraph diligently in his spare time. He was not very successful in completing the model of the telegraph, though he had a definite concept in mind. Finally, in 1836, after Morse had been appointed as professor of the Literature of the Arts of Design at the University of the City of New York (the present-day New York University), he asked a colleague Leonard D. Gale to help him out. Gale was a chemist who was also familiar with pioneering work done by the physicist and Princeton professor Joseph Henry. The prototype produced by Henry was helpful to Morse because it included the crucial electrical relay that boosted the signal for longer distances. Morse, however, designed an armature that was a recording instrument and utilized the electromagnetic relays that boosted the current. These innovations conceived by Morse made his electrical telegraph the most practicable concept available at the time.

Samuel Morse hired a young technician named Alfred Vail, who proved to be vital to the success of the telegraph prototype. A patent application was made in 1837, and Alfred Vail helped provide the funding for continued research, using the facilities at his family's ironworking factory in Morristown, New Jersey. During this time Morse and Vail were also working together on devising a code that could transmit letters and numbers through the telegraph. This would eventually become known as American Morse Code. Though Morse and Vail were lobbying the federal government to build a demonstration telegraph line, the country was suffering from an economic depression, called the Panic of 1837, and the government showed little interest in testing a new telegraphy device. But by 1843, the economy was recovering, and Morse was feeling bullish about the progress of his new electrical telegraph. He applied once again to the federal government for $30,000 (equivalent to about $10 million in today's dollars) to build a telegraph system that would connect Washington, DC, with Baltimore, Maryland, some 40 miles away. The funding was eventually approved by President Tyler, and the project was begun. Although the original plan was to bury the lines underground, defective wires prevented the successful completion in time, and the crew quickly erected poles along the route, which held the wires. The test of the new telegraph took place on May 24, 1844, when a message was sent from the Supreme Court in Washington, DC, to Alfred Vail in Baltimore, Maryland. The iconic first message, selected by Annie Ellsworth, the young daughter of a friend of Samuel Morse, was this Bible verse: "What hath God wrought!"

People were so excited about the transformative nature of the electric telegraph, some thought it would bring world peace!

Of all the marvelous achievements of modern science the electric telegraph is transcendentally the greatest and most serviceable to mankind . . . The whole earth will be belted with the electric current, palpitating with human thoughts and emotions . . . How potent a power, then is the telegraphic destined to become in the civilization of the world! This binds together by a vital cord all the nations of the earth. It is impossible that old prejudices and hostilities should longer exist, while such an instrument has been created for an exchange of thought between all the nations of the earth.

[Briggs, Charles F., and Augustus Maverick. 1858. *The Story of the Telegraph.* Accessed January 7, 2020. Quoted in https://www.elon.edu/u/imagining/time-capsule/150-years/back-1830-1860/

Briggs, Charles F. and Augustus Maverick. 1858. *The Story of the Telegraph and a History of the Great Atlantic Cable.* New York: Rudd and Carleton.]

SIGNIFICANCE

Samuel Finley Breese Morse was a polymath, a 19th-century Renaissance man who possessed multiple talents. His primary profession was as a painter, a career that he excelled at, though without much monetary success. He painted large, grand pieces that only the very wealthy could afford. He was also fascinated by new technology and encountered the revolutionary technique of daguerreotype photography on a trip to France, after meeting the inventor Louis Daguerre. Morse promoted the technique in the United States and taught it to Matthew Brady, who became the legendary photographic chronicler of the Civil War. Morse was also drawn to political realm and ran for office unsuccessfully three times, including once in 1835 for the mayor of New York City on the "Nativist" ticket. His politics, controversial at best, would be considered distasteful in today's society. After a run-in with an Italian on a trip to Italy, Morse developed an aversion to the Roman Catholic faith as an overly oppressive religion that was antithetical to liberty as conceived in the United States. Morse opposed immigration from Catholic countries and developed nativist views. He also strongly countered the views of many of his intellectual New England cohorts and was intensely opposed to abolitionism. In fact, he once publicly condemned the Emancipation Proclamation and claimed that "slavery, per se, is not a sin. It is a social condition ordained from the beginning of the world . . . by Divine Wisdom" (Morse 1863). But, despite his foibles and faults, Samuel Morse had a genius for recognizing a new technology, bringing together the requisite parties that could produce a commercial product and then persistently promoting it. That's what he did for the telegraph.

The invention of the telegraph revolutionized communication throughout the world. For the United States, it was especially significant, because the country was already vast and it was rapidly expanding. With the combination of the railroads and the telegraph system, disparate localities in the nation could immediately be connected. The installation of telegraph cables by a variety of private companies took off throughout the country. Morse maintained that the government should control the telegraph system, but the federal administration refused to take on the role. So the United States became the sole location in the western world where the telegraph system was managed by private corporations. There were many start-ups that installed the first sets of telegraph wires, but soon the industry consolidated, and by 1866, Western Union bought out its remaining rivals. Western Union became a long-standing monopoly, with what is known in economics as a "natural monopoly," due to the high start-up costs and the economies of scale, which are often seen in utilities and are heavily regulated. The government did recognize the critically important potential of the telegraph system when the Civil War broke out after the shelling of Fort Sumter in 1861. A system utilized by the Union military, which was called the United States Military Telegraph Corps (USMT), was created after the start of the Civil War, and it was run by civilian operators. The Union side already had a vast system of telegraph wires, while the South did not. This was a crucial benefit to the Northern cause. President Abraham Lincoln, fascinated by the communication advantages offered by the USMT telegraphs, spent countless hours in the telegraph room of his Secretary of War Edward Stanton, during the Civil War. For the first time in history, the commander in chief could communicate and strategize, virtually in real time, with his generals on the field of battle, who were able to dismantle and then reassemble their telegraph equipment very quickly as the battle ensued. This advantage constituted a fundamental difference in the course of the Civil War. In fact, the telegraph system may have influenced Lincoln in another fascinating way. According to historian Garry Wills, the pithiness required by the new technology of the telegraph, so admired by the technophile Abraham Lincoln, almost certainly influenced the president in his concise words, so carefully chosen, for his greatest speech, the Gettysburg Address.

FURTHER INFORMATION

Fitzgerald, Dorothy. February 1951. "The Painter Who Was Father of the Telegraphy." *Popular Economics*, 1(5): 37–42.

Gilmore, Paul. Fall 2002. "The Telegraph in Black and White." *ELH*, 69(3): 805–833.

"A History of Telegraphy." 2014. Tancia, Ltd. Accessed January 6, 2020. https://www.pens.co.uk/pen2paper/wp-content/uploads/2014/08/A-History-of-Telegraphy.pdf.

Hochfelder, David. 2012. *The Telegraph in America, 1832–1920*. Baltimore: Johns Hopkins University Press.

"Invention of the Telegraph." Samuel F. B. Morse Papers at the Library of Congress, 1793–1919. Accessed January 6, 2020. https://www.loc.gov/collections/samuel-morse-papers/articles-and-essays/invention-of-the-telegraph/.

Morse, Samuel. 1863. "An Argument on the Ethical Position of Slavery in the Social System, and Its Relation to the Politics of the Day." New York, Papers from the Society for the Diffusion of Political Knowledge (12). Accessed May 23, 2022. http://reader.library.cornell.edu/docviewer/digital?id=may922812#mode/1up

Silverman, Kenneth. 2003. *Lightning Man: The Accursed Life of Samuel F. B. Morse*. New York: Knopf.

Wills, Garry. 2006. *Lincoln at Gettysburg: The Words That Remade America*. New York: Simon & Schuster.

3 Telephone

INTRODUCTION

Before the invention of the telegraph, instant communication was not possible. However, the telegraph revolutionized communication throughout the United States and the world by the second half of the 19th century. Emergency messages could be conveyed, whether it was from one town to another or over thousands of miles. The telegraph was used most effectively for military purposes during the Civil War and influenced American business practices as well. Prominent inventors were all investigating the possibilities of an improved telegraph. After all, who would even want a different form of communication? The telegraph did it all—delivered messages over many miles almost instantaneously. Once again, the door was open for a new invention that no one even imagined that they would ever need. Henry Ford is purported to have commented in anticipation of his new invention, the automobile: "If I had asked people what they wanted, they would've said faster horses." The telephone is that quintessential product that anticipated demand for it before anyone realized that it existed. Although the telegraph was revolutionary, the telephone eventually brought the telegraph to its extinction.

DESCRIPTION

It was on June 2, 1875, that Thomas Watson fiddled with a transmitter spring to get it to vibrate, when he accidently sent a twang to Alexander Graham Bell listening in the next room. Bell recognized the twang as a complex sound, similar to a human voice. Watson went on to create a new type of machine the following day, which by the third day was a recognizable prototype of a telephone. Bell submitted his patent application on February 14, 1876. Bell and Watson demonstrated their new invention at the Centennial Exhibition in Philadelphia, a giant celebration of the 100th birthday of the United States, where examples of new technology were proudly displayed. Bell's telephone was one of them. The image shown here is one of the telephones that were demonstrated at the Centennial Exhibition. It features a single electro-magnet and was both a transmitter and a receiver. The telephone has a wood base, brass posts and brackets, and a tin mouthpiece. It measures 5 inches wide by 11 inches long by 6 ½ inches high.

The telegraph had met its limit by the 1870s when miles of telegraph wire had been strung throughout the world, but only one message at a time could be sent over the wires. This created enormous holdups and delays for messages waiting to be sent. Some of the most clever inventors were searching for a better system, among them Thomas A. Edison, who was striving to discover a method of sending several messages along the lines at the same time. One of the inventors who was working on the issue was a young Scotsman named Alexander Graham Bell. Born in Edinburgh on March 3, 1847, Bell moved to Canada at the age of twenty-three after the tragic death of his two brothers from tuberculosis in London. Bell came from a highly accomplished family. His grandfather, Alexander Bell, was a cobbler, tavern owner, and comedian who was known for his outstanding elocution and melodious voice. He gave popular staged readings and published several books on the subject of speech and moved to London where he opened a school of elocution. Alexander's father, Alexander Melville Bell, was a trained linguist and author. He also was an expert on speech and developed a system called "Visible Speech," which translated spoken sounds into thirty-four written codes and symbols, indicating the shape of the lips, tongue, and throat. The proposed purpose of the exercise was to aid in pronouncing foreign words. However, the system turned out to be extremely effective in teaching deaf people to learn how to pronounce words, without the benefit of hearing them. (There is a story that Grandpa Alexander's technique for improving diction and eliminating the grating London Cockney accent was picked up by George Bernard Shaw for his play *Pygmalion*, which was later turned into the musical *My Fair Lady*. Or was it father Alexander Melville's system of Visible Speech that was parlayed into a system used by Professor Henry Higgins in Pygmalion? No one really knows.)

The young Alexander Graham Bell (known to his family as Aleck) came from this prominent family, steeped in the world of elocution, speech, and linguistics. He also was keenly familiar with the world of the deaf, as his mother Eliza Symonds Bell had grown deaf. As a child, Aleck was ever curious and was fascinated by the nature of sound, after learning to play the piano and experimenting with tuning forks. After moving to London to learn from his grandfather, Aleck taught music and elocution at a boy's boarding school and later traveled with his two brothers demonstrating the benefits of the Visible Speech method created by their father. The Bell family relocated to London, and in 1870, the three Bell brothers contracted tuberculosis. After the tragic deaths of Alexander's two brothers, the family again relocated, this time to a 10-acre farm in Brantford, Ontario, Canada, where Aleck was encouraged to recuperate in the fresh Canadian air. Here Bell indulged his continuing fascination with sound, refining the symbols for Visible Speech and studying the unwritten language of the Mohawk Indians, who were located on a reservation nearby the farm. He also attempted to study the work of the German physicist Hermann von Helmholtz, who had written that vowel sounds could be reproduced through electrical tuning forks. Aleck, however, was a poor reader of German and misunderstood the texts and diagrams. He thought that Helmholtz had proposed that *all* speech could be transmitted over wires, a feat that Helmholtz had not even suggested. This mistaken belief gave Bell the confidence to experiment with the concept himself, though he was not trained in electrical engineering.

Aleck Bell recovered from tuberculosis and was ready to return to a paid position. His father was employed in Montreal teaching Visible Speech, and soon Aleck was offered a similar position in Boston at the Boston School for Deaf Mutes. He taught at a number of similar schools in the area, and in 1872, he opened his own school, which he called the "School of Vocal Physiology and Mechanics of Speech" in Boston. One of his deaf students, Mabel Hubbard, would eventually become his wife. Her father, Gardiner Greene Hubbard, a wealthy patent attorney, would become a lifelong benefactor and supporter of Alexander Graham Bell and his pursuits. Subsequently, Bell was offered a position as a professor at Boston University. Bell was known for his indefatigable drive, and he spent many hours after work in his laboratory experimenting with his attempts to transmit speech. He was still working on the harmonic telegraph, a method that could transmit multiple messages over the telegraph wires simultaneously. He traveled down to Washington, DC, in March 1875 to apply for a patent on the harmonic telegraph, where he also met with the preeminent American physicist and expert on electromagnetism, Joseph Henry. Henry had recently been appointed the secretary of the newly formed Smithsonian Institution. The neophyte scientist Aleck Bell demonstrated his prototype to the renowned Joseph Henry, asserting that he believed that it could be improved so that it would transmit voices directly through the telegraph wires. But, Bell confessed, he didn't have sufficient knowledge in electricity to complete the experiment and perhaps should let others take on the task. Henry famously responded to Bell the words he most needed to hear: if you don't have the knowledge, then "Get it!" Bell later stated, "But for Henry, I should never have gone on with the telephone." Bell soon hired an assistant who would become crucial to the invention of the telephone: Thomas Watson. Bell and Watson tirelessly toiled on the invention of the harmonic telegraph, which was the dream of Bell's financial backers. However, they pursued an alternate dream at night where they secretly performed experiments on transmitting human speech, a dream which was to become the first telephone.

When President Rutherford B. Hayes saw a demonstration of the new device called the telephone in 1896, this was his reaction:

That's an amazing invention, but who would ever want to use one of them?

["The Development of the Telephone: Imagining the Internet, a History and Forecast." Elon University School of Communications. Accessed January 12, 2020. https://www.elon.edu/u/imagining/time-capsule/150-years/back-1870-1940/]

SIGNIFICANCE

The demonstration of the telephone made quite a splash at the Centennial Exhibition. British physicist Lord Kelvin, enthralled with the potential of the new device, exclaimed, "I hear, I hear. It is the most wonderful thing I have seen in America." Many believe that Alexander Graham Bell, with his extensive training in human speech, was uniquely qualified to invent such a device. Although many other inventors quickly jumped on the bandwagon, and even sued Bell with patent infringement suits that lasted decades, the concept of a telephone that transmitted the human voice was not something that intrigued most inventors. It was the perfection of the telegraph that was the priority. As described by John Brooks in his book *Telephone: The First Hundred Years*,

> Human Speech, as opposed to dot-and-dash code, was considered sacred, a gift of God beyond man's contrivance through science. Public reaction to the very idea of telephony in the 1860's and 1870's wavered between fear of the supernatural and ridicule of the impractical. People were made uneasy by the very notion. Hearing voices when there was no one there was looked upon as a manifestation of either mystical communion or insanity. Perhaps reacting to this climate, most physicists and electricians took it as an axiom that electricity could not carry the human voice. To have the freedom of mind to take the last step, there was needed a man whose thought was centered not on electricity but on the human voice, and that man was Alexander Graham Bell. (Brooks, quoted in Stern and Gwathmey 1994)

Alexander Graham Bell went on to promote the new invention in the United States and in Europe, where he spent an extended honeymoon with his new wife Mabel. The first telephone exchange was constructed in New Haven, Connecticut, in 1878, licensed by the Bell Telephone Company, a company formed by Bell and his financial backers, Gardiner Hubbard and Thomas Sanders. Within three years, there were telephone exchanges in most American cities. The American Telephone and Telegraph (AT&T) Company was incorporated in 1885. The company pushed ahead with building the infrastructure, reaching to Chicago in 1899 and to San Francisco in 1915, making the first American transcontinental telephone service. There were 600,000 telephones by 1900 in the United States and 5.8 million by 1910. The first telephones were very expensive and were primarily installed in businesses of lawyers, bankers, doctors, and other commercial customers that could afford them. They were installed in very few residential properties, sometimes in the homes of the selfsame doctors, lawyers, businessmen, and the business elite who wanted to be connected to their offices. It was one of those new products that had to be marketed, and the public had to be convinced that they were necessary. Telephone entrepreneurs publicized novelties such as news reports, concerts, church services, weather reports, and store sales over the telephone lines to encourage families to sign on. After the first patents ran out for the Bell Company in 1893 and 1894, many smaller start-ups joined the fray and built local telephone companies that competed with Bell and reduced the costs. Even so, telephones were not utilized as a method to have long chats with friends and family until the 1920s and beyond. Until then, the device was most often used as the telegraph had been, as a means to contact someone in an emergency or to convey a business message. Meanwhile, Alexander Graham Bell spent the rest of his life inventing a number of new products, although the telephone was his most influential and most lucrative. He bought a home in Baddeck, on Cape Breton Island on the coast of Nova Scotia, Canada, where he spent much of his later life.

FURTHER INFORMATION

"Alexander Graham Bell and the Telephone." June 4, 1910. *Scientific American*, 102(23): 462, 470–471.

Berger, J. Joel. May 1976. "On the Centennial of the Telephone: Alexander Graham Bell: Inventor of 'Electric speech.'" *The Science Teacher*, 43(5): 36–39.

"The Development of the Telephone: Imagining the Internet, a History and Forecast." Elon University School of Communications. Accessed January 12, 2020. https://www.elon.edu/u/imagining/time-capsule/150-years/back-1870-1940/

Fischer, Claude. 1992. *America Calling: A Social History of the Telephone to 1940*. Berkeley: University of California Press.

Gray, Charlotte. 2006. *Reluctant Genius: Alexander Graham Bell and the Passion for Invention*. New York: Arcade Publishing.

"The Life and Legacy of Alexander Graham Bell." 2020. San Bernadino, CA: Charles River Editors.

Stern, Ellen, and Emily Gwathmey. 1994. *Once Upon a Telephone: An Illustrated Social History*. New York: Harcourt Brace.

Oh let me love
And loving you
I will be constant
Kind and true

4 Valentine's Day Card

INTRODUCTION

In American pop culture, February 14 is universally recognized as a special day. You'll know that it is coming when you make a quick trip to the pharmacy to pick up vitamins or cold medication on a cold winter's day. You'll suddenly be assaulted by gigantic displays of red hearts, flowers, candy, red roses, and cards, so many cards. This extravaganza begins soon after the Christmas displays are packed away, for, though it may be more than a month away, it is never too early to think about what to do about Valentine's Day. Considerations abound—should I send a Valentine to the entire family or just my spouse; should I buy candy (even though we are both endeavoring to lose that extra holiday poundage) or just flowers and a card? So many decisions, brought to you by the unrelenting advertising industry. You might imagine that the ultra-commercialization of American holidays is a modern invention. But, surprisingly, the birth of the American commercial greeting-card and gift-giving industry took place earlier than you might expect. It was the mid-19th century when the first American card and gift-giving craze began. And it all started with Valentine's Day.

DESCRIPTION

Valentine's Day celebration was a low-key holiday in both England and the United States until the middle of the 19th century. The continuing Protestant influence of the Puritans, who rejected the Catholic worship of saints, diminished the popularity of the holiday in the United States, though imported English Valentine cards did appear in American stationary shops in the early years of the century. But by the 1840s, new printing techniques that were used in England to produce manufactured Valentine cards were transported to the United States, and soon a Valentine's Day craze was born. The center for the fad was on the East Coast, most notably in New York, Philadelphia, and Boston, where there were many shops and a cadre of middle-class gentry with money and time to allocate to this whimsical endeavor. The fad for commercially produced Valentine's cards took off.

Stationary stores promoted the cards, and their store windows were bursting with Valentine's Day paraphernalia. A new type of offering, called a "valentine writer," appeared on the shelves. These were helpful books with pages of romantic Valentine rhymes that one could include on the Valentine card.

The Valentine card shown in this example dates from 1830 to 1835, which is an early example of the American valentine craze. It is from the collection at the Brooklyn Museum. It measures 4 ⅞ inches high by 7 ⅝ inches wide and is a collage made from paper and fabric. There is a colorful cut-out figure of a man and a woman facing each other in the center of the card. At the feet of the figures are applied green leaves, accented by gold leaves and a flower on each side. Surrounding the panel with the cut-out figures are paper doilies adhered to the card in both white and blue. Surmounting the doily on the left is a set of embracing white cupids. In an oval panel under the figures is a handwritten sentiment stating, "Oh let me love/And loving you/I will be constant/Kind and true." The origin of this card is unknown. It seems to be an early handmade card, assembled from various pieces of fabric and paper that were either found in the house or purchased. The card, instantly recognizable as a Valentine card, demonstrates the fondness for sentimental romantic sentiments as early as the 1830s.

The origin story of the celebration of love and romance that is the modern-day Valentine's Day is a bit unexpected. Valentine's Day was named after a Catholic martyr named St. Valentine. Though the history is hazy and there are several versions of the story, some things are undisputed. First, the holiday is named after the death of Valentinus, a Christian martyr, the patron saint of epileptics. Second, the holiday had nothing to do with love and romance. Valentinus (a name that is derived from the Latin *valeo*, meaning "be strong") was a popular name in early Christian times. In fact, there were over thirty Catholic saints named Valentine. However, the St. Valentine of the legend is based on two martyrs, both of whom were beheaded on February 14. The first St. Valentine was a priest in Rome who restored sight to a blind girl and converted the Roman family to Christianity. The second St. Valentine was a bishop in Terni, not far from Rome, who cured a boy who was crippled and could not speak. The boy's family, and others around them, subsequently converted to Christianity, which resulted in the bishop's death by decapitation at the hands of the Romans. Both these martyrs were buried along the Flaminian Way, an ancient road near Rome. These events took place in the 3rd century AD. These stories of the saints, called hagiographies, were retold over centuries and may actually be two versions of the same story. Another legend in the Valentine's Day origin story is its connection to the Roman celebration of Lupercalia. This rowdy ancient pagan fertility rite involved a carnival of mostly naked young men running through the town smearing blood from goats and dogs that had been ritually sacrificed onto the faces of pregnant young women yearning for healthy babies. When the Christian popes attempted to ban this raucous celebration, some historians contend that Valentine's Day was substituted as a Christian rite as a replacement for the lascivious holiday of Lupercalia. Although other pagan holidays were re-invented by early Christian popes, there is disagreement about whether this one was one of them.

The first indication that the St. Valentine's Day celebration would be transformed into a rite of love and romance came in the late Middle Ages. Geoffrey Chaucer, the English writer of *The Canterbury Tales*, penned a number of poems in the late 1300s that referred to Valentine's Day as the day that birds mated, comparing their courtship to human matchmaking. The tradition was born. In the 17th century, Shakespeare referred to Ophelia as "Hamlet's Valentine," and Valentine's Day developed into a romantic celebration of love, which endured over the next centuries. The celebrations varied, however. Courtly love was expressed by the European aristocrats

---

An equally popular form of Valentine's Day card in the mid-19th century was the comic or satirical card. These cards could be purchased alongside the hearts and flowers on the sentimental cards, and these nasty cards had extremely graphic, cartoonish images as well as nasty poems, often targeting women who did not conform to the Victorian sensibility. This is one example:

You ugly, cross and wrinkled shrew,
    You advocate of women's rights,
No man on earth would live with you.
    For fear of endless fights.

[*Comic Valentines*. The Library Company of Philadelphia. 1840–1880? Accessed May 23, 2022. https://digital.librarycompany.org/islandora/object/digitool%3A6321?solr_nav%5Bid%5D=48dbe5bd3ecf4b4a2571&solr_nav%5Bpage%5D=0&solr_nav%5Boffset%5D=0]

Another example:

Among the women who in history brightest have shone
Are those who have left the men's affairs alone,
Who in their homes have found their proper places,
And sought not in crowds to show their faces;
We see you seek a different line—
You are too bold to be my Valentine.

[*Comic Valentines*. Library Company of Philadelphia, After 1869? Accessed May 23, 2022. https://digital.librarycompany.org/islandora/object/digitool%3A5758?solr_nav%5Bid%5D=8716d0fff6283dacfd97&solr_nav%5Bpage%5D=0&solr_nav%5Boffset%5D=0]

through poems and gift-giving. Matchmaking games were the common themes in European peasant celebrations. The most outrageous Valentine's Day tradition took place in France in the 18th century. Unmarried young people would put their names into a hat, and matches would be made according to the name that was picked. The chosen young women would then prepare a meal for the men, and subsequently they would attend a town dance. If the man was not pleased with the woman's culinary and social skills, the unfortunate woman would be expected to go home and remain in seclusion for eight days. When the seclusion was over, the rejected women would gather in the town square and burn the unrequited lovers in effigy as a display of their vengeful fury. The whole messy process often resulted in riots in the town, and the French Parliament outlawed the practice in 1776.

SIGNIFICANCE

Despite the initial American reluctance to embrace the commemoration of the martyrdom of an early Christian Catholic saint, in its medieval make-over as a paean to romantic love and sentiment, the celebration of St. Valentine's Day prevailed as a hugely popular holiday in the Victorian era. In fact, it became the first manifestation of the triumph of the commercialization of American holidays. By the 1840s, printed cards were all the rage. The records show that postmen were overwhelmed with cards around February 14, as eager Americans began to send cards to their family members and friends in addition to their romantic targets. Another interesting facet to the Valentine craze was the alternate fad of sending comic or nasty valentines. This trend, which happily died out eventually, was as popular as the sentimental cards were during the 19th century. Many valentine cards, both the romantic and the nasty, were sent anonymously. Unfortunately, the negative ones could be really mean. This was the mid-19th century, when the Industrial Revolution was picking up steam, and the women's rights movement was gaining momentum as well. Some of the satirical cards were downright insulting and were often anonymously sent to women who were attempting to venture out of their prescribed roles in the strict Victorian society. This aspect of the Valentine's Day card trend could turn the holiday into a charivari, a carnival-like outburst of lewdness and insult.

The Valentine's Day card-sending craze of the mid-19th century heralded a new and enduring fashion in American popular culture—the purchase of a manufactured greeting card. Though one might think that the Christmas card is the quintessential American greeting card, in fact it was the Valentine's Day card that initiated the explosion of the greeting card fad. Christmas cards came later in the 19th century, in the 1870s and 1880s. Soon after that, in the early 20th century, Joyce C. Hall would launch the American company Hallmark in Kansas City, which would take ultimate advantage of the American partiality for manufactured sentiment. No holiday or life-changing event would be excluded—there would be a greeting card to mark them all. But the origin story of the icon of American consumer culture, the greeting card, actually began with the early Victorian craze for St. Valentine's Day cards.

FURTHER INFORMATION

Barth, Edna. *Hearts, Cupids, and Red Roses: The Story of the Valentine Symbols*. New York: Clarion Books.

Bitel, Lisa. February 14, 2018. "The Gory Origins of Valentine's Day." Smithsonian.com. Accessed October 12, 2019. https://www.smithsonianmag.com/history/gory-origins-valentines-day-180968156/.

Forbes, Bruce D. 2015. *America's Favorite Holidays: Candid Histories*. Oakland: University of California Press.

Nelson, Elizabeth W. 2004. *Market Sentiments: Middle-Class Market Culture in 19th Century America*. Washington: Smithsonian Books.

Schmidt, Leigh E. Winter 1993. "The Fashioning of a Modern Holiday: St. Valentine's Day, 1840–1870." *Winterthur Portfolio*, 28(4): 209–245.

Schmidt, Leigh E. 1995. *Consumer Rites: The Buying and Selling of American Holidays*. Princeton, NJ: Princeton University Press.

Cooking and Food

5 Butter Churn

INTRODUCTION

Think about those delicious childhood breakfasts—those crunchy slices of buttered toast. Or those summer barbeques with fresh corn on the cob dripping with butter. Everyone has bought a pound of butter divided into quarter-pound sticks at the supermarket. The ubiquitous sticks could be found in every family's refrigerator, competing with whipped butter or ersatz "I Can't Believe It's Not Butter" oleo margarine, which came in tubs. High in fat and cholesterol, real butter may be fattening, but it is an undeniably rich and tasty treat. But where did this yummy treat originate? First, it's a dairy product, made from cow's milk. It was very popular in 19th-century America, but it wasn't sold in quarter-pound sticks. The history of butter in the United States is a fascinating one—one that involves the business of rural life on the farm, the creeping urbanization of the nation, and, surprisingly, an early example of women's paid work.

DESCRIPTION

The artifact shown here is a dash or broomstick-type churn from the state of Pennsylvania. It originates from Bucks County. Although its maker is unknown, the style is Pennsylvania German. The date of the churn is between 1790 and 1820. The churn is made of redware, a popular form of earthenware pottery from the 19th century, and covered with a lead glaze. Inside the redware vessel is a wooden staff. The churn is 13 ⅞ inches high by 8 ⅛ inches in diameter. Pennsylvania was settled by immigrants from England, Germany, and Switzerland and had rich soil that lent itself to productive dairy farming. Pennsylvania became known as the "Butter Belt," the producer of the finest butter available by the end of the 19th century.

Butter is a product of the cream that separates from the raw cow's milk. Milking the cows had, for centuries, been part of the female realm on the farm. Men were responsible for the crops and the livestock, and women for the dairy work. Traditionally, in Europe, milking was the purview of women solely, as evidenced by the old English term "milkmaid." Milk, lactation, and

33

fertility were female attributes, which were associated with the milk of the female cows. In the early 19th century on small farms in the United States, the tradition prevailed. The practice of making butter was often handed down through families or among farm women. Never written down, the best methods were taught to the girls based on tradition. Experience, observation, and judgment weighed in on the successful practice of butter-making. Without scientific methodology, the production of butter from cow's milk generated a varied product that depended on the size of the farm, location of the farm, and the skill of the farm women. Even the temperament of the cow came into play as to the quality of the milk. Butter-making was a complicated process that required time, dexterity, and also muscle. Scrawny, wraith-like milkmaids would not be the most successful, as the milking of the cows and the effective use of the butter churn required plenty of strength.

The process of making butter began with the milking of the cows. The busiest time of the year for milking was in the spring when the calves were born, when the cows produce the most milk. In the spring the cows would be able to feast on the fresh green grass, and their butter would be a golden yellow. In the winter the cows were fed dry fodder, which produced a pale yellow butter. In addition, the specific items in the diet of the cow affected the taste of the butter. Woe to the unfortunate person who gets the butter made from a cow that munched on wild onions or garlic, for the taste would be extremely unpleasant. In addition, turnips or parsnips that made it into the cow's fodder would also unfavorably flavor the butter. When time came to milk the cows, the milkmaid would take a bucket and her three-legged stool out to the milking barn, where she would give the cow something to eat, which encouraged the cow to stand still. Then the milkmaid would sit on the stool at the cow's rear right leg, holding the bucket tightly between her legs, and wash and brush the udder of the cow in order to clean the area in preparation for milking. The next step would be to strain the milk through a fabric sieve into a jug. To separate the cream, the milkmaid would then pour the milk into "setting dishes," also called pancheons, which were round and shallow and made of either wood, enameled metal, or ceramic, and cover them with a cloth. It would take up to 24 hours for the cream to finish rising to the top. The cream would be skimmed off with a tool called a skimmer, which was a wide, shallow spoon with small holes that allowed the milk to fall back into the pan while retaining the thick cream. It was then set aside in a "sour cream tub," a covered container made of wood. A smaller farm would not have enough cream to produce butter daily, so the cream would sometimes sit for several days, depending on the time of year, before the churning was begun. The cream would ripen during that time and create a tangy flavor. If available, the milk pans would be placed in a springhouse, which would keep the ripening cream cool with the constant flow of cool water from the stream that flowed through the springhouse.

When there was sufficient cream in the sour cream tub, the milkmaid would begin the process of churning the butter. A number of variations of the butter churn were available by the 19th century, but the most popular on the small farms was the broomstick or dash churn. This type of churn consisted of a wood or ceramic tall, narrow bucket. The lid of the bucket had a center hole, which accommodated a wooden pole with a plunger or dasher at the end. The milkmaid would fill the churn to about half full with the cream before beginning the process. The pole and the plunger would be pumped up and down vigorously in order to splash the cream up along the sides and produce the butter. The agitation would separate the fat molecules in the cream and eventually produce pea-sized clusters of butter rising to the top of the churn. With a little more gentle agitation, the butter clusters would come together at the top. The liquid that remained at the bottom of the churn was buttermilk, and it was usually discarded. Then the butter would be washed with cool water several times. The process would take up to an hour to complete. Finally, the butter had to be "worked" with a butter paddle on a working table, which pushed out the remaining moisture until the remaining butter seemed dry. The milkmaid would sometimes add salt and then store the butter in a large tub or "firkin." When farm wives would sell their butter in small containers at the market, they would often stamp the top of the container with individual stamps of carved decorative wood designs. These were used to identify the farm where the butter was made. In addition to the dash churn, other types of churns became popular in the 19th century as farms became larger and demand for larger yields grew. The barrel churn was a popular version, as was the end-over-end churn, both of which produced more butter than the old dash churn.

English folk melody that was sung while churning butter in a rhythmic fashion:

Come, butter, come;
Come, butter, come,
Peter stands at the gate
Waiting for his buttered cake;
Come, butter, come.

SIGNIFICANCE

Work on early American farms was arduous and demanding. While the farmer and the boys on the farm were responsible for the crops, the farm equipment, and the livestock, the women were given many other tasks. These tasks included, but were not limited to, tending to the dairy side of the farm. Of course, women were also expected to plan for and prepare the meals for the family, raise and educate the children, make the clothing, and make the fabric for the clothing, among other tasks. The chore of spinning and weaving cloth to make clothing was eased as the textile industry developed in the 19th century and New England mills began to produce factory-made fabric that was inexpensive enough to buy. In the 19th century, rural families also began to send their children to school, even the girls. So there were fewer hands available on the farm to help out on a daily basis. With the availability of factory-made textiles and the onset of public education, however, farm women were no longer required to do two of the more onerous and time-consuming tasks on the farm.

Dairying remained an essential part of the farm wife's responsibilities. In the early 19th century, there were a number of economic downturns that negatively affected the economy. Undeterred, farm wives continued the relentless drudgery of milking the cows and making the butter. Individual families did not need large amounts of butter, so women began to sell their surplus butter at the local market. This became a small business for many farm women. At this time women had no property rights, but because the task of dairying was part of the women's realm, they were solely responsible for the sale of the farm's butter. In fact, this income became a crucial asset to many farm families. The wives would go to market with their butter, sold in pound tubs with the family's individual stamp, and use the profits to purchase necessary items for the family's use. The farms in the Pennsylvania counties near Philadelphia grew to be recognized as the premier butter producers. Farm women would produce butter that would not only be sold at the market but would be transported to Philadelphia and beyond. With this success, farm wives would often hire help for the butter production. Sometimes they would hire relatives or other assistants, which included Irish immigrant girls or African Americans. Although farm wives developed this lucrative business of producing and selling butter, their labor was not recognized. In fact, the Supreme Court of Pennsylvania affirmed in 1853 that a woman's "dependent condition" left her "unfit . . . for outdoor business life." In addition, interpreting the married woman's property law of 1848, the Pennsylvania Supreme Court affirmed that a husband was "still entitled to the person and labor of the wife, and the benefits of her industry and economy" (Jensen 1988: 827). Therefore, the success of many farm women in their butter production was not noted until research was done in the 20th century with the onset of the study of material culture and women's studies. As butter production became more and more valuable, men began to take over the tasks of producing butter, purchasing larger churns, or, eventually sending the cream to a factory called a "creamery," which produced the butter. Until then, the process of dairying continued to be denigrated as merely "women's work" even though it had been a crucial element in the economic success of the farms for decades.

FURTHER INFORMATION

Cowan, Ruth S. 1983. *More Work for Mother: The Ironies of Household Technology from the Open Hearth to the Microwave.* New York: Basic Books.

Douma, Michael, curator. 2008. *Butter through the Ages.* Institute for Dynamic Educational Development. Accessed April 30, 2019. http://www.webexhibits.org/butter.

Jensen, Joan. Summer 1988. "Butter Making and Economic Development in Mid-Atlantic America from 1750 to 1850." *Signs,* 3(4): 813–829.

Jensen, Joan M., and Johnson, Mary. 1983. "What's in a Butter Churn?" *Frontiers: A Journal of Women Studies,* 7(1): 103–108.

Khosrova, Elaine. 2016. *Butter: A Rich History.* Chapel Hill, NC: Algonquin Books.

Powell, Elizabeth A. 1974. *Pennsylvania Butter Tools and Processes.* Doylestown, PA: The Bucks County Historical Society.

Williams, Susan. 2006. *Food in the United States, 1820s to 1890.* Westport, CT; London: Greenwood Press.

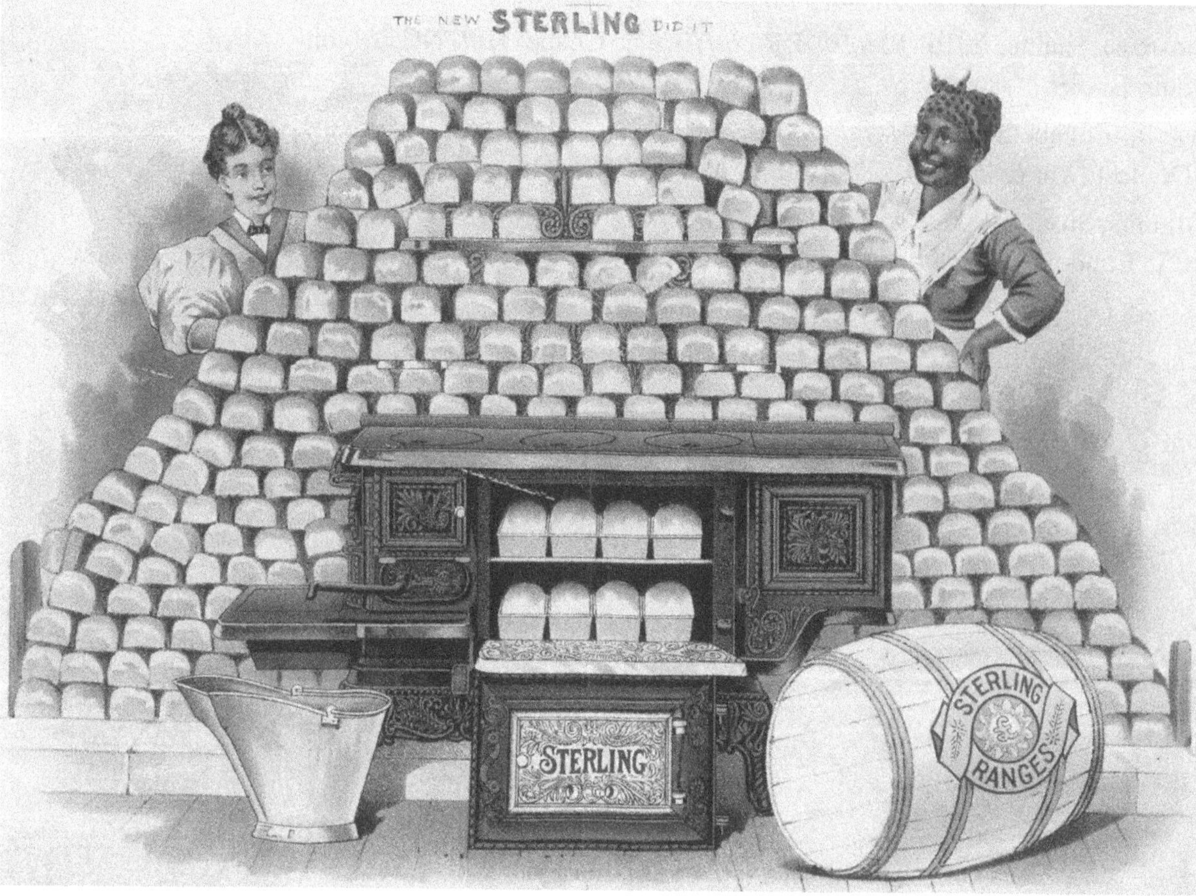

Library of Congress

6 Cookstove Advertisement

INTRODUCTION

In the kitchens of early 19th-century American middle- and working-class homes, life centered around the hearth. As perhaps one of the only heated rooms in the house, families gathered in the kitchen after the day's work was done, while the mother toiled and stooped over the hearth, keeping the fire lit and adjusting the cooking pots. For the housewife, every day was dominated by the tending of the hearth. Life for the housewife changed significantly after the cast-iron cookstove was invented and the fireplace was no longer needed as the sole source for preparing the family's meals. Though the Industrial Revolution was proceeding apace in the commercial realm, the cooking stove was one of the first labor-saving technologies that substantially improved the lives of American housewives. The cast-iron cookstove revolutionized the method of cooking and also eventually changed the style of cooking for American cooks.

DESCRIPTION

The artifact displayed here is a trade card produced by one of the prominent stove companies, Sterling Ranges. Trade cards were popular forms of advertising in the late 19th century. Trade cards were colorful and often funny, in their attempt to make the case for the usefulness of the product the company was promoting. This card shows two women, one white, one African American, proudly displaying a mountain of bread loaves behind a magnificent cast-iron Sterling cookstove. Inside the stove itself are another eight loaves of bread. The title says, "The New Sterling Did It," at the top of the card. At the lower right hand side is a logo design that says "Sterling Ranges," and on the stove itself is a large brand name label that says "Sterling." The obvious implication is that this amazing, almost magical new appliance served as the vehicle for baking all these loaves of bread. What a marvel! In the past, when cooking was done on the hearth, bread was difficult to make in the home. In the cities and towns, there were bakeries that made bread for purchase, but in smaller, rural areas, bread was not as readily available. Home cooks often made other types of replacements, like cornbread, johnny cakes, or pancakes. So this mountain of bread loaves must have been a sight to see for 19th-century home cooks. These cookstoves, especially the newer, larger ones, could accomplish amazing things. This trade card was produced circa 1896. The women depicted in the card, as implied by their forms of dress, are most likely an upper-middle-class housewife and her African American servant. Another version of this card shows a similar-sized cookstove and a similar stack of loaves of bread. The title says, "The Sterling did it, only one fire pot of coal, only one BBL of flour baked in 10 hours only 231 loaves." However, in this trade card, there is only one woman, who is dressed in much simpler garb. There is no servant in sight. One can infer that the two cards were published around the same time but with different audiences in mind (Accessed May 23, 2022. https://www.historicnewengland.org/explore/collections-access/capobject /?refd=EP003.003.008).

Until the invention of the cast-iron cookstove, cooking was done in a fireplace. The fireplace in the kitchen was higher and deeper than those in the other rooms of the house, which were built only for heating purposes. The cooking was done in this large fireplace, commonly called the hearth. It required a selection of skills and tools that were unique to that method of cooking. With the onset of the cooking stove era, these skills were eventually forgotten, and the special tools were put aside. The revolution of the new appliance called the cookstove changed the American woman's skills and chores. It also changed the American diet.

Hearth cooking was hot, dirty, and hazardous. It also required a strong back, as much of the cooking took place on the floor. Housewives were required to bend over and lift heavy pots that were either hung above the fire or were set at floor level among the ashes. The cooking was done with heavy iron pots, which were used to cook stews, soups, or boiled meat and vegetables. Because soups and stews were one-pot meals and could be left to cook for hours in the hearth, they were very popular with home cooks. To cook a soup or stew, an iron pot would be suspended above the flame by an iron crane or a lug pole, which stretched across the mouth of the fireplace. The pots would be hung on pothooks or trammels, which are adjustable hooks that allow for adjusting the height of the pot above the fire. As the cooking proceeded, the cook would lift or lower the pot, as it was the only way to control the heat. Other types of cooking took place on the floor of the hearth. Baking, toasting, and grilling would be done on the floor either in an old-fashioned type of Dutch oven with legs or with gridirons to grill. Some kitchens had a brick oven built into the chimney where baking could be done. There, the fire would be set, and the ashes would be removed. As the bricks maintained the heat for hours, the food would be placed inside the brick oven and baked. Sometimes several items could be baked in the brick oven in succession as the oven proceeded to cool down. An innovation called a tin kitchen or reflector oven allowed for cooking a roast on a spit. The reflector oven consisted of a tin screen device that would be set in front of the fire to reflect the heat back into the fireplace. Inside the reflector oven was a spit on which the roast would be skewered and then rotated in order to cook evenly. The delicious taste that resulted from roasting meat in this way continued to be popular even after the introduction of the cookstove oven, which technically baked the meat instead of roasting it. In addition to the various riggings required for cooking in a fireplace, the hearth cook required a number of other tools that aided in successful cooking. These included tongs, pokers, shovels, and irons.

Stoves were becoming available in the early 19th century. In 1741, Benjamin Franklin invented the legendary Franklin stove, a device that, after some crucial design improvements, maintained its popularity for decades. It was a device that could be placed in the fireplace or away from the fireplace in the middle of the room. The Franklin stove was more efficient than the traditional fireplace and therefore burned less firewood. But it retained the look of an open fireplace, with the fire on view. Families did utilize the Franklin stove for a few cooking purposes, including heating a tea kettle or as a warming plate. However, its use was not primarily for cooking; it was meant to heat the room and was often located in the living room or parlor, not the kitchen.

The first cooking stoves were on the market in the United States by the 1820s. The early cookstoves were fueled by wood, though coal soon become more popular, especially in the urban areas where wood was less available. The tradition of cooking on the hearth as well as the expense of these new devices slowed the expansion of the cookstove into American homes. However, by the mid-century, they were gaining in popularity, and by the end of the century, the cast-iron cookstove was a standard feature in most American kitchens. The cookstove, whether fueled by wood or coal, maintained a significant advantage over cooking in the hearth. First, the cooking method was significantly more efficient than using a fireplace. The heat was retained inside the firebox of the stove, and therefore, a smaller amount of fuel was required. The tiresome chore of bringing in the fuel from the storage bin was thus mitigated. The new stoves boasted both an oven and a cooktop. Depending on the style and size of the stove, it could have as few as two cooking burners or as many as eight, often with more than one oven. In addition, a popular accessory was a hot water tank that would be connected to the stove. With these new cooking appliances, cooks could now bake in the oven while boiling or frying several items on the top of the stove. Home cooks were given the opportunity to create more varied and creative meals with the marvelous new stove. New cookbooks were published with standardized measurements taking the place of the vague measurements utilized in the past. Cooks began to follow cookbook recipes and made more elaborate meals with numerous courses. The cookstove industry grew exponentially in the decades of the 19th century, as the appliance gained prominence as the first mass market durable appliance in the American household. It even took on a symbol of the modernization of American life.

SIGNIFICANCE

The significance of the invention of the cast-iron cooking stove has been cited by a number of historians of women's history. As interest in the study of women's work, especially housework, has piqued starting in the late 20th century, the nature of women's work has been analyzed. As discussed, the drudgery of toiling all day long at a hearth, bending over, lifting, poking, moving, adding wood, and tending the fire in order to provide the meals for the family, was a given in 18th-century America. New inventions like the Franklin stove provided more efficient use of firewood but did not alleviate the grind at the kitchen hearth. As the cooking stove was introduced and proceeded to improve during the first half of the 19th century, home cooks were provided with an easier method to cook the family's meals. The availability of servants waned as the 19th century progressed, and the importance of labor-saving devices grew. However, as is true with many technological improvements, the effect was not wholly clear-cut. Home cooks did enjoy a more efficient and effective appliance, but the work involved did not disappear. Stoves required a different but not entirely uncomplicated set of skills. The homemaker still had to carry in the fuel, though the load had decreased. The method of cooking on a cookstove required learning how to use the various gadgets on the stove that made it perform properly, like the dampers, and flues. A chemical called "blacking" had to be purchased and used regularly on the cast iron to prevent rust. In addition, a social backlash took place as the popularity of the new cookstove grew and began appearing in many American homes. The nostalgia of the Romantic movement that was sweeping through American culture made it possible for some social critics to condemn the cast-iron cooking stove as a symbol of the collapse of American family values. Stoves were vilified in some American press as agents of the destruction of the moral principles symbolized by the family gathering around the hearth. With the cooking stove in the kitchen, there was no longer any need for the great roaring fireplace. With the progression of technology, central heating systems were installed in most modern homes. While greatly increasing the comfort level of the house's occupants, many Americans yearned for the radiant warmth of the fireplace flames. By the end of the 19th century, the Colonial Revival movement commenced and many homes were designed with fireplaces, which, however unnecessary, were very popular. And they remain so today.

FURTHER INFORMATION

Brewer, Priscilla J. Spring 1990. "'We Have Got a Very God Cooking Stove': Advertising, Design, and Consumer Response to the Cookstove, 1815–1880." *Winterthur Portfolio*, 25(1): 35–54.

Cowan, Ruth S. 1983. *More Work for Mother: The Ironies of Household Technology from the Open Hearth to the Microwave*. New York: Basic Books.

Ellin, Phyllis M. 1985. *At Home with the Range: The American Cooking Stove, 1865–1920*. Master's thesis, University of Pennsylvania, Philadelphia, PA.

McGaw, Judith A. Summer 1982. "Women and the History of American Technology." *Signs*, 7(4): 798–828.

McLean, Alice L. 2006. *Cooking in America, 1840–1945*. Westport, CT: Greenwood Press.

Strasser, Susan. 1982. *Never Done: A History of American Housework*. New York: Henry Holt and Company.

7 Oyster Plate

INTRODUCTION

Raw oysters are a popular delicacy on the menus of today's top restaurants. Connoisseurs can order oysters from various locations around the country and delight in their assorted sizes and tastes. But today's oyster production and consumption pale in comparison to the millions of oysters that were harvested and consumed at the height of the American oyster craze in the second half of the 19th century. From 1880 to 1910, a total of 160 million pounds of oyster meat was harvested every year. And during that time period, the oyster was one of America's favorite foods; it was prepared in a variety of methods apart from the familiar raw oyster on the half shell. Recipes abounded in 19th-century cookbooks for oyster stew, fried oysters, broiled oysters, oyster fricassee, oyster fritters, oyster Newberg, oyster pie, pickled oysters, oyster stuffing, and countless more. The oyster craze eventually ended when the nation's waterways succumbed to the pollution that had been spewed into them unchecked for decades, only to be resurrected, to a lesser degree, in the 20th century after the passage of the Clean Water Act in 1972.

DESCRIPTION

A special piece of tableware, called the oyster plate, was a delightful accessory to the standard fine china of a 19th-century home. Households would have a set of these plates to utilize at large dinner parties. These ornately decorated and colorful plates often contained seafood-related themes and were produced by the finest china manufacturers available in the American market, which included the European companies such as Sevres, Dresden, and Wedgwood, as well as the American manufacturers Lenox, Picard, and Union Porcelain Works. In the 1870s, an oyster plate service for twelve could cost a family as much as $500 or as little as $35, which still made it a costly trifle. An oyster plate would typically contain four to six depressions in the shape of an oyster shell, at times with another depression that would hold cocktail sauce. The oysters would be taken out of the shell before plating, as the shells had various shapes and often had sharp edges that could scratch the delicate plate. The oysters would be served on the plates accompanied by special silver forks. The oyster plate shown in this example, from the Metropolitan Museum of Art in New York, was produced by the Union Porcelain Works in Greenpoint, Brooklyn, and sold by Tiffany and Company in New York. The Union Porcelain Works was the first American producer of true porcelain, based on French and English manufacturing techniques. The colorful plate, dating from 1881, measures 8 9/16 inches by 6 ½ inches. Similar to other oyster plates, this one has marine themes. It is shaped like a clam shell and hand painted with depictions of a mussel, snail, skate egg case, lobster claw, whelk, baby clam, and seaweed. The plate has four depressions that resemble oyster shells and one that resembles a scallop shell. Surrounding the white oyster and scallop shells, the plate is painted in a naturalistic sea-blue, with a dark blue mussel, red lobster, pink snail, and green seaweed. The plate is finished off with decorative gold-painted edging.

The consumption of oysters has a long history. The Ancient Greeks ate oysters, as did the Romans, who considered them a symbol of wealth, even placing a representation of the oyster on one of their coins. They are also credited with advancing the theory that oysters are an aphrodisiac. The 18th-century Venetian writer and infamous womanizer Giacomo Casanova opined in his memoir that his copious consumption of oysters aided him in his seduction of over one hundred women. The French also historically craved the bivalve mollusk, harvesting them incessantly until, by the 19th century, the French oyster beds had been decimated. In North America, the story of the consumption of oysters is also a prolonged and fascinating tale. Indigenous Americans were known to harvest and consume oysters for upward of nine thousand years. The local tribes in New York, known as the Lenni Lenape, offered Henry Hudson oysters when he sailed into the New York harbor in 1609. Oyster shell trash pit piles, called middens, have been discovered all over the eastern coastal region.

The oyster that was consumed by 19th-century Americans is a mollusk whose family is "ostreidae" and species is "ostreidae Crassostrea virginica," also known as an Eastern oyster. It is a part of the family of "true oysters," which are not pearl-producing, and can be found all along the North American eastern seaboard and the Gulf of Mexico. Although oysters from all regions in the United States are biologically identical, they vary in size and taste due to the surrounding environment. Oysters are salt-water bivalve mollusks that live in brackish, coastal waters. They are filter-feeders and can filter out pollutants. The reason that oysters vary so much in size and flavor is the variance of the water temperature, amount of salt in the water, availability of food, and amount of crowding. Warmer water produces larger oysters, which often have a milder flavor.

Oysters were a popular local delicacy in the coastal regions of the eastern United States throughout the 18th and early 19th centuries. By the mid-19th century, technological advances provided new opportunities for expanding the reach of the popular mollusk. Transportation and preservation of fresh oysters were not possible until the construction of the railroad lines that were able to transport the oysters to western regions. Fresh oysters were packed in ice and shipped to Cleveland, Cincinnati, Detroit, Chicago, and St. Louis where an appreciation for the delicacy also developed. In addition, canning techniques allowed for easy transport for the popular delicacy, and the canning industry soon took off in eastern cities. A new harvesting technique also increased the size of the oyster catch. Instead of the traditional oyster tongs, which were used by an individual to rake up the oyster beds, a technique called dredging was used. This method combed the ocean floor with iron mesh bags. It sucked up many more oysters at deeper depths. With the availability of oysters, the price plummeted. By the mid-1800s, the price of oysters was one half that of beef. In fact, the ubiquitous oyster establishments in the large eastern cities served oysters at bargain basement prices. In New York, the so-called Canal Street Plan, named after a street in Lower Manhattan, was popular in the oyster saloons. These "oyster cellars," located down a few steps from street level, were indicated by a red balloon hung outside the door. A customer could consume "all you could eat" oysters for six cents, as a salty snack to go with a beer. The prominence of the oyster saloons even offered opportunity to unexpected entrepreneurs. The oyster industry was an integrated one; many oyster fishermen from the Chesapeake were freed slaves. Although no longer slaves, they were not allowed by law to own their own boats or even to fish without a white escort. Because of these restrictions, many relocated to New York before the Civil War in order to receive more opportunity in a northern state. Many black oystermen settled on the south shore of Staten Island where the oyster industry thrived, in a settlement called Sandy Ground. Prejudice was still an issue in New York, of course, and there were still constraints on African American businesses. However, many African American oystermen made a good living in the industry. One very successful African American businessman was Thomas Downing, who opened an oyster saloon in 1825. Running a café or oyster saloon was an accepted business for a black man in New York because African Americans were already often employed as waiters. Downing became a prominent member of New York society, serving the most powerful New York bankers, politicians, and businessmen, a surprising success for a son of a freed slave from Virginia.

The oyster cellars and saloons were everywhere, and many were located in poor areas with questionable clientele. However, the narrative of 19th-century oyster consumption is unexpectedly democratic. Although oysters were exceedingly inexpensive and were gobbled down by the poorest members of society as a nutritious and tasty snack, the wealthiest class also signed on to the oyster craze. In the second half of the 19th century, the Victorian upper class served oysters as one of the many courses in their extravagant dinners. The overly elaborate nature of Victorian culture and design was evident on the dinner tables of the Victorian family. Formal dinners often had up to nine courses, with separate china pieces for each course. Dinner service sets could max out at 514 pieces. In addition to the standard various plates, bowls, cups and saucers, and serving dishes, there were specialty pieces that were made for a specific purpose. Of course, with the passion for eating oysters in full swing, the finest of households always included a set of oyster plates for the use of their guests. These "luscious bivalves," a nickname for the oyster when served at Victorian dinner parties, became a requisite part of the meal.

Charles Mackay, a popular Scottish songwriter, visited New York City in 1857. During his visit, he raved in his diary about the accessibility and popularity of the oyster:

In walking up Broadway by day or by night—but more especially by night—the stranger cannot but remark the great number of "Oyster Saloons," "Oyster and Coffee Saloons," "Oyster and Lager Beer Saloons," which solicit him at every turn to stop and taste . . . In these (saloons). . . oysters as large as a lady's hand are to be had at all hours, either from the shell, as they are commonly eaten in England, or cooked in twenty, or perhaps, in forty or a hundred ways. Oysters pickled, stewed, baked, roasted, fried, and scalloped; oysters made into soups, patties and puddings, oysters with condiments and without condiments; oysters for breakfast dinner and supper; oysters without stint or limit—fresh as the fresh air, and almost as abundant—are daily offered to the palates of the Manhattanese, and appreciated with all the gratitude which such bounty of nature ought to inspire.

[Quoted in: Kurlansky, Mark. 2006. *The Big Oyster: History on the Half Shell*. New York: Random House Trade Paperbacks (155).]

SIGNIFICANCE

Oysters played an important role in the culinary traditions of American life in the 19th century. The abundance of the bivalve provided residents of the coastal states delicious sustenance for millennia, from the age of the Native American tribes to the bustle of a burgeoning city like 19th-century New York. The technology that allowed for the transportation of the popular oyster to locations far afield, from the American Midwest to Europe, continued to satisfy the voracious appetites of a growing population. The oyster industry was efficient in its harvesting of the mollusk along the coastal beds of the New York City region. When the numbers began to reduce, the resourceful New York oystermen learned to seed the local beds with oysters from the Chesapeake region. The industry continued to expand as the number of oysters grew and the price dropped. Americans were eating oysters for breakfast, lunch, and dinner, and even the wealthiest among them were delighting in their delicate flavor and serving them on special pricey plates. But even with the ingenious advances that provided more oysters for public consumption, there was dark cloud on the horizon. Consumers were unexpectedly coming down with serious bacterial infections including typhoid. Raw sewage had been dumped into New York harbor for years, and the industrial waste along the New York and New Jersey coasts was also seriously polluting the eastern coastline. Oyster fishermen continued to harvest the mollusk into the 20th century, but by 1927, the last oyster beds in the New York City region were closed due to pollution. The passage of the Clean Water Act in 1972 led to cleanups of the coastal waterways, but New York is still too polluted with heavy metals and polychlorinated biphenyls (PCBs) to allow for harvesting. Oysters are farmed in various locations around the country and provide a reduced number for today's more limited consumption. A program called Baykeeper in New York has begun to build oyster reefs in various locations in the harbor where oyster beds can grow. After all, the hearty little bivalve is a filter-feeder and actually helps rehabilitate the harbor as it filters pollution from the water. The wonderful oyster is still with us and working hard!

FURTHER INFORMATION

Grimes, William. 2006. "Before There Were Bagels, New York Had the Oyster." *New York Times*. March 6. https://www.nytimes.com/2006/03/01/books/before-there-were-bagels-new-york-had-the-oyster.html.

Kurlansky, Mark. 2007. *The Big Oyster: History on the Half Shell*. New York: Random House Trade Paperbacks.

Lobel, Cindy R. 2014. *Urban Appetites: Food and Culture in Nineteenth Century New York*. Chicago: University of Chicago Press.

Nigro, Carmen. 2011. "History on the Half-Shell: The Story of New York City and Its Oysters." *New York Public Library* blog post. June 2. https://www.nypl.org/blog/2011/06/01/history-half-shell-intertwined-story-new-york-city-and-its-oysters.

Royte, Elizabeth. 2006. "The Mollusk That Made Manhattan." *New York Times Book Review*. March 5. https://www.nytimes.com/2006/03/05/books/review/the-mollusk-that-made-manhattan.html.

Shepard, Barnett. 2008. *Tottenville: The Town the Oyster Built*. New York: Preservation League of Staten Island and Tottenville Historical Society.

Simpson, Richard. June 1997. "Setting the Altar of Gastronomy: Victorian Dinnerware—Oyster Plates." *Antiques & Collecting Magazine*, 102 (4): 36.

Watman, Max. 2016. "The Oyster Makes Its Return to the Hudson and the Chesapeake." The Daily Beast, New York. August 15. https://search.pro quest.com/docview/1819476107.

Entertainment

Baseball Card

Buffalo Bill's Wild West Poster

Godey's Magazine

Piano

Souvenir from the Centennial Exhibition

JOHN M. WARD.
ALLEN & GINTER'S
Cigarettes.
RICHMOND. VIRGINIA.

8 Baseball Card

INTRODUCTION

Baseball is known as America's "national pastime." References to the game turn up in an overwhelming variety of common American expressions: "Getting to first base," "hitting it out of the ballpark," "grandstanding," "playing hardball," demanding that someone "play ball," "touching base" with someone, being "caught off base." These are all familiar phrases that originate with baseball. America's game, played by "the boys of summer," maintains its popularity after over 150 years. With the onset of the game of baseball came the beginning of the craze for baseball cards, a tradition almost as old as the game itself.

DESCRIPTION

The baseball card shown here, from the large collection at the Library of Congress, is part of a set of baseball cards issued in 1887 by the Allen & Gintner Tobacco Company. It is a chromolithograph and measures 2.5 inches high by 1.5 inches wide. The Allen & Gintner Tobacco Company was launched by a former Confederate officer Lewis Gintner, with his partner John Allen, in Richmond, Virginia, in 1865. These cigarettes are believed to be the first to include a set of collectible baseball cards in their "World's Champions" series of chromolithograph cards. The series did not exclusively portray baseball players, however. There were ten baseball players in the fifty-card set, which also included stars of rowing, wrestling, boxing, shooting, billiards, and pool. The cards were printed by Lindner, Eddy & Claus of New York City. The images were colorful, painted portraits of the players and were very popular collectibles from the time that they were first issued. Allen & Gintner Tobacco Company provided a bound album for collectors to organize and arrange the fifty cards. This handsome set marked the inauguration of the baseball card collecting craze.

The Allen & Gintner card in the photo depicts John Montgomery Ward, an influential early baseball player who was inducted into the Baseball Hall of Fame in 1964. Ward was born in 1860 in Bellefonte, Pennsylvania, in the

Nittany Valley, not far from State College, the location of the Pennsylvania State University. Both his parents passed away when Ward was a young teenager, and the precocious Ward was sent to the Penn State campus to study in its prep school program. He soon showed remarkable pitching ability on Penn State's first baseball team. After an unfortunate incident regarding a theft of chickens from a nearby farm, Ward was expelled and forced to support himself with various jobs. However, his true love was baseball, and he soon became a semi-pro player on a number of local teams. He joined his first major league team, the Providence Grays, part of the new National League, in 1878, at the age of eighteen. His pitching ability was outstanding, but he also excelled as a position player and as a hitter. Ward had the distinction of being the second major league pitcher to have pitched a perfect game, when he pitched for Providence in 1880. Ward's pitching arm soon gave out, but he continued to play in various field positions and took over as player-manager. In the off-season, the intellectually gifted Ward completed law school at Columbia in 1885. He received a political science degree from the same university in 1886. He was instrumental in founding the first players' union, called the Brotherhood of Professional Baseball Players in 1885, with which he fought for the rights of players against the dreaded "reserve clause" that allowed management to maintain control of a player's contract even after their contract had expired, binding that player to a team indefinitely. The reserve system remained entrenched for eighty years, finally ending with the onset of the "free agency" rules in the 1970s. Ward also lobbied, without success, for the New York Giants to hire a talented pitcher, George Stovey, from the Negro Leagues. It would be another sixty years before another Negro League player, Jackie Robinson, would join the Brooklyn Dodgers as the first African American Major League baseball player. Ward went on to a long and storied career in law. He often represented the rights of individual players against the corporate ownership and in 1887 was quoted as stating, "There was a time when the National League stood for integrity and fair dealing. Today, it stands for dollars and cents . . . Players have been bought, sold and exchanged as though they were sheep instead of American citizens" (Devereaux 2018: 59).

The game of baseball evolved from a British game called "rounders." This game was similar to a number of children's games that were played in the late 18th and early 19th centuries with noteworthy names like "stool ball," "one-old-cat," "feeder," "town ball," or even "base ball." All these children's games used a ball and a stick and involved running back and forth to "bases." The game of rounders was closest to the game of modern baseball. Rounders had four bases in a diamond configuration, where a "feeder" (pitcher) threw to a "striker" (batter). The striker had three opportunities to hit the ball or else he was "out." He would also be out if he hit the ball and the ball was caught or if the striker was hit with a ball while running to base. The English game of rounders was the direct antecedent to baseball. This fact was not in dispute until the late 19th century, when a group of American businessmen colluded to construct a false narrative that could prove that baseball was truly an "American" game. At a baseball banquet held at the historic New York City restaurant Delmonico's, an argument ensued between Albert G. Spalding, former baseball player, official, team owner, and sporting-goods entrepreneur, and Henry Chadwick, a distinguished baseball writer and the originator of the baseball scoring system. Chadwick insisted that the popular game was based on the British game of rounders, while Spalding, in agreement with Abraham G. Mills, president of the National League, contended that the game was invented in the United States and was therefore thoroughly American. A commission was set up to study the issue. As chair of the commission, Mills made sure that his and Spalding's position prevailed. Locating an elderly gentleman from Cooperstown, New York, who contended that General Abner Doubleday had drawn up a diagram showing a baseball diamond in 1839, the commission decreed that the answer had been found. Baseball was invented by an American military hero from the Civil War, General Abner Doubleday. The fact that he was long dead and that there was no diagram, or other existing evidence of this claim, was manifestly ignored. The myth had been created. Baseball was invented by Abner Doubleday in Cooperstown, New York. Baseball historians have totally debunked the claim, but the myth lived on, as myths do. This phenomenon is vividly described by baseball historian Warren Goldstein as "the intransigent persistence of untruths" (Goldstein 1989). Legions of Americans still believe that baseball was invented by Abner Doubleday in Cooperstown, New York, and historians are still combatting the false claim that was made over a century ago. Not helping the matter is the fact that the Baseball Hall of Fame is, to this day, located in the small, rural hamlet of Cooperstown, New York.

The British game of rounders did evolve into the American game of baseball, and New York City was where it started. The Knickerbocker Base Ball Club used the first written rules of the game, developed by Alexander Cartright and Daniel "Doc" Adams in 1845. These two are considered the true originators of the American game of baseball, for, though the rules have changed over the years, the basic structure of the game has remained the same. There were nine players on each team, there was a diamond-shaped base configuration, and a batter (called a "Striker" at the time) had three chances to hit the ball before being called "out." The nine-innings game was initiated in 1857. Baseball spread through the northeastern states, played by gentlemen members of a variety of social clubs. While modern-day baseball still uses the term "clubs" to describe the professional teams, the earliest baseball clubs were actual men's social clubs or fraternal organizations with members who paid dues and met in taverns or on playing fields. It was a popular though still amateur sport. During the Civil War, the popularity of the game broadened throughout the country. A famous lithograph shows the game being played by Union soldiers at a Confederate prison camp in North Carolina.

Along with the newfound popularity of the game of baseball came the enduring love for baseball memorabilia, especially the baseball card. The first baseball cards were included in cigarette packages, on heavy cardstock, which served as a necessary stiffener for the soft cigarette packets. The use of tobacco was growing in popularity in both the United States and Europe in the first half of the 19th century. Tobacco was sold in packets with brand names by the mid-century. But at that time cigarettes still were hand-rolled. In the 1880s, an automated cigarette-rolling machine was invented, and James Buchanan Duke of North Carolina invested in the machine, creating the cigarette company W. Duke & Sons. Other manufacturers soon jumped on the bandwagon. With industrial development came improved printing capabilities, and the advertising industry boomed. Soon multiple cigarette

---

CASEY AT THE BAT: THE BATTLE OF THE REPUBLIC SUNG IN THE YEAR 1888

By Ernest Lawrence Thayer

Written in 1888, this (abridged) bit of comic verse has been a perennial favorite and is often recited by men in Mudville baseball uniforms on the streets of Cooperstown, New York, outside of the National Baseball Hall of Fame.

The outlook wasn't brilliant for the Mudville nine that day;
The score stood four to two with but one inning more to play.
And then when Cooney died at first, and Barrows did the same,
A sickly silence fell upon the patrons of the game.

The sneer is gone from Casey's lip, his teeth are clinched in hate;
He pounds with cruel violence his bat upon the plate.
And now the pitcher holds the ball, and now he lets it go,
And now the air is shattered by the force of Casey's blow.

Oh, somewhere in this favored land the sun is shining bright;
The band is playing somewhere, and somewhere hearts are light,
And somewhere men are laughing, and somewhere children shout;
But there is no joy in Mudville—mighty Casey has struck out.

[Thayer, Ernest. 1888. Originally published anonymously in the San Francisco Examiner (then called the Daily Examiner), June 3, Accessed October 6, 2019. https://www.poetryfoundation.org/poems/45398/casey-at-the-bat.]

companies started advertising their various brands. Inside the packages, companies inserted promotional materials on the cardboard stiffeners that were included in the package. Cards with pictures of famous actresses and other celebrities (sometimes shown in provocative poses) were the first to be included in the packets. These colorful cards, using chromolithography, were instantly popular. By 1886, after strong criticism of the provocative images damaged the industry, images of popular baseball players took their place. One brilliant innovation was the strategy of offering sets of cards that could be collected. By giving people the option to collect a whole set, consumers were encouraged to demonstrate brand loyalty. Card collectors were often young boys who would beg their fathers for the cards when their dads would purchase a new pack of cigarettes. These cards appealed to the growing American middle-class families that enjoyed newfound leisure time and were able to devote precious hours to the collection of cards and the study of baseball statistics that were included on the back side of the card.

SIGNIFICANCE

Baseball cards have a long history. Beginning in the 1880s in cigarette packaging, they were soon sold in bubblegum packets to the delight of the young collectors. Today's collectors relish the value of certain historical baseball cards, which can reach values of over a million dollars. Although in the internet age, contemporary baseball cards have been reduced to a niche market, rare historical cards still garner big payoffs. The game of baseball, as America's national pastime, has also had its ups and downs in popularity. It has, however, continued to maintain an almost mythical status as the quintessential American sport. Much has been written about baseball, and there have been a multitude of baseball films, including the biographical, historical, and the mystical, like *Field of Dreams* and *The Natural*. Baseball has been described by the late baseball historian Bruce Catton as a "pageant and a ritualized drama, as completely formalized as a Spanish bullfight, and although it is wholly urbanized it still speaks of the small town in the simple rural era that lived before the automobile came in to blight the landscape. One reason for this is that in a land of unending change, baseball changes very little" (Bruce Catton, quoted in Berkow 1981).

FURTHER INFORMATION

Berkow, Ira. 1981. "What Is Baseball's Meaning and Its Effect on America?" *New York Times*. May 31. Accessed October 1, 2019. https://www.nytimes.com/1981/05/31/sports/what-is-baseball-s-meaning-and-its-effect-on-america.html.

Buckley, James, Jr. 2010. *Eyewitness Baseball*. London; New York: DK Publishing.

Devereaux, Peter. 2018. *Game Faces: Early Baseball Cards from the Library of Congress*. Washington, DC: Smithsonian Books/Library of Congress.

Goldstein, Warren. 1989. *Playing for Keeps: A History of Early Baseball, 20th Anniversary Edition*. Ithaca, NY; London: Cornell University Press.

"John Ward." n.d. National Baseball Hall of Fame. Accessed October 5, 2019. https://baseballhall.org/hall-of-famers/ward-john.

Lamb, Bill. 2017. "John Montgomery Ward." *Society for American Baseball Research*. Accessed October 5, 2019. https://sabr.org/bioproj/person/2de3f6ef.

Ritter, Lawrence. 2010. *The Glory of Their Times: The Story of the Early Days of Baseball Told by the Men Who Played It*. New York: Harper Perennial Modern Classics.

9 Buffalo Bill's Wild West Poster

INTRODUCTION

The United States was primed to emerge as an economic powerhouse by the last quarter of the 19th century. No longer an agrarian, raw, and young nation, it was rapidly transforming into a formidable, urban, industrial one. The United States was changing. With the intensification of the Industrial Revolution came labor unrest and violent strikes that disrupted the economy. Society was shifting as the middle class grew and many workers exited farms in rural areas to commence work as clerks in urban businesses. As of the 1890s, the frontier was declared closed, but Americans still felt a longing for its limitless opportunities. The myth of the American West had not yet been created, but it soon would be, performed by an authentic member of the cowboy class, the Indian fighter Buffalo Bill Cody, in his beloved *Wild West* show.

DESCRIPTION

The artifact shown here is a poster of Buffalo Bill's Wild West and Congress of Rough Riders of the World, a version of the show that Buffalo Bill initiated in 1893. This show included a variety of military units from foreign lands, including Cossacks and gauchos. The poster dates from 1899 and depicts a group of Indians attacking a wagon train, with a large portrait of Buffalo Bill in an insert on the right side of the poster. The poster is 40 inches wide by 28 inches high. At the top of the poster in large red lettering is the title "Buffalo Bill's Wild West," and underneath it in smaller blue lettering, it states, "And Congress of Rough Riders of the World." Under the depiction of Buffalo Bill is the text, in white letters, "Col. W. F. Cody, Buffalo Bill, Will Appear at Every Performance." At the bottom of the poster, also in white lettering, it states, "A Congress of American Indians. Representing Various Tribes, Characters and Peculiarities of the Wily Dusky Warriors in Scenes from Actual Life Giving Their Weird War Dances and Picturesque Style of Horsemanship." Buffalo Bill's popular shows were beloved in the United States and even spent several years touring Europe.

The show performed at Queen Victoria's Golden Jubilee in London and continued on to France, Spain, Italy, Austria, and Germany. The European audiences adored the shows, eager to see the depiction of the exotic American West and the Indians with their "weird war dances and picturesque style of horsemanship." In 1893, Buffalo Bill set up shop in Chicago where the magnificent World's Columbian Exposition was taking place.

It was on May 19, 1883, in Omaha, Nebraska, that Buffalo Bill Cody introduced the legendary show that would make him a celebrity throughout the world. This outdoor spectacle, which he entitled *Buffalo Bill's Wild West*, was a unique invention that brought together live cowboys and Indians, horses, and all sorts of entertainers into an outdoor event that had elements of a circus but was something new. Outdoor spectacles using live animals were not unheard of: horse shows had made the rounds in the United States since the 18th century. Circuses also utilized live animals, of course, and sometimes included skits about Native American life. But *Buffalo Bill's Wild West* was different: it was bigger, and it purported to convey the story of the American West, as told by some of its actual participants. Bill Cody devised this Wild West story as a narrative, retelling tales from his own life and the lives of others. Much of it was exaggerated, of course, and even apocryphal, but it was irresistibly appealing to the American public.

The *Wild West* show was a phenomenal success. In 1886, between one and two million people, half the metro New York City population came to see the electrically lighted show performed on Staten Island. The show was performed twice a day for six days a week (excluding Sundays.) Each performance cost fifty cents, twenty-five for children, and the horseshoe-shaped grandstand accommodated twenty thousand people. After the audience was seated, the "Star-Spangled Banner" was played by the Cowboy Band. The first up was Annie Oakley, the diminutive sharpshooter who performed at the *Wild West* show for decades, joining in 1886 at the tender age of fifteen. After her performance came a demonstration of "Cow-boy's Fun," which included roping and bronco riding. Then Buffalo Bill entered the arena, riding on a white stallion, with his shoulder-length hair blowing in the wind beneath his cowboy hat. He always made a commanding impression on the enthusiastic crowd as he expertly shot clay pigeons while galloping through the arena. After Buffalo Bill, the Lakota Indians thundered in on horseback, attacking the historic Deadwood stagecoach in a recreation of an Old West stagecoach attack. The breathless pace of the *Wild West* show left the audience enthralled. It continued for 2 hours, interspersed with additional demonstrations of Native American ceremonial dances, as well as roping by Mexican vaqueros. The finale of every show was the showstopping Indian attack on the settler's cabin, after which Buffalo Bill saluted his huge cast and invited the audience to wander around the surrounding encampment where the cast members lived during the show's tenure. And this encampment was vast: by the 1890s, the show employed as many as five hundred cast members and staff, who were fed three meals per day and lived in walled tents.

But Bill Cody was not born into celebrity. When William Frederick Cody was born in 1846, his hometown of Le Claire, Iowa, was still part of the Iowa Territory. The frontier was pressing forward inexorably to the west, with all the uncertainty and risk that implied. Members of Cody's family experienced much of the peril and danger of the old frontier in their pursuit of a stable homestead. After leaving the Iowa Territory, they moved to Ontario, Canada, to the hometown of Bill Cody's father Isaac, before settling near Fort Leavenworth, in the Kansas Territory in 1853. Kansas was deep in the throes of the "Bleeding Kansas" slavery wars. Congress had passed the Kansas-Nebraska Act in 1854, which called for the Kansas Territory to decide by popular vote whether to become a slave or a free state. This led to seven bloody years of fighting between the pro-slavery "Border Ruffians" and the anti-slavery "Free-Staters," which lasted until Kansas entered the union as a free state in 1861. By declaring himself a Free-Stater, Isaac Cody became the target of violent attacks and was nearly fatally stabbed on September 18, 1854. Life became unbearable on the Cody farm, as his father had to hide out. Permanently weakened by the effects of the knife attack, Isaac died in 1857, leaving the family impoverished. Bill had to leave school at the age of eleven to work. His first job was as a messenger on horseback for a wagon train. Bill took a number of jobs in his early working years, including as an ox driver, and he also claimed to have briefly worked as a rider for the short-lived but legendary Pony Express. This was an assertion that he made throughout his adult life, and it became a standard theme of his *Wild West* show. He became an experienced stagecoach driver and wagon master and also tried his hand as a gold prospector at Pike's Peak during the gold rush of 1858–1860. Bill Cody subsequently joined the army and fought for the Union during the Civil War, working as a Union scout, and then with the Seventh Kansas Cavalry. He married Louisa Frederici in 1866, continuing to work as a scout for the army. In 1867, Bill Cody was offered a job by the Kansas Pacific branch of the Union Pacific Railroad to procure meat for the workers constructing the railroad. Here's where Bill Cody earned his nickname "Buffalo Bill." He was estimated to have killed more than four thousand buffalo in an eight-month period.

In 1868, Bill was hired by General Eugene Carr as a chief of scouts for the U.S. Fifth Cavalry. Bill worked as a scout as well as a dispatch rider for four years. He participated in sixteen battles with Native Americans during this period, but his most celebrated battle was against the Cheyenne in the Battle of Summit Springs, in the Colorado Territory, on July 11, 1869, for which he received the Medal of Honor in 1872. Bill Cody was beginning to gain acclaim as a horseman and Indian fighter by this time, and the writer Ned Buntline chose the romanticized character of "Buffalo Bill" to star in a serialized story published in Street and Smith's *New York Weekly* on December 23, 1869. Buntline had met Bill Cody in Fort McPherson, Nebraska, and was impressed with his exploits. This story would be the first of over 1,700 Buffalo Bill stories and dime novels, written by Buntline and Colonel Prentiss Ingraham, as well as others. These stories, extremely popular at the time, constituted a cornucopia of both glamorized fact and total fiction. They also created a media celebrity in Buffalo Bill Cody, hero of the West. Buntline persuaded Bill Cody to appear in a stage show that Buntline was producing, so in 1872, Buffalo Bill made his debut as an actor in the show *The Scouts of the Prairie*. He continued performing in shows in a theatrical troupe he called the Buffalo Bill Combination for eleven seasons, polishing up his stage persona, transforming himself from a diffident performer to a consummate showman. During the off-season, Cody would return to the prairies to hunt, often escorting wealthy clients, including the Grand Duke Alexis of the Russian royal family, on expeditions.

SIGNIFICANCE

Buffalo Bill Cody became one of the most famous personalities in the world by the end of the 19th century. He is considered a hero by many despite his reputation as an Indian fighter and buffalo hunter. His treatment of his troupe and his staff was extremely generous. Native Americans sought positions as part of his troupe, because the pay was equal to that of the white performers and they received more respect than in other areas of society. Bill Cody respected Native American culture and encouraged the troupe members to retain their languages and their rituals. Women were also treated with uncommon respect in Buffalo Bill's *Wild West* shows. Bill believed strongly in women's rights and women's suffrage, long before the Nineteenth Amendment was passed in 1920. Even African Americans were represented in the shows, a few as cowboys and many in the concert band. And despite the fact that Buffalo Bill was known as a killer of buffalos, he worked to save the buffalo in his later years.

Buffalo Bill had an innate sense of showmanship, an understanding of the zeitgeist and what the world was anxious to see. He bemoaned the fact that the majority of members of the audience in his earlier shows were men, and specifically men of the working class. Bill saw that the culture was changing before his eyes, that the rough and tumble world of the old frontier was fading fast, while the comfortable life of the American bourgeoisie was replacing it throughout the country. Part of his genius was to recognize that middle-class women, who increasingly developed control over family and household affairs in the Victorian era, desired a night out for themselves and their families. Buffalo Bill was constantly searching for new and larger audiences. The scrappy male audiences of his early shows were not going to grow; however, the middle class was expanding exponentially. The brilliance of his creation was somewhat counterintuitive: women might not be expected to willingly attend violent shoot-em-up events. But by the end of the 19th century, the frontier was closing, as identified by Frederick Jackson Turner in his celebrated thesis in 1893. The American myth that there would always be a western frontier was no longer justifiable. Even the members of the Buffalo Bill troupe, many of whom included actual participants, were aging, and the whole concept of the taming of the West was rapidly transforming into a form of nostalgia. This spectacle was beloved because the *Wild West* had in fact ended; it was never coming back. What the Buffalo Bill's *Wild West* show did, however, was to create the enduring myth of the Wild West. Cowboys, Indians, the freedom of the west, all were part of the creation myth shaped by Buffalo Bill and his troupe and the other multifarious shows that imitated his. The shows maintained their popularity despite the fact that Buffalo Bill went bankrupt due to the unfortunate aftereffects of his poor investments and his inveterate generosity and died a relatively poor man at the age of seventy in 1917. By that time, the spectacle of the *Wild West* show was losing popularity as movies were becoming the chosen entertainment of the day. But the myth of the old west soon became the theme of many a Hollywood western.

FURTHER INFORMATION

"Being Buffalo Bill: Man, Myth and Media." n.d. National Cowboy and Western Heritage Museum. Accessed May 24, 2022. https://national cowboymuseum.org/explore/buffalo-bill-man-myth-media/.

Carter, Robert A. 2000. *Buffalo Bill Cody: The Man behind the Legend*. New York: John Wiley & Sons.

Fees, Paul. 2019. "Wild West Shows: Buffalo Bill's Wild West." Buffalo Bill Center of the West. Accessed December 19, 2019. https://centeroft hewest.org/learn/western-essays/wild-west-shows/.

Fleming, Candace. 2016. *Presenting Buffalo Bill: the Man Who Invented the Wild West*. New York: Roaring Brook Press.

Warren, Louis S. 2006. *Buffalo Bill's America: William Cody and the Wild West Show*. New York: Alfred A. Knopf.

Warren, Louis S. 2008. "Was He a Hero: Buffalo Bill Cody—a Legend in His Own Time, and Ours." *True West*. April 1. Accessed December 19, 2019. https://truewestmagazine.com/was-he-a-hero/.

Wilson, Andrew. 2016. "Found Staten Island Stories 3: Buffalo Bill's Wild West, Mariners' Harbor, 1886 and 1888." *New York Public Library*, blog post. September 23. Accessed December 19, 2019. https://www.nypl. org/blog/2016/09/23/clone-found-staten-island-stories-3-buffalo-bills -wild-west-mariners-harbor-1886-and.

GODEY'S MAGAZINE

FOR SEPTEMBER

TEN CENTS A COPY
ONE DOLLAR A YEAR

THE WOMAN THAT SAVED THE UNION

ANNA ELLA CARROLL, "Secret Member of Lincoln's Cabinet"

10 *Godey's Magazine*

INTRODUCTION

During the 20th century, the era of the glossy magazine reigned supreme. Large-format magazines with stunning photographs, like *Life*, chronicled American popular culture throughout the century. Other magazines performed different roles: *Time* and *Newsweek* were dedicated to news and politics, and literary magazines like *The New Yorker* appealed to the intellectual elite. Other magazines had a political slant. There were very popular women's magazines as well: *Vogue, Ladies Home Journal*, and *Cosmopolitan* were favorites for women. But long before any of these popular magazines hit the newsstands, there was another magazine, *Godey's Lady's Book*, which was published from 1830 to 1898. This magazine had a profound and enduring influence in many aspects of society throughout the 19th century.

Godey's Lady's Book, later known as *Godey's Magazine*, was a monthly publication that had 150,000 subscribers during the 1860s, a remarkable number that had grown from just 10,000 twenty years earlier. The journal was intended for an audience that was expanding, a cohort of educated middle-class American women who had the time and the inclination to devote to a hundred-plus-page magazine chock-full of every conceivable subject that a curious modern housewife could possibly fathom. These magazines were published in Philadelphia but were shipped throughout the growing nation, promoting contemporary 19th-century American cultural values, all the way from the stately homes of New England to the sod houses of the prairie.

The magazine was founded by Louis Antoine Godey in 1830. Godey was a Philadelphia businessman who had published a small magazine called *The Lady's Book*, which was filled with stories and poems reprinted from British magazines, as well as a number of fashion plates and songs. In 1837, he approached Sarah Josepha Hale, the editor of a Boston publication called *The Ladies' Magazine*, which was struggling, and offered to purchase it, changing the name to *Godey's Lady's Book and American*

Ladies' Magazine. Hale would be the new editor. This was a match made in heaven, for, though Godey was a shrewd businessman, Hale had a distinct understanding of middle-class American women and what interested them. Sarah Hale was born in 1788 in Newport, New Hampshire, daughter of Gordon and Martha Whittlesey Buell. She learned to read from her mother but, as was the custom at the time, did not have any formal schooling. Her most significant education came through her brother, who attended nearby Dartmouth College, and shared his textbooks with his eager sister. Sarah began teaching at age eighteen and, at twenty-five, married a New Hampshire lawyer named David Hale. The intellectually curious couple enjoyed a happy marriage, spending evenings either studying together or meeting with a local literary club whose members critiqued their own literary works as well as current published authors. Soon after the birth of their fifth child, David Hale died suddenly of pneumonia, leaving Sarah to care for the young family all on her own. Sarah Hale, with help from her husband's Masonic brothers, first ran a hat shop but soon realized that her particular gifts were in the literary realm. With help from her Mason friends, she published a novel entitled *Northwood* in 1827, which enjoyed some success. With that wind behind her back, Hale was offered a position as editor of a magazine for women that was being launched by a Boston clergyman. It was after ten years at the *Ladies' Magazine* that Louis Godey made the offer to Sarah Hale to purchase the magazine, launching the influential monthly *Godey's Lady's Book*. The pair of Godey and Hale continued to cooperate at the magazine for forty years. Godey sold the publication in 1877, when the name was changed to *Godey's Magazine*. Hale retired the same year and passed away in 1879, at the age of ninety, after spending forty years as editor.

DESCRIPTION

Topics in the magazine ranged throughout the interests of the day. The image shown here is a cover for the September 1895 issue of *Godey's Magazine*: a striking three-color, red, white, and blue image of a woman seated in a chair at a table, wearing what appears to be a military uniform, with a lamp on the table. She is surrounded by a number of maps, which were most likely military maps. Above the drawing of the woman there is a title that states, "The Woman That Saved the Union." At the bottom of the cover in red lettering is another title: "Anna Ella Carroll, 'Secret Member of Lincoln's Cabinet.'" The title of the magazine is at the top in bold red lettering "Godey's Magazine." Underneath, it states, "For September, Ten Cents a Copy, One Dollar a Year." The artist of this print is H. W. Phillips. The subject of this article is a woman named Anna Ella Carroll, a highly respected political tactician, friend, and advisor to Abraham Lincoln both before and during the Civil War. Daughter of the governor of Maryland and cousin of the last surviving signer of the Declaration of Independence, Anna Ella Carroll was steeped in the intricacies of politics, literature, and law. A staunch supporter of the Union cause and of President Lincoln, Carroll convinced the governor of Maryland, which was a slave state, to remain in the Union, thereby protecting the District of Columbia from being surrounded by enemy Confederate

MARY HAD A LITTLE LAMB

Sarah Josepha Hale was also known as the author of the nursery rhyme "Mary Had a Little Lamb," which is a children's poem purportedly based on an incident that happened when Sarah was teaching school in the hamlet of Newport, New Hampshire, when a young student arrived with a little lamb in tow. Published in 1830, it became a popular rhyme, which later was recited by Thomas Edison as his first audio recording on his new invention, the phonograph.

MARY'S LAMB.

Mary had a little lamb,
Its fleece was white as snow,
And every where that Mary went
The lamb was sure to go;
He followed her to school one day—
That was against the rule,
It made the children laugh and play,
To see a lamb at school.

And so the Teacher turned him out,
But still he lingered near,
And waited patiently about,
Till Mary did appear;
And then he ran to her, and laid
His head upon her arm,
As if he said—'I'm not afraid—
You'll keep me from all harm.'

"What makes the lamb love Mary so?"
The eager children cry—
"O, Mary loves the lamb, you know,"
The Teacher did reply;—
"And you each gentle animal
In confidence may bind,
And make them follow at your call,
If you are always kind."

[Hale, Sarah Josepha. May 24, 1830. *Poems for Our Children*. Boston: Marsh, Capen & Lyon.]

states. During the Civil War, Carroll has been credited with giving crucial military advice to Lincoln's cabinet for the Tennessee River campaign. She has become more of a controversial figure in the last century, however, and historians are still at odds about whether she performed such a pivotal role or was merely an expert at self-promotion.

SIGNIFICANCE

The ubiquity of *Godey's Lady's Book* in 19th-century middle-class homes gave it an outsized influence in many aspects of American Victorian society. Among the abundance of oddments in a cluttered Victorian home would be at least one copy of *Godey's Lady's Book* nestled on the magazine rack next to the voluminous whatnot, a large Victorian etagere popular for displaying the family's favorite knickknacks. And these magazines were often passed around among families, so even those families that could not afford the annual subscription rate could benefit from its multifaceted articles, stories, and illustrations. The influence of this magazine was broad. Hale, a widow with five children to support, was an inveterate defender of women's education. She was not, however, a feminist. She did not participate in the women's rights movements or the suffragette movement. Though she was a staunch supporter of the Union before the Civil War, she did not include political articles in the magazine. Godey, ever the astute businessman, eschewed politics, especially the discussion of slavery, in his nationwide magazine. He feared losing his southern subscribers. Hale, however, sneakily included multiple references to the tragedies of war and the universality of motherhood in her magazine's articles and stories. Hale hoped that by appealing to women's aversion to war, she could help prevent the secession of the South that eventually did take place. Sarah Hale has been criticized by 20th-century feminist scholars as a champion of the "cult of true womanhood," also known as the "cult of domesticity," a values system that promoted the institution of two gender realms in society. The woman's sphere was in the home, the domestic realm. Here the woman exhibited the four cardinal virtues: piety, purity, submission, and domesticity. The man's realm was outside in society, in the commercial and business world. However, although Hale was not a radical feminist, she was an advocate for women's education, for the promotion of women as physicians, and for the publication of female authors. Sarah Hale was, in fact, the quintessential professional woman, toiling for forty years as editor of *Godey's Lady's Book*. She was a woman who worked within the system but understood what impact she could have. As Laura McCall states, "The massive bulk of her aggressively worded editorials calling for women's seminaries and colleges, woman physicians, expanded physical activity, and less restrictive dress indicates she was not a conservative mouthpiece for an ideology dictated by men. Not only her writings but her very existence prove that she neither espoused passivity nor lived a life confined to the home" (1989: 222).

Probably the most lasting contribution of Sarah Josepha Hale to the preservation of a national union was her commitment to instituting Thanksgiving as a national holiday. She discussed it in her early novel *Northwood*, written in 1827, and she continued to strongly advocate, both in the magazine and politically, for the holiday as the nation was wracked by the fears of a Civil War. Hale wrote editorials in *Godey's Lady's Book* promoting Thanksgiving as a national holiday. At the time, the only national holidays were George Washington's birthday and the Fourth of July. Thanksgiving was a New England tradition that was expanding into western outposts where New Englanders had relocated. Hale, however, saw it as a nationalistic American celebration and included references to it in every November issue of the magazine. Recipes, poems, and short stories about families gathering for Thanksgiving were included every year. But Hale did not stop there. Every year she wrote personal letters to every governor, and to the president, knowing that if every state instituted the holiday, the national government might be forced to follow. By 1860, Thanksgiving was officially celebrated in thirty of the thirty-three states. In 1863, with the Civil War raging, Abraham Lincoln proclaimed the last Thursday of November as a day of thanksgiving, a proclamation that he repeated the following year. After his assassination, subsequent presidents continued the practice. Sarah Hale has been credited with establishing the national family holiday we now celebrate. Surprisingly, Hale has also been given the credit for the American tradition of celebrating Christmas with a Christmas tree. After an illustration of Queen Victoria, Prince Albert, and their children gathered around a Christmas tree, with gifts under the tree, was published in the *Illustrated London News* in 1848, Sarah Hale knew what to do. Aiming to influence Americans to celebrate Christmas as a family holiday, Hale took the happy royal scene, removed Victoria and Albert's tiara and sash, and published the selfsame picture in her magazine in 1850. Christmas trees would soon be the new fad in both England and in the United States, thanks to the wily advocacy of Sarah Josepha Hale.

It would be difficult to overestimate the influence of *Godey's Lady's Book* in 19th-century middle-class American culture. Its impact ranged from ideas on literature to music education to home design to fashion to politics to, above all, women's role in society. *Godey's Lady's Book* published a variety of female authors, and also a panoply of prominent American authors like Nathanial Hawthorne and Edgar Allen Poe, insisting, for the first time, on copywriting each issue in order to prevent other magazines from reprinting the stories and articles. Louis Godey and his stalwart editor Sarah Hale held the reins of this influential magazine for forty years, and the magazine continued to hold sway for another twenty years, until the

20th century dawned. Although *Godey's Lady's Book* has faded from institutional memory in the popular culture, in academic circles the name keeps popping up, in scholarly writings about feminism, the "cult of domesticity," 19th-century design, fashion, fancywork (19th-century needlework), music and music education, food, travel, and, of course, the celebrations of Thanksgiving and Christmas.

FURTHER INFORMATION

Forbes, Bruce D. 2015. *America's Favorite Holidays: Candid Histories.* Oakland: University of California Press.

Hoffman, Nicole T. Fall 1990. "Sarah Josepha Hall (1788–1874)." *Legacy,* 7(2): 47–55.

McCall, Laura. Summer 1989. " 'The Reign of Brute Force Is Now Over': A Content Analysis of Godey's Lady's Book, 1830–1860." *Journal of the Early Republic,* 9(2): 217–236.

Nelson, Elizabeth W. 2004. *Market Sentiments: Middle-Class Market Culture in 19th Century America.* Washington, DC: Smithsonian Books.

Schmidt, Leigh E. 1995. *Consumer Rites: The Buying and Selling of American Holidays.* Princeton, NJ: Princeton University Press.

Sommers, Joseph M. Summer 2010. "Godey's Lady's Book: Sarah Hale and the Construction of Sentimental Nationalism." *College Literature,* 37(3): 43–61.

11 Piano

INTRODUCTION

Music has played a fundamental role in human society for millennia. Scientists don't know the origin of music in human history, but they are uncovering clues to the use of music in early societies as they unearth more examples of early instruments. The oldest known instruments were recently found in a cave in Germany and date from approximately forty-two thousand years ago. These early examples were wind instruments, a type of flute made from bird bone and mammoth ivory. Researchers hypothesize that the early *homo sapiens* traveled to Europe through the Danube River and used these instruments for recreational or religious purposes, expanding their societal influence throughout Europe. Music has continued to play a role in sustaining cultural connections, in both religious and secular realms. A relatively recent introduction to the musical scene, the piano, has had an enormous impact on both European and American societies. As the piano grew progressively more popular, it eventually represented the quintessential symbol of economic and social achievement in Victorian households.

DESCRIPTION

The Industrial Revolution allowed production of many types of pianos at a variety of price ranges. Certain manufacturers were becoming very popular. The piano shown in this example was produced in 1835 by the company Firth, Hall and Pond, located at 1 Franklin Square in New York City. This company was founded by John Firth, an immigrant from England, and William Hall, in 1821. They established a company called Firth and Hall. As a manufacturer of a variety of musical instruments, they were moderately successful. In 1833, Sylvanus Pond became a third partner, and the firm was renamed Firth, Hall and Pond. The company continued to produce pianos and other instruments and branched out into the sheet music publication field. Over the years, the Firth company, later known as Firth, Pond and Company, and even later as Firth, Son and Company, saw growing success in the music business until the firm was sold in 1867 to the Oliver Ditson

Company. The photo of the piano shown here is an upright cabinet piano from the collection of the Metropolitan Museum of Art. It is described as being made of wood and various materials. Its dimensions are 84 ⅞ inches high by 47 ¼ inches wide and 23 ⅞ inches deep.

The piano was invented a little over three hundred years ago in Florence, Italy, by a musical craftsman named Bartolomeo Cristofori. Although there had been keyboard instruments available in Europe before 1700, they were limited in their range. The harpsichord, an instrument dating back to the Middle Ages, resembled a small grand piano in appearance. The sound, however, was distinct. The strings that are connected to the keys were actually plucked, and the dynamics (the loudness and softness of the sound) could not be controlled. Another precursor of the piano was the clavichord, which was a smaller, tabletop instrument and made a sound through a brass strip, which touched the string when the key was struck. This permitted some control over the dynamics, but the sound was very soft. The craftsman Bartolomeo Cristofori worked for the Grand Prince of Tuscany as part of the Medici court. He made and repaired harpsichords for the popular musical performances at the court. A consummate inventor, Cristofori relentlessly tinkered with the instruments, striving to improve their sound. His magnum opus was his new instrument that he called the *gravicembalo col piano et forte*, which means "keyboard instrument with soft and loud." Cristofori's new innovation created sound through leather hammers striking the strings after a key was depressed. This novel instrument, surprisingly, was no longer in the family of stringed instruments; it was now a type of percussion instrument. Because of the hammers, the new keyboard instrument was able to moderate the dynamics, depending on how forcefully the key was struck. This was a radical change, for, not only could it be soft and loud but the sound was also robust enough to perform with other instruments. The courts of Europe were duly impressed with this new musical contrivance; they purchased the instruments as fast as Cristofori could produce them. The courts of the kings of Portugal, Spain, and eventually Prussia eagerly acquired them. This is where Johann Sebastian Bach was first introduced to the rare and precious instrument. The instrument soon lost its awkward and cumbersome name, dropping the multiword mouthful to the one-word "pianoforte." Eventually it was further simplified to merely "piano."

The expensive and rare pianoforte continued to be a prestige addition to wealthy and aristocratic homes of Europe. It was even showing up at salons of the well-to-do in the American colonies. Instrument makers began to produce more of them. The first journalistic mention of a piano performance in colonial America was in Boston in 1771. An announcement of a concert included a line about "select pieces" being played during the intermission on a new type of instrument. The name of the instrument was misspelled on

the program, however. It called the mysterious instrument a "forte, piano."
A young Thomas Jefferson, however, never to be one behind the times in
either fashion or culture, must have been introduced to the pianoforte at
about the same time, probably in the salon of one of his wealthy neighbors
in Virginia. Jefferson was in the process of ordering a number of items from
England through his agent Thomas Adams. He requested a clavichord as a
gift for his soon-to-be wife Martha Skelton. Jefferson changed his order,
however, in a later missive to Adams, when he wrote, "I must alter one
article in the invoice. I wrote therein for a Clavichord. I have since seen
a Forte-piano and am charmed with it. Send me this instrument instead of
the Clavichord . . . let [it be] worthy of the acceptance of a lady for whom
I intend it" (Loesser 1954).

As pianos became more prevalent in Europe and European classical
composers like Mozart and Beethoven began writing specifically for the
piano, different types of pianos reached the market. Both "grand" and
"square" pianos were popular options. The first successful piano merchant
in the United States was John Jacob Astor, a man who subsequently made
his name and fortune in the fur trade. Astor began to import pianos from
England in 1786. These precious instruments soon would accompany many
of the westward pioneers on their perilous journeys into the various outposts
of the Western territories. By the middle of the century, pianos had reached
into the homes and lives of both upper- and middle-class Americans. The
instrument became the first luxury household item that American families
strove to acquire. Even members of the working class were introduced to
the skill of reading music, and, specifically, piano playing. When Charles
Dickens made a trip to the United States in 1842, he visited the thriving textile mills in Lowell, Massachusetts. There, Dickens was astonished by the
level of literacy in the factory girls who worked the long hours in the mills.
Though these girls were daughters of local farmers, they were schooled
in reading, writing, and music. In the boarding houses where they lived, a
piano was provided for them to play in their free time. Dickens found this
to be a uniquely American trait, for in England, the children of the wealthy
might have been tutored in the arts, but factory workers were neither literate
nor musically trained. The fact that the factory girls were musically trained
pointed to a distinguishing characteristic in American life. Musical training
was, increasingly, becoming a feature of proper preparation for entry into
the American middle class. Harriet Beecher Stowe, author of *Uncle Tom's
Cabin*, wrote the influential book *The American Woman's Home*, with her
sister Catherine Beecher, in 1869. Along with a variety of household tips
and design suggestions for a modern home, the Beechers included a sketch
of a drawing room (or parlor) with a piano located in the corner of the room
across from the sofa as a proposal for a proper middle-class home.

In a speech given to the Piano and Organ Manufacturers' Organization in 1890, President Grover Cleveland unambiguously stated the cherished and sentimental place of the old upright piano in the Victorian family home.

In many a humble home throughout our land, the piano has gathered about it the sacred and tender associations. For it, the daughters of the household longed by day and prayed in dreams by night. For it fond parents saved and economized at every point and planned in loving secrecy. For it, a certain Christmas Day, when the arrival of the piano gave a glad surprise, was marked as a red-letter day in the annals of the household.

With its music and with simple song each daughter in her turn touched with love the heart of her future husband. With it, the sacred hymn and the family prayer are joined in chastened memory. With it, closed and silent, are tenderly remembered the days of sickness, the time of death, and the funeral's solemn hush.

When the family circle is broken and its members are scattered, happy is the son or daughter who can place among his or her household goods the old piano.

[Grover Cleveland, 22nd and 24th President of the United States

(Address of the Piano and Organ Manufacturers' Banquet, New York, April 24, 1890)]

SIGNIFICANCE

In 1886, seven out of ten pupils in the public schools were being taught to read music, and many of them had a piano or organ in their parlors. In the second half of the 19th century, there were a number of additional piano manufacturers. Kimball, Washburn, Crown, and others, many of which were located in the new mass market manufacturing centers in the Midwest, sold millions of pianos in the $200 range. Sears advertised three pianos in its 1897 catalog, ranging in price from $125.00 ("a regular $300.00 instrument") to "Our Special" $179.00 Upright Cabinet Grand Piano. In addition, six decorative parlor organs were on sale for between $38.95 and $56.00. The importance of having a piano, or the cheaper version, the parlor organ, was evidence of what's known as the "cult of domesticity" in American Victorian society. Men and women occupied differing realms in society at that time. Men worked and ventured out into the world. Women stayed at home and were responsible for taking care of the home and the children. But more than that, women were given the task of monitoring the moral lives of the family. Without any external power, no ability to make money outside the home or even to own property, women were expected to wield the moral power within the private domain of the home. The piano held a critical position in this domain, where women acted as a conduit for the family's cultural education. Women were encouraged to learn to play the piano as an element of their proper domestic training. As the first mass market luxury good to enter the homes of many working and middle-class households, the piano held an exalted place. It became a badge of respectability and success in the Victorian quest for upward mobility. It also represented a symbol of the feminine accomplishment. Though women were not permitted to work, they were encouraged to learn to play the piano and to entertain family and friends within the home. Craig H. Roell, in the book *The Piano in America, 1890–1940,* powerfully describes the situation this way: "To Victorians, home was both a shelter *from* the anxieties of industrial society and a shelter *for* the moral and spiritual values that the commercial spirit was threatening. 'Home Sweet Home' was called an 'oasis in the desert,' a sanctuary where man could recover his humanity from the selfish degrading, immoral business and industrial world. The home nourished love, morality, religion, and culture" (1989). This ideal of womanhood and of shelter was often represented by the family gathered around the piano for a pleasant evening at home, as depicted in many paintings and advertisements of the day.

Women had few choices in Victorian America. However, for women, one occupation that was allowed in the restrictive Victorian environment was that of the piano teacher. As the 19th century waned and the 20th century loomed, the number of female music teachers grew. African Americans also suffered during these years of Jim Crow discrimination. By the end of the 19th century, pianos had become a standard feature in American homes and were affordable, even for working-class African Americans. Gospel music developed in African American churches, and pianos played a crucial role. One other development was the invention of ragtime. Scott Joplin wrote the *Maple Leaf Rag* in 1899, and soon ragtime became the rage in American popular culture. With its syncopated rhythms, it was the first African American music to cross over into white mainstream culture. After World War I, jazz soon eclipsed ragtime in popularity and influence. Both styles of music, however, depended on the availability of the piano to reach an eager audience. Finally, the piano, a precious and rare instrument at the beginning of the 19th century, was, by the dawn of the 20th century, a ubiquitous and beloved feature in many American homes.

FURTHER INFORMATION

Ames, Kenneth L. 1992. *Death in the Dining Room & Other Tales of Victorian Culture.* Philadelphia: Temple University Press.

Clark, Clifford E., Jr. 1986. *The American Family Home: 1800–1960.* Chapel Hill: University of North Carolina Press.

"Firth." 2017. Antique Piano Shop. Accessed September 5, 2019. https://antiquepianoshop.com/online-museum/firth/.

Good, Edwin, Cynthia A. Hoover, and Patrick Rucker. 2001. *Piano 300: Celebrating Three Centuries of People and Pianos*. Washington, DC: National Museum of American History.

Holmquist, Donald C. Winter. 1965. "Pride of the Pioneer's Parlor: Pianos in Early Minnesota." *Minnesota History*, 39(8): 312–326.

Loesser, Arthur. 1954. *Men, Women and Pianos: A Social History*. New York: Dover Publications, Inc.

Parakilas, James. 1999. *Piano Roles: Three Hundred Years of Life with the Piano*. New Haven, CT: Yale University Press.

Roell, Craig H. 1989. *The Piano in America, 1890–1940*. Chapel Hill: University of North Carolina Press.

12 Souvenir from the Centennial Exhibition

INTRODUCTION

It was the late 1860s, and the United States was still smarting from the wounds of the recently ended Civil War. The South was defeated, and the resentment engendered by the war and the subsequent Reconstruction era in the southern states was intense. However, the 100th birthday of the nation was imminent, and a number of patriotic citizens began lobbying to sponsor a big celebration. Maybe such an event would help heal the wounds of the war, these enthusiastic promoters suggested. Besides, the United States of America was a new type of country, a nation based on ideals of liberty, democracy, and opportunity, which had recently fought a war that ensured freedom for all its citizens. The country was also advancing as the Industrial Revolution continued to provide technological breakthroughs and bought more labor-saving devices to the American public. There was much to celebrate. A centennial exhibition could serve as a vehicle to bring the nation together once again and celebrate its founding as well as its future.

DESCRIPTION

The Centennial Exhibition, held in 1876 in Philadelphia, Pennsylvania, was a celebration of the first one hundred years of American independence. Many visitors to the Centennial Exhibition willingly spent their limited funds on small souvenirs as reminders of their experiences at the fair. Numerous fair souvenirs have survived and can be found in museum collections. This artifact shown here is a commemorative handkerchief that features images of the five major buildings at the fair. These buildings, in clockwise order, were the Main Exhibition Building, the Machinery Hall, the Horticultural Hall, and the Agricultural Hall, with the Memorial Hall depicted in the center. There is a patriotic theme in the piece, with stars depicted on three sides and a version of the Great Seal of the United States at the top. The Great Seal depiction includes a bald eagle with its wings outstretched, holding a scroll that states "E Pluribus Unum," the motto of the United States that means "out of many, one." Under the eagle is the American flag in the shape of a shield with stars on the top and the stripes on the bottom. To the left of the shield are three olive branches, which symbolize peace, and to the right are arrows, which symbolize the thirteen original states (although in this version there are only ten). The eagle has its head facing the olive branches, which indicate a preference for peace. Under the seal is the title, "Centennial International," which continues under the depiction of Memorial Hall, "Exhibition, Fairmount Park, Philadelphia, 1776–1876." The handkerchief is made of plain weave printed cotton and is 24 ⅞ inches by 24 ¼ inches. The text and the buildings are depicted in sepia tones, and there is a dark red border around all four edges.

As the site where American independence was declared and the Constitution was written, Philadelphia seemed like the ideal location to hold the nation's hundredth birthday celebration. The city was large enough to host the expected crowds of visitors and was accessible and centrally located. The band of supporters convinced Congress to set up a commission to oversee the planning of the exhibition in 1871. The proposal called for eliciting private funding for the fair. However, a severe economic downturn that occurred after the Panic of 1873 depressed much of the hoped-for private investment. Eventually the organizers lined up funding from a variety of sources, including federal, state, and international backers, as well as universities and churches. The final saving grace for the completion of the fair was a loan from the federal government. None of the supporters of the newly reunited Union wanted this grand, patriotic gesture to fail.

When the Centennial Exhibition, formally called the "International Exhibition of Arts, Manufacturers and Products of the Soil and Mine," opened on May 10, 1876, throngs of visitors streamed in through turnstiles that ticked off each and every one with a newly invented counter. The president of the United States, Ulysses S. Grant, formally opened the fair. The exhibition was a huge operation, a combination of world's fair, state fair, and exposition of the latest in technological advancements. The grounds were located on 185 acres in Fairmount Park in Philadelphia, Pennsylvania, overlooking the Schuylkill River. There were over two hundred buildings on the site. Admission to the fair was fifty cents. The fair was open six days a week and closed on Sunday. Using their lobbying power "Sabbatarians" vetoed the opening of the fair on Sunday, and prohibitionists likewise barred alcohol from being sold at most of the popular exhibits. However, right outside the official fair grounds, bars and cafés were erected that drew large crowds and served plenty of alcohol to thirsty patrons. Although the organizers would have preferred nighttime hours for the fair, the use of gas light (electric light was not available in 1876) stoked fears of damaging fires, so the closing time was set for 6 p.m. By the time the Centennial Exhibition closed after a short stint of only six months, on November 10, 1876, a whopping 9,910,966 visitors had passed through calculating turnstiles. With the U.S.

population maxing out at forty-six million people at the time, attracting a total of almost ten million visitors in six months was an amazing feat. The Centennial Exhibition may have started out on shaky ground, but it ended as an enormous financial and cultural success.

FROEBEL'S GIFTS

As part of the Women's Pavilion, there was a demonstration of novel idea that was imported from Germany called a "kindergarten" or children's garden. The German educational theorist who was responsible for this innovation was Friedrich Froebel. He theorized that children learn through play. One of the tools designed by Froebel for this directed play was a selection of "gifts," or play materials that were introduced to the kindergarten children systematically. Some of these materials were sets of specially designed maple building blocks. When the family of legendary architect Frank Lloyd Wright was living in the area, his mother attended the fair and purchased the blocks for her young son. Wright has credited the blocks with helping to spark his imagination to create his innovative style of architecture.

SIGNIFICANCE

Although ostensibly a celebration of the nation's first hundred years, the Centennial Exhibition was transformed into a proclamation of the nation's future. Most of the exhibits showcased new technological achievements. The largest building, the vast iron-frame and glass Main Exhibition Building, at 1,880 feet long by 464 feet wide, was purported to be the largest building in the world. The exhibitions inside were a combination of American themes, with a variety of foreign exhibits as well. Many items in the Main Hall were for sale, and eager American consumers snatched them up. The most popular exhibit was in the huge Machinery Hall, which boasted the amazing new Corliss Engine, built by George H. Corliss, a forty-foot high steam engine, which was the world's largest and that powered all the machinery exhibits at the fair. The great Corliss engine went on to power machinery in the Pullman railroad car factory in Chicago after the fair closed. The Agricultural Hall displayed new farm equipment and livestock, which fascinated the many Americans who still lived on small family farms. The Horticultural Building displayed a variety of gardens, which attracted the middle-class suburban families who were becoming entranced with exotic Victorian gardens. Memorial Hall, the smallest of the main buildings, was built as an art museum and displayed over three thousand paintings and six hundred sculptures. Memorial Hall was constructed as a permanent structure, and after the fair it became the Philadelphia Museum of Art. It is presently used as a children's museum. There was even a Women's Pavilion, built by the Women's Centennial Committee, which was led by Elizabeth Duane Gillespie, great-granddaughter of Benjamin Franklin. The pavilion displayed products designed by and for women, including many new labor-saving devices that could free the housewife from the daily drudgery of housework and allow her to engage in outside pursuits. In fact, this prescient pavilion promoted a feminist agenda with its multiple pamphlets and posters advocating for women's rights. Although the Women's Centennial Committee was not encouraged to include this pavilion at the fair, their sublimely successful effort at fundraising for the fair drove the organizers to allow the committee to build it.

Americans streamed into the Centennial Exhibition during its six-month run. Because the fair was not open on Sunday, it wasn't easy to get to for workers who had typical six-day workweeks. Some companies gave their staff time off to visit it, and some even sponsored trips to the fair for their workers. Other families took vacations to travel to Philadelphia and stayed in the temporary hotels that were developed in the neighborhood around Fairmount Park to accommodate the throngs of visitors. But what did these visitors see? In many respects, they saw a vision of the country's future. The gigantic and powerful Corliss engine was a symbol of the industrial growth that the nation was beginning to experience. New innovations were on display at the fair, including Alexander Graham Bell's original telephone, the typewriter, and linoleum flooring. An elevated monorail carried people over a ravine. Elevators were a novel invention and were on display in various locations around the fair including one that lifted forty people up 185 feet to an observation platform. New food offerings included hot popcorn, bananas (served in tin foil as a snack), and root beer. The Statue of Liberty's hand and torch was also on display, and visitors could pay to climb up to the top of the torch. Monies collected at the Statue of Liberty exhibit were used to help finance the construction of the statue's base, which was eventually dedicated in 1886. One of the few exhibits that celebrated the past and not the industrial future was a reconstruction of a "New England kitchen of 1776," which fascinated visitors who had graduated to many labor-saving gadgets in their kitchens that included the cast-iron cooking stove. The colonial historical reference appealed to Americans and led to the nostalgic and popular design movement called the "Colonial Revival." The Philadelphia Centennial Exhibition of 1876 was a celebration of the nation's birthday. However, the country was in the throes of an industrial boom that would leapfrog the United States from an industrial backwater to an industrial juggernaut. Much of the evidence of this transformation was right there to see in the multiple exhibits at the Centennial fair. This fair was America's introduction to gleaming technological future.

FURTHER INFORMATION

Cashman, Sean D. 1993. *America in the Gilded Age: From the Death of Lincoln to the Rise of the Theodore Roosevelt.* New York; London: New York University Press.

Greene, Elizabeth B. 2017. *Buildings and Landmarks of 19th Century America: American Society Revealed.* Santa Barbara, CA: Greenwood.

Howe, Jeffery. October 2002. "A 'Monster Edifice': Ambivalence, Appropriation, and the Forging of Cultural Identity at the Centennial Exhibition." *Pennsylvania Magazine of History and Biography*, 126(4): 635–650.

Pizor, Faith K. April 1970. "Preparations for the Centennial Exhibition of 1876." *Pennsylvania Magazine of History and Biography*, 94(2): 213–232.

Schlereth, Thomas J. 1991. *Victorian America: Transformations in Everyday Life, 1876–1915.* New York: Harper Perennial.

Smeins, Linda E. 1999. *Building an American Identity: Pattern Book Homes and Communities, 1870–1900.* Walnut Creek, CA: AltaMira Press.

Grooming, Clothing, and Accessories

Portable Bathtub

Corset

Mourning Jewelry

Native American War Shirt

Shaving Mug

Beaver Fur Top Hat

13 Portable Bathtub

INTRODUCTION

Americans love their bathrooms.

American homes have bathrooms, and many have multiple bathrooms. By the onset of the 21st century, homes in the United States were being built with at least two, and often four or five, bathrooms. And the bathtubs play an essential role in our bathrooms. But this was not always the case. In the beginning of the 19th century, homes did not have running water, and bathrooms did not exist. By the end of the century, the availability of running water piped into the house, and waste water discarded through the sewer pipes, made bathing accessible to many American families. But in addition to the change in the availability of water, it was the attitude toward bathing that was also transformed over the decades.

DESCRIPTION

The portable bathtub shown in this example dates from the period when Americans were rediscovering the benefits of dunking oneself into a tub of water. It is called a "plunge bath" and dates from between 1840 and 1880. It is constructed of painted tin, with a cork stopper and a wood and iron handle. According to the Smithsonian's National Museum of American History, it measures 7 ¾ inches by 50 ⅜ inches by 20 ¾ inches at the narrow end and 8 inches by 50 inches by 21 inches at the wider end. It was most likely used for a water cure. Many bathtubs of the time were small affairs; some were called a "sitz bath," a portable tub where the person sat in a semi-reclining position, partially immersed with the legs and head exposed to the air. These were believed to help inflammation of the brain, internal organs, and nervous fevers. The large plunge bath, however, was most likely utilized for another type of cure. It was possibly used with herbs and hemlock branches, which were steeped in a vapor with scalding hot water. The bather would lie or sit in the bathtub wrapped in blankets soaking up the aromatics. The bathtub could also have been used for a cold plunge, which was another popular healthy procedure recommended at the time. Soap was not used for these types of baths. In fact, soap was not commonly available until late in the 19th century. Instead of soap, the use of bran, oat, or almond meal was suggested, or even borax or ammonia for scrubbing greasy skin.

In world history, the practice of bathing varied with different ancient cultures around the globe. Asian cultures had long traditions of bathing, as did the aboriginal peoples of Mesoamerica. However, with the onset of the Middle Ages in Europe, the habit of bathing that was practiced for centuries by the Greeks and Romans was summarily discarded by the newly dominant Christian church. The idea of washing oneself seemed self-indulgent to the spiritual teachings of Christianity. Besides, the luxurious public baths provided in late Roman society were considered dens of promiscuity and decadence to the church. The Romans spent hours in the baths; it was a social and communal activity for all classes of people. The baths were part of a large building complex where a Roman would first enter the tepidarium (warm bath,) then the caldarium (hot steam bath,) followed by the frigidarium (cold bath) for a bracing cold dip. Afterward, the bather would return to the tepidarium to calm the body down and receive a massage with oils, which was then scraped off with a tool called a strigil. This process sounds hedonistic, almost like indulging in a visit to a modern spa—so it is no wonder the early Christians rejected its use. Besides, the early Christians were determined to reject any and all facets of pagan Roman culture. Religious Christians were advised to concentrate on one's spiritual journey to the afterlife, while the indulgences in bodily pleasures were absolutely discouraged. In the early medieval period after the 3rd century, baths and bathhouses were eschewed. It wasn't until the 11th century, during the Crusades, that Europeans rediscovered the advantages and pleasures of bathing. Though the Crusaders' attempts to regain control of the Holy Land from Muslim hands would ultimately fail, they were successful in returning with a number of discoveries that would enhance their daily life. These included silk, cotton, mirrors, and the hammam or Turkish bath. The European version of the Turkish bath included a steam bath and a seat in a large, round bathtub. These bathhouses were available for a broad range of classes, and their popularity spread through Central Europe up until the 16th century. In England, the ubiquitous bathhouses were dubbed "stews," or "stewhouses," which referred to the body being "stewed" in the hot water. The popularity of these bathhouses, combined with the patrons' absence of bodily cover, did, however, lead to a level of bawdiness and a dearth of decorum. Eventually, they evolved into places where prostitution was commonly practiced. The reputations of the public baths devolved into seediness by the 16th century. However, the final demise of the public bathhouses occurred with the scourge of the bubonic plague, or Black Death. The plague invaded Europe in the mid-1300s, with smaller outbreaks occurring through the 1700s. The Black Death pandemic killed upward of half the population of Europe. At the time it was thought that disease could enter the body through the pores, and a hot bath caused the pores to open, thereby allowing the disease to enter the body. So, because of the fear of this deadly disease, European public bathhouses were systematically shut down by the mid-16th century.

The following centuries in Europe and in North America were the truly filthy ones. Water developed a downright dangerous reputation. Because of the belief that disease could enter the body through the pores, the condition of preserving one's dirty, blocked pores was the optimal one. Baths were to be avoided at all costs. In the 1700s in Europe, clothing was opulent; those who could afford it wore heavy damasks, silks, and linens. In fact, linen was believed to be a healthy fabric that actually absorbed sweat and removed it from the body. A wealthy man, instead of having a luxurious bath, would have a closet full of luxurious linen shirts, which he would change frequently. The concept of bathing achieved a minor comeback during the 18th century, though it was not widespread in European culture. By the beginning of the 19th century, some enlightened Europeans began to consider the bath as a possible healthy option. Certain medical professionals recommended that taking a short, cold bath or shower would be good for the health. However, as the Industrial Revolution brought many new migrants to the large cities in Europe and in the United States, severe crowding occurred. Before the installation of water and sewer systems, poor people lived in filthy conditions and rarely, if ever, bathed. Cultural traditions proved enduring, as well. In certain countries, France in particular, the peasant population resisted the recommendations for better hygiene, accepting old adages like the one that stated, "People who take baths die young." Public bathhouses were constructed, and students in high schools were encouraged to take baths or showers at least once a month. Eventually, the reluctant French population began to wash themselves almost as often as they washed their clothes.

Americans, however, developed an interest in bathing for healthful reasons even before the access to water and sewer systems transformed the cities and towns. An interest in dousing one's body in a bath took hold with the quasi-scientific concept of the "water cure." Also known as hydropathy, the water cure fad came to the United States in the 1840s through a Central European village in Silesia, with a farmer named Vincenz Priessnitz. This enterprising farmer claimed to have cured a sick cow as well as his own injuries through a treatment with cold water and wet bandages. The spa he opened soon served as a magnet for ailing European princes, counts, and other prominent folk. Wealthy Americans also caught wind of this treatment, and some traveled to Silesia to partake of the water cure. The idea caught on with many reform-minded Americans who were always looking for practical and ingenious new methods for curing aches and pains. By the 1850s, there were two hundred water cure centers across the country, and a biweekly journal called the *Water-Cure Journal* had over one hundred thousand subscribers. Harriet Beecher Stowe, author of *Uncle Tom's Cabin*, partook of a water cure in Vermont where she spent ten months taking several cold-water baths and showers per day. She claimed that the process renewed her. Of course, the rest, relaxation, exercise, good food, and refreshing water certainly contributed to her cure. Beecher went on to cowrite with her sister, Catharine Beecher, one of the most influential books of the mid-19th century, *The American Women's Home*, in 1869. In it they discussed at length the importance of including a bathroom in the house as well as bathing, although using soap and keeping a full-size tub were still not a recommended part of the routine. The influential magazine called *Godey's Lady's Book* also lobbied for adding bathrooms to newly built suburban homes, as well as encouraging American families to have once-weekly baths. The debate persisted, however, in the mid-19th century: Was it healthier to submerge oneself in cold or warm water, and for what maladies? And of course, soap was rarely included in the conversation.

An important factor in the growing acceptance of the salubrious effects of personal hygiene resulted from the consequences of the bloody American Civil War, which started in 1861 and continued until 1865. The U.S. Sanitary Commission was set up in 1861 with the mission to standardize care in the Union military hospitals and all the Union camps. The concept of the "Sanitary" was based on the British Sanitary Commission, which was established after the success of the famous nurse Florence Nightingale during the Crimean War. Nightingale developed and utilized novel hygienic methods to prevent deadly infections, by washing patients, keeping the walls and floors in the hospital clean, and laundering sheets and clothing. Back in the United States, following Nightingale's lead, the Sanitary Commission encouraged soldiers to wash and brush their teeth. When they appeared at the war hospital with severe injuries, they were kept clean by an army of nurse volunteers who worked tirelessly throughout the war. The success of the Sanitary Commission had beneficial results after the Civil War. Soldiers still died more often from infections than from gunshot wounds, but the percentage was significantly reduced. The thousands of Union veterans who survived the onslaught went home with a totally new concept of personal cleanliness. The respect that was displayed for the "Sanitary" and its indefatigable nurses led to a new nationwide admiration for sanitation as a patriotic endeavor. With a new appreciation for personal hygiene, Abraham Lincoln was the first president of the United States to install a bathtub in the White House. Unfortunately, the Confederacy did not have a similar organization to standardize care for its troops. The Confederate troops had no coordinated effort and were forced to depend on the care of a disparate number of women's volunteer aid groups.

MENCKEN'S HISTORY OF THE BATHTUB HOAX

The famous journalist H. L. Mencken wrote an article on December 28, 1917, in the *New York Evening Mail* titled "A Neglected Anniversary" that falsely claimed to identify the first bathtub ever installed in the United States, on December 20, 1842, in Cincinnati. This lead-lined tub supposedly weighed 1,750 pounds. Mencken went on to assert that bathtubs were so controversial that several cities tried to officially ban them based on the fact that they were unhealthful and undemocratic, an "epicurean luxury." He goes on to say that President Millard Fillmore visited Cincinnati on a campaign trip and was offered the opportunity to try out the famous bathtub. Impressed, Fillmore went on to install a bathtub in the White House in 1850, the first ever.

The entire story was false, totally made up from whole cloth. But there was enough in the story that sounded plausible enough to general readers that it was never fact-checked. The story was reprinted over and over and was eventually included in encyclopedias and textbooks, to the chagrin of Mencken himself. In 1926, he offered a mea culpa and an explanation for the hoax. Mencken was testing the endurance of rumors and false claims, which, once stated, can live on in perpetuity. Mencken's claims persisted much longer than he expected. In fact, in 2001, an article in the respected newspaper the *Washington Post*, repeated the false myth once again.

SIGNIFICANCE

In the United States, European traditions persisted in the new nation for many decades. At the onset of the 19th century, Americans adhered to the same standards of personal hygiene as their European compatriots, that is, a near total absence of concern for personal hygiene. This lasted up until the middle of the century, when a variety of reformers took on the crusade for healthy bathing, influenced by the water cure movement, as well as other scientific and medical advances, like the Sanitarian movement and Louis Pasteur's discovery of the germ theory. The United States, unlike most of the more tradition-bound European societies, accepted the idea of personal hygiene as a novel idea that enriched one's way of life. Hotels in large cities took the lead and installed plumbing, which included toilets and baths, surprisingly early in the 19th century. The Astor House in New York, which opened in 1836, included toilets and bathrooms on each floor. In fact, with the end of the Civil War, the concept of bathing and keeping clean became a patriotic and moral prerequisite. In addition, with the burgeoning growth of industrial cities in the United States, reformers pushed for the installation of water and sewer systems to be installed in the teeming slums, and requirements for plumbing and toilets were eventually enshrined into various tenement house laws. Bathtubs, however, were not included in the first tenement laws, and crowded families in tenements in New York were still obliged to use portable tubs in the kitchen. The solution for many of these families was the return of the old bathhouse, of which many were built in the slums of the large northern cities like New York. Reformers at the turn of the 20th century encouraged immigrant families to reject their European traditions of personal hygiene and use the bathhouses. At the same time, middle-class American families were flocking to the new "streetcar suburbs" in the last decades of the century. The pleasant single-family houses in these developments commonly included a bathroom, with a sink, toilet, and tub. By the end of the century, soaps of many kinds were universally available and were advertised relentlessly. Americans began their love affairs with their bathrooms as well as their obsession with cleanliness. The transformation of the American concept of personal hygiene into "cleanliness is next to godliness" was almost complete.

FURTHER INFORMATION

Ashenburg, Katherine. 2007. *The Dirt on Clean: An Unsanitized History.* New York: North Point Press.

Heifer, Harold. 1954. "A Bathtub Chronicle." *Challenge*, 2(6): 36–38.

Mencken, H. L. 1917. "A Neglected Anniversary." *New York Evening Mail* (Reprint). December 28. http://hoaxes.org/text/display/a_neglected _anniversary_text.

Nelson, Libby. 2016. "What a 1917 Prank about the History of the Bathtub Can Tell Us about Modern Hoaxes." *VOX.* April 1. https://www.vox .com/2016/4/1/11346940/bathtub-history-prank-april-fools.

Smith, Virginia. 2007. *Clean: A History of Personal Hygiene and Purity.* Oxford: Oxford University Press.

Wilke, Jacqueline S. Summer 1986. "Submerged Sensuality: Technology and Perceptions of Bathing." *Journal of Social History*, 19(4): 649–664.

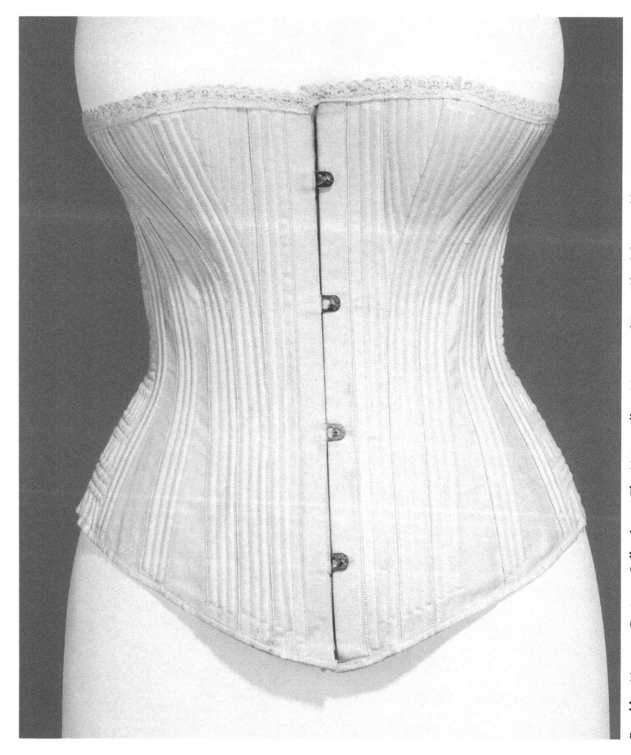

14 Corset

INTRODUCTION

Consider the aches and pains you endure with certain fashion choices. Men have to suffer tight dress shirts and shoes, ties, and warm suit jackets. Women have numerous fashion choices that can be immensely uncomfortable—high heels, Spanx, tight clothing. Imagine this: tight-laced corsets that squeeze your waist down to 19 inches. A stick shoved down the front of your dress that prevents you from bending over. Metal cages, called crinolines, extend your voluminous skirts out to a circumference of 150 inches and hamper your walking through a doorway, into a carriage, or could even burst into flames from errant sparks from a fireplace. Nineteenth-century women suffered from a variety of constricting and dangerous garments that constrained their movements and their lives. The ubiquitous corset was one of the most restrictive and controversial of women's undergarments. And yet it survived, in various forms throughout the 19th century and into the 20th.

DESCRIPTION

By the late 19th century, a selection of different corset types appeared on the market. The variety of the corset types included so-called healthful corsets that were designed for use by active women. The Ball's corset shown here, dating from about 1885, is an example of this type of corset, targeted to the horseback rider. The garment is made of white cotton, with metal, elastic, and whalebone. It boasts shirred elastic sections that cover an interior coiled wire spring system. The elastic and wire springs were advertised as "health preserving," and the claim was that the undergarment represented a "revolution in corsets." Of course, the touted comfort of the Ball's corset was questionable at best. The wearer still had to attempt a strenuous activity while wearing a restrictive garment that cinched the waist with various types of stays.

The corset has had a long history. The word "corset" comes from the Old French word *corps*, meaning "body," which in turn derived from the Latin word for body, *corpus*. The modern use of the word "corset" describes a very tightly fitted undergarment that envelops the torso from the breast to the hips and is usually secured at the front with hooks and loops and tightened up with laces in the back. It typically contains some type of "stays" or inserts made of whalebone or other rigid material. The 19th-century corset was designed to create the appearance of a tiny waist. It was used primarily by women, although in certain eras men wore them as well. The modern concept of the corset as a shape-forming undergarment was first commonly used in 16th-century Europe. However, it was the 19th century when the popularity and notoriety of the corset reached the height of absurdity. The century also served as its swan song.

Clothing in the early medieval era had been loose fitting. Styles evolved and became more tailored with the invention of buttons, lacing, and seams. The fashions that subsequently developed emphasized the contrast between men's and women's body shapes. One of the developments was the bodice, which was a front-laced, snugly fitted garment worn over a blouse. When heavier fabrics like brocade and velvet were introduced, the tight bodice became even more fitted, and it began to function like a corset. It wasn't until the first half of the 16th century that corsets with rigid stays made of whalebone, horn, or buckram appeared on the scene, originally surfacing in either Spain or Italy and soon spreading throughout Europe. The busk, which was the rigid stay inserted at the center front of the neckline, was the earliest inflexible element used in corsets. Eventually, other stays were developed and added to the corsets around the sides to lend further support to the garment. The corset, a complicated and expensive undergarment, was worn primarily by the members of the court or other prosperous ladies whose wealth allowed them to follow the emerging fashion trends. This state of affairs persisted throughout the 18th century, when fashionable women wore more restraining corsets, even resorting to the concept of "tight lacing," an extreme form of corsetry. Poor and working-class women made do with what they were able to conjure up, using leather or other materials as stays to fashion a corset-like garment, over their petticoats. These simple lace-up bodices also accentuated the bust, waist, and hips to form the preferred hourglass silhouette. With the arrival of the Enlightenment in the late 18th century, philosophers as well as doctors began questioning the purpose of the restricting corset. Controversy abounded, as the new emphasis on science and reason encouraged detractors to criticize the artificial constraint of the waist that was possible with a whalebone corset. The styles evolved to reflect a new fascination with the classics, as the neoclassical style of art and architecture influenced fashion as well. The fashion for women in Europe and the United States was influenced by the French Empire style, and the dresses were white, with high waists and flowing skirts. Corsets may have been worn as a form of undergarment but were not as tightly laced, because the natural waist was not displayed.

As the 19th century wore on, the role of the corset grew as the size of the waists shrank. At the beginning of the 19th century, the influence of the French Empire style was still evident, with high waists, low-cut necklines, and simple flowing skirts. The preferred color was still neoclassical white. By the 1820s, there was a backlash to the openness of the Enlightenment, and the French Empire influence waned. The dresses began to be fitted to the natural waistline. In so doing, the emphasis on the waist led to the impulse to exaggerate the smallness of the waist and the width of the skirt. Colorful clothes came back into style, and surface decoration abounded. By the 1830s, women were wearing large bonnets with long ribbons. The dresses boasted wide, V-shaped necklines and huge leg o'mutton sleeves. As the dresses accentuated the broad shoulders and a low but tiny waist, corsets became the fashion once again. These corsets were long and continued over the hips, with whalebone strips that gave the corsets more structure. The pièce de résistance was the busk, a wood or metal flat bar that was inserted down the front of the corset to ensure a smooth bodice all the way to below the waist. Anyone who has seen the film *Gone with the Wind* can recall the unforgettable scene where Scarlett O'Hara hangs onto the bedpost while her slave Mammy tugs on the strings of the corset to squeeze in Scarlett's waist to the desired diminutive circumference. The fashion in the 1860s demanded such sartorial restraints.

By the second half of the 19th century, the manufacturing boom engendered by the Industrial Revolution and the invention of the sewing machine made the corset a ubiquitous element in the American woman's wardrobe. Though corsets were expensive handmade accessories utilized by members of the upper class in previous eras, the situation was about to change. New manufacturing plants began to produce thousands of corsets in various sizes and styles and at affordable prices. This is what has been called the "democratization" of the fashion industry, making the corset accessible to the growing number of women in the fashion-conscious middle class. Women of all ages and economic backgrounds wore corsets on a daily basis. It was simply a requisite element in a women's regular dress routine. The corset demanded a second set of hands to help put it on and tighten the laces at the back, although the hooks and loops on the front made it possible for a woman to remove the corset by herself or even put it on. Of course, it could not be tightened except from the back by a second person. The woman wearing a corset faced many obstacles. She could not bend from the waist. Deep breathing was impossible. Even sitting in a deep chair was not manageable, because the busk, the rigid support that was inserted down the front of the corset, would pop out when the woman sat down. So, she was forced

THE DRESS REFORM MOVEMENT

In the 1850s, a movement began that attempted to modernize the byzantine collection of garments that women were wearing in polite American society. This became known as the Dress Reform Movement. The movement was started by a group of feminists who were advocating for the women's vote, as well as temperance and abolition. A young woman named Elizabeth Smith Miller, the cousin of Elizabeth Cady Stanton, began to wear a version of trousers under her skirts as a protest to the severe and constricting garments that contemporary women were obliged to wear. Her friend, Amelia Bloomer, also began to sport the new type of outfit and published a description of it in her feminist magazine, *The Lily*. The reformed clothing began to attract publicity, and the outfit developed a moniker—"bloomers." Advocates of women's rights started wearing them, and the coverage of the style by the press intensified. Much of the coverage wasn't positive, however, and the advocates were accused of being extremists, and even threats to society. After being ridiculed by newspaper articles and cartoons, the women in the movement ceased to wear the bloomers publicly. They had become too much of a distraction, and the Dress Reform Movement was, for the moment, dead.

to perch on the edge of the chair. For the same reason, climbing stairs was also hard to manage.

SIGNIFICANCE

The corset has remained one of the most controversial and iconic garments in fashion history. Though a mainstay of high style for centuries, it became the symbol of western women's place in society during the 19th and early 20th centuries. As fashion democratized, allowing for members of the middle and working classes to easily purchase readymade undergarments from department stores and catalogs, the stakes were raised. If all women were sporting the restrictive corset, the fashionistas had to differentiate themselves somehow. This led to the exaggeration of the tiny waist, sometimes dubbed a "wasp waist" and to the phenomenon of tight-lacing. Although in fact most women did not insist on lacing their corsets to create a pinched 19-inch waist, many did. The medical profession continually protested the use of tight corsets, maintaining that the force of the tight garment damaged the internal organs. Others joined the protest, including feminists, health advocates, and artists. Their cries did not make much of a difference in the popularity of the corset, however. It wasn't until the 1920s that the revolution in fashion precipitated by the new, more permissive post–World War I society led to the demise of the corset and the invention of the less restrictive undergarments, the girdle and the brassiere.

But what was the significance of the corset in society? Books have been written about this subject, and the controversy continues. Some historians have insisted that the ubiquity of the corset in the 19th century persisted because of the enforcement of sex roles and the segregated realms of women and men. Whereas women's fashions became ever more decorative, frivolous, and complicated as the century progressed, men's fashions went the opposite way. Veering away from the ruffled, colorful waistcoats worn by so-called dandies in the early part of the 19th century, men started wearing somber colors, black and brown, with a simple style that contrasted markedly from the flamboyance of the women's dress. This divergence in style has been identified as a symbol of the domination of men over women. The fashions demonstrated it: Men were serious and strong; women were frivolous and submissive. Men were also active—they could actually move more freely in their clothes, whereas women could not. Women's back and core muscles would atrophy after long-term corset use, so in reality their bodies were weakened. The corset prevented proper breathing and led to shortness of breath. It was dangerous to wear a corset during pregnancy, but women did wear it anyway. Why did women continue to wear the corset? Despite the entreaties of the dress reformers and other health advocates, women did wear corsets for more than a century. Victorian society enforced divergent sex roles during the 19th century. Women were relegated to submissive roles and had very little power in society. Thorstein Veblen, famous 19th-century economist and social commentator, and writer of the book *Theory of the Leisure Class*, coined the term "conspicuous consumption" to describe the extents to which women were able to flaunt their newfound wealth with their conspicuous displays of flamboyant and elaborate dress. Women played the role of a decorative bauble. They weren't allowed to seek employment, and they relied on servants to complete housework tasks. But were women also complicit in this affectation? Corsets and the other tortuous garments worn by women in the 19th century were considered a moral imperative. The erect posture that was forced onto the woman wearing a corset exemplified a morally "upright" person. Such a person must, by necessity, be disciplined and controlled. The women not wearing a corset were considered "loose" and immoral. The corset symbolized the position women held in society, and many women desired to show off their respected role; it was ultimately all they had. They had no autonomy in this society. Yes, social pressure played a role, as did tradition and the desire to be fashionable. When the roles of women began to blur at the end of the 19th century, as women began to work outside the home and take up sports like cycling, tennis, and swimming, and as households no longer had servants, the tyranny of the corset began to fray. As the ubiquity of the corset subsided, the strange garment took on another role, in fetishistic role-playing. The compulsory garment that represented moral rectitude in a sexually repressed society has become associated with sexual fetishism in modern culture.

FURTHER INFORMATION

Kelly, Lori D. 1991. "Bipeds in Bloomers: How the Popular Press Killed the Dress Reform Movement." *Studies in Popular Culture*, 13(2): 67–76.

Kunzle, David. 1982. *Fashion and Fetishism: A Social History of the Corset, Tight-Lacing and Other Forms of Body-Sculpture in the West.* Totowa, NJ: Rowman and Littlefield.

Lord, W. B. 1868 [2007]. *The Corset and the Crinoline: An Illustrated History.* Mineola, NY: Dover Publications.

Miller, Leslie S. 2000. "The Many Figures of Eve: Styles of Womanhood Embodied in a Late-Nineteenth-Century Corset." Ed. Jules David Prown and Kenneth Haltman. *American Artifacts: Essays in Material Culture.* East Lansing: Michigan State University Press, 129–147.

National Park Service. "Vicksburg: Fashion Sense—or Sensible Fashion? Clothing in the 19th Century." Accessed May 25, 2019. https://corpora .tika.apache.org/base/docs/govdocs1/229/229742.pdf

Prown, Jules D., and Kenneth Haltman (eds.). 2000. *American Artifacts: Essays in Material Culture.* East Lansing: Michigan State University Press.

Roberts, Helene E. Spring 1977. "The Exquisite Slave: The Role of Clothes in the Making of the Victorian Woman." *Signs*, 2(3): 554–569.

Schoeny, Marlise. 2000. "Reforming Fashion, 1850–1914: Politics, Health, and Art." The Ohio State University Historic Costume and Textiles Collection. Accessed June 2, 2019. https://costume.osu.edu/2000/04/14 /reforming-fashion-1850-1914-politics-health-and-art/.

Steele, Valerie. 2001. *The Corset: A Cultural History.* New Haven, CT; London: Yale University Press.

Victoria and Albert Museum. "19th-Century Fashion." Accessed May 25, 2019. http://www.vam.ac.uk/page/0-9/19th-century-fashion/.

15 Mourning Jewelry

INTRODUCTION

Did your mom assemble a baby scrapbook that contained pictures, statistics, newspaper announcements, greeting cards, and even a lock of hair from your first haircut? These types of scrapbooks are still popular, as are memento scrapbooks of weddings and other important life events. However, have you ever heard of a scrapbook that commemorates a death? Many types of remembrances of the dead were popular during the 19th century, especially after the Civil War in the Victorian era. *Memento mori*, Latin for "Remember you shall die," is a term used for symbols of death used in medieval through Victorian eras. These symbols often included skulls, skeletons, or images of the Grim Reaper (Death). During the 19th century, a "cult of death" emerged that employed various means to remind families of the imminence of death and the remembrance of their deceased loved ones. Though the most macabre symbols were eschewed by this time, personal reminders of the lost loved one often replaced them.

DESCRIPTION

Mourning products were produced in the late 19th century that accompanied the Victorian cult of death. In addition to photos, other things were utilized to create mementos of a deceased loved one. One of the most important relics was a sample of the loved one's hair. Family members cut hair from the deceased, or trimmed their hair while they were still alive, or sometimes both. This hair was safely kept so that the family could later use it to create decorative household items or jewelry for the family's use. This so-called hairwork was one of the most bizarre and peculiar traditions of the Victorian age. Hair was used to create many forms of jewelry, as well as watch chains for pocket watches, and even elaborate wreaths. Hairwork was a skill that originated in the 16th century in Sweden, where women spent the long winter nights threading hair into various types of jewelry. The craft soon traveled to Russia and Europe and later to the United States. The skill was handed down through families. By the second half of the 19th century, the popularity of hairwork had increased. The ever-popular ladies' magazine, *Godey's Lady's Book*, published a series of articles that described the techniques for creating hair jewelry, which included some general directions and sample patterns. In order to make the trinket, the hair was grouped to form usable strands, tied to bobbins, or weighted bags, and woven around a frame. It was then boiled and removed from the frame and taken to a jeweler to add the clasps or necessary fasteners. But though the skill of making hair jewelry and decorative items had traditionally been the bailiwick of close family members who remembered and mourned the deceased, the growth of the industrial economy in the 19th century began to change that. The designs became heavier, larger, and more ornate as per the popular elaborate Victorian style. They also became more sentimental. Professional jewelers learned the skill, got into the field, and were often hired by families to create the desired trinket. Advertisements for these jewelers were found in local magazines and newspapers.

The hairwork trinket shown here is a charm, originating from Pennsylvania, probably Philadelphia. The artist is unknown. The charm is made from gold and woven hair. The cylindrical, snare drum-shaped charm is only ⅝ inches across and ⅝ inches tall. It is engraved on the top in gold with the inscription "Malvern Hill, Bull Run 2d, Fredericksburg, Va." The top and bottom of the charm are gold, with gold roping connecting the top and bottom. The dark brown hair is woven in between the gold, forming the shaft of the drum. The charm was produced to commemorate Major William B. Hubbs, a painter from Germantown, Pennsylvania. Major Hubbs died in the Civil War as a member of the 95th Pennsylvania Infantry, in 1862.

Humans mourn their dead. This practice has endured as long as human society has existed. But the observance of mourning has shifted over the centuries as rituals around death have changed. Wearing black as a form of mourning dress has a long history in western culture. But the use of black clothing to represent mourning peaked in the second half of the 19th century. The long-lived British monarch, Queen Victoria, survived for forty years after the death of her beloved husband, Albert. In respect for his memory, she continued to wear nothing but mourning apparel for the rest of her life. The practice of donning mourning dress had been gaining in popularity in England and in the United States by the mid-19th century. But the abiding influence of Queen Victoria on both sides of the Atlantic brought on an even stricter adherence to the mourning dress code for the proper Victorian. In the United States, the catastrophic mortality of the Civil War also contributed to the ubiquity of the various mourning rituals of the time.

The Victorian era embraced a so-called cult of death. Unlike in 21st-century society, the specter of death was haunting every house, ominously hovering over each and every family. It never really went away. Children died; one-third of all babies died before reaching the age of ten. Adults died also, from infections, diseases, accidents, and of course, war. The ubiquity of death was not something new in the Victorian age; in fact, the certainty of death had been reflected on for centuries by Christians who utilized "memento mori" to remind humans of the definitive nature of impending death. But the Victorians celebrated death in a new way. Technology and the availability of new consumer products presented opportunities to recognize a loved one's passing. Photography, available in mid-19th century America, was a common tool to document the death of a loved one. Photos were taken in deathbeds and even in coffins. These pictures were used to populate the omnipresent scrapbooks. Photos were taken of younger family members, dressed in mourning garb, holding a photo of the deceased loved one. Photos were taken of babies who had died in infancy, often with a parent holding the deceased baby as if it were asleep. These photos could be displayed prominently in the parlor or could be tucked neatly into the mourning scrapbook that was further decorated with sentimental stickers that depicted angels, flowers, hearts, or happy children in memory of the departed. Sentimentality was the foundation for all the mourning paraphernalia that was popular in the Victorian era. The 19th-century Romantic period in the fine arts seeped into the popular culture with heart-rending tales of child death, cute animals, romantic love, and other themes that evoked emotion in the viewer.

SIGNIFICANCE

The cult of death was endemic in American Victorian society. Death was also endemic, and the certainty of death was recognized as a facet of life that must be acknowledged and celebrated. When a loved one passed away, certain procedures were typically followed. The curtains would be drawn in the house, and a black bunting and wreath would be placed on the door. Inside, the mirrors and any other reflective or shiny item would be covered with a black drape, often black crepe fabric. During the Victorian times, most Americans died at home, and the clock in the room where the loved one died would be stopped at the time of death. Cards would be sent out to inform family and friends of the death; in addition, funeral invitations would be sent out. There were also memorial cards made up that stated the name of the deceased, date of death, and a sentimental message. These would be used as keepsakes and would often be saved for the mourning scrapbook or photo album. The coffin would be set in the parlor, surrounded by flowers, and the typical wake time was three days. Many people feared that they could wake up and could be buried alive, ergo the waiting time and the term "wake." Women took on the major responsibility of mourning the family member. Mourning clothing was worn for extended periods: for a husband, a wife wore mourning apparel for up to two and a half years. The first period of mourning was deep black, but the colors lightened up as time passed. Men wore black suits and often sported black bands on their hats but otherwise were allowed to return to work. Women, as the so-called vessels of grief, were generally constrained to the home for the mourning period.

The concept of grief as a public acknowledgment was an idiosyncrasy of the Victorian era. Women wore veils to cover up their teary faces, yet they were expected to weep in grief. The black crepe bunting inside and outside the house announced to the world that the family was in mourning. There were rituals that allowed the family to grieve and to accept the grief. Some traditions, like the interminable wearing of mourning clothes for women, were onerous. However, the modern rejection of the recognition of grief has led to a paucity of memorial symbolism and a general uneasiness with grief. In modern society, many people are discomfited with the Victorian mourning trinkets, the hair jewelry and wreaths, the deathbed photographs, and the sentimental scrapbooks. But maybe we have turned too far in the opposite direction. Mourning is currently out of style, but it doesn't go away.

FURTHER INFORMATION

Lutz, Deborah. 2011. "The Dead Still among Us: Victorian Secular Relics, Hair Jewelry, and Death Culture." *Victorian Literature and Culture*, 39(1): 127–142.

Margulis, Marlyn I. May 2002. "Victorian Mourning Jewelry." *Antiques and Collecting Magazine*, 107(3): 20–23.

National Park Service. 2011. "The Custom of Mourning during the Victorian Era." https://www.nps.gov/jofl/learn/historyculture/upload/Mourning Article2011.rtf.

Rahm, Virginia. Summer, 1974. "Human Hair Ornaments." *Minnesota History*, 44(2): 70–74.

Scheumaker, Helen. 2008. *Love Entwined: The Curious History of Hairwork in America*. Philadelphia: University of Pennsylvania Press.

16 Native American War Shirt

INTRODUCTION

In the over five hundred Native American tribes within the landmass of the United States, there were no common religions practiced by all the tribes. There was a true diversity of beliefs. However, none of the languages spoken by the various tribes included a specific word that can be translated into "religion." Such a concept was foreign to the Native American tribes. A separation of secular and religious life did not exist; the two were emphatically integrated into what is often called the "life-way." These beliefs became a way of life to the various tribes, though the individual beliefs differed depending on the region and the landscape of the area. One of the common beliefs for the Native American tribes was that they, as humans, shared the world with a number of supernatural beings and forces "who rewarded and punished them and whom they encountered directly and indirectly through nature" (Butler 2000: 17). Nature was all-powerful and sacred.

Native Americans used many symbols in all aspects of their culture. Almost all the symbols refer to elements of nature. Some symbols are universal in many of the tribes; others are used specifically by a certain tribe. For instance, bears are sacred for many Native American tribes and revered for their spiritual and physical power and courage. The circle shape is symbolic of the four natural elements: water, earth, wind, and fire. It also can represent the cycle of birth and death. All the art that has been produced by Native American tribes contains symbols in the choice of material, the design, and the items represented. It is not created just as "art for art's sake." In addition, the clothing worn by Native American tribes often had symbolic meaning related to their spiritual beliefs.

DESCRIPTION

The item of clothing depicted here is a war shirt from the Upper Missouri River Tribe in Missouri that dates from between 1830 and 1840. Women in the tribe sewed the war shirts, and it was considered a sacred activity. The shirt was a symbolic garment, endowed with spiritual power and strength,

113

using the supernatural force that emanates from plants and animals. War shirts were important items of clothing for Native American tribes. They were indicative of the wearer's social status. In order to have the right to wear a war shirt, a Native American warrior had to prove himself to be brave in combat. In the Lakota tradition, the warriors who wore the shirt were called "the shirt wearers." But the right was not given indefinitely; if the wearer demonstrated weakness or cowardice, the warrior could be deprived of the right to be a shirt wearer. As a symbol of bravery and status, many chiefs in early photographs are shown wearing a highly decorated war shirt.

War shirts were made of tanned hides, from white-tailed deer, pronghorn, or bighorn sheep. The war shirt shown here is made of deer hide. The shirt was constructed of two to four hides, depending on the pattern. The front and rear of the shirt had one hide each. The sleeves were constructed from different hides. Early war shirts retained the natural contours of the animal as a show of respect, with the legs of the animal hanging down on either side, as is shown in this example. The shirt resembled a poncho, placed over the head and loosely hanging around the torso. Later versions showed the legs trimmed off to create a more boxy shape, with the sleeves and the sides enclosed, showing the influence of European clothing. The two hides were sewn at the top of the shoulders, hanging loosely. A common feature of typical war shirts was four embroidered strips, two over each shoulder and two more down the sleeves. The strips were highly decorated before attaching to the shirt. The decorations consisted of beadwork and quillwork. This example has glass pony beads and porcupine quills. The bold black-and-white beadwork recalls porcupine quill panels from earlier versions. These elaborate embroideries were produced by women in the tribe. The most skilled were highly respected artisans. The work was considered sacred. The patterns were symbolic, related to the tribe, and adhered to very precisely. The patterns were believed to contain spiritual powers, as a gift from the Spirits. In addition to the beadwork and quillwork, fringes, pelts, and lock of human hair were added to the war shirt. This war shirt contains ermine tails that signify wealth and authority. The human hair fringes were from the owner and his warrior friends as a token of brotherhood. The hair of a beloved warhorse might have also been added to the shirt. The large round medallion

NATIVE AMERICAN WAR SHIRT AT AUCTION

In 2012, the war shirt worn by Chief Joseph, leader of the Nez Perce tribe, was sold at auction for $877,500. The shirt was made famous by a portrait by Cyrenius Hall painted in 1878 and later depicted on a six cent U.S. postage stamp produced in 1968. Chief Joseph was known for his heroic retreat and eloquence in surrender, after a battle against U.S. soldiers in 1877.

in the center represents the circle of the universe. The wearer of the shirt and the tribe he represents are believed to be at the center of the universe. The war shirts, revered by the tribes, were typically worn ceremonially, although some less elaborately decorated shirts were also worn in battle.

SIGNIFICANCE

The war shirt is an example of the spiritual symbolism that permeated Native American daily life. What we in non-Indigenous culture deem to be beautiful art are items of deep symbolic meaning to the tribes that created them. The art is imbued with significance of their spiritual beliefs. Their abstract beauty can be appreciated by itself, but for the creators, it remains an interpretation of the natural world and an attempt to gain insight from it.

FURTHER INFORMATION

Butler, Jon, Grant Wacker, and Randall Balmer. 2000. *Religion in American Life: A Short History*. New York: Oxford University Press.

Dufrene, Phoebe. Fall 1990. "Exploring Native American Symbolism Journal of Multi—Cultural and Cross—Cultural Research in Art Education." *Columbia*, 8(1): 38–50.

Feder, Norman. 1965. *American Indian Art before 1850*. Denver: Denver Art Museum.

Horse Capture, Joseph D., and George P. Horse Capture. 2001. *Beauty, Honor, and Tradition: The Legacy of Plains Indian Shirts*. Minneapolis: Minneapolis Institute of Art.

"Introduction to Native People's Traditions." 2021. The Pluralism Project. Harvard University. Accessed July 28, 2021. https://pluralism.org /introduction-to-native-peoples%E2%80%99-traditions.

Lanford, Benson. October 2010. "A Sioux Quilled War Shirt." Bonhams. Accessed July 26, 2021. https://www.bonhams.com/auctions/18407/lot/ 2234/.

Navrátil, Lukáš. 2019. "Plains Indians War Shirts." February 11. Accessed July 28, 2021. https://www.matotope.com/plains-indians-war-shirts/.

Spivack, Emily. 2012. "The Long Journey of Chief Joseph's War Shirt." *Smithsonian Magazine*. July 25. Accessed July 28, 2021. https://www. smithsonianmag.com/arts-culture/the-long-journey-of-chief-josephs -war-shirt-7146932/.

"The Use of Symbols in Native American Art." May 8, 2019. The Faust Gallery. Accessed July 28, 2021. https://www.faustgallery.com/the-use -of-symbols-in-native-american-art/.

"What Did the Native Americans Wear? The Religious and Cultural Significance." August 8, 2011. Accessed July 28, 2021. https://www .brighthubeducation.com/social-studies-help/122796-clothing-of-indige nous-native-american-people/

17 Shaving Mug

INTRODUCTION

The work of barbers has had a long and storied history through the centuries. The word "barber" comes from *barba*, Latin for "beard." And of course, until the onset of the 20th century and the invention of Gillette's disposable safety razor, the ubiquitous barber shop was the place to get a shave as well as a haircut. In fact, from the Middle Ages until the 18th century, barbers were known as barber-surgeons and performed a number of surgical procedures, including dentistry, bloodletting with leeches, enemas, and extraction of teeth. A group of Greek barbers from Sicily introduced the barbering profession to Rome in the 3rd century AD, and the fashion in Rome was to be clean shaven. The fashions change, however, and a variety of beard types were seen by European men off and on up until the beginning of the 18th century when the beard disappeared from the polite society. Beards were considered unrefined and coarse, and a gentleman would not be seen with one. Being clean-shaven was considered a manly attribute, because shaving required patience and grit. It was not easy or even safe to get a shave, whether at home or at the barber shop. However, by the middle of the 19th century, the style changed, and beards of all sorts appeared in Europe and in the United States. One of the early advocates of the beard in the United States, of course, was Abraham Lincoln. A clean-shaven man until after he won the presidential election in 1860, Lincoln received a letter from an eleven-year-old girl in New York City who had seen him in photographs and decided that his lanky, wizened, angular face would benefit from some facial hair. Her suggestion was that "you would look a great deal better for your face is so thin." He became the first bearded U.S. president.

Beards became all the rage during the Victorian period. Much has been written about the reason for this. Society was in flux as the Industrial Revolution was affecting gender roles. Men were leaving the farms with their families and settling in the cities and suburbs, commuting to factory or office jobs. The work was hard and stressful but not as physical as working on the farm or in a trade. Also, all of a sudden they were working for a boss and giving up their independence and self-sufficiency for a wage. Women were given the responsibility of managing the household and the family. Women's rights were also becoming an issue, and the women's rights movement advocated for education, admission into the professions, gaining rights to property, divorce, and child custody. All of a sudden, men didn't feel so manly anymore. If women could perform the tasks that men had traditionally done, what differentiated the two genders? A beard, of course! And the bigger and scruffier the beard, the better. Another factor mentioned by historians is the endemic racism exhibited by the white majority. Scientists believed at the time that certain races and ethnic groups did not have enough facial hair to grow a beard. The flaunting of the huge whiskers in white society was an implicit expression of white supremacy. If a full beard demonstrated manliness and virility, the lack of one was its antithesis. All U.S. presidents from Lincoln until William Howard Taft, who served from 1909 until 1913, had beards or large mustaches. None have since.

With the turn of the 20th century, a number of factors influenced the waning of the beard fad. By the 1890s, the concept of having a full beard ran up against a new scientific belief that men could transmit infectious particles residing in the beard. Especially with the scourge of tuberculosis, newly discovered to be transmitted by germs, a clean-shaven man could demonstrate cleanliness and sanitation. The concept of exercising and bodybuilding also became popular, encouraging men to show their manliness with muscles instead of whiskers. When the safety razor was introduced in 1904, the beardless trend began to take off. Now, men could shave themselves at home with a safe, reliable, disposable razor. The complete dissolution of the 19th-century beard craze came with the onset of World War I. Soldiers were required to wear bulky gas masks, which didn't fit properly over a big beard.

DESCRIPTION

The artifact shown here demonstrates the popularity and ubiquity of the barber shop in late-19th-century America. In 1880, there were forty-five thousand full-time barbers in a nation that still had only fifty million people. Barber shops were a local hangout for the neighborhood men, a place where one could get a shave, a trim, as well as the sports news, local gossip, and business news, or even smoke a cigar. (The earlier habit of drinking and gambling at the barber shop was fading by this time.) Men usually went to the barber at least three times a week to get a shave. One of the fascinating artifacts dating from this time was the shaving mug. An upgrade from the previous method, a hand basin and a soap ball, the mug was able to contain more soap so the barber could use it for the next customer. In the 1840s, "shaving compounds" in porcelain containers were introduced and, in the 1870s, paper-wrapped soap to use with shaving mugs. The fad of the individualized painted mugs began in the 1870s. (It was believed that mugs that were shared were responsible for the rashes that customers sometimes got after a shave. It was, in fact, most likely the unsanitary razor that was responsible for the rash, however.) The mugs were often hand-painted with the name and a charming scene describing the man's occupation drawn on the mug. They were considered a status symbol, both for the barber, who displayed the mugs, and for the customer.

These mugs were imported from France or Germany. They came in three sizes: small, medium, and large. The mugs were delivered blank and were hand-painted locally for the individual buyer. The mug shown here was made by Haviland, a French Limoges porcelain producer. It is cylindrical with a shaped base, rolled rim, and a loop handle. It measures 3.75 inches in height, with a diameter of 4 inches. It is inscribed with gold lettering: "Niagara Engine Co. No 5 / T. Cornell." Niagara Engine Co. No. 5 of Tompkinsville, established in 1878, was part of the Edgewater Fire Department of Staten Island, New York. It has an image of a 19th-century fire pumper and painted flowers. The maker's mark is printed on the underside, "CFH," a mark used by Charles Field Haviland, Limoges, France, from 1870 to 1882. The date of the mug is estimated to be between 1878 and 1882. It is part of the collection of the Staten Island Historical Society.

SIGNIFICANCE

Barbers retained their popularity throughout the 19th century despite the beard fad. Barber shops were everywhere and stayed open long hours. They became a center for local men to gossip and hang out. In the early days of the 19th century, they even provided gambling and drinking opportunities, adding to an aura of licentiousness for the barber establishments. During slavery, slave men were taught the tonsorial arts, and the masters were shaved by their slaves. After the slaves were set free in the northern states, many became professional barbers and set up barber shops. Some even became wealthy. But their success didn't last. Several factors were responsible for this. The temperance movement and the Second Great Awakening led to a reaction to the conviviality and liquor enjoyed inside the shops. Epidemics and the subsequent fear of disease led some people to shave at home. White resentment of the growing wealth of the black barbers was a large factor as well. This was a period of scientific racism in the United States, and many scientists promulgated racist theories on black intelligence and propensity for violence. All of a sudden white men started to eschew the razor blade–wielding black barbers. By the middle of the century, German immigrant barbers flooded the cities, pushing out all but the most celebrated barbers who served elite white clientele. And this was the time that the new fad was the full beard. The days of the successful professional African American barbers who served the white community were over. However, many black barbers settled in African American neighborhoods, and even today, the black-owned barber shops have remained a mainstay of the community. Today there are approximately 109,000 barber shops for a population of 329 million in the United States.

FURTHER INFORMATION

Adams, Russell B. 1978. *King C. Gillette, the Man and His Wonderful Shaving Device*. Boston: Little, Brown and Co.

Barlow, Ronald S. 1996. *The Vanishing American Barber Shop: An Illustrated History*. St. Paul, MN: William Marvy Co., Inc.

Oldstone-Moore, Christopher. 2016. *Of Beards and Men: The Revealing History of Facial Hair*. Chicago; London: University of Chicago Press.

Peterkin, Allan. 2001. *One Thousand Beards: A Cultural History of Facial Hair*. Vancouver: Arsenal Pulp Press.

Powell, Robert B. 1978. *Occupational & Fraternal Shaving Mugs of the United States*. Hurst, TX: Robert Blake Powell.

Smithsonian Institution. "Hair Removal." Accessed September 23, 2021. https://www.si.edu/spotlight/health-hygiene-and-beauty/hair-removal.

Trainor, Sean. 2014. "The Racially Fraught History of the American Beard." *The Atlantic*. January 20. Accessed September 23, 2021. https://www.theatlantic.com/national/archive/2014/01/the-racially-fraught-history-of-the-american-beard/283180/.

Withey, Alun. 2018. "A Brief History of Beards." History Extra. May 21. Accessed October 26, 2021. https://www.historyextra.com/period/victorian/a-brief-history-of-beards/.

18 Beaver Fur Top Hat

INTRODUCTION

For centuries, the hat was an essential element of a man's wardrobe. In the 19th century, the hat that had star status in the man's closet was the top hat. Also known as a topper or a stovepipe, it was a tall, brimmed, flat-crowned hat. A commonly told, but likely apocryphal, story about the top hat ascribes its origin to a London hat maker named John Hetherington. When he wore the hat on the streets of London, it apparently caused a riot, and in the *St. James Gazette* newspaper in January 1797, it was recounted this way: "[Hetherington] appeared on the Public Highway wearing upon his head a tall structure having a shining lustre and calculated to frighten timid people." He was subsequently charged with breach of the peace and inciting a riot and required to post a $500 bond. This inauspicious introduction of the top hat into society did not prevent the scary "tall structure" from becoming a staple of every well-dressed man's wardrobe.

DESCRIPTION

The hat pictured here is a beaver top hat dated 1832. It is a tall hat, measuring 8 ¼ inches by 9 inches by 10 ⅞ inches high. The hat was manufactured by Peck and Company, a Boston, Massachusetts, hat manufacturer. Peck and Company was located on Cornhill, a 19th-century street in Boston. The area is now part of the redevelopment of City Hall Plaza that was completed in the 1960s. An engraving dating from 1836 of the shops on Cornhill shows Peck and Company with building signs that state, "Boston and New York, Fashionable Hat Warehouse. Peck and Co. Wholesale and Retail Hat Manufacturers."

Beaver pelts were used for a number of types of hats, but the most enduring was the top hat. The beaver hat was the most valued item in a man's wardrobe and was often handed down in families as an inheritance. The Puritans in 17th-century England and America wore an unadorned, tall, narrow brimmed hat made of beaver pelt that was plain and extremely durable. The Puritan hat served as the predecessor to the top hat and was a reaction to the elaborate men's hats of the 18th century that sported feathers and big brims. The top hat was popularized in the early 19th century by the British George Brummell, known as "Beau" Brummell. The stylish Brummell was known for his introduction of sophisticated and elegant fashions for men. He was dubbed a "dandy," a term that described an exquisitely well-dressed, refined man. His taste in clothes became highly influential in Europe and North America. In addition to the top hat, Brummell's influence on men's fashion included understated but finely tailored jackets in dark colors, eschewing the formerly popular knee breeches in exchange for long pants, with white shirts and cravats. The fashion for men in the 19th century, in contrast with the exaggerated styles for women, featured a tailored, toned down, and sophisticated style.

Making a beaver hat took time and consisted of several stages. First, the beaver had to be trapped, and the local Native American tribes did much of the trapping. The tribes traded the pelts with the Europeans for pots, pans, and other useful items. The beaver, North America's largest rodent that survives in the cold regions of the northern United States and Canada, has two types of fur—the coarse guard hair and the soft underfur. The underfur, or beaver wool, is the desirable, soft, and waterproof fur that is used to make the felt for the hats. When preparing the beaver pelt for shipping, two different types of pelt could be produced—castor sec or castor gras. Castor sec (meaning dry beaver in French) was also known as parchment beaver. The beaver was skinned, and its skin was scraped clean. But the coarse guard hairs remained on the pelt and had to be removed later in the process. The other process was called castor gras (meaning fat beaver in French). The Native American trappers who worked with the fur traders in the United States and Canada often took five to eight pelts, sewed them together, and wore them for twelve to eighteen months. The rubbing of the fur against the skin, combined with the wearer's perspiration, produced a softer, more pliable skin that lost its guard hairs. The castor gras method was preferable and therefore sold for more money but took longer to produce. When the pelts were prepared for shipment by either the castor sec or castor gras method, they were shipped to Paris, London, or North American cities to the hat manufacturers.

One beaver hat required from one to five full-grown male beaver pelts, and the process to complete the hat involved over thirty procedures. When the hat makers received the pelts, the next step was to pull and shave the beaver wool off the pelt. Any remaining guard hairs were removed, and then the fur was shaved off to create beaver fluff. The subsequent part of the process of making a beaver hat was onerous; in fact it was downright dangerous. It was called "carroting," and it was a technique that involved using mercury salts diluted in nitric acid in which the fluff was soaked in a chemical bath. The carroting softened the fur and made it easier to create the felt.

It turned the fur tips an orange color, however; hence the term "carroting." When applying steam to the fur to produce the felt, mercury vapors were released into the air, which was toxic for the hat makers. The old expression "mad as a hatter" originated because the makers of beaver hats often went mad after long-term exposure to mercury in the hat production. The mercury damaged the nervous system and often resulted in dementia, involuntary muscular contractions, difficulties in speech, and loss of hearing, eyesight, teeth, and nails. Tremors that were caused by the mercury poisoning were dubbed "hatter's shakes." By the end of the 19th century, the risk of using mercury salts in hat making was identified. Recommendations such as better ventilation and the use of protective clothing ameliorated the exposure, and in the 20th century, an alternative hat making method was found.

DESCRIPTION OF THE IMPORTANCE OF THE FUR TRADE IN AMERICA'S WESTWARD DEVELOPMENT

The history of North American Expansion might almost be written in terms of the fur trade. Europeans were early attracted to the North American coast by the hope of reaping profits from this trade, and after the beginning of settlement revenue from it was the principal means of sustenance to the early English, French, and Dutch colonies. . . . Many a nameless trader, discoverer, has been the first white man to set foot upon lands credit for the discovery of which has gone to others. . . . Before him was the wilderness; behind him, over paths he himself had made, poured in an ever advancing tide of settlement. . . . This the fur trader has blazed the way across the continent.

[Arthur H. Buffinton, paper presented to the Colonial Society of Massachusetts by Samuel Eliot Morrison, January 1916.

From: Dolin, Eric J. 2010. *Fur, Fortune, and Empire: The Epic Story of the Fur Trade in America*. New York: W.W. Norton & Company, Inc.]

SIGNIFICANCE

The story of the beaver hat is a tale of European fashion, animal extinction, and North American trade. The beaver hat became a fashion craze in the late 16th century in London and Paris. It was snatched up by wealthy bourgeoisie men who wore it as a badge of rank. Beaver had been a sought-after commodity for centuries, especially prized for its warmth, softness, and water resistance. The Vikings produced beaver pelts, and later on, it became a favorite of European royalty, so much so that the European beaver, the *castor fiber*, neared extinction on the continent by 1500. Things were not looking good for the beaver hat aficionados. But trade for the nearly identical North American beaver, the *castor canadensis*, was soon to bring beaver fur back to eager European consumers. And, surprisingly, a share of the early beaver trade came from the Pilgrims of the Plymouth Colony in Massachusetts. When the Pilgrims set off from England in 1620 on the Mayflower, they were fleeing religious persecution. They practiced a form of Calvinist Christianity that had broken away from the all-powerful Church of England, and they were seeking a location where they could practice their religion freely. But as a result of their dire financial need, the Pilgrims employed a business model to fund their trip to the New World. They summoned a group of London sponsors to invest in their new colony. Eventually, after negotiation, a joint stock company was formed, and the investor group was named "The Company of Merchant Adventurers of London." The presumption was that the investors could turn a profit off these courageous religious adventurers. The merchant adventurers lent the Pilgrims the funds to purchase a boat and supplies, but the Pilgrims were expected to send back valuable products in order to pay back the debt. Life didn't go well for the first year of the colony, but the Pilgrims realized the following year that the prized beaver fur could be obtained by working with the local tribes. The prime beaver region was in Maine, north of the Plymouth colony. The Pilgrims made an agreement to trade with the Abenaki tribe, by providing them with corn, as well as other commodities, in exchange for beaver pelts. As a result, the Pilgrims began sending back the coveted pelts and had completely paid off their debt by 1636. The intrepid Pilgrims of the Plymouth colony not only saved themselves from disaster but also launched a trading business that spread as the new colonies grew. In fact, as the beaver population in the Northeast dwindled, trade moved west, and much of the development of the northern United States and Canada was a result of the growing demand for beaver pelts both in Europe and in the colonies. Canada benefited from the beaver trade, with the Hudson Bay Company, which was chartered in 1670 as a fur trading business and still exists as a

---

ABRAHAM LINCOLN'S TOP HAT

Although he stood at a hulking 6 by 4 inches tall, Abraham Lincoln chose to sport an extra-high stovepipe top hat for much of his adult life. This serious hat made Lincoln appear even taller and more imposing. Some historians suggest that he began wearing it as a gimmick, but it became his signature hat. He was wearing a silk top hat on April 14, 1865, Good Friday, when he took his wife, Mary, to Ford's Theatre to see the play *Our American Cousin*. That was the day he was assassinated by John Wilkes Booth. The hat, adorned with a 3-inch mourning band in remembrance of the death of his son Willie, was preserved by the War Department and is now on display at the Smithsonian Institution in Washington, DC.

retail business today. In fact, the national symbol of Canada is the beaver. The popularity of the beaver top hat continued into the first half of the 19th century. The declining population of the beaver, even in North America, and the introduction of the less expensive silk top hat in the 1840s struck the final death knell to the enduring popularity of the beaver top hat.

FURTHER INFORMATION

Bunker, Nick. 2011. *Making Haste from Babylon: The Mayflower Pilgrims and Their World*. New York: Vintage Publishing.

Crean, J. F. August 1962. "Hats and the Fur Trade." *Canadian Journal of Economics and Political Science*, 28(3): 373–386.

Dolin, Eric J. 2010. *Fur, Fortune, and Empire: The Epic Story of the Fur Trade in America*. New York: W.W. Norton & Company, Inc.

Feinstein, Kelly. March 2006. "Fashionable Felted Fur: The Beaver Hat in 17th Century English Society." History Department, UC Santa Cruz. Accessed June 19, 2019. https://humwp.ucsc.edu/cwh/feinstein/Main%20Page.html.

Kurin, Richard. 2013. *The Smithsonian's History of America in 101 Objects*. New York: Penguin Books.

McNight, David. 2001. "In Pursuit of Adventure: The Fur Trade in Canada and the North West Company—The Beaver and Other Pelts." McGill University. Accessed June 10, 2019. http://digital.library.mcgill.ca/nwc/history/01.htm.

Payne, Alice. 2014. "The Story of . . . the Top Hat." May 7. Accessed June 11, 2019. https://theconversation.com/the-story-of-the-top-hat-26215.

Shrimpton, Jayne. 2016. *Victorian Fashion*. Oxford: Shire Publications.

Wallace-Wells, David. 2011. "Puritan, Inc." *The New Republic*. https://newrepublic.com/article/75603/puritan-inc.

Health and Medicines

Civil War Surgical Instruments and Case

Nightmare Turtle Magic Lantern Slide

Patent Medicine—Cocaine Toothache
Drops

Phrenology Head

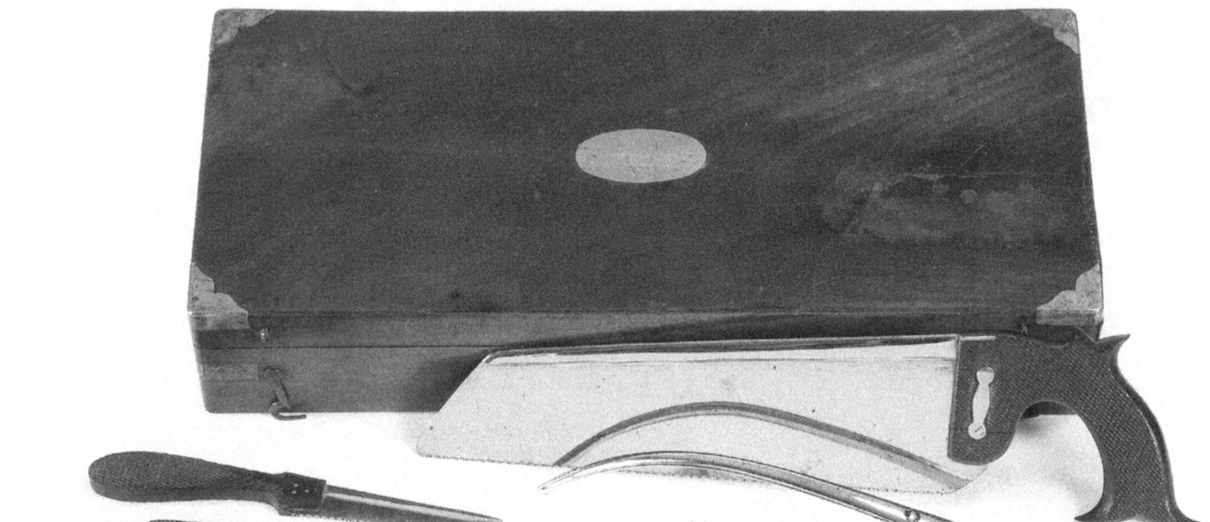

Minnesota Historical Society

19 Civil War Surgical Instruments and Case

INTRODUCTION

An operating room in one of today's modern hospitals is jam-packed with all types of highly specialized equipment. And today's surgeons are blessed with the finest of instruments. Most important, operating theaters are kept sanitized and germ-free. The doctors and nurses don masks and gloves. Practitioners of modern medicine understand that an antiseptic environment is crucial to preventing a potential life-threatening infection. But during the Civil War, according to one historian, American medicine was "in the very last years of the medical middle ages" (Devine 2016: 151). The revolution in science and medical technology that predated modern medicine would come toward the end of the 19th century. But the Civil War took place during the 1860s. American physicians and surgeons were hampered by primitive tools and antiquated theories of medicine. Nevertheless, the medical field benefited from the dogged toil of its doctors, as well as from a hospital system designed to accommodate the unremitting crush of war injuries caused by the violence of the Civil War battlefield.

DESCRIPTION

The surgeons who treated the wounded during the Civil War had few tools at their disposal. What they did have was a small surgical kit that contained a number of instruments. Surgeons were required to provide their own instruments, and their kits were their most prized possessions. The kit shown here had twenty-two surgical instruments. The instruments were nestled into a walnut case with brass fittings. The kit belonged to William H. Leonard, MD, an assistant surgeon of the Fifth Minnesota Regiment. The instruments have steel hardware and checkered ebony handles. Ebony was a dense dark brown or black hardwood. The kit includes the following instruments: two bone saws, flexible saw blade with linked teeth and detachable handles, scalpel, forceps, bone nippers, tourniquet with brass compress and red canvas strap, two brass and steel trepanning tools with a detachable handle, surgical wire, and an envelope containing eight suture needles. The bone saw, also called a capital saw, was used to saw through large bones in the leg or arm for amputations. The flexible saws were used to amputate smaller bones, like ribs, fingers, tows, ankles, or wrists. The scalpel was a sharp knife used to make incisions into the skin. The surgeon would use the scalpel to cut down to the bone before using the saw to complete the amputation. Forceps, the instrument that looks like a pair of scissors with a curved end, were most often used to extract a bullet. Bone nippers, the instrument that looks like pliers, were utilized to remove splinters of bone after the bone was sawn off. It could also be used for amputating small appendages like fingers. The tourniquet was a commonly used tool that temporarily cut off blood supply while the surgeon performed an amputation. The trepanning tools made small round holes in the skull, an ancient technique still occasionally used today to alleviate bleeding on the brain. The surgical wire and needles were used to close up wounds after surgery.

Understanding the tools that were in the medical kit of a Civil War surgeon, it is evident that amputations were some of the most common surgical procedures performed as a result of the bloody conflict. Records from the landmark 6-volume *Medical and Surgical History of the War of the Rebellion* (MSHWR) indicate that there were close to thirty thousand amputations performed during the war. Despite the fact that these operations were performed in a germ-infested, nonsterile environment, only 26.3 percent of the amputees died from infection. The surgeons realized that performing an amputation within 48 hours after the injury occurred saved many lives. The tools of the Civil War surgeon were very primitive. However, one of the newer tools in the arsenal of the Civil War surgeon was general anesthesia. Ether was used as a form of general anesthesia as early as 1846, and chloroform was discovered in 1847. So, the myth of the Civil War soldier "biting the bullet" while a surgeon amputated his leg is apocryphal. The vast majority of surgeries were performed on soldiers using a general anesthetic.

SIGNIFICANCE

The Civil War took place several decades before the widespread academic professionalization of American occupations. By the end of the 19th century, doctors, lawyers, architects, and other professions were offered the opportunity to study in well-funded academic institutions. The United States eventually developed licensing requirements for all types of professions. But in the 1860s, American doctors did not attend a medical school as we know it today. The only medical schools available were independent, privately owned institutions that were not affiliated with universities. Under the influence of President Andrew Jackson, during the 1830s and 1840s, there was a pervasive attack on elitism and professionalism, and the states that did have licensing requirements eliminated them. The medical schools in antebellum America were primarily owned and run by private physicians. They were not competitive—an academically poor student who was rejected by one of the nation's universities could be accepted to a medical school, providing that the family could pay the tuition. College degrees were not required to be accepted to medical school, and some accepted students were barely literate. School was limited to two four-month terms, taught by the owner-physicians in subjects they preferred. Little or no training was done in the hospital, and the medical students therefore had almost no experience with actual patients. One of the most egregious faults of the American medical training was the paucity of anatomical lab work. Because of the religious influence in the country, dissections of human cadavers were banned. In fact, the few cadavers made available to American medical students were ones stolen from fresh graves. This was not the same situation in certain countries in Europe, however. Medical students who could afford an elite medical education traveled to Paris, where they would prepare at the Paris Clinical School. France was years ahead of the United States in its medical knowledge, not least of all because of the availability of cadavers, which helped them to clearly understand human anatomy. The handful of Parisian-trained American doctors formed a tiny core of top physicians in the United States. This was the state of affairs of the medical profession that the country faced at the onset of the Civil War. However, the backbreaking work performed by the field surgeons during the war gave them experience that they never had in medical school or in their previous practice. By the end of the war, American surgeons became experts in various types of surgery.

Another advantage gained by the medical profession during the Civil War was the influence of the Sanitary Commission, at least on the Union side. In 1861, Congress authorized the establishment of the U.S. Sanitary Commission, modeled after the British Sanitary Commission. During the Crimean War, Florence Nightingale, the founder of modern nursing, was celebrated for limiting deaths from infection through improved sanitation. Although scientists had not yet discovered that germs caused infection, they were learning that through better hygiene, deaths from war injuries could be reduced. Baths were encouraged, as was the frequent cleaning of sheets, bed clothes, as well as hospital walls and floors. The U.S. Sanitary Commission appointed Frederick Law Olmsted, who would famously design Central Park and other parks as the world's first professional landscape architect, to head the Commission. Although the work of the Commission was opposed stridently by the War Department, who considered the group "a respectable body of supposed fanatics and philanthropists, backed by a large class of anxious and sympathetic women" (Ashenburg 2007: 209) by the end of the war, the Commission was an unmitigated success. The number of deaths due to injury and disease during the Civil War, though still alarmingly high, had been substantially reduced from the fatality counts in earlier wars. And for the first time, an army of trained female nurses was utilized to aid in the treatment of the battle wounded, under the direction of Dorothea Lynde Dix as superintendent of women nurses for the Union army.

Another medical advance that was a result of Civil War was the hospital system organized by Lincoln's new surgeon general, Dr. William A. Hammond, who initiated a series of reforms. Because of the size of the armies, the scope of the battles, and the chaos on the battlefields, Hammond realized that there had to be an escalating system of medical and hospital facilities to handle the thousands of battle-wounded soldiers. The system he created served the patients first at a field station, then at a field hospital, then a division or corps hospital, and then finally, if necessary, at a major Army hospital in a nearby city. Although the system could still be overwhelmed, at the battle of Antietam, on "America's bloodiest day," the complex system saved many lives as hordes of support personnel performed their duties in this indelible scene described by Alfred J. Bollet: "Stretcher bearers . . . removed the wounded from the front line and took them to regimental assistant surgeons located just behind the front line. These surgeons triaged the wounded, stopped bleeding, administered opiates, and dressed wounds. Trained ambulance attendants then moved the wounded to field hospitals set up in existing buildings or tents just beyond artillery range" (Rostker 2013: 81). The method was further improved at the Battle of Gettysburg, which took place on July 1–3, 1863, with over fourteen thousand wounded Union soldiers and seven thousand Confederates left behind on the battlefield. The Sanitation Commission, coupled with the work of the U.S. Surgeon General, organized and improved the conditions for the wounded soldiers and the attendant surgeons during the Civil War. The Confederacy did not benefit from these reforms and was forced to depend on local charities with fewer hospitals and nurses.

Germ theory wasn't accepted science during the Civil War, when surgeons were still reusing dirty instruments and performing invasive surgery using their bloodied and grimy hands. The instruments that surgeons used in the field hospitals were primitive. But the experience gained through the misery was invaluable. Doctors who had scant training before the war were now experts. The role of hygiene and sanitation lived on beyond the war, as soldiers as well as surgeons went home and demanded running water, sewers, toilets, and bathtubs. The system of hospitals also lived on past the war, and many state-run veterans' hospitals were built as a result of the war. The revolution in technology was about to transform medicine forever, but the Civil War had primed the profession for change.

FURTHER INFORMATION

Albin, Maurice S. 2000. "The Use of Anesthetics during the Civil War, 1861–1865." *Pharmacy in History*, 42(3/4): 99–114.

Ashenburg, Katherine. 2007. *The Dirt on Clean: An Unsanitized History.* New York: North Point Press.

Bollet, Alfred J. 2002. *Civil War Medicine: Challenges and Triumphs.* Somerville, NJ: Galen.

Burns, Stanley B. 2020. "Surgery in the Civil War." Public Broadcasting Service. Accessed June 8, 2020. http://www.pbs.org/mercy-street/uncover-history/behind-lens/surgery-civil-war/.

Devine, Shauna. 2014. *Learning from the Wounded: The Civil War and the Rise of American Medical Science.* Chapel Hill: University of North Carolina Press.

Devine, Shauna. June 2016. "To Make Something Out of the Dying in this War: The Civil War and the Rise of American Medical Science." *Journal of the Civil War Era*, 6(2):149–163.

Gilchrist, Michael R. April 1998. "Disease & Infection in the American Civil War." *American Biology Teacher*, 60(4): 258–262.

Rostker, Bernard. 2013. *Providing for the Casualties of War: The American Experience through World War II.* Santa Monica, CA: Rand Corporation.

Shryock, Richard H. Summer 1962. "A Medical Perspective on the Civil War." *American Quarterly*, 14(2) Part 1: 161–173.

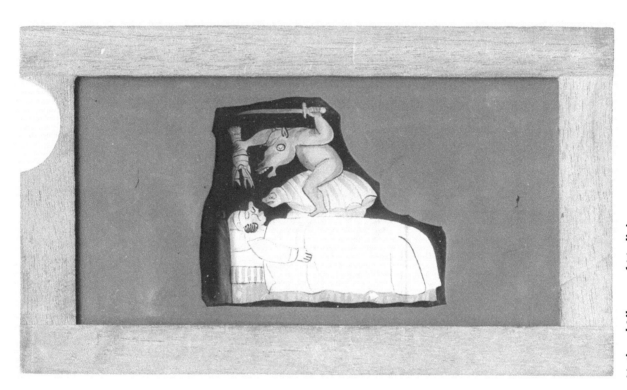

20 Nightmare Turtle Magic Lantern Slide

INTRODUCTION

The scourge of mental illness has always been with us. Successful treatments for diseases of the mind have eluded humanity for centuries. In many societies, a mentally ill person was believed to be possessed by the devil. The word "lunatic" is derived from the Latin *lunaticus*, which meant "moon-struck" or influenced by the moon in displaying periodic insanity. In Western cultures, individuals who exhibited signs of mental illness were often shunned by the public. While Europe and the United States were still primarily rural societies, families kept their mentally ill family members safely ensconced at home. And these families were not rare; current statistics indicate that almost half of the population will experience some form of mental illness within their lifetime. As the Industrial Revolution brought more population into the cities, keeping mentally ill family members at home became unsustainable, and another solution had to be found. Because the mentally ill were often accused of exhibiting moral or spiritual failure, they were typically treated like prisoners and were actually held in city jails, or in unregulated private asylums where they were often mistreated.

DESCRIPTION

The first institution in the United States to address the growing need to accommodate the mentally ill in an organized way was the Pennsylvania Hospital. In 1752, it opened a section to house mentally ill patients. As demand grew further, the hospital constructed a separate ward. In the early 19th century, many hospitals proceeded to construct wards for the mentally ill in other cities. These were not happy places; in many wards, the patients would be chained to the wall, ostensibly so that they would not hurt themselves or others. It wasn't until a small number of reformers reacted to the horrendous conditions in the jails and asylums that the situation began to improve. One of the first reformers to influence asylum conditions was Dorothea Dix, a teacher from Maine who, after visiting a jail in Boston that housed the insane, resolved to tackle the support of the mentally ill as her lifelong mission. Dix had an enduring influence on the treatment of the mentally ill in the 19th century. She convinced state legislatures to fund hospitals for the mentally ill; this was a revolutionary change. Dix was also able to convince Congress to pass a law in 1851 to federally fund mental hospitals. However, President Franklin Pierce vetoed it, contending that the care of the mentally ill remained a concern of the states. The effect of the veto was long-lasting; it is still in the jurisdiction of state hospitals to house the mentally ill. Dorothea Dix's lobbying effort was uniquely successful, however; she was responsible for the construction of thirty-two state mental hospitals by the time of her death in 1887.

Another transformative figure in the field of the care of the mentally ill was Thomas Story Kirkbride, a Quaker physician from Philadelphia. Kirkbride was bursting with ideas about improving the conditions and even possibly curing the mentally ill. After a visit to England where he visited a Quaker hospital called York Retreat, Kirkbride determined to provide the same type of environment in the United States. At York Retreat, a British Quaker physician named Samuel Tuke devised a method of caring for the mentally ill that he dubbed "Moral Treatment." A philosophy that espoused the humane precepts of the Quaker creed, Tuke recommended using compassionate care within comfortable surroundings, a radical shift in the common practice of the American medical profession. Kirkbride went further, devising architectural designs for mental hospitals that could practice Moral Treatment. In 1854, Kirkbride published *On the Construction, Organization, and General Arrangements of Hospitals for the Insane*, which delineated specific layouts and design specifications for the building of a hospital, including large, encompassing grounds that surrounded it. Kirkbride was not an architect, but he had a vision of his theory of Moral Treatment that he called "The Kirkbride Plan" or a "linear plan." The plan placed a hub in the center of the building that housed the offices, dining room, medical offices, and other administrative functions. On either side of the central hub were two spokes that extended out on the right and left sides, with a number of stepped sections. These sections contained patients' rooms and common areas and were narrow, with large windows that allowed for ample light and air. This was a crucial factor in Kirkbride's theory. He believed that bright and pleasant conditions would help a patient recover from any type of mental illness. The opposing wings of the building were assigned for men and women on either side. The tiered sections separated the patients by seriousness of illness; the least severe would be closest to the central hub, and the most severe patients would be at the farthest so as not to provide a negative influence on the others. All patients, however, were to be provided with the same level of comfort. Kirkbride believed that a professionally designed landscape surrounding the hospital would also inspire medical improvement for the patients. He also recommended that the patients spend their days in productive work, and a small farm was included in the plans for his hospitals where the patients could work and also provide usable food for the facility.

Another aspect of the Kirkbride plan for Moral Treatment was his emphasis on the total environment for the mentally ill patient. In addition to the importance of the physical comfort of the patient, Kirkbride maintained that showing kindness and consideration for the individual promoted mental health. In the past, harsh punishments using restraining devices were the standard treatment for mental illness. Kirkbride's concept of providing home-like environments and kind treatment was a radical one in the 19th century. Michel Foucault, the French philosopher and social theorist and author of *History of Madness*, described how the asylums of the 18th century were almost like zoos, where curious onlookers would gape at the raving lunatic patients who performed for the audience like chimps behind bars in a cage. This type of boorish conduct was what the reformers like Kirkbride endeavored to counteract. Whereas earlier medical theories classified insanity as "madness," the reformers like Kirkbride took a more clinical approach, believing that insanity was a disease of the brain. The disease of mental illness, it was believed, could be cured by separation from society, still in an institution, but in one that treated the patient with respect and love. Another theme of Kirkbride's form of Moral Treatment was to encourage the patients to be busy at all times. In addition to the daily exercise and work projects, Kirkbride agonized about the free hours for the patients between dinner and bedtime. He considered boredom to be the enemy of successful treatment. So Kirkbride's plan included nightly activities that he called "Evening Entertainments" that would stimulate and entertain the mind. These programs included lectures on science and musical performances, as well as a technology that was known as the magic lantern show. Kirkbride dubbed this type of program "magic lantern therapy." Kirkbride was one of the first serious promoters of the use of early photography. He became friends with two early photographic pioneers, Frederick and William Langenheim. Kirkbride amassed a huge collection of photographic slides in his psychiatric hospital in Philadelphia that were produced by the Langenheim brothers. At the hospital Kirkbride would present magic lantern shows in a room specifically designed for that purpose, with rows of benches and a podium that housed the magic lantern machine. The magic lantern show was a precursor of the modern slide show, as the glass photographic or hand-colored slides would be projected on the wall behind the machine. Photos of a wide variety of subjects would be presented, including international travel, art, religious subjects, science, classical history, and others. What was prohibited by Kirkbride was any photo of the patients themselves. Kirkbride was cognizant of the previous conditions of lunatic asylums, where curious spectators would gawk at the crazy lunatic patients, and he was determined not to allow anything like it to reoccur. That was another reason that he recommended siting the hospitals in suburban locations where it was difficult for inquisitive onlookers to gain entrance.

The magic lantern slide presented here dates from 1855, from one of the Kirkbride hospitals, St. Elizabeth's Hospital, in Washington, DC. It is one of a pair of wood-framed slides in the hospital's collection. The first slide (not shown) is a drawing of a man sleeping peacefully in a bed, shown from the side, with his head resting on a pillow and a blanket covering his body. The second slide (shown here) depicts a nightmare scene, with the same man sleeping in the same bed, but this time he is in the midst of a terrible nightmare. The man is confronted by a huge green turtle parked on his chest on which is sitting a bright blue mare holding a sword above his head and a red lobster dangling over the man's face. This frightening night "mare" scene was used as part of Kirkbride's treatment program at his psychiatric hospitals. Though it is not known exactly what this slide was utilized for, it is an example of Kirkbride's theory of the connection between the eye and the mind. He contended that the magic lantern slides could transmit images directly from the eye to the brain and target the segment of the brain that was malfunctioning. It was possible that Kirkbride believed that the second slide would startle the patients into a cure for their mental illness. Kirkbride wrote that his slides could help alleviate "delusions and morbid feelings, at least for a transitory period" (Leavitt 2017).

SIGNIFICANCE

There has been a long and checkered history of the treatment of mental illness. Many dangerous and unsuccessful treatments have been tried. Bloodletting was considered an effective treatment for many diseases, including mental illness, and the practice persisted for centuries. Placing patients in asylums where they were effectively separated from society was a tactic that was utilized for centuries as well. While the first asylums treated patients with cruel punishments like ice baths and tying them down with a variety of torturous restraints, Thomas Kirkbride relied on the humanitarian beliefs of his Quaker religion to transform the treatment of the mentally ill. His plans for the construction of large state-run mental hospitals, funded through the efforts of his fellow reformer Dorothea Dix, were designed to alleviate the horrendous conditions that existed in the asylums for the mentally ill. The hospitals built to the specifications of the "Kirkbride Plan" in the mid-to-late 19th century boasted clean, bright rooms; large well-tended grounds; and a number of productive activities offered to patients. The concept was to treat the patients with respect and love and, hopefully, to cure their illness. The first hospitals using the Kirkbride plan served a small population, with the staff housed within the facility. Here they would get to know all the patients and be able to deal with them on a personal level. But this idyllic situation, alas, would not last. State-funded facilities, with increasing demand and decreasing budgets, endorsed the idea of isolating the patients in large facilities away from large population centers. This concept was devised by Kirkbride to prevent the bedlam that took place in the previous zoo-like asylums. But it soon became another method of warehousing the mentally ill in crowded, impersonal, unhealthy institutional settings. Though intended as home-like facilities, these mental hospitals were soon transformed into miserable storehouses for an unhappy and sick population. Novel therapies were tried, some no better than the ancient blood-letting. Surgical lobotomies, seizure-inducing Metrazol therapy, electric shock therapy, and other ineffective treatments were tried in order to "cure" patients suffering from various forms of mental illness. As conditions in the state mental hospitals deteriorated in the 20th century, biomedical drug treatments as well as psychotherapy have been used to successfully treat many mental disorders. The days of the large, institutional state hospital are over, and many of them now sit idle, silent vessels of their countless tales of sickness and despair. Kirkbride had some prescient and innovative ideas for the care of the mentally ill. Though groundbreaking at the time, as society has advanced, his pioneering plans have unfortunately entered the dustbin of history.

FURTHER INFORMATION

Godbey, Emily. Spring 2000. "Picture Me Sane: Photography and the Magic Lantern in a Nineteenth-Century Asylum." *American Studies*, 41(1): 31–69.

Greene, Elizabeth B. 2017. *Buildings and Landmarks of 19th Century America*. Santa Barbara, CA: Greenwood, an imprint of ABC-CLIO, LLC.

Hussung, Tricia. 2016. "A History of Mental Illness Treatment: Obsolete Practices." Concordia University St. Paul. October 14. Accessed September 5, 2019. https://online.csp.edu/blog/psychology/history-of -mental-illness-treatment.

Layne, George S. April 1981. "Kirkbride-Langenheim Collaboration: Early Use of Photography in Psychiatric Treatment in Philadelphia." *Pennsylvania Magazine of History and Biography*, 105(2): 182–202.

Leavitt, Sarah A. 2017. "Illuminating St. Elizabeths at the National Building Museum." *Circulating Now from the Historical Collections of the National Library of Medicine*. April 20. Accessed August 27, 2019. https://circulatingnow.nlm.nih.gov/2017/04/20/illuminating-st-elizabeths -at-the-national-building-museum/.

Meier, Allison. 2017. "A 19th Century Magic Lantern Designed to Quell Patients' Delusions." *Hyperallergic*. June 8. Accessed August 26, 2019. https://hyperallergic.com/383981/magic-lantern-slides-as-mental-therapy/.

Scull, Andrew. 2015. *Madhouses, Mad-Doctors, and Madmen*. Philadelphia: University of Pennsylvania Press.

Yanni, Carla. 2007. *The Architecture of Madness*. Minneapolis: University of Minnesota Press.

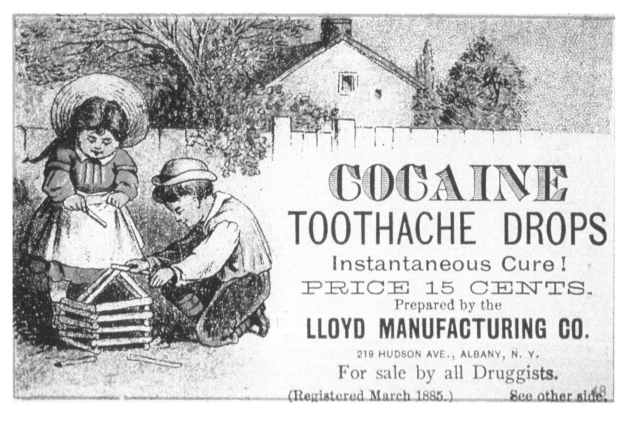

21 Patent Medicine— Cocaine Toothache Drops

INTRODUCTION

Life expectancy improved by almost ten years in the United States in the last thirty years of the 19th century. During this period, however, doctors still had few effective medicines that could treat the common and deadly diseases that were affecting the population at the time. Most of the life-saving medicines we know today were discovered after the 20th century began. Aspirin was synthesized in Germany in 1899 and became available as tablets in the United States in 1915. Antibiotics weren't discovered until 1928, when penicillin was first created by the Scottish microbiologist Alexander Fleming from a fungus he was growing in his lab. The remarkable increase in life expectancy in the United States during the last years of the 19th century was most likely caused by another factor—the newly discovered germ theory, which led to significant improvements in sanitation. The role of doctors during the 19th century was different from what it is today—families did not seek out medical advice until absolutely necessary. And doctors did not possess many tools to alleviate medical symptoms. Though, due to the advances in the study of pathology, they often were able to diagnose common diseases, they had few options to cure the disease once diagnosed. The most common life-threatening diseases—influenza, tuberculosis, diphtheria, typhus, smallpox, and yellow fever—had no cure. However, during this dark period in medical history, a variety of alternative medicines were promoted by certain medical professionals. These practitioners included hydropaths, who believed in the curative effects of water treatments; homeopaths, who created solutions using tiny, diluted amounts of the substance that caused the disease in order to cure the disease; and eclectics, who used herbal and botanical remedies in treating disease. None of these specialties have been proven to be worthwhile in the long run, but in the absence of any effective remedies for deadly diseases in the late 19th century, they were trumpeted by many as miracle cures.

Nonetheless, desperate families searched for therapies that could assuage their pain and cure their ills. This led to a burgeoning business in

145

over-the-counter medications, called patent medicines, which many Americans eagerly purchased and used. The term "patent medicine" is really a misnomer, because most of these remedies were not patented. The medications that were sold as patent medicines were usually trademarked or proprietary. Originating in Europe, "letters patent" (from *patens* in Latin for "open") were issued by the king and granted monopoly privileges to companies to produce a certain product. In England, the term was extended to makers of medications that were endorsed by the royal family. Some of these medications were exported to America in the 18th century. The term "patent medicines" stuck even though most of the subsequent products that were produced in the booming 19th-century patent medicine industry were not approved through the American patent system. The companies that produced the patent medicines were often small, family-run businesses. Many of the manufacturers were not medically trained. Many more were simply swindlers. As the nascent American advertising industry developed in the late 19th century, the patent medicine industry took full advantage of it. In fact, those manufacturers are considered the pioneers of many modern advertising techniques. They were advertised through every possible means: in newspapers and magazines, on calendars, pamphlets, advertising cards, cookbooks, on walls and barns. One of the most lucrative methods to promote these medicines was through traveling "medicine shows" that included a variety of entertainments in addition to the plugging of the product, which was offered for sale, of course. The advertising appealed to lowest instincts of its audience: it was prurient, with sexy women promoting products that restored sexual vitality to aging men; it appealed to one's fear of death, depicting people on their deathbeds. Patriotism was another common theme in these advertisements.

In the 19th century, there were no federal regulations concerning pharmaceutical products, so these patent medicine producers could claim whatever they pleased. And claim they did. They hawked that these products were cures for cancer, tuberculosis, and whatever deadly disease was terrifying the public at the time. Many of the products were targeted at more minor ailments, like constipation, headache, "female complaints," and the like. During the late 19th century, two diseases captured the popular imagination and became targets of the patent medicine industry. A neurologist named Dr. George Bard published a report in 1881, claiming that a new illness called "neurasthenia" was rampant in the United States among the upper and middle classes. This malady had the following symptoms: headache, insomnia, depression, hopelessness, palpitations, and fidgetiness. Modern psychiatrists would call it neurosis. The other popular malady was dubbed "dyspepsia," which was a disease of the well-fed. Its symptoms included stomach pains, cramps, and intestinal complaints. Many patent medications were aimed at relieving this disease. It often flared up as a result of too much heavy food. Victorian dinners were known for their enormous, multiple course feasts.

DESCRIPTION

One particularly mystifying product to modern sensibilities is a toothache remedy called Cocaine Toothache Drops, seen in the photo shown here. Dating from about 1885, this trade card touted the medication on the back side of the card this way: "This preparation of Toothache Drops contains cocaine, and its wonderful properties are fully demonstrated by the many recommendations it is daily receiving." This product was originated from an Albany, New York, pharmacy in 1885. It cost fifteen cents. The use of cocaine for numbing tooth pain was known at the time. It was used for toothaches, as well as for dental procedures. The pharmacy was in Albany, and the product was produced by Charles E. Lloyd and his partner S. Dexter Pilsbury. Lloyd was a clerk at the pharmacy, and his neighbor Pilsbury had inherited a large fortune and may have been the principal investor in the product. The advertising card measures at 2.36 by 3.94 inches. It colorfully depicts two young children playing in front of a white fence with a house and trees in the background. The text of the front of the card states: "Cocaine Toothache Drops; Instantaneous Cure! Price 15 Cents; Prepared by the Lloyd Manufacturing Co.; 219 Hudson Ave, Albany, NY; For sale by all Druggists.; (Registered March 1885); See other side." The depiction of the children in the advertising card implies that the product could be used with children, even for babies with teething pain.

Cocaine was a popular additive to a number of products during the 19th century. In 1860, it was first isolated from the coca leaf. After the discovery that South American Indians used to chew the leaves to increase energy and stave off hunger, doctors showed an interest in using it for medical purposes. It in fact was an effective anesthetic, and it was used for surgery. At that time, however, it was not known to be addictive. Cocaine was an ingredient in a very popular wine that was called "Vin Mariani." With the influence of Women's Christian Temperance Union and other prohibitionists, Atlanta, Georgia, passed a prohibition law in 1886. John Pemberton, an Atlanta pharmacist, created a nonalcoholic drink as an alternative to his other product, Peruvian Wine Coca, another cocaine-soaked wine. This product was dubbed Coca-Cola and soon became so popular that a variety of other cocaine-infused cola drinks soon hit the market. The Coca was a reference to the South American coca plant, and the Cola was a reference to the kola nut from Africa, which contained caffeine. The drink was originally intended as a type of patent medicine. Coca-Cola contained cocaine, in reduced amounts, until 1929.

SIGNIFICANCE

The patent medicines of the 19th century contained all sorts of dangerous products. Some of them had some medicinal value; some had none. Products like the Cocaine Toothache Drops contained actual anesthetic properties, but the drug cocaine was dangerously addictive. In 1905, procaine, commonly known by the trade name Novocaine, was developed as a nonaddictive alternative. Opioids like morphine and heroin were also commonly used in many patent medicines. Most of patent medicines contained alcohol. But there was no law or regulation for these drugs and no requirement to list the ingredients in the medication. For many years a comprehensive food and drug law had been proposed by members of Congress. The first one was introduced in 1879 but went nowhere. But in 1906, the landmark legislation unofficially called the "Wiley Act," after the indefatigable chemist from the Department Harvey Washington Wiley who fought for regulation, was passed that finally regulated food and drugs. After Upton Sinclair's exposé of the meat-packing industry, *The Jungle*, shone an unvarnished light on the dangers of the unregulated marketplace, President Theodore Roosevelt met with his socialist rival Sinclair to collaborate on the passage of a set of laws that became the Meat Inspection Act and the Pure Food and Drug Act. But it wasn't until 1938 under Franklin D. Roosevelt that a stronger law was passed called the Food, Drug and Cosmetic Act. A scandal had rocked the nation in 1937 when a so-called wonder drug, which was really a form of antifreeze, was marketed to children and over one hundred of them died. Finally, the government took a stand in regulating the products that purported to be lifesaving drugs.

FURTHER INFORMATION

Blum, Deborah. 2018. *The Poison Squad*. London: Penguin Books.

McCoy, Bob. 2013. "Overview: The Great American Fraud." Museum of Quackery.com. April 13. Accessed March 9, 2021. http://www.museumof quackery.com/ephemera/overview.htm.

Ross, Meghan. 2014. "Vintage Pharmacy Ad Promoted Cocaine Toothache Drops." *Pharmacy Times*, 80(12). December 18. Accessed March 9, 2021. https://www.pharmacytimes.com/view/vintage-pharmacy-ad-pro moted-cocaine-toothache-drops.

Schlosser, Eric. 2018. "The Man Who Pioneered Food Safety." Book Review. *New York Times*. October 16. Accessed March 9, 2021. https:// www.nytimes.com/2018/10/16/books/review/poison-squad-deborah -blum.html.

Srivastava, Veena. 2019. "Cocaine Toothache Drops Were Once Used to Relieve Tooth Ache." *Quack Track*. May 21. Accessed March 9, 2021. https://quacktrack.org/cocaine-toothache-drops-were-once-used-to -relieve-tooth-ache/

U.S. Food and Drug Administration. 2018. "Background: Research Tools on FDA History." January 31. Accessed May 26, 2022. https://www.fda.gov/about-fda/fda-history-research-tools/background -research-tools-fda-history.

Young, James H. 2015. *The Toadstool Millionaires*. Princeton, NJ: Princeton University Press. Project Muse. Accessed March 8, 2021. Muse.jhu. edu/book/38642.

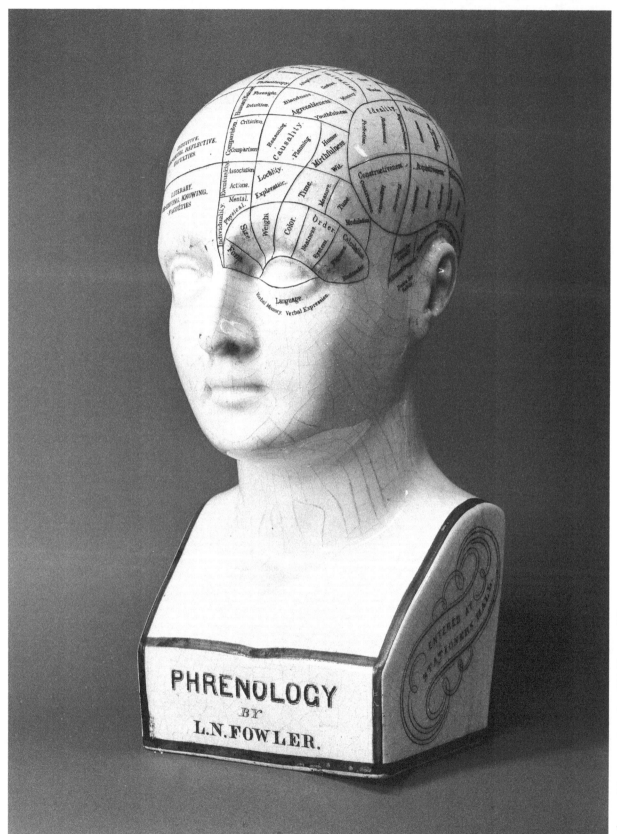

22 Phrenology Head

INTRODUCTION

Have you ever heard someone say something like this: "She needs to get her head examined!" or "She has highbrow tastes, she likes opera and symphonies. Me, I like lowbrow stuff like wrestling." Have you ever commented that someone was "well-rounded"? All these phrases refer to anatomical traits of a person's head. And they originate from a surprisingly popular 19th-century discipline that was called phrenology. Although it was called a science at the time, it is now recognized as a pseudoscience, and its teachings have been universally debunked. However, these phrases that refer to the shape of one's head emerged from this fake science and are still used today.

DESCRIPTION

The artifact displayed in the image here is a plaster bust that is clearly labeled with the "organs of the brain." Each organ is delineated by black outlines on a generic life-sized bust of a human head. This bust was a very popular souvenir for aficionados of phrenology. It sold for $1.25. This bust dates from between 1880 and 1910. It measures 12 ½ inches high by 5 ½ inches wide by 5 ½ inches deep and is made of white ceramic with black and blue outlines and text. On the front of the bust is written "PHRENOLOGY By L. N. Fowler." On the left side of the head, in a decorative scroll, is the text "Entered at Stationary Hall." On the right side of the head, in a decorative scroll, is the text "L.N. Fowler, Ludgate Circus, London." On the back is a paragraph of text attributed to Lorenzo Niles Fowler stating: "For thirty years I have studied Crania and living heads from all parts of the world and have found in every instance that there is a perfect correspondence between the conformation of a healthy skull of an individual and his known characteristics. To make my observations available I have prepared a bust of superior form and marked the divisions of the organs in accordance with my researches and varied experience." Inscribed on the bust are the presumed locations of the psychological characteristics within the brain, which are determined by the size and proportion of each so-called organ.

151

By carefully measuring the skull and any protuberances or bumps on it, a person's intelligence and character could be deduced, according to the precepts of phrenology. The characteristics are called "faculties." Of the faculties, there are two "orders," one being "feelings." Of the feelings, "propensities" are characteristics shared with all animals and are located at the back of the brain. "Sentiments" are peculiar to humans only and are located at the top of brain. The second order is "intellectual faculties," which are located at the front of the cranium. These faculties include the senses (like taste and smell) and language. The shape of the skull indicated intellectual capacity. If a person had a large skull with a high brow, it would indicate high intelligence, hence the terms "highbrow" and "lowbrow." These are broad generalities about the study of the head; phrenologists used more detailed analysis to produce a report for each individual being examined.

In the 1830s a young man from upstate New York named Orson Squire Fowler embarked on a journey that would make him both famous and rich. A bright student from Cohocton in the western part of the state, he left home at the age of seventeen and walked the 400-mile trek to Amherst, Massachusetts, home of the newly formed Amherst College, where he hoped to become a Congregational minister. He worked his way through school and made friends with one of his classmates, Henry Ward Beecher. A member of the prominent Beecher clan, Henry would go on to become one of the most famous 19th-century preachers and an American celebrity. During his stay at Amherst, Beecher developed an interest in a new import from Europe, the study of phrenology. This so-called science, now known as a pseudoscience, was a direct antecedent to psychology. Phrenology was gaining popularity among the intellectual elite of New England and, with the direct help of Orson Squire Fowler, would soon be a nationwide sensation throughout popular culture as well.

The name "phrenology" comes from the Greek, "phreno" meaning "mind" and "logos" meaning "the study of" making it "the science of the mind." The concept was invented by a German physician working in Vienna in the late 18th century, Franz Joseph Gall. He deduced that his student classmates who exhibited large foreheads and prominent eyes had the most acute memorization abilities and concluded that the area of the brain right behind the eyes must be associated with verbal memory. He further theorized that the entire shape of the head could forecast one's intellectual capacity. Gall conceived of the brain as a collection of "faculties," with each area of the brain governing certain traits. The shape of the brain was thought to match the shape of the skull that surrounded it. One of his students, Johann Gaspar Spurzheim, refined Gall's theories and proposed that all personality traits as well as intelligence could be ascertained by studying the bumps on one's head. This formed the basis for the new study of phrenology.

Spurzheim and Gall had a professional falling out, and Gall went on to study neurology, while Spurzheim went full steam ahead with international advocacy for the study of phrenology. After relocating to Great Britain, where he enjoyed phenomenal success, Spurzheim took a trip to the United States in 1832 to further publicize his theories. The popularity of phrenology in the United States had already been gaining ground among medical practitioners, but it was the arrival of Spurzheim that truly spurred its popularity. Spurzheim gave a number of lectures around Boston to huge crowds. But the pace exhausted him, and he died of typhoid in Boston at the age of fifty-five. His death made the news, and his brain and skull were preserved and now reside at Harvard University. Spurzheim's visit, though short, had a lasting influence on the acceptance of the theories of phrenology in the United States. Another proponent of phrenology, a Scottish disciple of Spurzheim, named George Combe, also made an extended visit to the United States in 1838. His visit had even greater influence, as he traveled throughout the country giving sold-out lectures about phrenology. Combe's peripatetic travels resulted in the creation of phrenology societies that sprang up in cities all across the United States. In addition, Combe returned to Scotland and wrote a three-volume book called *Notes on the United States of North America during a Phrenological Visit in 1838–1839–1840* that included detailed descriptions of life in the United States.

As the science of phrenology was gaining popularity in the United States due to the proselytizing of both Johann Spurheim and George Combe, the Amherst student Orson Squire Fowler began to exhibit an intense fascination with the field. No longer anxious to train as a Congregational minister, Fowler enlisted as a missionary in the cause of promoting phrenology. He, like many other reform-minded Americans of the period, was captivated by the appeal of the self-improvement aspect of the science. The idea, as advocated by Spurzheim and Combe, was the ultimate perfectibility of the individual. Although the science purported to predict the individual's intelligence and personality traits, it also allowed for the individual to work on training the brain to improve its qualities. By publicizing these attractive aspects of the science, Fowler was able to boost its popularity. At the tender age of twenty-five, Orson Squire Fowler and his brother, Lorenzo Niles Fowler, began their campaign to promote phrenology to the American population. First, the two evangelist phrenologists would invite the public to a free lecture. The crowds that would appear would enjoy the lecture and were enthralled with the prospect of learning all about themselves with a reading of their head bumps and shapes. These readings, of course, were not free, and this is where the Fowler brothers began to see real profits. They were natural salesmen. In addition to thousands of ordinary Americans, the Fowlers examined the heads of numerous contemporary celebrities, including Horace Greeley, Brigham Young, and P. T. Barnum. Much of the intellectual elite and members of the various reform movements of the period were in thrall with this new and exciting science and supported the Fowlers' efforts. The Fowlers, joined by Orson's sister Charlotte, her husband Samuel Wells, and his sister-in-law Lydia, opened up an office in New York, which they called the Fowlers & Wells Phrenological Cabinet. The enterprise soon became a resounding success. Here a visitor could attend a variety of lectures and get his or her head examined with a phrenological examination, costing between $1 and $3. One could also purchase a bust similar to the one shown in the photo, with the "organs" of the brain outlined. The Cabinet had rooms that were overflowing with shelves of busts, casts, skulls, and paintings that depicted the various types of heads. Some were busts of famous talented people; others were busts of famous criminals.

MARK TWAIN SEES A PHRENOLOGIST

The famous American writer and humorist Mark Twain was staying in London in 1873. Twain always showed an interest in the pseudoscience, but he also demonstrated a clear skepticism in its claims. Here Twain recounts a pair of visits to Lorenzo Niles Fowler's office in London:

> In London 33 or 34 years ago, I made a small test of phrenology for my better information. I went to Fowler under an assumed name and he examined my elevations and depressions and gave me a chart which I carried home to the Langham Hotel and studied with great interest and amusement-the same interest and amusement which I should have found in the chart of an impostor who had been passing himself off for me and who did not resemble me in a single sharply defined detail. I waited 3 months and went to Mr. Fowler again, heralding my arrival with a card bearing both my name and my nom de guerre. Again I carried away an elaborate chart. It contained several sharply defined details of my character, but it bore no recognizable resemblance to the earlier chart. These experiences gave me a prejudice against phrenology which has lasted until now.

[Stern, Madeleine B. May 1969. "Mark Twain Had His Head Examined." *American Literature*, 41(2): 210.]

SIGNIFICANCE

There was a burst of reformist fervor in the years before the Civil War in the United States. Movements such as the Second Great Awakening and the New England Transcendentalist movement influenced an American society that soon developed a mounting appetite for novel self-improvement schemes. Abolition, vegetarianism, the importance of physical fitness, women's rights, temperance, prison reform, education reform, and new therapies such as hydrotherapy were all topics that were emerging in popular culture in the mid-19th century. Orson Squire Fowler and his family-run phrenology business were definitely on the forefront of many of these reformist concerns. Phrenology as a technique was right in the epicenter of these American reforms. Americans fell in love with the theory of phrenology. Fowler and his associates sold the practice to the public as a method of self-improvement. Although the character of the individual was analyzed by the phrenological head examination, the result was not necessarily inevitable. Fowler spent years exhorting his customers to improve themselves through exercising their brain. They were given advice about their character, scientifically analyzed by a well-trained professional, and with it came guidance about how to develop the facets of one's character that needed improvement. It was the ultimate of self-help schemes. And it appealed to all elements of society: it was embraced not only by the intellectual elite and the wealthy but also by America's burgeoning middle class. Fowler, the ultimate entrepreneur, had found a winner, and he and his family became household names.

Orson Squire Fowler pursued reform in many directions. Orson, his brother Lorenzo, and his brother-in-law Samuel Wells expanded their operation in New York City, opening a publishing house that published a popular journal called the *American Phrenological Journal*, as well as numerous books and pamphlets written by Orson. Fowler & Wells Publishers was responsible for a multitude of reformist literature and advice books. The Fowlers endorsed many of the popular reform initiatives including educational reform, vegetarianism, women's rights, sex education, the condemnation of tight-laced corsets, the temperance movement, and hydrotherapy. Another innovation of Orson's was his interest in residential architecture. His novel idea was to build an octagonal or eight-sided house. He built one for himself in Fishkill, New York, that was enormous, boasting sixty rooms. He wrote a book exhorting the benefits of an octagonal house, and a number of them were built in the mid-19th century. However, the fad did not last long.

Fowler and the science of phrenology had its heyday in the antebellum period. By the end of the 19th century, these theories were outstripped by newer, more modern scientific theories. When psychology was introduced, the theories of a relationship between the cranium and one's brain became outdated. However, the concept of identifying certain discrete areas of the brain led to the modern sciences of neurology and psychology. The theories of phrenology, though innovative in the early to mid-19th century, have now been discredited. The study of phrenology as a science was in some ways an example of biological determinism, a theory that contends that human behavior is innate and determined by biological attributes and not by environmental causes. This determinism would include the phrenological theories that the size and shape of the brain are determinative of character or intelligence. This assertion by the 19th-century phrenological advocates has resulted in the contemporary allegation that phrenology is a racist science and has been deemed an example of scientific racism. In fact, Fowler, for all his modern reformist ideas, believed, as many others did in the 19th century, that racial differences were immutable and that the white race was inevitably superior. Although he supported the abolition of slavery, he believed that the black race had a smaller brain and lower intelligence. Despite his innovative mind and his inveterate reforming spirit, his racist theories have relegated Fowler and his famous phrenological family to irrelevance and ridicule in contemporary society.

FURTHER INFORMATION

Branson, Susan. Winter 2017. "Phrenology and the Science of Race in Antebellum America." *Early American Studies: An Interdisciplinary Journal*, 15(1): 164–193.

Gura, Philip F. 2017. *Man's Better Angels: Romantic Reformers and the Coming of the Civil War*. Cambridge; London: The Belknap Press of Harvard University Press.

Janik, Erika. January 2014. "The Shape of Your Head and the Shape of Your Mind." *The Atlantic*. Accessed November 18, 2019. https://www.theatlantic.com/health/archive/2014/01/the-shape-of-your-head-and-the-shape-of-your-mind/282578/.

Parssinen, T. M. Autumn 1974. "Popular Science and Society: The Phrenology Movement in Early Victorian Britain." *Journal of Social History*, 8(1): 1–20.

Poskett, James. 2019. *Materials of the Mind: Phrenology, Race, and the Global History of Science, 1815–1920*. Chicago; London: University of Chicago Press.

Stern, Madeleine B. May 1969. "Mark Twain Had His Head Examined." *American Literature*, 41(2): 207–218.

Young, Dwight L. Spring 1990. "Orson Squire Fowler: To Form a More Perfect Human." *Wilson Quarterly*, 14(2): 120–127.

Household Items

Electric Light Bulb

Reclining Chair Patent Model

Sampler

Sewing Machine

Sideboard

23 Electric Light Bulb

INTRODUCTION

By the late 19th century, human society had advanced past the agricultural revolution and was well into the Industrial Revolution. Technology was transforming society at an unprecedented rate. The railroads and the telegraph system were connecting the continent from sea to sea. Corporations were becoming nationalized, white-collar jobs were multiplying, and the middle class was growing, creating a huge pool of potential consumers with disposable income. But one thing was still hindering development, both in the home and in the factory: the dearth of artificial light. Work was performed when the sun permitted it; on a winter's day, it ended early; on a gloomy day, it was difficult to see. Imagine a world where darkness fell in mid-afternoon and there were no clean, reliable, and bright artificial lighting sources to read by. This was the world of the mid-late 19th century.

DESCRIPTION

This state of affairs was about to be transformed with the introduction of the electric light bulb. The bulb shown here was produced in 1886 by Thomas Alva Edison in his Menlo Park, New Jersey lab. Edison had been perfecting the electric light bulb for over six years since he first filed for a patent for a bulb that he created in his lab in November 1879. This 1886 bulb has a simplified screw base, with a thread pitch, which is still used today. The filament is made of treated cellulose, which was an innovation made by Joseph Swan, Edison's British rival. Edison hired semiskilled laborers to blow the glass for the bulbs into iron molds. With these innovations, the price of Edison's bulbs had been reduced from his original patent bulb, from $1.00 each to $.30 each. This bulb comprises brass, plaster, glass, and carbon and measures 5 $^{19}\!/\!_{32}$ inches by 2 $^{5}\!/\!_{32}$ inches.

The bulb shown here and its subsequent improvements soon altered life in American society. The various types of artificial lighting had remained mired in the past for much of the 19th century. Yes, there were various attempts to improve it. But candles were still the standby method for lighting for many in the 19th century, despite the explosion of other inventions that were sparked by the Industrial Revolution. Fire was still the primary source of light, ever since it was discovered by humans hundreds of thousands of years ago. And it continued to be, using variations of candles, gaslights, oil, or kerosene lamps. Fire was dangerous, it was dirty, and it was dim. It was also expensive to provide enough light to read or work by. That's what makes the harnessing of electricity for use as an artificial light source so revolutionary. Candles were used for centuries. The Phoenicians invented wax candles, which were highly prized and used by the wealthy who could afford them. The average family was forced to purchase tallow candles, made from animal fat. These candles gave off an unpleasant smell and often irritated the eyes. Not an enjoyable way to read or sew at night! Even the best of candles gave off a flickering, dim light. A breakthrough came with the invention of the Argand lamp in 1783. Ami Argand, a Swiss physicist, created an oil lamp with a meshed wick, which was inside of a cylindrical glass funnel. The intensity of the flame was greater, and the flickering was reduced, providing a more pleasing, constant, and brighter light. These lamps became extremely popular in the early 19th century. Families would gather around a circular table with the Argand lamp proudly posted at the center of the table. Here they could read, write, play a game, or sew relatively comfortably. But even with this highly practical invention, this was still one small lamp. The rest of the house remained in virtual darkness.

The oil lamp developed further during the century, as new types of oils were discovered. Whale oil was used in the United States for Argand lamps. Kerosene was invented after the discovery of petroleum in 1859. The kerosene lamp was game-changing, because of its high intensity light. However, it was still a fire, and it produced heat, and house fires often resulted from the use of kerosene lamps. A new way of lighting was introduced in the mid-19th century: gaslight. This light, produced from a mixture of gases made from the distillation of coal, was first used only in outdoor, public areas. This restriction of its use was due to public resistance, because of the supposed danger of coal gas. If burned incompletely, the gas could cause drowsiness and smelled bad. It was used in public buildings and factories, but not in homes until later, when the technology improved. Although it took some time to be fully accepted, the introduction of gaslight into American homes by the 1880s constituted a welcome change. For one thing, once gas was piped into the house, light was available throughout the house, through light fixtures called gasoliers, instead of from one portable lamp. Also, the light was brighter than any other option available at the time. In addition, the introduction of the gas delivery system, through a system of gas lines, ushered in a new era, an era of utility infrastructure that would presage the period of electricity soon to come. For, by the time that most of the middle-class urban households were enjoying the benefits of gas lighting in their homes, Thomas Edison and others would be tinkering with the new, completely revolutionary lighting method called "electric light."

The middle class and the wealthy alike in the United States saw a benefit from a reliable system for providing artificial light, and gaslight was popular, though it was still sooty, required ventilation, and could be dangerous. One of the advantages of a gas line system was for the alternate uses for gas, like heating and cooking, which gained in popularity after the introduction of electric lighting. However, frontier and rural families, as well as poor urban dwellers, still relied on lamps fueled by various types of oil and kerosene. The artificial lighting revolution had not yet begun. But it soon would. Several inventors in Europe and in the United States were experimenting with electricity for use as an artificial lighting source. Early in the 19th century, an English inventor named Humphry Davy invented an electric light called an arc light that would be useful in public installations. The arc light, which was lit by an electrical current passing between two carbon rods, produced a very bright arc of light from the carbon vapors. The light only lasted a few hours, and it was tricky to assemble properly. The harsh, bright light that it produced was not practical for any interior installation. However, it was utilized for outdoor applications and in the maritime industry in ships and lighthouses.

By the 1870s, a number of scientists were researching the concept of harnessing electricity in order to create a usable electric light bulb. Two inventors, Thomas Alva Edison in the United States and Joseph Wilson Swan in England, were working concurrently but independently on the design of an electric light bulb. Both men understood from previous research that a light bulb required a vacuum in order to prevent the light from darkening the inside of the bulb and burning out too quickly. They were both researching the most effective material to use for the filament inside the bulb. Though Edison and Swan could each be credited with inventing the light bulb, Edison got the patent first and received credit. Swan, after being sued by Edison for patent infringement, demonstrated to Edison that he had actually done prior research on the product. Swan eventually teamed up with Edison to launch a corporation in Britain called the Edison and Swan United Electric Light Company that successfully marketed a fusion of the two inventors' products.

So in the United States, it was Thomas Edison who was given credit for inventing the electric light bulb. Edison was a tireless inventor who created the first industrial research lab in his facility in Menlo Park, New Jersey. He was born in 1847 in Milan, Ohio, the youngest son of Samuel and Nancy Edison. Samuel, a failed political activist, was born in Canada and escaped to the United States after taking part in an unsuccessful rebellion in Upper Canada, now known as Ontario. He ended up in Ohio, where Thomas was born. Thomas was an extremely curious child but did not take well to public school. His mother, Nancy, a former teacher in Canada, recognized the child's inquisitive nature and homeschooled him. Young Thomas was perennially determined to figure things out. At age six, after some rumination on the problem, he attempted to help a mother goose hatch her eggs. He theorized that if a goose's rump helped the eggs to hatch, then a larger rump like his could work faster, so he sat on them. The mother goose was not happy when she found him there, though Thomas' mother was amused by her son's imaginative reasoning. This was merely one of the many early tales of Thomas Edison's unstoppable curiosity. In 1853, the family moved to Port Huron, Michigan. Here young Thomas began experimenting with chemicals in a lab he set up in the basement of his parents' home. His mother, Nancy, encouraged his (at times risky) research, and the inventor eventually praised her for her appreciation of his intellect as a child. "If it had not been for her appreciation and her faith in me at a critical time in my experience, I should very likely never have become an inventor" (Winchell 2019: 25).

Thomas Edison realized that he would require additional funding for his inveterate experimentation, and, at age twelve, he took a job as a newsboy on the train that ran from Port Huron to Detroit. It was during this time that Edison lost his hearing while working on the Grand Trunk Railway. According to Edison, a conductor lifted him up into the train by his ears when he was standing outside of a train with his arms loaded down with newspapers. Edison felt something snap, and from then on, his hearing was permanently damaged. He became progressively deaf after that time. Edison later asserted, however, that his hearing loss was not a disabling handicap. He was able to concentrate without the distraction of outside noise and also did not have to put up with "all the foolish conversation and other meaningless sounds that normal people hear" (Edison, quoted in Stross 2007: 9). While he was working on the Grand Trunk Railway, Edison was fascinated with the telegraph offices that were in the railroad stations. The concept of electricity and the use of Morse code to send messages along electrical wires captivated him. But, as a young newspaper boy, he did not have the skills to send messages through Morse code, and, despite his eager enthusiasm to learn it, he was not able to figure it out on his own. One day, Edison happened to see a young boy thoughtlessly playing on the tracks when a train car started rolling toward him. Edison jumped up and rescued the toddler from the train. His father, the station agent, was so grateful to Edison that he offered to teach him telegraphy. Thomas Edison practiced incessantly and soon became proficient enough to be a professional telegraph operator. Edison spent the next five years peripatetically traveling around the Midwest honing his skills as a telegraph operator while cogitating about the uses of electricity in his spare time. These deliberations often included playing pranks on his fellow operators, using batteries to give them an electrical shock.

In 1868, Edison arrived in Boston to work as a night-shift operator for Western Union. Here he was able to devote time to his experimental operations. He soon commenced his full-time career as an inventor, quitting his job at Western Union in 1869 to focus on filing patentable inventions. He applied himself tirelessly to this task, and in fact, by the end of his life, Edison would have filed a record 1,093 U.S. patents. His first patent was for a vote recorder, to be used by Congress and other legislatures. This accurate device would record the ayes and nays and tabulate them quickly. Edison tried to sell the device to the Congress, but it was roundly rejected. The representative for the Congress explained that any quick tabulation would not allow for additional lobbying for votes by the opposing side. The sale was dead. Edison learned a lesson from this venture: never invent something that people don't already want, or at least can be convinced that they need; in his words, "Anything that won't sell, I don't want to invent" (Time 1979). After this commercial failure, Edison pursued other avenues for his inventions. In 1871, he invented the Edison Universal Stock Ticker, for which he was paid handsomely. With the cash in hand, Edison relocated to Newark, New Jersey, where he set up a lab with two scientists, Charles Batchelor and John Kruesi. His partners had the scientific training that Edison lacked and helped him make models and detailed drawings. In 1873, Edison invented both the diplex and quadruplex telegraphs. Jay Gould, the millionaire railroad tycoon, bought the quadruplex from Edison. This infusion gave Edison more cash, which he used to build his new laboratory in Menlo Park, New Jersey, the world's first industrial research lab, which opened in 1876. This is where Edison invented the phonograph, the invention that first brought him fame. When he presented the new device at the National Academy of Sciences in Washington in 1878, two women fainted from astonishment.

Edison's newfound notoriety gave him the opening to apply his team to the biggest test of all: inventing a reliable, safe, long-lasting electric light bulb. The multiple moguls of the Gilded Age had the resources and aspirations to help Edison in this venture. John Pierpont Morgan and a few of his financier cronies got together to sponsor Edison to research this persistent puzzle. Edison and his team discovered that carbon remained stable in a perfect vacuum, and Batchelor shaped it into a horseshoe to form a filament, which formed the crucial tweak that created a bulb that lasted for a revolutionary 16 hours. This feat took place on November 17, 1879. Edison and his crew continued perfecting the bulb in order to extend its useful life, lower costs, and increase production.

SIGNIFICANCE

Thomas Alva Edison went on to manufacture light bulbs in his facility. But this may not have been his most significant contribution. Edison had a vision that propelled him miles ahead of most of his rival inventors. He knew that a light bulb in itself could not create the transformation to society that he foresaw. A system was needed to distribute the electricity to the light bulbs, or they would be useless. Generators were necessary, as well as a method to deliver the current to a cohort of consumers. Edison envisioned what we now call the electric grid, and he made an intriguing proposal to J. Pierpont Morgan, the Vanderbilts, and other New York industrialists. He launched a company called the Edison Illuminating Company in 1880 and proposed to build a central electrical station in the financial district of downtown Manhattan at Pearl Street. Though the task was difficult in a crowded city, Edison was determined to prove that that his system, which he called direct current, DC, could deliver electrical service to the businessmen and newspaper offices that resided in that area. Though delayed and over the budget, Edison completed his project in 1882 with the opening of the First District, in a small neighborhood of ancient narrow streets surrounding Wall Street. The Pearl Street station continued to add more powerful dynamos and jumbos, which were types of generators, and by 1884, it supported ten thousand bulbs in the First District.

Edison's revolutionary system of delivering electricity to businesses and homes was slowly catching on but was spawning a series of competitors. First of all, the existing gas companies feared the introduction of electric light would destroy their business, which had been slowly gaining ground over the previous decades. The expensive gas infrastructure, which had been piped into urban and suburban buildings, could be made obsolete by an electric grid. The gas businesses unsuccessfully fought off the onslaught of electricity. However, they eventually realized that the coal gas infrastructure could be reoriented to be utilized for central heating and cooking. Ultimately, the most formidable competitor for Edison was a Serbian American immigrant named Nikola Tesla, a brilliant but eccentric physicist, engineer, and futurist. Tesla discovered an alternative system for delivering electricity, which he called alternating current, or AC. This system had definite advantages over Edison's direct current. When Tesla teamed up with Pittsburgh businessman George Westinghouse in 1888, they battled with Edison's company in what has been called the "War of the Currents." In order to standardize the electrical delivery system, one of the two currents had to win the war, and the one that won was Tesla's AC current. Though Edison's was usable in small areas like the original First District, DC lost power as it traveled along the wires. It was not efficient and could only be transmitted a mile from an electrical power station. Tesla's system manipulated the voltage so that high-voltage electricity could be transmitted over long distances and then stepped down at a transformer for delivery into homes and businesses. This system is still used today.

Thomas Alva Edison, through brilliance, hard work, and a large dollop of self-promotion, has remained the most famous and revered inventors in American history. The 19th-century American magazine *Puck* described Edison in 1880: "Edison is not a humbug. He is a type of man common enough in this country—a smart, persevering, sanguine, ignorant show-off American. He can do a great deal and he thinks he can do everything" (Cashman 1993: 13). In fact, he didn't do everything, but he did an astonishing amount. He invented the phonograph, the motion picture, and various improvements to the telegraph and the telephone, among hundreds of other useful products. But the most transformative product that he invented and promoted was the light bulb and with it the electrical distribution system. It changed life throughout society, in homes and businesses alike. People were no longer living in the dark, which altered the human biological clock. People could read or attend school both day and night, improving literacy. Manufacturing plants lit up and could now be run on 24-hour basis, with two extra 8-hour shifts, expanding production exponentially. Although Edison's first use of electricity was for the light bulb, soon a huge variety of new uses would be invented, which would improve the quality of life for the average American consumer. Sewing machines, Christmas tree lights, irons, washing machines, and many other appliances were electrified. Home décor changed as the clean bright light provided by electrical lamps allowed for a new light and spare aesthetic. It was no longer necessary for the dark, heavy Victorian furniture and textiles that obscured the dust and soot that sullied the 19th-century household lit by gaslight. Skyscrapers, lit by electric light and serviced by electric elevators, expanded skyward. This was a brave new world, a world introduced by Edison's light bulb.

FURTHER INFORMATION

Bailey, Diane. 2016. *How the Light Bulb Changed History*. Minneapolis: Abdo Publishing.

"Business: The Quintessential Innovator." 1979. TIME, October 22. Accessed January 20, 2020. https://content.time.com/time/subscriber/article/0,33 009,947523,00.html

Cashman, Sean D. 1993. *America in the Gilded Age: From the Death of Lincoln to the Rise of Theodore Roosevelt*. New York: New York University Press.

Josephson, Matthew. November 1959. "The Invention of the Electric Light." *Scientific American*, 201(5): 98–118.

Rybczynski, Witold. 1986. *Home: A Short History of an Idea*. New York: Penguin Books.

Schlereth, Thomas J. 1991. *Victorian America: Transformations in Everyday Life*. New York: Harper Perennial.

Stross, Randall. 2007. *The Wizard of Menlo Park: How Thomas Alva Edison Invented the Modern World*. New York: Crown Publishers.

Winchell, Mike. 2019. *The Electric War: Edison, Tesla, Westinghouse and the Race to Light the World*. New York: Henry Holt and Company.

24 Reclining Chair Patent Model

INTRODUCTION

What's your dad's favorite chair? It's likely to be the Barcalounger or other behemoth of a reclining chair that dominates your living room. It may be hideous, but one thing can be said for it—it's comfortable. What type of chair was popular in the living rooms of the Victorian era? Reclining chairs did exist, but they were substantially different from today's versions. And the rooms were different too—houses didn't have living rooms; they had parlors, which were formal and utilized primarily for entertaining guests. Most parlors in middle- and upper-class homes contained a so-called parlor suite of matching furniture. This set consisted of a man's arm chair, a smaller lady's arm chair, a sofa, and four armless parlor chairs. These pieces were upholstered and featured elaborate carved wood trim. Though they were upholstered, they were not comfortable, with a hard seat and a very straight back. Owing to the Victorian emphasis on strict moral rectitude, lounging or slouching in a chair was frowned upon in a public venue. In a large Victorian house, the multiple rooms had assigned uses. The parlor was a public room, but many other rooms were used as private spaces exclusively for the family's use. In those rooms, a different, more comfortable type of furniture was allowed. The recliner was one of these pieces.

The concept of a reclining chair dates back to Queen Elizabeth I in the 16th century, who had a reclining "stool." Such a luxurious custom item was not available to the general public, however. Other royalty of the time were also accommodated with comfortable, reclining chairs, including the Spanish king Philip II and the English king Charles I. The original development of a reclining chair for the mass market was designed to assist the old and infirm. An invalid chair or a "sleeping chair" was developed during the 17th and 18th centuries in Europe, though it was not commonly available. However, things changed in the mid-19th century as interest in such an item grew, and England's cabinetmakers applied for over twenty patents for a mechanical reclining chair, often called an "easy chair." The most famous of the British reclining chair prototypes was the Morris chair. First designed in 1866 by Warrington Taylor of Morris & Company, the Morris chair had a wooden frame and upholstered seat, back, and arms. The reclining feature consisted of two bars that could be pegged at various angles. Later versions of the Morris chair, produced by Liberty and Company, were imitated widely by designers of the Arts and Crafts movement both in England and in the United States.

The United States had an enduring affection for the rocking chair and developed a similar fondness for the reclining chair. Various patents for the mechanisms were granted during the 19th century. Many of these chairs were based on designs of dentists' chairs, barbers' chairs, and especially, train seats. The network of railroads was expanding throughout the country in the mid-late 19th century, and the interiors of the train cars were becoming increasingly comfortable and luxurious. One of the signature features of the train seat was its ability to recline. Using and enjoying this type of seat on a train, many Americans saw a use for these comfortable chairs in their homes. More and more opulent versions of these chairs were patented by the end of the century. In 1888, a chair called the "Rip Van Winkle Reclining Rocking Chair" was patented by P. C. Lewis of Catskill, New York. This huge, plush, upholstered reclining chair had "twenty-seven combinations and by counting each recline or change of seat, back or foot-rest, as other reclining or adjustable chair makers do, it could make over two hundred changes of position" (Edward 1998–1999). The famous Morris chair from England was the most common and popular reclining chair in the United States. By the turn of the 20th century, living rooms were supplanting parlors in middle-class homes, and the Morris chair found its place there. It was handsome, comfortable, and affordable.

DESCRIPTION

The reclining chair seen here is an actual patent model for a chair designed by George A. Schastey in 1873. At this time the U.S. Patent Office required that a working model of a proposed invention be submitted in addition to the full set of drawings. The model, with its original upholstery and paper identification tags, was acquired by the Metropolitan Museum of Art in New York. A miniature chair with complete working parts, it is 10 inches high by 6 inches wide by 7 inches deep. It is made of walnut with yellow and black striped silk upholstery and braided guilloche trim. The patent was filed on July 10, 1873, and described as an "improvement in adjustable reclining-chairs" (Frelinghuysen 2016). It used catch-bolts and springs to keep the arms in plane, giving the user more stability as the chair was pushed back. The patent was granted in December 1873.

The designer, George A. Schastey, was a popular interior designer for the rich during the Gilded Age. Though his work was sought-after during the last quarter of the 19th century, Schastey is little known today. The Metropolitan Museum of Art has recently opened a period room called the Worsham-Rockefeller Dressing Room, originally inside a house on Manhattan's West 54th Street. This room dated from 1881 to 1882 and was designed by Schastey for Arabella Worsham, who later married the railroad tycoon Collis P. Huntington. George Alfred Schastey was born in Merseburg, Prussia (now Germany) on May 4, 1839, and immigrated with his family to the United States in 1849 at the age of ten. Many Germans fled the country at that time to escape the political upheaval roiling the region. He began working as an apprentice to an upholsterer in New York before enlisting in the 68th New York Volunteer Infantry Regiment during the Civil War, rising to the rank of captain. After the war, the residential housing market boomed, and the Industrial Revolution brought an expanding economy. Soon the rich industrialists would look forward to spending their money on magnificent new mansions with luxurious and glittering interiors. Schastey was able to take advantage of that boom. He worked for several of the most prestigious cabinetmaking and interior decorating firms in New York, including the Herter Brothers, Pottier & Stymus, and Cottier & Company. In 1873, Schastey opened his own cabinetmaking factory and decorating firm on West 31st Street in New York. He worked with a number of the other decorating firms on a number of commissions in Northern California for the enormously wealthy railroad tycoons. Schastey would secure commissions for Leland Stanford, Mark Hopkins Jr., Charles Crocker, and Collis Huntington, known as the "Big Four." This group, who financed the Central Pacific Railroad, became the most influential men in the development of Northern California. With their broad reach and expansive wealth, members of the group became renowned philanthropists. As Schastey's reputation grew, he expanded his factory, and toward the end of the century, he was one of the most respected custom cabinetmakers in the nation. Unfortunately, in 1893 a fire destroyed his New York factory at a loss of $200,000 (five million in today's dollars). Though he attempted to rebuild it, he died in 1894 onboard a ship bound for Germany, at the age of fifty-five. His brothers tried to relaunch the business, but the attempt failed, and it went bankrupt in 1897.

ALL IN THE FAMILY

In 1971, the recliner hit the big time with the launch of the sitcom *All in the Family*. Archie Bunker would sit on his yellow recliner and pontificate about all the world's troubles. The recliner would come to represent the white working-class man in 1970s America.

SIGNIFICANCE

George A. Schastey is being rediscovered as one of the most prominent cabinetmakers and decorators for the well-heeled during the Gilded Age. He is known for his fine workmanship and taste. In addition to his cabinetmaking skills, Schastey had an inventive mind, submitting a design for an improved adjustable reclining chair and receiving a patent for it. Reclining chairs were evidently gaining in popularity during the 1870s, and Schastey was searching for a new design. It was more complex than the simple Morris chair that came over from Britain some ten years before. Over the years many patents have been filed for improvements on the reclining chair. Despite the fact that it was not proper to recline in the Victorian parlor, the recliner gained in popularity in other rooms of the house. It was most often a man's chair, and printed advertisements of the period show contented men sprawled across an overstuffed recliner. As the Victorian ethos faded, American culture became more relaxed. Living rooms replaced parlors, and recliners often joined the sofa as part of the living room suite. The present-day recliners are even more complex—they can be heated, include cup holders, have wi-fi connections, and even have motorized lift mechanisms that lift you right out of the chair.

FURTHER INFORMATION

Ames, Kenneth L. 1992. *Death in the Dining Room*. Philadelphia: Temple University Press.

Edwards, Clive. Fall–Winter 1998–1999. "Reclining Chairs Surveyed: Health, Comfort, and Fashion in Evolving Markets." *Studies in the Decorative Arts*, 6(1):32–67.

Frelinghuysen, Alice C., Nicholas C. Vincent, and Moira Gallagher. Winter 2016. "Artistic Furniture of the Gilded Age." *Metropolitan Museum of Art Bulletin*, 73(3): 1–2, 4–48.

Johnson, Ken. 2016. "Peeking into the Gilded Age at the Met." *New York Times*. January 7. Accessed January 21, 2021. https://www.nytimes.com/2016/01/08/arts/design/peeking-into-the-gilded-age-at-the-met.html.

Pynt, Jennifer, and Joy Higgs. Autumn 2008. "Nineteenth-Century Patent Seating: Too Comfortable to be Moral?" *Journal of Design History*, 21(3): 277–288.

Sophia Dyer ae
14 years
Portland 1819

GENEALOGY 1819

Caleb Dyer Born Dec 23 1768
Mary Randall Born March 3 1765

Married Sept 14 1780

Mary Dyer Born Nov 25 1781
Caleb Dyer Born Nov 29 1783
Bessie Dyer Born Jan 9 1786
Eliott Dyer Born Feb 16 1788
Sarah Dyer Born April 3 1790
Octavia Dyer Born Aug 6 1792
Aphia Dyer Born Aug 6 1792
Storer Dyer Born Sept 13 1794
Almira Dyer Born July 16 1796
Ellen Dyer Born July 9 1798
Seth Dyer Born June 13 1800
Nathan Dyer Born Dec 10 1802
Sophia Dyer Born Nov 10 1805

Seth Dyer Died June 16 1805
Storer Dyer Died Sept 28 1812
Bessie Dyer Died July 6 1816
Aphia Gould Died Oct 8 1838
Caleb Dyer Died Mar 11 1842
Ellen Willard Died Oct 20 1865
Almira Chester Died Jan 15 1854

Seth Dyer
Storer Dyer
Bessie Dyer

25 Sampler

INTRODUCTION

Before the invention of the mechanical sewing machine, hand sewing was an essential domestic craft. Girls were taught to sew and embroider at a young age in order to prepare them for the domestic tasks that they were expected to pursue as homemakers. For centuries, one of the most common endeavors for teen and preteen girls was the creation of a sampler. The word "sampler" derives from the Latin word *exemplum* and the old French word *essemplaire*, which means "example." These embroidered sheets served as physical examples of varieties of sewing techniques that could be reproduced for other applications. Museums worldwide have a few early examples of these once common yet extremely delicate and rare textiles. Samplers have been identified that were included in Egyptian burial grounds dating back to the 14th or 15th century. There are some European examples from the 16th century. Pattern books were printed in the 1500s in Germany, Italy, France, and England. However, because of the expense of books, most families would have relied on the samplers themselves to teach young girls the art of embroidery.

Because of the tradition of creating embroidered samplers in Europe, the practice was brought over to the American colonies. The earliest extant sampler was produced by Loara Standish of the Plymouth Colony in Massachusetts in 1645. The custom continued through the 18th century and up through the mid-19th century in the United States. Young girls, relegated to the domestic sphere, were expected to know how to sew. The sewing lessons were combined with the schoolwork for these girls. In the United States, with its appreciation for education, girls were taught to read, write, and do simple arithmetic. (This practice applied to white girls. Slaves were statutorily denied the right to an education, though some free blacks were educated in specially designated schools, like the African Free School in New York City.) In the first half of the 19th century, many girls would create two samplers during their childhood. For young girls, often aged five or six, a first sampler was undertaken. This was often done at home under their

173

mother's or grandmother's watchful eye. In some cases, the girls would be sent to a local school, a so-called dame school, which was attended by both girls and boys and managed by a single woman or a widow. As there were no standardized public schools at this time, the dame school would serve as an elementary school for these local children. These were not free, however. They also served as one of the few socially acceptable ways for a spinster or widow to earn a living. Consequently, these schools were attended by only the families that could afford them. The children in these schools learned the basics of reading, writing, and arithmetic. As part of this education, either at home or at school, the girls were instructed to create a "marking sampler," which was a simple sheet that demonstrated the various embroidery techniques in bands of letters and numbers. Girls were expected to know rudimentary arithmetic as well as embroidery, because, as homemakers, they were obliged to know how to keep track of their (very valuable) linens by marking them with a cross-stitched number and their initials. During this time, girls were often not sent for further education. The lucky ones, however, were likely sent to a girls' boarding school, where they would attempt another, much more elaborate sampler. Often these would be decorative pictorial samplers, indicating not only the girl's sewing skill but also her preparation to be a proper, refined wife. They would often contain religious verses or verses written by the girl herself. They also frequently depicted mourning scenes, remembering lost family members, an important factor of life during the 19th century. Some samplers depict the family's genealogical record, which might be accompanied by a landscape scene. From the girls who attended the most advanced schools, sometime the samplers would even depict scientific themes, geographical maps, or civics lessons, but these were much less common. Though these more elaborate samplers were not specifically designed to teach basic education, they demonstrated that the girl had mastered the womanly arts of patience and obedience and that the family had enough wealth to educate the daughter to be a virtuous wife. These samplers were usually signed by the creator, with a date, and sometimes included the name of the school she attended. A girl's sampler was generally framed and proudly hung in the family's parlor as a symbol of the family's status.

DESCRIPTION

In the first decades of the 19th century, there were a number of girls' academies that taught the art of creating a fine needlework sampler. In fact, as in any art form, there were distinct regional styles that emerged from different areas of the country. The example shown here is from Portland, Maine, a center of an idiosyncratic style of sampler in the early years of the century. Maine was settled by English Puritans in the mid-1600s. It was not, however, one of the original thirteen colonies. It remained part of the Commonwealth of Massachusetts until 1820, when it seceded from Massachusetts and became the 23rd state under the Missouri Compromise of 1820. The city of Portland became the commercial center of Maine at the beginning of the 19th century and briefly its capital in 1820. There were a number of girls' academies in Portland, and they developed a signature style during the first four decades of the 19th century. Two of these schools were the School of the Miss Mayo's and Elizabeth Hussey's School. The most prominent and long-lasting of these schools was the Misses Martin School, run by the sisters Penelope, Catherine, and Elizabeth Martin. The Martin family emigrated from England to Boston in the 1783 and later relocated to Portland. After financial losses adversely affected the family, they were compelled to open a school, which was the most prestigious in town and ran from 1804 to 1834. All the samplers from Portland during this period have a similar style, and many of them depict genealogies, though some depict the typical letters, numbers, and verses of the marking sampler. These samplers were not simple, though. They typically included a wide border of rose vines, which were stylized in the earlier samplers and lushly naturalistic in the later ones. Besides the text, these samplers also depicted typical federal-style buildings or street scenes.

The sampler illustrated here was sewn by Sophia Dyer at the age of fourteen in 1819, using silk thread on linen. The school that Sophia attended is not known; however, the style of the sampler is typical of the type produced in the Portland girls' schools at the time. The various stitches displayed on this sampler include cross stitch, buttonhole stitch, double running stitch, chain stitch, split stitch, eyelet stitch, satin stitch, and the slanting Gobelin stitch. As was typical with this style, it has a wide rose vine border, with roses, rosebuds, and leaves. The lower left and upper right depict a town scene with white federal-style buildings. On the lower right is a mourning scene, characteristically depicted with a grave monument and a weeping willow tree curving down over it symbolizing mourning for the three family members whose names are listed on the grave. Lambs are shown in front of the monument, symbolizing purity and innocence, indicating that the lost family members were children. The rest of the panel is a genealogical list of the Dyer family, showing birth and marriage dates of the parents and the names and dates of each of the children. On the upper right side of the panel, above the mourning picture, is a list of the children who passed away. This family record shows how large these families could be—there are thirteen children listed, of which seven had already died when this sampler was completed.

SIGNIFICANCE

Samplers were prevalent in American households before the onset of public education. They were treasured by the family and were actually sometimes used as valid family records. In fact, some families provided samplers to the U.S. government to prove family relationships to Revolutionary War veterans when they applied for war pensions between the years of 1818 and 1878. Though precious family heirlooms, samplers were not considered high art. However, the development of material culture studies, folk art appreciation, and especially, the growth of women's studies have made the study of American samplers a key to the exploration of daily life and the history of female education in the early years of the United States. These charming pieces of art, similar yet displaying regional and personal differentiation, are fonts of information about the lives of these girls and their families. They include the girls' own names and ages and the names, birthdates, marriage dates, and death dates of the family members. In fact, in many cases these samplers may be the only record of these girls' lives. The study of the samplers that are still extant has led to more research in women's diaries, letters, account books, and other records that have brought to life the everyday existence of a typical American woman in ways that weren't known before. When public education became available for boys and girls in the United States in the second half of the 19th century, girls' academies were no longer as necessary. Letters and numbers were taught in school on blackboards and with paper and pencil. Also, with the advent of mass-produced clothing and the popularity of the home sewing machine, hand sewing did not serve such a crucial purpose. By the end of the 19th century, the age of the charming hand-embroidered sampler had ended.

FURTHER INFORMATION

Boggon, Sharon. 2005. "A Brief History of Embroidery Samples." Accessed November 10, 2020. https://web.archive.org/web/20150822122126/http://inaminuteago.com/articles/samplerhist.html.

Krueger, Glee F. 1978. *A Gallery of American Samplers: The Theodore H. Kapnek Collection*. New York: E. P. Dutton, in association with the Museum of American Folk Art.

Manseau, Peter. 2017. *Objects of Devotion: Religion in Early America*. Washington, DC: Smithsonian Institution.

Mascolo, Frances McQueeney-Jones. 2013. "'I My Needle Ply with Skill: Maine Schoolgirl Needlework' at Saco Museum." *Antiques and the Arts Weekly*. January 21. Accessed November 10, 2020. https://www.antiquesandthearts.com/1-25-13-cover-needlework/.

Peck, Amelia. October 2003. "American Needlework in the Eighteenth Century." Heilbrunn Timeline of Art History. New York: The Metropolitan Museum of Art. http://www.metmuseum.org/toah/hd/need/hd_need.htm.

Ring, Betty. 1987. *American Needlework Treasures: Samplers and Silk Embroideries from the Collection of Betty Ring*. New York: E.P. Dutton, in association with the Museum of American Folk Art.

Ring, Betty. 1993. *Girlhood Embroidery: American Samplers & Pictorial Needlework, 1650–1850*. New York: Alfred A. Knopf.

"V&A Embroidery—A History of Needlework Samplers." Victoria and Albert Museum. Accessed November 12, 2020. https://www.vam.ac.uk /articles/embroidery-a-history-of-needlework-samplers.

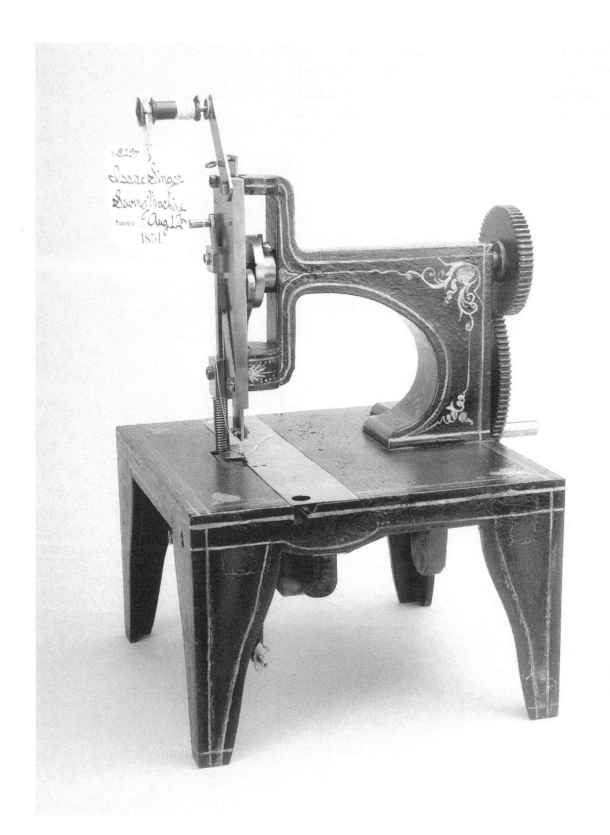

26 Sewing Machine

INTRODUCTION

Inventions of the early Industrial Revolution were shaping the American textile industry in manifold ways. Two 18th-century British inventions, the flying shuttle loom and the spinning jenny, were already altering the industry on both sides of the Atlantic. The flying shuttle allowed looms to produce much wider fabrics, and the spinning jenny replaced the spinning wheel and produced multiple lengths of yarn on the same apparatus. These advances were early innovations that spurred the growth of the textile industry, as factories began to spew out more and more fabric in both Britain and the United States. Though the yarn and the fabric could now be factory-made, the finished product, whether it was clothing, tents, or bedding, still had to be hand-sewn. In this era of innovation, there were still no machines that could sew a piece of clothing together.

DESCRIPTION

There were a variety of attempts to invent and produce a machine that could improve on the speed and efficiency of hand-sewing. It wasn't until the mid-19th century that one was invented that changed the industry forever. The artifact shown here is Isaac Merritt Singer's sewing machine patent model. It was Patent No. 8,294, and it was issued on August 12, 1851. Although Singer went on to successfully promote the sewing machine for home use, this one was a heavy-duty commercial model manufactured in his friend Orson Phelps' machine shop in Boston, Massachusetts. It is made of metal and iron and measures 16 inches high by 17 inches wide by 12 inches deep. Singer was a performer as well as an inventor and quite the showman. He successfully used his talents to promote his new machine. He would take his sewing machine to events where he would demonstrate the sewing machine's ease of use to an enthusiastic group of housewives. One of his most pioneering tactics was to convince the women, who were still severely constrained by the societal restrictions put on them by the 19th-century emphasis on the cult of domesticity, that they could easily learn to use this complicated but highly useful piece of machinery. Soon the sales of this newfangled contraption grew exponentially.

But the invention of this sewing machine did not appear out of the blue. Many attempts had been made to devise a method of reproducing hand-sewing faster and more effectively mechanically. One of the major stumbling blocks was that the inventors expected that a machine that sewed would have to imitate the human hands and fingers. However, a number of inventors embraced the challenge. In 1790, a London cabinetmaker named Thomas Saint received a patent for a number of items, which had the following cumbersome title: "An Entire New Method of Making and Completing Shoes, Boots, Splatterdashes, Clogs, and Other Articles, by Means of Tools and Machines Also Invented by Me for That Purpose, and of Certain Compositions of Nature of Japan or Varnish, Which Will Be Very Advantageous in Many Useful Appliances." The patent included, among other things, a description of a machine that was for "stitching, quilting, or sewing." The title of the patent, while exhausting, was not the primary reason that the machine was basically ignored for eighty-three years. The major confusion was that the patent was filed under "apparel." Also, there is no evidence that it was ever built by the inventor. In 1873, the patent was discovered by William Newton Wilson, and the machine was constructed according to the plans. Though it didn't function perfectly, with minor changes it could have been a usable sewing machine.

The next attempt at creating a viable sewing machine was in France, some forty years after Thomas Saint. Barthelemy Thimonnier was a tailor who mused about the fact that sewing took so long to complete, while weaving could be done so quickly. He was inspired by the hooked needle used by local embroiderers, and he created a machine that used a similar needle to sew a chain stitch. In 1830, Thimonnier received a patent for a sewing machine. Unlike Saint's attempt in England, Thimonnier's patent was not ignored, and he received a contract from the French Army to produce uniforms. He manufactured eighty machines in Paris in 1841, which successfully produced the clothing. However, one night he was confronted by an angry mob of torch-wielding tailors who were fearful for their livelihoods and burned down the factory. Thimonnier just barely escaped himself. The determined inventor pursued and improved his machine, setting up another factory, but the throng of frenzied tailors struck again. This time Thimonnier was able to escape with one machine in hand, and he fled to England. Unfortunately, he was unable to repeat his success, and he died a broken and penniless man.

The next inventor that made an attempt at a usable sewing machine was an American, Walter Hunt. Born in New York, the "Yankee mechanical genius" (Cooper 1976) was an inveterate and brilliant inventor. His most famous invention was the safety pin. But he is not credited with inventing the sewing machine because his design was never patented. In 1834, Hunt invented a sewing machine that created a lockstitch using two threads, one from above and one from below. This was the first attempt that eschewed the concept of imitating hand sewing by inventing a completely new type of stitch. Hunt, though he did receive twenty-six patents in his thirty-three-year career, never filed a patent for the sewing machine. He was dissuaded by his friends and colleagues who were fearful of undermining the tailor and seamstress industries, and besides, he didn't consider it to be very promising. It was too bad, because it was virtually identical to the one invented by Elias Howe in 1846.

Elias Howe was born in 1819 on a Massachusetts farm to a family that was barely surviving. He had little schooling, attending school only during the winter months and working on the farm the rest of the year. However, he showed an interest in tools and machinery. He left for Lowell, Massachusetts, to work as a machinist in the cotton mills at the age of sixteen but left two years later for a machinist position in Cambridge. His next job was in Boston where he worked for Ari Davis who had a shop that repaired precision machinery. After discussing the concept with his boss and after seeing the weaving done by the cotton looms, he became obsessed with the idea of a machine that could sew. He convinced his friend George Fisher to lend him $500, and he set up shop in his friend's attic to work on the project. Inspired by the flying shuttles on the looms in Lowell, he created a machine that used a lockstitch, powered by a hand crank, similar to the one invented twelve years earlier by Walter Hunt. This stitch consisted of a needle carrying a thread through a piece of cloth, which a second thread was laced through. The needle was withdrawn, and the thread was carried back to the other side of the cloth. Elias Howe submitted his patent application and received the patent in 1846. In order to promote the new device, Howe arranged for a competition between five of the faster seamstresses in the region and his one sewing machine. The machine beat the seamstresses in both quality and speed. However, Howe struggled to attract any buyers or backers to get his machine manufactured. At $300 each, his machine was extremely expensive. Also, the question of taking work away from the respected tailors and seamstresses was still a concern in the mid-19th-century American society. So Howe made the fateful decision to try his luck on the British market.

Howe's British endeavor was not as successful as he had hoped. It looked promising at first. He sent his brother Amasa to London to try to drum up backers. The only one he found was a corset maker named William Thomas who bought the rights for 250 pounds with 3 pounds more for each machine sold. He requested that Elias come over to specialize the machine for corset making. Howe came and later sent for his family. Howe, once again unsuccessful in promoting the machine, quarreled with Thomas and sent his family back to the United States. He struggled to get enough money to secure passage back to the United States himself. Upon returning home, penniless once again, he discovered that his wife was on her deathbed. Though a brilliant inventor, Howe was not a brilliant businessman. However, his luck would soon change. With Howe in England trying to elicit interest in his invention, other inventors in the United States ignored Howe's patent and manufactured and sold a variety of sewing machines, some almost exactly like his patented one to a now-interested public. Howe was depressed and discouraged by the death of his wife and his persistent poverty, and he pondered how he could combat his rivals who were using his patented designs.

Meanwhile, a rival of Howe's named Isaac Merritt Singer produced a machine that made definite improvements to Howe's original machine though using some of Howe's patented designs. Singer, born on October 27, 1811, was the eighth child of German Jewish immigrants from Pittstown, New York. He worked as a mechanic and a cabinetmaker, but his first love was the theater. He formed his own theatrical troupe, which he dubbed the Merritt Players. But unfortunately, it wasn't successful enough to pay the bills. He relocated to Fredericksburg, Ohio, to work for a small manufacturing plant that produced wooden type for printers. It was here that Singer began his career as an inventor, creating an improved type-carving machine. He moved to Boston to promote his machine and seek financial backing. There he befriended Orson C. Phelps, who was tinkering with an innovative design for a new sewing machine that was based on Howe's. Phelps was in search for some improvements to the machine, and Singer invented some enhancements that advanced the efficiency and precision of the machine. One of these innovations was a forward-moving shuttle that moved in a straight path and tightened stitches. The original design called for a curved horizontal needle, which traveled in a complete circle. The revolutionary new design had a straight, vertical needle that moved in an

---

THE SONG OF THE SHIRT

"The Song of the Shirt," written by Thomas Hood in 1843, describes the life of a poor seamstress in Victorian England before the invention of the sewing machine.

With fingers weary and worn,
With eyelids heavy and red,
A woman sat in unwomanly rags,
Plying her needle and thread—
Stitch! Stitch! Stitch!
In poverty, hunger, and dirt,
And still with a voice of dolorous pitch
She sang "The Song of the Shirt!"

[Hood, Thomas. 1843. Originally published in anonymously in Christmas edition of *Punch Magazine*.]

up-and-down path. Other improvements on the Singer machine included a friction pad that controlled the tension of the thread from the spool and an adjustable arm that permitted the spooled thread to be changed as needed. These improvements created more reliable and continuous stitching (Kurin 2013: 147). The machines produced by Phelps and Singer were heavy-duty, with the head, base cams, and gear wheels made of cast iron, which were filed and ground by hand. The packing crate served as a stand.

SIGNIFICANCE

The sewing machine was one of the most significant inventions of the 19th century. It affected the home lives, employment, and the textile industry. The invention also sparked a legendary patent war, dubbed "the Sewing Machine War." Elias Howe, still destitute and incensed that the three elements of his patent were being copied, determined to seek redress. He noticed a demonstration of an I. M. Singer sewing machine in a New York City storefront window in 1850. Having obtained fresh financial backing, Howe sued Singer for patent infringement and went to trial in 1854. The trial was lengthy; it generated 3,575 pages of records, but in the end Howe prevailed. However, there were another collection of companies that were successfully obtaining patents for innovations in sewing machines, creating what is known as a "patent thicket," meaning that a number of parties can lay claim to key parts of an invention. This situation could lead to endless litigation, which would use up the precious resources of the various entities. An attorney named Orlando Brunson Potter, who was the president of one of the rival companies, came up with an idea that would fix the situation. He recommended setting up a cooperative agreement between Howe, Singer, and a number of other manufacturers. They formed a "patent pool," a type of cartel, which provided a lower price for licensing for the patents to a limited number of participants. The patent pool was known as the Sewing Machine Combination, or the Sewing Machine Trust. For every machine that was manufactured by the pool participants, Howe received $5.00. For each nonmember of the pool, the price for a patent license was $15.00. For the manufacturers that ignored the pool and produced sewing machines without the license, they faced a sure patent suit. As a result of the patent pool, both Howe and Singer became millionaires. All the members of the Sewing Machine Combination prospered, as did the sewing machine business, from 1856 until 1877, when the last patent expired.

The Singer Sewing Machine Company went on to become one of the most influential companies of the late 19th century. It used innovative marketing techniques, placing the new machines into homes of the newly emergent American middle class. Isaac Singer, a brilliant but unstable administrator, was eventually squeezed out of active management by Edward Clark, who formed the Singer Manufacturing Company in 1863. He expanded the door-to-door sales that Singer had introduced and initiated the first "hire-purchase plan" or installment plan that allowed families to pay for this rather expensive appliance in $5 monthly installments. The Singer Manufacturing Company also marketed their products through an extensive advertising campaign and began a successful buyback program to encourage customers to upgrade their sewing machines to the newest models. The Singer Manufacturing Company opened up factories in many foreign countries, became one of the first multinational corporations, and built a skyscraper in New York City in 1908 that was, for a short time, the tallest building in the world.

Called "the Queen of Inventions" by the influential and ubiquitous magazine *Godey's Ladies' Book*, the sewing machine became a status symbol in the parlors of the 19th-century homemaker. It also indelibly altered the textile industry. When the sewing machine was first introduced, many were skeptical of its general usefulness. But when the Civil War started, all of a sudden thousands of uniforms and tents were needed for Union and Confederate soldiers. For the first time, all the recruits were measured for uniforms, and a standard sizing was introduced. Inexpensive ready-made clothing was now available to all. By the 1880s a new type of manufacturing facility was introduced—the sweatshop. Women, many of them young immigrants who were struggling to get by, were hired to work at low wages for long hours in unsafe conditions, sewing the ready-made clothing that was increasingly in demand. By the turn of the 20th century, the unsafe conditions in many sweatshops became unsustainable. The infamous Triangle Shirtwaist fire of 1911, which killed 136 workers, sparked public outrage that resulted in legislation that regulated sweatshop conditions. By the dawn of the 20th century, the sewing machine, no more than half a century old, had become an essential tool, used by homemakers and a newly dominant textile industry alike.

FURTHER INFORMATION

Bellis, Mary. February 23, 2019. "The Sewing Machine and the Textile Revolution." Accessed February 1, 2020. https://www.thoughtco.com /textile-revolution-sewing-machine-1991938.

Connolly, Marguerite. Spring 1999. "The Disappearance of the Domestic Sewing Machine, 1890–1925." *Winterthur Portfolio*, 32(1): 31–48.

Cooper, Grace R. 1976. *The Sewing Machine: Its Invention and Development*. Washington, DC: The Smithsonian Institution Press.

Eves, Jamie H., Beverly L. York, Carol Buch, and Michele Palmer. 2019. "Sewing Revolution: The Machine That Changed the World." Windham Textile and History Museum. Accessed January 23, 2020. https://mill museum.org/sewing-revolution/.

Godfrey, Audrey M. Fall 2006. " 'The Queen of Inventions': The Sewing Machine Comes to Utah." *Journal of Mormon History*, 32(3): 82–103.

Kurin, Richard. 2013. *The Smithsonian's History of America in 101 Objects*. New York: Penguin Books.

Mossoff, Adam. 2009. "The Sewing Machine War—How vs. Singer." *The Volokh Conspiracy*. May 1. Accessed February 6, 2020. http://volokh .com/posts/1241141796.shtml.

Op Den Kamp, Claudy, and Dan Hunter. 2019. *A History of Intellectual Property in 50 Objects*. Cambridge: Cambridge University Press.

Palmer, Alex. 2015. "How Singer Won the Sewing Machine War." *Smithsonian Magazine*. July 4. Accessed February 4, 2020. https:// www.smithsonianmag.com/smithsonian-institution/how-singer-won-sewing -machine-war-180955919/.

Pusey, Allen. 2015. "Sept. 10, 1846: The Sewing Machine Patent War." *ABA Journal*. September 1. Accessed February 6, 2020. http://www.abajournal. com/magazine/article/sept._10_1846_the_sewing_machine_patent_war.

Stamp, Jimmy. 2013. "The Many, Many Designs of the Sewing Machine." *Smithsonian Magazine*. October 16. Accessed January 23, 2020. https://www.smithsonianmag.com/arts-culture/the-many-many-designs -of-the-sewing-machine-2142740/.

"Stitches in Time: A Hundred Years of Machines and Sewing." 2004. The Museum of American Heritage. Accessed February 1, 2020. http://www .moah.org/stitches/index.html.

Strasser, Susan. 1982. *Never Done: A History of American Housework*. New York: Henry Holt and Company.

27 Sideboard

INTRODUCTION

It was the mid-19th century, a decade before the paroxysm of the Civil War ripped the country apart. The United States was expanding west in its quest for what newspaper editor John O'Sullivan purportedly dubbed its "Manifest Destiny," the mission of this nation to transport freedom and the Founders' ideals from sea to sea. The west was still a frontier, but the eastern states were growing in population and in wealth as the construction of railroads, and the production of mills and factories brought booming industrial development to the region. As trade with Europe grew, so did the wealth. European examples of styles of dress, architecture, and furniture were imported to the American elite who bought them up as soon as they arrived. In addition, a new influx of European immigrants came ashore as the political unrest roiling Europe in 1848 resulted in a new type of immigrant, many of them educated and experienced craftsmen from Europe. The styles of dress and design that were in vogue in the United States were most often based on French originals, although German influence was seen as well.

The American elite had cash to spare and built extravagant, baronial houses in this early Victorian era. The expanding middle class also built large homes to exhibit their growing affluence. One of the new additions to these homes was the separate dining room. During the colonial and early American period, family dining was done in the kitchen or multi-use common room. Formal dining rooms were rare. As the 19th century progressed, houses grew in size with many more rooms, most of which were identified by their specific use. The dining room was one of these. In the nation's early years, table manners were almost nonexistent as people ate with a knife, often eschewing forks, and spit, wiped their mouths with their sleeves, and emitted blasts of bodily functions with abandon. As the American culture evolved, families had more disposable income and craved more elaborate spaces, and a new focus on civility reigned. With the new formal dining room, specific furniture pieces were developed as well as more elaborate

187

serving pieces and utensils. Family members were now expected to use forks, keep their bodily outbursts to themselves, and use napkins instead of sleeves. With the spread of Victorian culture in the United States, the separate spheres of men and women were defined, as the woman took on the responsibility of the home and the man was encouraged to venture out into the world. With this change in the second half of the century, the home became more "feminized." In the mid-19th century, however, the dining room was still a relatively new development in American homes. Furniture designed for this room still exhibited "masculine" elements—large, ponderous, heavy pieces. The most noticeable of these pieces was the dining room sideboard, a massive piece of furniture that sat against the wall adjacent to the dining table. The sideboard, originally called a side table, was used for the purpose of storing dishes and utensils for dining as well as holding serving dishes and beverages during dinner. The massive wood sideboards in many homes of the mid-19th century were idiosyncratic. They were unique in that they depicted scenes of the hunt, sculptural reliefs of dead game, fish, and wildfowl. Ostensibly these depictions were scenes that encouraged diners to appreciate the abundance of riches to be consumed, as a metaphor for the natural order. The natural order deemed that humans were in charge, confirming that, as per Genesis 1:28, humankind should "have dominion over the fish of the sea, and over the fowl of the air, and over the cattle, and over all the earth, and over every creeping thing that creepeth upon the earth" (Ames 1992: 71). Not only did these unusual pieces symbolize the God-given dominance of human beings over all other creatures, but these ostentatious and over-the-top sideboards also represented the apotheosis of the masculine influence in the Victorian home.

DESCRIPTION

The sideboard shown in this example, part of the collection of the Cleveland Museum of Art, demonstrates the apex of this mid-19th century style. Built circa 1855, this massive walnut masterpiece was most likely executed by the French-born American sculptor Joseph Alexis Bailly. It was most likely made in Philadelphia, where Bailly lived and worked. Bailly was born in Paris, France, in 1825 and died in 1883. According to the obituary in the *New York Times*, he participated in the French Revolution of 1849 and was subsequently compelled to leave the country. He settled in Philadelphia where he lived for thirty years. He was a well-known sculptor, known for his statues of a number of famous Americans including George Washington, Benjamin Franklin, and Ulysses S. Grant. This grandiose sideboard may have been exhibited in one of the many international expositions that were popular during this era. Many of the most elaborate sideboards that are still extant today were designed to be shown in an international exhibition, where countries displayed their best furniture designs in a friendly rivalry.

This sideboard is an example of the Renaissance Revival style, a mid-19th-century revival style that was believed to symbolize wealth, seriousness, and authority. It most likely was influenced by another sideboard, shown in the famous London Crystal Palace exhibition of 1851 by the Parisian firm of Fourdinois. The French were the leaders of the design field during this period, and the enormous and extravagantly detailed Fourdinois sideboard enjoyed wide influence over later designs. The Bailly sideboard is similar in many ways to the Fourdinois example. At 114 inches long by 83 inches high by 27 inches deep, it is smaller than the French piece. But it has the same three-storied, three-bayed design, topped by a broken pediment. Also both pieces have a carved relief of a dead deer, almost life-sized in the upper central panel. Fruits, including a pineapple, are carved into a central tondo. Native Americans are carved on either side of the piece, joining the hunting dogs, putti, and dead game depicted on the sideboard. The inclusion of the Native Americans as part of the depiction of fruits and animals indicates that the carver considered them part of the natural world and not true members of the human race. The presence of the Native Americans also implies that the piece was part of an international exhibition, identifying it as uniquely American.

SIDEBOARD IN THE RUTHERFORD B. HAYES WHITE HOUSE

Soon after President Rutherford B. Hayes and his wife, Lucy, moved into the White House in 1877, they announced that they would not be serving wine or other alcoholic beverages during President Hayes' presidential term. A teetotalers' group gave them a gift of a round-ended sideboard that did not feature a space to display wine bottles or decanters. After Hayes' tenure, it was donated to a local Washington DC restaurant.

SIGNIFICANCE

This sideboard is significant because it represents a transitional period in American design. Though the country was growing in wealth and power, it was still influenced by the more primitive table manners of the earlier period. Civility was the new watchword in the newly crafted dining rooms. However, the culture had not moved past the metaphorical proximity to killing one's food before eating it. As the century progressed, two factors agitated against this popular design feature, a feature that was common on sideboards in dining rooms of both the elite and the middle class. First, with the Victorian cultural shift of the two separate gender spheres that appointed the woman as the ruler of the home, dining rooms as well as the other rooms in the house took on a simpler, more feminine countenance.

The post-Bellum period in the United States saw a gradual simplification of the dark, heavy furniture of the early Victorian era, which culminated in the radically simplified style of the Colonial Revival at the turn of the 20th century. The women in charge of the home most likely did not appreciate the rawness of the naturalistic depictions of dead deer and wildfowl staring at them during a formal dinner. The second factor in play was the development of industrial food processing, which became widespread in the third quarter of the 19th century. Chicago developed a huge meat processing industry, aided by the invention of the refrigerated railroad car. The population was migrating to cities as fewer families subsisted on farms, and they were no longer dependent on hunting or sacrificing farm animals for their meat. So this was the beginning of the cultural shift that created the vast cultural distancing between the killing of the animal and its consumption, a distance that has grown ever wider today. This depiction of suffering animals seems rather off-putting to a modern eye. However, the view of stricken or dead game in full view of elegant diners was still considered totally appropriate, a symbolic contrast between the savagery of the animal and the human refinement of the cooked meal in the eyes of the mid-19th-century family. These quirky and peculiar massive sideboards represent a moment in time in a world that was changing fast.

FURTHER INFORMATION

Ames, Kenneth L. 1974. "Battle of the Sideboards." *Winterthur Portfolio*, 9: 1–27.

Ames, Kenneth L. 1992. *Death in the Dining Room*. Philadelphia: Temple University Press.

Hawley, Henry. May 1987. "American Furniture of the Mid-Nineteenth Century." *Bulletin of the Cleveland Museum of Art*, 74(5): 186–215.

"Joseph Allexis Bailly." USPatterns.com. Accessed January 13, 2021. https://uspatterns.stores.yahoo.net/josalbail.html.

Ormsbee, Thomas H. 1952. *Field Guide to American Victorian Furniture*. New York: Bonanza Books.

Peck, Amelia. 2004. "American Revival Styles, 1840–76." Heilbrunn Timeline of Art History. Metropolitan Museum of Art. Accessed January 15, 2021. https://www.metmuseum.org/toah/hd/revi/hd_revi.htm.

"Sculptor Joseph A. Bailly's Death." 1883. *New York Times*. Obituary. June 18. Accessed January 13, 2021. https://timesmachine.nytimes.com/timesmachine/1883/06/18/102945823.pdf.

Stott, Annette. Winter 2002. "The Dutch Dining Room in Turn-of-the-Century America." *Winterthur Portfolio*, 37(4): 219–238.

Political and Civic Life

Civil War Draft Wheel

Confederate Battle Flag

Frederick Douglass Frontispiece

Political Equality Spoon

28 Civil War Draft Wheel

INTRODUCTION

Conscription is defined as the compulsory induction into a nation's armed forces. Though often used interchangeably with the term "draft," it is not exactly the same concept. Conscription is the enforced induction into the military, while the draft is the process by which it is enforced. Conscripts are selected through a procedure called the draft. Many baby boomers remember the trepidation that accompanied the use of the draft during the Vietnam War. Although there has not been a draft since 1973, young men are still required by law to register with the Selective Service at age eighteen, just in case the draft is reinstituted. Though the controversial issue of conscription has faded from view, it hasn't really disappeared. Ever since the suspension of American military conscription in 1973, the United States has relied on totally volunteer armed services. An all-volunteer military has historically been preferred; however, conscription has been utilized several times in American history, beginning with the Revolutionary War. It was utilized on a temporary basis, as was the short-lived conscription effort during the Civil War. In 1917 during World War I, the Selective Draft Act was passed, officially creating a governmental office that handled conscription. It wasn't until 1940 that the United States passed a peacetime conscription law, the Selective Training and Service Act. Though when it was passed, the country was not involved in a war, it was used to amass a powerful military force during World War II. In 1948, the Selective Service Act was passed, which conscripted troops necessary for the Korean and Vietnam Wars. Since the act was repealed in 1973, no one has been conscripted into the U.S. military.

DESCRIPTION

During the Civil War, an emergency draft process to conscript inductees was used because of the dire shortage of manpower that the Union faced after two years of bloody and ineffective battles against the Confederacy. General Robert E. Lee's forces had won a series of victories, depleting the Union army. On June 27, 1863, Lee's armies surged north through the

193

Shenandoah Valley in Virginia, setting up the momentous battle that would take place at Gettysburg, Pennsylvania, on the first of July. Troops were sent out of New York to join General Meade's army at Gettysburg, depleting the forces available to defend New York. According to General John Wool, there were only 550 men and no military ships left in the city, leaving the great metropolis defenseless if the Battle of Gettysburg was lost and General Lee's Confederate forces were able to march through Pennsylvania up to New Jersey at the city's western edge. The war was inching frighteningly close to the New York City, the business capital of the nation, and the populace was becoming nervous.

Due to a fall in recruitment, an increase in desertions, and battle losses, the number of available troops was dropping. The federal government had passed the National Conscription Act in March 1863. Through this new law, government agents were authorized to do house-to-house canvassing to register all those men who were eligible for the draft. The law subjected all single men aged twenty to forty-five and all married men up to age thirty-five to a draft lottery. Federal provost marshals were also appointed, with vast powers to arrest draft dodgers, resisters, or deserters in each congressional district. Draftees who could afford it were permitted by law to be exempted from serving in the military by paying $300, a sum that was equal to a year's salary of the local Irish laborers. Or, alternatively, they could propose someone to take their place. This means of exemption allowed the wealthy and well-connected to avoid the draft, whereas the poor and working-class men were forced into serving in a conflict that many didn't fully support.

The method used to select these new draftees was through a lottery. Eligible men were enrolled by filling out registration cards, which were placed in large wooden cylinders called draft wheels. The example shown here is an actual relic utilized on the Lower East Side of Manhattan, between Rivington and 14th Street. It is a made of wood, with cylindrical drum on a trestle frame with bracket feet and a decorative turned stretcher. There is a large handle made of iron and wood, which was used to make the drum spin. There is a lockable rectangular hatch, which opens up to receive the draft cards. There were 3,606 draft cards inside this draft wheel, which had been filled out with the names of eligible men from the district. There is also a brass plate on the side of the drum next to the handle. The plate is engraved with this statement: DRAFT WHEEL/ USED JULY 13, 1863/ WITH NAMES OF RESIDENTS IN THE/ 7TH CONGRESSIONAL DISTRICT N.Y. CITY/COMPRISING THE 11TH AND 17TH WARDS/ PRESENTED BY FREDERIC C. WAGNER/ CAPTAIN AND PROVOST MARSHALL/ JUNE 20TH 1865. The draft wheel measures 23 inches wide by 25 ½ inches high by 21 ¾ inches deep. This draft wheel was used in the July 13, 1863, draft lottery. This type of draft wheel was deemed the "wheel of misfortune" by contemporary New Yorkers.

SIGNIFICANCE

The draft lottery of July 1863 in New York led to the most violent civil disorder in American history. Known as the draft riots, these ferocious disturbances were also vicious race riots. There was a backstory to these uprisings. Even though there was a growing support for abolition among the Republicans in New York, the city had a long history of political support for the Democrats, the anti-abolitionist party. The city had supported the Democratic candidate in almost all the presidential elections from 1832 until 1868 and gave Abraham Lincoln only 35 percent of its vote in both the 1860 and 1864 elections. For decades, New York had cultivated a strong business engagement with the South. Cotton from southern slave plantations was funneled through the city's businesses and exported or sent to upstate or New England cotton mills for processing, producing huge profits for the city. In addition, resentment against fighting a war to abolish slavery was growing exponentially among the poor and working-class white population in New York, a population that consisted of mostly Irish and German immigrants. In a more and more teeming and turbulent city, these immigrants found themselves competing for the lowest-paid jobs. They were anxious about being forced to share these low-level jobs with newly freed slaves moving in from the South. When President Abraham Lincoln enacted the Emancipation Proclamation in January 1863, their fear intensified. The Emancipation Proclamation, coupled with the onerous draft laws recently enacted, created a roiling cauldron of seething resentments among the working class in New York City that was primed to boil over.

Congress had passed the National Conscription Act on March 3, 1863. The draft was to be used only in communities where enrollment targets were not met, and many New Yorkers regarded the enrollment targets for the New York area to be onerously high. Although New York had sent many recruits to serve in the Union army at the beginning of the war, enthusiasm was flagging, and the enacting of the Emancipation Proclamation exacerbated the suspicion. Antipathy against this despised new draft law was building. Despite the fact that the draft agents understood the risk that they were taking, they nonetheless scheduled the first draft lottery on Saturday, July 11. No federal troops were on hand to back up the local police force. In order to keep possible violent protest at bay, the decision was made to have the first draft lottery at the outskirts of the city, uptown on 47th Street and 3rd Avenue, in area of Manhattan that had many vacant lots and fewer residents. The lottery took place without incident, and 1,236 men were chosen as draftees. However, the quota of 2,000 men had not yet been met, and so another lottery was scheduled for Monday morning, July 13. This one-day hiatus allowed residents of the working-class neighborhoods to gather in the streets and taverns to mull over the fact that conscription was taking place. Many were becoming more and more incensed.

Monday dawned as hundreds of the city's laborers advanced uptown banging copper pans as they went. They carried "NO DRAFT" signs, cut telegraph wires, and gathered weapons on the way to the office on 47th Street and 3rd Avenue. Members of the Black Joke Engine Company No. 33, a company of volunteer firemen, furious over the fact that they no longer had exemptions from military service, determined to destroy all the evidence that there ever was an enrollment for the draft. They threw stones at the building, scared off the police, destroyed the draft wheel, and, after pouring turpentine throughout the building, set it on fire. Throngs of protesters were now mobbing the streets as the violence swelled, with skirmishes taking place throughout the midtown and downtown areas. The mobs targeted the 5th Avenue mansions of the city's Republican elite, which they looted and then set on fire. The unrest devolved from draft protest and class war into a brutal race riot, as the riotous throngs of mostly Irish laborers began chasing down any African American they could find, shouting, "Kill all niggers!" At 4 p.m. on July 13, rioters attacked the Colored Orphan Asylum on 5th Avenue between 43rd and 44th Streets, yelling, "Burn the niggers' nest!" The 233 orphans were saved by a young Irishman, Paddy McCafferty, who escorted them out to the relative safety of the 20th Precinct, as the mob burned the furniture and then set fire to the large stately building. The orphanage building could not be saved. As night fell, the attacks intensified. African Americans were lynched, burned, and tortured. Homes and businesses occupied by African Americans were torched, and the furniture inside was brought out into the street and set on fire. Racially mixed couples and prostitutes who had African American men as clients were particularly targeted, as the disdain for miscegenation, or "amalgamation" as it was called at the time, was intense among the New York Irish. The violence continued throughout the day, as the mobs set their sights on Newspaper Row, across from City Hall Park. Staff members of several of the well-connected newspapers were able to defend their buildings with Gatling guns obtained from the army. However, the less well-defended *Tribune* building was set on fire and stoned. The day ended with a cooling downpour.

Tuesday, July 14, began with continuing attacks on institutions and shops frequented by the well-to-do and federal offices. But the worst offenses were directed toward African Americans, who were hunted down in the streets and attacked. Gangs set up barricades in several locations throughout the area and proceeded to sever the telegraph lines in adjacent districts, eliminating communication. The local police were ineffectual and could not contain the vicious mobs. The city's leaders knew that something had to be done. The Democrats and their Tammany leaders endorsed negotiating with the mob, and Governor Seymour actually sent emissaries into the breach to broker a peace. The Republicans, which included politicians as well as many of the wealthy elite, on the other hand, were incensed by the violent mobs.

They were worried that a concession to the mob would demonstrate weakness to a surging Confederacy, and, in fact may even have led to a European intervention. These powerful and influential members of the city's elite considered the out-of-control rioters to be an existential threat to the nation. The headline of the *New York Times* howled: "Crush the mob!" Calls were made for the federal government to impose martial law. The mayor of New York, George Opdyke, a Republican, called on Edwin Stanton, secretary of war, pleading for troops. Fortunately for Opdyke, the Battle of Gettysburg had finally ended with a Confederate defeat, and General Lee retreated across the Potomac on Monday night. Stanton sent five regiments to New York to quell the violence. The troops used howitzers loaded with grapeshot to disperse the rioters. They entered buildings to clear them, charging up the stairs to the roofs, where many of the rioters proceeded to jump off to their deaths. The soldiers tore down the barricades, using bayonets to fight the fierce but frightened mobs. The six thousand troops were able to stop the rioting by Thursday night. It had been four days of brutal, unbridled unrest.

Although the official death toll is 119, contemporaries believed that closer to 1,000 people died. It was the worst riot in American history. Twenty percent of the resident African Americans fled the city permanently, while thousands more hunkered down in temporary bunkers on the city's outskirts. The perpetrators got off with light sentences, as the incumbent Democrats were not inclined to incite more resentment among their constituents. Lincoln refused to impose martial law, worried about alienating the Democrats. He turned control as commander of the Department of the East over to General John Adams Dix, a Democrat. The draft was reinstituted, but the rules were changed, and the New York City quota was cut to less than half the original number of draftees.

FURTHER INFORMATION

Burrows, Edwin G., and Mike Wallace. 1999. *Gotham: A History of New York City to 1898*. New York, Oxford: Oxford University Press.

"Disaster!" 2001. Virtual New York. New Media Lab at the Graduate Center, City University of New York. Accessed May 16, 2020. https://virtualny .ashp.cuny.edu/index-2.html.

Harris, Leslie M. 2003. *In the Shadow of Slavery: African Americans in New York City, 1626–1863*. Chicago: University of Chicago Press.

Holzer, Harold. 2013. *The Civil War in 50 Objects*. New York: Viking.

Joyce, Toby. Summer 2003. "The New York Draft Riots of 1863: An Irish Civil War?" *History Ireland*, 11(2): 22–27.

S.v. "Military Conscription." *West's Encyclopedia of American Law, edition 2*. Accessed May 27, 2022 from https://legal-dictionary.thefree dictionary.com/Military+conscription

29 Confederate Battle Flag

INTRODUCTION

What does the Confederate Battle Flag signify today? Undoubtedly, it means different things to different people. But it is unquestionably divisive. In the third decade of the 21st century, the flag still induces rage, hurt, and in some circles, pride. To many Americans, it represents the symbol of the treasonous Confederates who fought against the United States in a bid to secede from the Union and pursue a slave-holding agenda. To others, it evokes history and heritage, the ancestors who fought valiantly for states' rights, and the freedom from a tyrannical federal government. The battle against the use of the Confederate Battle Flag rages on, with vicious outbreaks every several years. But many Americans don't know the history of the flag or understand the story behind the flag's use in the past 160 years. Sadly enough, the flag is still a lightning rod in the American culture wars.

DESCRIPTION

The four-foot square wool Confederate flag that is pictured here dates from 1861. It was flown in the bloody Battle of Gettysburg in Pennsylvania that took place in July 1863. The battle flag was not the original flag of the Confederacy. Though it is often called the "Stars and Bars" flag, that nickname actually refers to the first national flag of the Confederacy. The Stars and Bars flag, adopted by the Confederate Congress in March 1861, is a version of the American "Stars and Stripes" flag. It has a navy blue square canton at the upper left, surrounded by three stripes, two red and one white. Inside the blue field are seven stars, representing the seven states that seceded to form the Confederacy. As with the Stars and Stripes flag, the number of stars increased as more states joined the Confederacy. Eventually, there would be thirteen stars, representing the eleven states that seceded, and two of the three states that never actually joined the Confederacy—Maryland, Kentucky, and Missouri. It was wishful thinking on the part of the Confederate administration. The Confederacy planned to use the Stars and Bars flag during the battles of the Civil War. However, after the battle of Bull Run, it proved impractical and even potentially dangerous for the soldiers on the battlefield. The soldiers were confused by the similarity of the two flags amid the chaos that surrounded them. They needed a flag and symbol that they could easily distinguish through the bedlam and smoke. Confederate Congressman William Porcher Miles suggested creating a flag that would be flown expressly for battlefield use. General Pierre T. Beauregard designed a flag based on the cross of St. Andrew. This flag, known as the Confederate Battle Flag, or the Southern Cross, is the flag that is represented here. It has a blue cross edged with a white band on a red field, with three stars on each arm of the cross and one star in the center, totaling thirteen stars, which, like the Stars and Bars, optimistically represented two additional states that never joined the Confederacy. Unlike the Stars and Bars flag, which has a 2:3 aspect ratio, the Southern Cross is square. There were a number of other battle flags introduced by the Confederacy during the Civil War, but they were not as distinctive as the Southern Cross. The popularity of the battle flag affirmed the new nationalism of the Confederate population as the affection for the Union's Stars and Stripes subsided. This was the symbol of their independence. The Confederate Battle Flag had become the symbol of the Confederacy, while the national flag of the Confederacy, the Stars and Bars flag, eventually faded into obscurity.

MISSISSIPPI'S DECLARATION TO SECEDE FROM THE UNION (1861)

A DECLARATION *OF THE IMMEDIATE CAUSES WHICH INDUCE AND JUSTIFY THE SECESSION OF THE STATE OF MISSISSIPPI FROM THE FEDERAL UNION*

Our position is thoroughly identified with the institution of slavery—the greatest material interest of the world. Its labor supplies the product which constitutes by far the largest and most important portions of commerce of the earth. . . . There was no choice left us but submission to the mandates of abolition, or a dissolution of the Union.

[https://en.wikisource.org/wiki/A_Declaration_of_the_Immediate_Causes_which_Induce_and_Justify_the_Secession_of_the_State_of_Mississippi_from_the_Federal_Union]

SIGNIFICANCE

The Confederate Battle Flag signified a soldier's loyalty to the Confederacy as opposed to the Union during a battle in the bloodstained years of the Civil War. However, in the century and a half that has passed since the Civil War, the flag has transformed into a symbol of much more. In the 20th century, people from the South began using the flag to indicate their identity. During World War II, soldiers used the flag to classify themselves as

Southerners. After the war, Southern collegiate football teams began using the Southern Cross to represent the teams. Beginning with the Kappa Alpha Order, a fraternity founded at Washington and Lee University, a college founded in 1865, and where Robert E. Lee served as president, Confederate symbols, including the battle flag, were introduced. But use of the flag had, in fact, been appropriated by white supremacists. The Ku Klux Klan began flying the Confederate Battle Flag during the third rebirth of the racist organization in the 1930s and 1940s. The flag was also used by the States' Rights Democratic Party, commonly known as the Dixiecrat Party, a party formed by Senator Strom Thurmond from South Carolina in protest to the adoption of a civil rights plank in the Democratic Party in 1948. President Harry Truman had ordered the integration of the military after the end of World War II and called for other civil rights actions, acknowledging the injustice felt by returning African American veterans who fought bravely for the country only to return to segregation, discrimination, and Jim Crow laws. The Dixiecrat Party championed that segregation and those Jim Crow laws and selected the Southern Cross as their symbol. In addition, the flag was adopted by southern states for use as their state flags. The last state to fly its image is Mississippi, which even today incorporates the battle flag on its state flag. Many other southern states still incorporate allusions to the Confederacy in their state flags.

Though the Dixiecrat Party's tenure was short-lived, the proliferation of the Confederate Battle Flag continued. It was used by many during the 20th century as an adopted flag that served as a symbol of a certain type of youth-driven, rebellious culture, creating what became known as the "flag fad" during the 1960s. Even popular television shows like the *Dukes of Hazzard* promoted the flag. The hugely popular NASCAR car racing circuit promoted the use of the Confederate Battle Flag until May 2020 after the killing of George Floyd in Minneapolis set off a protest movement against the treatment of African Americans by the police while also protesting the use of racist Confederate symbols. The historian John Coski, in his book *The Confederate Battle Flag: America's Most Embattled Emblem*, describes the ubiquity of the flag in popular culture this way: "The Confederate flag's meaning in the 1960s was logical and historically consistent with its meaning in the 1860s, as a symbol of opposition to the employment of federal authority to change the south's racial status quo. There could be no more fitting opposition than the Confederate battle flag. Although segregationists lost their battle and their cause was discredited, attitudes of white supremacy live on." (Coski 2005: 294.) In fact, though the flag was appropriated by self-styled "rebels" in the late 20th century and onward, it remained a symbol of white supremacy in the eyes of both its promoters and its detractors.

In the larger view, the symbolism of the Confederate Battle Flag is ensnared in a mythological, false narrative promulgated by the South after the Civil War that is known as the "Cult of the Lost Cause." This myth explains why there were some seven hundred monuments and fifteen hundred symbols erected and endorsed that glorified Confederate heroes in thirty-one states throughout the country during the many decades since the Civil War ended. What was the Cult of the Lost Cause? The Lost Cause narrative originated in the American South after the Civil War. Suffering a stinging defeat, many Southerners refused to accept their loss and proceeded to concoct a myth of the war as a saga of great heroism and courage, a clash of civilizations. The war had not been fought for the perpetuation of slavery, but for the mighty cause of states' rights, and the doomed but noble fight came to be dubbed the Lost Cause. The cause was lost, but it was a valiant effort on the part of the South, to sustain the fine society that was based on "veracity and honor in man, chastity and fidelity in women." The North, according to this narrative, had been "invigorated by constant struggle with nature, had become materialistic, grasping for wealth and power" (Landrieu 2018). The narrative of the Civil War being fought primarily for states' rights became an accepted, though false, canard promulgated by some Americans for many years. However, research by Ta-Nehisi Coates reveals the truth. In his article "What This Cruel War Was Over: The Meaning of the Confederate Flag Is Best Discerned in the Words of Those Who Bore It," he quotes Confederate writings that lay bare the true troubling cause of the Civil War. One editorial in a Richmond-based newspaper soon after the war proclaimed: " 'The people of the South,' says a contemporary, 'are not fighting for slavery but for independence.' It is a . . . new-fangled heresy—a heresy calculated to do us no good . . . Our doctrine is this: WE ARE FIGHTING FOR INDEPENDENCE THAT OUR GREAT AND NECESSARY DOMESTIC INSTITUTION OF SLAVERY SHALL BE PRESERVED" (Coates 2015).

The Cult of the Lost Cause has endured, but evidence is clear that there were several flare-ups of the cause of white supremacy in the years since the Civil War ended. Used as propaganda to promote the Lost Cause, erection of the Confederate monuments, use of the Confederate flag, as well as the naming of streets and even military installations after Confederate generals have proliferated throughout the nation. But attention to the date of these Confederate symbols is revealing: their use has always surged during times of attempted advancement by African Americans. There was a huge spike in erection of monuments from the 1890s to the 1920s when segregation and Jim Crow laws were at their height. Another spike occurred during the 1950s after the *Brown vs. Board of Education* decision and in the 1960s during the civil rights movement. These symbols were used as emblems of the preservation of white supremacy. They sent a message of intimidation to the African Americans—don't forget who is in charge and who will continue to be.

FURTHER INFORMATION

Coates, Ta-Nehisi. 2015. "What This Cruel War Was Over." *The Atlantic.* June 22. Accessed June 11, 2020. https://www.theatlantic.com/politics /archive/2015/06/what-this-cruel-war-was-over/396482/.

Coski, John M. 2005. *The Confederate Battle Flag: America's Most Embattled Emblem.* Cambridge: Belknap Press of Harvard University.

Cox, Karen L. October 2006. "Review: The Confederate Battle Flag: America's Most Embattled Emblem." *American Historical Review*, 111(4): 1181–1182.

Landrieu, Mitch. 2018. "How I Learned About the 'Cult of the Lost Cause.'" *Smithsonian Magazine.* March 12. Accessed June 19, 2020. https://www.smithsonianmag.com/history/how-i-learned-about-cult -lost-cause-180968426/.

Loewen, James W. 2015. "Why Do People Believe Myths about the Confederacy? Because Our Textbooks and Monuments Are Wrong." *Washington Post.* July 1. Accessed June 18, 2020. https://www.washingtonpost.com /posteverything/wp/2015/07/01/why-do-people-believe-myths-about -the-confederacy-because-our-textbooks-and-monuments-are-wrong/.

Martinez, J. Michael. November 2005. "Review: The Confederate Battle Flag: America's Most Embattled Emblem." *Journal of Politics*, 67(4): 1301–1302.

National Trust for Historic Preservation. 2020. "National Trust for Historic Preservation Statement on Confederate Monuments." June 18. Accessed June 18, 2020. https://savingplaces.org/press-center/media-resources /national-trust-statement-on-confederate-memorials.

Simpson, John A. Winter 1975. "The Cult of the 'Lost Cause.'" *Tennessee Historical Quarterly*, 34(4): 350–361.

Southern Poverty Law Center. 2019. "Whose Heritage? Public Symbols of the Confederacy." February 1. Accessed June 18, 2020. https://www.splcenter .org/20190201/whose-heritage-public-symbols-confederacy#lost-cause.

Frederick Douglass

MY BONDAGE

AND

MY FREEDOM.

Part I.—Life as a Slave.   Part II.—Life as a Freeman

By FREDERICK DOUGLASS.

WITH

AN INTRODUCTION.

By DR. JAMES M'CUNE SMITH.

By a principle essential to christianity, a PERSON is eternally differenced from a THING; so that the idea of a HUMAN BEING, necessarily excludes the idea of PROPERTY IN THAT BEING.   COLERIDGE.

NEW YORK AND AUBURN:
MILLER, ORTON & MULLIGAN.
New York: 25 Park Row.—Auburn: 107 Genesee-st.
1856.

30 Frederick Douglass Frontispiece

INTRODUCTION

A man born into slavery in the early 19th century was not expected to learn how to read and write; in fact it was illegal to educate slaves in most southern states before the Civil War. It's not surprising—if you consider your slaves as chattel, mere property, then it redounds to your benefit to keep them ignorant so they don't grasp uncomfortable realities like freedom. The fact that Frederick Douglass not only learned to read and write but also became an orator, scholar, and a statesman seems miraculous even from our vantage point two centuries hence. The implausible success story of Frederick Douglass has gradually transformed into an American myth. But the remarkable fact is that most of it is true, and much of the myth was self-consciously shaped by Frederick Douglass himself through three separate autobiographies that recount different stages of his life.

DESCRIPTION

The artifact shown here is the frontispiece and title page of Frederick Douglass' second autobiography, *My Bondage and My Freedom*. The original publication was in 1855, but this one was published in 1856. The frontispiece is defined as the page facing the title page of a book, often depicting a decorative illustration. This frontispiece has an engraving that is based on a daguerreotype that is now lost. The original photograph, using the early daguerreotype method of photography, is the engraver's interpretation of the original. Douglass was actively aware of marketing his image as a method of branding himself, and he was the most photographed person in the 19th century. He had his photograph taken 160 times over his lifetime. He never smiled in his photographs, affirming his image as a serious person and eschewing the racist tropes of happy "darkies" depicted in minstrel shows. Douglass is finely dressed in formal daywear that was typical for a well-dressed man of the period, wearing a double-breasted jacket over a waistcoat with a satin puff tie. His hair is long and parted on the left side, showing a bit of gray. Douglass was thirty-eight years old at the time this autobiography was published. As he aged, Douglass' visage would show more and more gray hair. Douglass did not treat his hair, and it remained kinky. Under Douglass' image is the signature of Frederick Douglass. Across from the image is the title page, which contains this text: "Seventeenth Thousand. My Bondage and My Freedom. Part 1.—Life as a Slave. Part II.—Life as a Freeman. By Frederick Douglass. With an Introduction by Dr. James M'Cune Smith. 'By a principle essential to christianity, a PERSON is eternally differenced from a THING; so that an idea of a HUMAN BEING necessarily excludes the idea of PROPERTY IN THAT BEING. Coleridge.' New York and Auburn: Miller, Orton and Mulligan. New York: 25 Park Row.—Auburn: 107 Genesee—st. 1856."

Samuel Taylor Coleridge was a British Romantic poet of the early 19th century who influenced the New England Transcendentalists. The quote from Coleridge was weighty enough to Douglass that he placed it on the title page of his autobiography. He was emphasizing that slaves were just as human as any other human being. As described by his biographer David Blight: "The humanity of his people must be demonstrated before a racist world" (2018). This fact was unfortunately in dispute at the time, when there was a common belief in various quarters that African Americans were not fully human and, because of that, were not required to be treated as humans in a Christian sense. This was one of the truths that Douglass endeavored to prove in all aspects of his life: that African Americans were as fully human as anyone else, with desires, hopes, and dreams like anyone else, and deserved the same freedom that was promised in the founding documents of the United States. Dr. James McCune Smith, whom Douglass asked to write the introduction to this autobiography, was a close friend of Frederick Douglass. Smith was born into slavery in New York City but was set free on July 4, 1827, when New York enacted the Emancipation Act of the state of New York. He later became the first African American to possess a medical degree, although he had to travel to Scotland to get it. He became a very prominent physician and abolitionist.

My Bondage and My Freedom had 464 pages and was four times as long as his first autobiography, the *Narrative of the Life of Frederick Douglass*, written ten years earlier. He was a more mature writer by this time, revising and expanding on the tale he had told of his life in slavery. He divided the book into two parts: the first was a retelling of his struggles as a slave, and the second was a chronicle of his life story as he remade himself into the celebrated orator and abolitionist. The book was published in August 1855, although the frontispiece shown here is from a reprint from 1856, after seventeen thousand copies were already in print. The book sold for $1.25, and it sold astonishingly well, with fifteen thousand sold in the first three months.

Douglass serialized it in his abolitionist newspaper, *Frederick Douglass' Paper*, and also sold it for the discounted price of $1.00 at his public lectures as he traveled the country with his sons.

FREDERICK DOUGLASS' INDEPENDENCE DAY SPEECH

Frederick Douglass was asked to give a speech regarding the Fourth of July Independence Day celebration on July 5, 1852. He gave a memorable sermon on the immorality of slavery and the hypocrisy of the American people to embrace independence while denying freedom to the slaves.

The blessings in which you, this day, rejoice, are not enjoyed in common. The rich inheritance of justice, liberty, prosperity and independence, bequeathed by your fathers, is shared by you, not by me. The sunlight that brought light and healing to you, has brought stripes and death to me. This Fourth July is yours, not mine. You may rejoice, I must mourn. . .

What, to the American slave, is your 4th of July? I answer; a day that reveals to him, more than all other days in the year, the gross injustice and cruelty to which he is the constant victim. To him, your celebration is a sham; your boasted liberty, an unholy license; your national greatness, swelling vanity; your sounds of rejoicing are empty and heartless; your denunciation of tyrants, brass fronted impudence; your shouts of liberty and equality, hollow mockery; your prayers and hymns, your sermons and thanksgivings, with all your religious parade and solemnity, are, to Him, mere bombast, fraud, deception, impiety, and hypocrisy—a thin veil to cover up crimes which would disgrace a nation of savages. There is not a nation on the earth guilty of practices more shocking and bloody than are the people of the United States, at this very hour.

[Accessed July 1, 2020. https://www.pbs.org/wgbh/aia/part4/4h2927t.html.]

SIGNIFICANCE

Frederick Douglass lived the most unlikely life for a slave born in the early 19th century in the United States. He was born on a plantation, as Frederick Augustus Washington Bailey, on the Maryland Eastern shore in 1818. Actually he didn't know his birthdate or birth year because that information was generally not divulged to slaves. However, birth records later revealed that a boy was born to the slave Harriet Bailey in 1818. The day, however, was never discovered, and Frederick Douglass chose February 14 as his birthday. Slave children were not permitted to bond with their mothers, and Frederick barely knew his, as he was shipped to a different plantation 12 miles away. His mother died when he was a young boy, and he never knew his father, who was white, and may have been his mother's master. He was sent to Baltimore at the age of eight. A bright and curious child, he was introduced to reading by his master's wife, Sophia Auld, who was soon chastised by her husband for introducing a slave to literacy. However, Frederick soon determined that literacy was his ticket to freedom, and he taught himself to read whatever he could get his hands on. With the few coins he could save, he purchased a book called *The Columbian Orator*, which was a popular collection of political essays, poems, and speeches that was used in schools at the time. Douglass not only read this book but he rather devoured it, memorizing every word and practicing the speeches. He was twelve at the time, but soon he would grow into a strapping, 6 inches by 2 inches man with a sonorous voice. What he learned from that book would change his life.

At the age of fifteen, Douglass was sent back to the plantation where he no longer enjoyed the minimal freedoms and urban sophistication of the city life. He was now laboring as a field hand, a job that he despised. The slave owner was dissatisfied with Douglass' work production and sent him to a "slave-breaker" named Edward Covey who beat him mercilessly. Douglass tells the story in his autobiographies that Covey was close to destroying his will, when one day Douglass resolved to fight back. He won the fight, and Covey never bothered him again. A weak and ineffective slave-breaker could never admit his failure to others. That gave Douglass his first sense of empowerment. He was now determined to escape. His first attempt at escape was unsuccessful and landed him in jail, although his owner had him released. It would be two more years before he gave it another try.

Proving to be an unproductive and undependable field hand, Douglass was sent back to Baltimore to work for Hugh Auld, the brother of his master Thomas Auld. Put to work in the shipbuilding industry, Douglass was taught the trade of ship caulking. However, he was still determined to escape to the north and met a free black woman named Anna Murray who agreed to help him. On September 3, 1838, at the age of twenty, he assumed the role of a free black sailor with borrowed papers, boarded a train north, and within 24 hours had arrived in New York City where he declared himself free. He married Anna and then proceeded to New Bedford, Massachusetts, where he took whatever odd jobs he could find. The former slave named Frederick Augustus Washington Bailey changed his name to Frederick Douglass after the main character in Sir Walter Scott's poem "Lady of the Lake," after a suggestion from a friend. Soon Douglass began attending meetings of the abolitionists, who were very active in the area. He was discovered by William Lloyd Garrison, the founder of the abolitionist group, the Massachusetts Anti-Slavery Society, and editor of the abolitionist newspaper, *The Liberator*. Douglass, who had shown himself to be a magnetic speaker, was hired by Garrison to give lectures around the states as he secured subscriptions to *The Liberator*.

This was the beginning of the political life of Frederick Douglass, who would spend his long life fighting for civil rights. He moved to Rochester, New York, where he published his own newspaper, which he called *The North Star*. He aligned himself with the women's rights movement and, briefly, with the radical abolitionist John Brown. When the Civil War broke out, the now celebrated former slave worked tirelessly for emancipation and for the rights of African Americans to serve in the military. Douglass traveled to Washington, DC, to meet with Abraham Lincoln to advocate for equal rights for the black troops and further fought for the postwar Thirteenth, Fourteenth, and Fifteenth Constitutional Amendments, which officially abolished slavery and guaranteed citizen rights and voting rights to all African American men. In 1872, he moved to Washington, DC, where he would spend the rest of his life in the political realm. He served five presidents in various positions, including consul general to Haiti from 1889 to 1891. His wife of forty-four years, Anna, passed away in 1882, and in 1884, he married Helen Pitts, a white woman who was an activist in the abolitionist cause. Douglass passed away in 1895, at the age of seventy-seven.

The story of Frederick Douglass' life was told three times by himself in his three memorable autobiographies. In them he told his life story as he lived through the three major periods of his life: his life as a slave and his escape from slavery, his life as an abolitionist and orator, and his life as an elder statesman and politician. He is remembered as a remarkable human being, a man brimming with courage and intelligence, eager to expose injustice wherever he found it. As a young man, he aligned himself with radicals, and as he aged, he aligned himself more with the political status quo. But his story remains one of extraordinary accomplishment.

FURTHER INFORMATION

Blight, David W. 2018. "Bondage and Freedom: Frederick Douglass." *The Yale Review*. October 12. Accessed June 29, 2020. https://onlinelibrary.wiley.com/doi/abs/10.1111/yrev.13414.

Douglass, Frederick. 1845. *Narrative of the Life of Frederick Douglass, an American Slave, Written by Himself*. Boston: Published at the Anti-Slavery Office.

Douglass, Frederick. 1855. *My Bondage and My Freedom*. New York; Auburn, AL: Miller, Orton and Mulligan.

Finkenbine, Roy. 2018. "Would Frederick Douglass Take a Knee?" *History News Network*. October 28. Accessed May 28, 2022. https://historynews network.org/article/170202

Frederick Douglass Heritage. Accessed July 2, 2020. http://www.frederick-douglass-heritage.org.

Kennedy, Randall. 2018. "The Confounding Truth about Frederick Douglass." *The Atlantic*. December. Accessed November 1, 2021. https://www.theatlantic.com/magazine/archive/2018/12/the-confounding-truth-about-frederick-douglass/573931/.

Matlack, James. 1979. "The Autobiographies of Frederick Douglass." *Phylon*, 40(1): 15–28.

National Park Service. "Frederick Douglass—Frederick Douglass National Historic Site." Accessed June 24, 2020. https://www.nps.gov/frdo/learn/historyculture/frederickdouglass.htm.

Quarles, Benjamin. March 1963. "Frederick Douglass." *Negro History Bulletin*, 26(6): 182, 201–203.

Szalai, Jennifer. 2018. "A Big New Biography Treats Frederick Douglass as Man, Not Myth." *New York Times*. October 17. Accessed June 24, 2020. https://www.nytimes.com/2018/10/17/books/review-frederick-douglass-prophet-of-freedom-david-blight.html.

Westerbeck, Colin L. 1999. "Frederick Douglass Chooses His Moment." *African-Americans in Art: Selections from the Art Institute of Chicago Museum Studies*, 24(2): 44–161, 260–262.

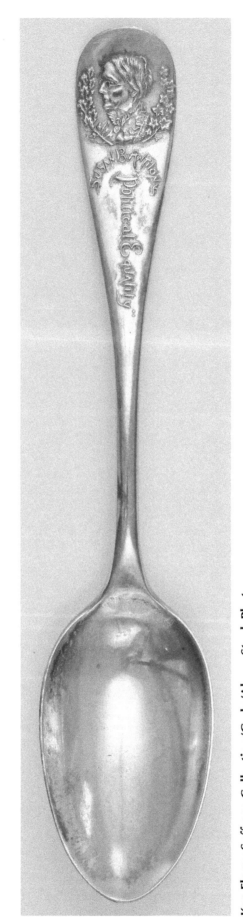

31 Political Equality Spoon

INTRODUCTION

It was on July 19 and 20, 1848, when a group of women's rights advocates, mostly women but with a sprinkling of male supporters, convened the first women's rights convention in Seneca Falls, New York, which launched the women's suffrage movement in the United States. Women had not been given the vote in the Constitution. Without that right, women had virtually no power or leverage in society, legally, socially, or politically. This was 1848, and there was an outbreak of activism worldwide. In Europe, republican revolts against the monarchies took place in Sicily, Italy, France, Germany, and the Austrian Empire. Here in the United States, 1848 brought the signing of the Treaty of Guadalupe Hidalgo, ending the Mexican-American War and enlarging the land mass of the nation. In 1848, there was also the discovery of gold in California and the election of Zachary Taylor as president. It was a period of social ferment here as well as in Europe. The newly ascendant movements for abolition, temperance, prison reform, public education, and even world peace were percolating around the nation. Many of these social movements were grounded in the religious revivals that were part of the Second Great Awakening that erupted in the United States during the first half of the 19th century. But there was one offshoot of these reform efforts that was the most radical and revolutionary of all: the fight for women's right to vote. There was such a hostile response from both men and women that it took over seventy years to attain that goal. It was 1920 when the United States passed the Nineteenth Amendment to the Constitution, which guaranteed women's suffrage. The world had been transformed during those years. In 1848, there were no electric lights, virtually no indoor plumbing or heating, no transcontinental railroad, no telephone, and no cars. In 1920, the United States was in the modern era. Women no longer wore corsets, and skirts were getting short. The world had suffered through its first world war, and much of the country enjoyed modern conveniences like electricity, telephone, and automobiles. It had been a long battle.

213

DESCRIPTION

The artifact shown here is a souvenir demitasse spoon. It is sterling silver and dates from 1892. It was designed by Millie Burtis Logan and produced for the American market. The spoon is 4 ½ inches long and has a plain bowl. It is decorated with a profile portrait of Susan B. Anthony at the obverse end of the handle. The profile is surrounded by oak branches, a symbol of strength and achievement. Under the profile in raised relief on the obverse end is her name, "Susan B. Anthony," written in a semicircle. And under that is the inscription, "Political Equality," also in raised relief. The spoon was made by Frank W. Smith, a silver manufacturer from Gardner, Massachusetts. Millie Logan was related to Susan B. Anthony. Her mother was Anthony's cousin. The spoon was most likely created as souvenir from a suffrage fundraiser. There were at least four types of spoons besides this one that were sold with this design: a 4 ½-inch grapefruit spoon; a 4 ½-inch scalloped, slotted bonbon spoon; and a 5 ¾-inch dinner spoon.

The women's suffrage advocates began to identify with popular culture as the movement matured at the end of the 19th and the beginning of the 20th centuries. As the consumer economy began to take control, production of collectibles and memorabilia exploded in popular culture. Souvenirs of various types with all sorts of messages could be purchased at every type of event. Knickknacks were king in the Victorian and Edwardian eras, and specific varieties of furniture were designed to display the knickknacks, like the corner etagere and the so-called whatnot shelf. Scrapbooking was very popular as was collecting stamps and postcards. Shopping in department stores became one of the favorite pastimes of the middle-class and upper-middle-class housewife. And the suffrage movement used the commercial world to advertise their political and social goals. Printing and manufacturing had advanced to the point where cheap trinkets were available to be sold or given away. The political button, first used in the presidential campaign of William McKinley and William Jennings Bryan, was made of celluloid. The suffragists eagerly seized on this advertising ploy to promote their cause. The concept of using the popularity of a mercantile culture to bring people into their movement was useful. What we see as suffrage memorabilia today, which include buttons, postcards, badges, playing cards, posters, and other ephemera, was often used to inform the public of an event, although it often was saved as a memento. These spoons were some of the earliest collectibles that were manufactured to promote the suffragists' cause.

SIGNIFICANCE

Susan Brownell Anthony was born in Adams, Massachusetts, in 1820, the daughter of Quaker farmer. The family moved to Rochester, New York, in 1845 and became active in the local abolitionist movement. Anti-slavery activists would meet at their farm every Sunday, sometimes joined by abolitionist leaders Frederick Douglass and William Lloyd Garrison. As a young person, Anthony was instilled with the Quaker beliefs in social justice and equality. She joined the workforce in 1848 as a teacher in Canajoharie, New York, where, she was disappointed to discover, she earned one-fourth of the salary of the male teachers. Anthony joined the local teachers' union and became active in the abolitionist and temperance movements. Though Susan B. Anthony did not attend because she was employed in Canajoharie, both her parents and her sister Mary attended the first women's rights convention in Seneca Falls in 1848, organized by Lucretia Mott and Elizabeth Cady Stanton. In 1851, Susan was introduced to Stanton, the woman who would be her lifelong friend and ally in the suffrage movement. Influenced by Stanton and Lucy Stone, Susan B. Anthony, the staunch abolitionist, was soon won over to the suffragists' cause. Lucy Stone was another early advocate for women's rights. She was an effective orator and the first woman from Massachusetts to earn a college degree.

Anthony and Stanton formed the American Equal Rights Association (AERA) and, in 1868, became editors of the association's newspaper the *Revolution* in 1868. Anthony was disciplined and organized, with excellent leadership skills. Stanton was the intellectual of the two and an outstanding writer. They both traveled around the country giving speeches promoting women's suffrage. This was a controversial topic at that time. After all, women had virtually no rights and would not gain any until given the right to vote. Women had no right to own property, to earn money, sign contracts, or even be the guardian of their own children. Because Anthony never married, she was allowed to be responsible for her own life and signed her own contracts for all her business dealings. She was disappointed when women were not included in the Fourteenth and Fifteenth Amendments to the Constitution that were passed after the Civil War. For the first time, women were specifically excluded from voting by constitutional amendment. This created a rift between the abolitionists and some of the women's suffragists. A few of the suffragists agreed that giving black men the vote should be first and that the women's vote would soon follow. Some knew better, and in fact the vote for women was so radioactive that the amendment would never have passed if women's suffrage was included. It took over fifty more years to succeed.

Susan B. Anthony and Elizabeth Cady Stanton continued their quest to enfranchise women. In 1872, Anthony was arrested for voting. She was tried and fined $100 and received national media coverage. Several new women's rights organizations were formed, and in 1888, Anthony helped merge the two leading organizations into one, the National American Women's Suffrage Association, which she led until 1900. Although she was considered a strange and controversial figure when she began her decades-long campaign for the women's right to vote, she became a respected national leader, even meeting President McKinley at the White House to celebrate her 80th birthday. Susan B. Anthony died in 1906 at the age of eighty-six. The movement continued with a series of new advocates, with a split between the radical feminists, led by Alice Paul, and the moderate ones, led by Carrie Chapman Catt. With the one-two punch of these competing organizations battling for a constitutional amendment, and the transformation of society as World War I ended, the campaign was finally successful with the passage of the Nineteenth Amendment to the Constitution in 1920.

FURTHER INFORMATION

Cashman, Sean D. 1993. *America in the Gilded Age: From the Death of Lincoln to the Rise of Theodore Roosevelt.* New York; London: New York University Press.

Finnegan, Margaret. 1999. *Selling Suffrage: Consumer Culture and Votes for Women.* New York: Columbia University Press.

Florey, Kenneth. 2013. *Women's Suffrage Memorabilia: An Illustrated Historical Study.* Jefferson, NC; London: McFarland & Company, Inc.

Hayward, Nancy (ed.). 2017. "Susan B. Anthony." National Women's History Museum. Accessed August 10, 2020. https://www.womenshistory.org/education-resources/biographies/susan-b-anthony.

Leach, William R. September 1984. "Transformations in a Culture of Consumption: Women and Department Stores, 1890–1925." *Journal of American History*, 71(2): 319–342.

McMillen, Sally G. 2008. *Seneca Falls and the Origins of the Women's Rights Movement.* New York: Oxford University Press.

Schlereth, Thomas J. 1991. *Victorian American: Transformations in Everyday Life, 1876–1915.* New York: Harper Perennial.

Stanton, Elizabeth C., Susan B. Anthony, and Matilda J. Gage (eds.). 2009. *History of Woman Suffrage, Vol. II.* February 9. Accessed August 11, 2020. http://www.gutenberg.org/files/28039/28039-h/28039-h.htm.

Zinn, Howard. 2005. *A People's History of the United States.* New York: Harper Perennial Modern Classics.

Religious Life

THE

FALL OF MAN.

~~~~~~~~

AMERICAN
SUNDAY-SCHOOL
UNION.

32 *The Fall of Man* Title Page

INTRODUCTION

In late-18th-century Britain, the agricultural economy was giving way to the insurgent Industrial Revolution as hordes of indigent farmworkers flooded into the cities to take jobs in the new factories. These families crowded together, often living in squalid housing conditions. The whole family went to work, including the children. Their only day off was Sunday, and the children were often left to their own devices, roaming around the neighborhood and getting into trouble. School was not an option, as there were no free public schools and the children worked all week anyway. Some religious leaders, incensed by this situation, explored new approaches to teach moral lessons to these unsupervised children. Robert Raikes, publisher of the British *Gloucester Journal*, became consumed with the notion of providing a method that could improve the morals of these children. Raikes, who became known as the "father of the Sunday School," opened a school in Gloucester around 1780, hiring a teacher and a housekeeper to run his new school. This school served the indigent poor, who were not being served by any type of free public school. These humble schools, open only on Sunday and located in houses, barns, chapels, and even on front porches, provided a crucial educational environment to an otherwise unschooled economic group. Classes in basic reading, writing, and arithmetic would reduce ignorance and inculcate moral structure for these wild and unruly kids. Soon the concept of the free Sunday School spread throughout the industrial north in England. The educational historian Frank Smith wrote: "The success of the Sunday Schools is an event of enormous significance . . . for two generations they were the chief means of giving secular instruction to the new working class in the factories." He goes on to explain that "it was through the Sunday School that the idea of universal education was first conceived possible. While discussion was still raging whether the laboring poor would be taught to write, a knowledge of reading was spreading throughout the country . . . the Sunday School was all-embracing and free . . . the faith of these early promoters was heroic" (Smith 1931, quoted in Snell 1999: 124). By

1833, the number of children attending Sunday Schools outnumbered those attending weekday schools. In 1851, three-quarters of the working-class children between the ages of five and fifteen attended Sunday Schools in England and Wales. The purpose of these British Sunday Schools was not to eradicate the entrenched class system that was a fixture in British society, however. As stated by one of the English founders of these schools, "There is no intention of raising them (the children) above their common level; for in that case, how would our manufactories be carried on, our houses erected and our table furnished?" (Jameson 1982: 186).

The phenomenally successful Sunday School program that originated in the northwestern industrial regions of Britain soon migrated to the fledgling nation across the Atlantic. The illiteracy rate was high in this country as well, and though we did not have an entrenched class system, many children from all social classes did not attend school. Religious education was also down. In 1790, Bishop William White and a few friends from Philadelphia founded the First Day Society, organized "for the benefit of such persons of either sex (and of any age) as cannot afford to educate themselves" (Boylan 1979: 321). This group aimed to provide moral education to the indigent children in the city by setting up Sunday Schools. The teachers who were hired were paid. The concept spread throughout the nearby cities, including one in Boston and one in Pawtucket, Rhode Island, the site of Samuel Slater's first American textile mill. These First Day Society Schools were not affiliated with any particular church and were nondenominational. They taught reading, writing, and arithmetic. These schools also endeavored to teach proper behavior and speech as well as cleanliness. They even often provided appropriate "Sunday go-to-church" clothing to the children. Though no specific religious teaching was included, most of the reading lessons were from the Bible, as knowledge of the Bible was considered essential to leading a moral life. Since these were once-a-week classes and time was limited, sectarian religious education was bypassed. Eventually, the realization that American children were for all intents and purposes still unschooled led to a drive to provide free public schooling that soon spread from Philadelphia to the whole country.

As public schools became more commonly available, the demand for Sunday Schools to teach the basics to children began to fade. By 1820, new Sunday Schools were being set up throughout the country that focused more broadly on religious education, more specifically evangelical religious education. Sunday School societies formed unions of the various groups. In 1817, the Sunday and Adult School Union was formed in Philadelphia uniting these groups. In 1824, the American Sunday School Union, known as the ASSU, was founded, combining unions from ten states and the District of Columbia into a national organization. This organization, though evangelical in nature, was not connected to any particular sect and considered itself nondenominational. The Protestant denominations that supported the group included the Presbyterians, Episcopalians, Congregationalists, and Methodists. For the first time, various social classes were included in the Sunday Schools, and instead of focusing on the poor children, children of the middle class were also included. As the curriculum became more religious, many Sunday School classes began to be held within the church grounds. Churches were happy to have young, pliable minds on their property, and many of the children eventually became church members.

Another factor that influenced the Sunday School movement in the United States was the so-called Second Great Awakening that took place in the first few decades of the 19th century. A reaction to the secular emphasis of the American Enlightenment and the leaders of the American Revolution of the 18th century, the Second Great Awakening was a religious revivalist movement based on evangelical beliefs. The (first) Great Awakening that took place in the 1730s and 1740s was a revitalization of religious piety at a time when secular ideas were at the forefront. The Second Great Awakening appealed to the growing American populace, as the population expanded hundreds of miles west. The Erie Canal's construction and the invention of the steamboat increased transportation options for trade, and the Industrial Revolution took families off the farms and into the factories and offices. The center of the nation moved from the East Coast to the Midwest. The altered social landscape led to an anxiety and isolation, which made evangelical Christianity, an emotional, personal type of religion, appealing to many Americans. The rural western territories couldn't support churches, so itinerant preachers would travel the region and set up camp meetings where hundreds, or even thousands, of attendees would be converted to a personal form of Christianity through fervent and animated preaching style. The populist orientation of this type of religious movement influenced the Sunday School movement, as evangelical converts were eager to spread the word through missionary work and religious tracts. Very often Sunday Schools were opened in rural areas where no church yet existed. Trained teachers, men and women alike, would teach religion as well as reading and writing if necessary. Because of the vast areas of the growing American land, the nationwide ASSU required literature and educational materials that could be provided for all the local schools. So, the ASSU became a publisher of Protestant tracts. The goal of the publishing arm of the organization was to disseminate moral and religious material to young readers. These included books, periodicals, and pamphlets for the Sunday School audience. The content was strictly enforced by a Publications Committee. The content was most often nonfiction and had to be moral and religious, age appropriate, good literature, and American in origin. Representatives of at least three denominations served on the Publications Committee so as not to show sectarian bias. The publications included history, biography, poetry, hymns, and didactic teachings, provided either for free or at nominal cost. The ASSU also provided entire libraries at a reduced rate to schools in rural areas where there were no circulating libraries.

DESCRIPTION

The artifact shown here is the title page of a small eight-page booklet published by the ASSU any time between 1827 and 1853. It is 3 ⅝ inches tall. The text of the page says, "The Fall of Man; American Sunday School Union." The engraved title page also depicts a boy sitting down leaning against a tree with a girl resting her head on his lap. It was most likely awarded as a Sunday School "prize" for attendance, a correct answer, or for winning a contest. The short booklet tells the story of Adam and Eve and the serpent in large type, simple language, almost like a child's reader. At the end of the booklet is the publication page. Its text states, "Upwards of One Thousand Varieties of Publications, Designed Especially Children and Youth, Published by the American Sunday-School Union, 146 Chestnut Street, Philadelphia. Published and for Sale at the Depositories of the American Sunday-school Union. G.S Scofield, 146 Chestnut St, Philadelphia. Henry Hoyt, 9 Cornhill, Boston. J.C. Meeks, 147 Nassau St., New York. W.H. Bulkley, 103 Fourth St., Louisville. C.T. Cherry, Rochester, N.Y. No. 17 Chalmers St., Charleston, S.C."

FINAL WORDS OF "THE FALL OF MAN" PUBLISHED BY THE AMERICAN SUNDAY SCHOOL UNION

How did Adam and Eve sin against God? And how were they punished? What was done to the serpent? What did God say of the ground? Is it not a dreadful thing to sin against God? Do you then pray and watch against sin, and love the Lord Jesus Christ, who died to save sinners?

SIGNIFICANCE

Though it is not well-known today, the Sunday School movement had a central role in the education of children in the 19th century, both in Britain and in the United States. In England and Wales, the lack of a free public school system in addition to the use of child labor during the Industrial Revolution made the Sunday School movement an essential tool in teaching literacy to young children. In fact, the success of the schools led to a more educated workforce that eventually joined the labor movement in demanding better working conditions for the workers. The British model continued to focus on teaching basic skills to the children, and left the task of religious education to the individual churches. The dominance of the Church of England precluded using the Sunday Schools for religious teaching by the various smaller sects. In the United States, however, the Sunday School movement was equally influential, but it became a conduit for the inculcation of teaching Protestant values as well as American nationalism to children both in the cities and on the frontier. The ASSU served as an institution builder for the evangelical movement just at the time that the Second Great Awakening was lighting revivalist fires throughout the country. The reformist zeal that started with the Sunday School movement led to many other religiously based movements, like abolitionism, temperance, the YMCA, and prison and asylum reform movements. American Sunday Schools relied on volunteers and on the ASSU for materials and support and benefited from many of the children joining congregations, helping cement the Protestant values into American culture.

FURTHER INFORMATION

Ahlstrom, Sydney E. 2004. *A Religious History of the American People.* New Haven, CT: Yale University Press.

Boylan, Anne M. September 1979. "Sunday Schools and Changing Evangelical Views of Children in the 1820s." *Church History*, 48(3): 320–333.

Boylan, Anne M. 1990. *Sunday School: The Formation of an American Institution, 1790–1880.* New Haven, CT: Yale University Press.

Butler, Jon, Grant Wacker, and Randall Balmer. 2000. *Religion in American Life: A Short History.* Oxford; New York: Oxford University Press.

Canary, Robert H. Fall 1968. "The Sunday School as Popular Culture." *Miscontinent American Studies Journal*, 9(2): 5–13.

Jameson, J. Parker. June 1982. "The Sunday School in the National Period." *Historical Magazine of the Protestant Episcopal Church*, 5(2): 185–189.

Snell, K. D. M. August 1999. "The Sunday-School Movement in England and Wales: Child Labour, Denominational Control and Working-Class Culture." *Past and Present*, 164: 122–168.

33 Birth and Baptismal Certificate

INTRODUCTION

According to the U.S. Census, German Americans are the largest self-reported ancestry group in the country with an estimated population size of over forty-four million. The first Germans to immigrate to the American colonies were a band of Quakers and Mennonites from the Krefeld region of the Rhineland in western Germany. They settled in eastern Pennsylvania and founded the city of Germantown, now part of Philadelphia, in 1683. The colony of Pennsylvania was founded in 1681 when Charles II granted a charter to William Penn, the founder of Pennsylvania. Penn was himself a Quaker and had been on a missionary trip to Germany, where he encouraged these religious pacifists to relocate to the new colony. In Penn's colony of Pennsylvania, religious tolerance was practiced, a notable departure from the Puritan colonies to the north. Germans felt at home in the city of Germantown, and soon many more Germans arrived from various regions in southwestern Germany: the Rhineland, Palatinate, Wurttemberg, Baden, and the German section of Switzerland. Two large waves of German immigrants landed on the shores of Pennsylvania between the years of 1727 and 1775, and by the time of the Revolutionary War, there were approximately sixty-five thousand to one hundred thousand residents of German descent in the Pennsylvania colony. These Germans brought with them a number of religious traditions. Between 5 and 10 percent of the immigrants, so-called "Plain people," members of Anabaptist sects like the Amish and the Mennonites, were fleeing religious persecution. The majority of the immigrants, referred to as "Fancy people," were affiliated with Lutheranism and the Reformed church, which were both culturally accepted German faiths. Unlike the religious dissenters, these Protestant immigrants were seeking better opportunities after the devastation of various wars with France that had taken a toll on the German economy. They assimilated more readily into the American culture. An even larger flood of German immigrants from northern and eastern Germany immigrated to the United States in the mid-19th century, and the majority of those settled in New York and the

225

Midwest. The Germans who settled in Pennsylvania came over in family groups and were mostly farmers and artisans. In the late 1700s, there were twice as many German immigrants arriving in family groups as English immigrants, who most often came into the country as single adults. Many of the German artisans were known for their printing skills, cabinetmaking skills, and their fine carpentry. The design and production of the famous Conestoga wagon were attributed to the artisans in the German community from Lancaster County. German families that could afford land outside of Philadelphia took up farming in the counties west and northwest of the city. These farmers were also known for their introduction of modern farming methods into the region. Pennsylvania Germans were also known as the Pennsylvania Dutch, a misnomer because they did not come from the Netherlands and did not speak Dutch. The language they spoke was a local Palatine-area dialect of German called Deitsch. A related term, Deutsch, is the name for the modern German language. Another possible explanation for the term "Pennsylvania Dutch" is that in that time period, people from the regions adjacent to the Netherlands were often called Dutch, even if they spoke a dialect of German. Pennsylvania Germans sometimes referred to themselves as Pennsylvania Dutch, in order to distinguish themselves from the German immigrants who immigrated in the mid-19th century. Those Germans included a large cohort of political refugees who emigrated from Germany to the United States after the revolution of 1848.

DESCRIPTION

The Pennsylvania Germans were devoted to education, and it is said that a schoolhouse was often erected in a village before the church. However, the schools were parochial and run by the religious leaders. The German culture was also known for its artistic traditions, and one of the most vibrant and distinctive was the practice known as "fraktur." The term refers to the decorated and printed documents that were produced to celebrate significant life milestones. The word is derived from the Latin *fractura*, which means "breaking." The Gothic typeface used in these documents is called *fraktur* in German, which describes the broken or fractured style of lettering that is utilized. So, though technically describing the typeface, the term "fraktur" has come to describe all the highly decorated illuminated manuscripts that use the fraktur font but are also festooned with a variety of colorful and charming figures, animals, and designs. The fraktur style has become one of the most iconic and beloved forms of American folk art. The rights of passage records that were recorded in fraktur documents include house blessings ("Haussegen"), reward of merit or penmanship sample ("Vorschrift"), confirmation certificate ("Confirmationsschein"), wedding certificate ("Tausfchein"), and memorial ("Denkmal"). By far the most common of the fraktur documents were the Tausfchein and Vorschrift. The

Taufschein celebrates the baptism of a child, and the pieces that still exist are some of the most delightful and charming examples. Some of the documents record both the birth and the baptism, and they are called "Geburts und Taufschein." These documents were produced between 1750 and 1860, with popularity reaching its peak during the period 1800–1835. The artists who produced the fraktur were most often the schoolmasters in the parochial school, although itinerant artisans or the farmers themselves sometimes created the folk art after being taught calligraphy in school. Most of the documents were unsigned, although some examples can be attributed to a specific artist through their identifiable stylistic components. A few artists are known because they signed the documents.

The example shown here, from the Philadelphia Museum of Art, is a so-called Geburts und Taufschein produced by the artist Francis Portzline between the years 1840 and 1855. It was made in Pennsylvania, in either Snyder County or Union County located at the central part of the state. The document is made of "wove" paper, decorated with ink and watercolor wash, pigments in gum medium. It is 12 $\frac{13}{16}$ inches high by 15 $\frac{9}{15}$ inches wide. Like many other Taufschein examples, this one is dominated by a central heart-shaped element that contains the text, written in German. Charming decorative elements include flowers, birds shown in profile, and butterflies adorning the two sides of the document, which accentuate the celebratory nature of the document. Additionally, two motifs on the document are characteristic of Portzline's work: the calligraphic scrolls resembling Celtic knots and the cluster of hearts arranged in concentric circles at the center of the page. Francis Portzline was born in Germany and lived from 1771 to 1857. He immigrated to Pennsylvania in the late 1700s and lived in York County in 1801 where he worked as a storekeeper and surveyor. He relocated in 1812 to the southern section of Union County, which became Snyder County in 1855. Trained in calligraphy, Portzline began work as a schoolmaster and soon became skilled in the folk art of fraktur, written in both English and German.

SIGNIFICANCE

Religion played a significant role in the lives of the early Americans. Many had come to the New World to seek freedom from religious persecution. The ones who didn't immigrate for that specific reason still relied on religion to guide their lives. Fraktur documents most often celebrated religious rites of passage, like baptisms, confirmations, and weddings, and were likely produced by the schoolmaster employed by the local church. The Pennsylvania Germans who produced the fraktur were primarily members of the Lutheran or Reformed Church, though the "Plain people," who practiced separation from the world and simple living, also produced these joyous and delightful documents. These so-called primitive works have become some of the most popular forms of American folk art. The fraktur typeface, originating in the German-speaking regions of Europe in the 1500s, was expanded on by talented folk artists who decorated the documents with fanciful designs. The production of these fraktur manuscripts endured in the German community in Pennsylvania until the beginning of the 20th century.

FURTHER INFORMATION

Bronner, Simon J., and Joshua R. Brown. 2017. *Pennsylvania Germans: An Interpretive Encyclopedia*. Baltimore, MD: Johns Hopkins University Press.

Carlson, Janice H., and John Krill. Autumn 1978. "Pigment Analysis of Early American Watercolors and Fraktur." *Journal of the American Institute for Conservation*, 18(1): 19–32.

Conner, Paul, and Jill Roberts (eds.). 1988. "Introduction by Don Yoder." *Pennsylvania German Fraktur and Printed Broadsides: A Guide to the Collections in the Library of Congress*. Washington: Library of Congress.

Grubb, Farley. Winter 1990. "German Immigration to Pennsylvania, 1709–1820." *Journal of Interdisciplinary History*, 20(3): 417–436.

Kenney, Alice P. January 1970. "Private Worlds in the Middle Colonies: An Introduction to Human Tradition in American History." *New York History*, 51(1): 4–31.

Manseau, Peter. 2017. *Objects of Devotion: Religion in Early America*. Washington, DC: Smithsonian Books.

Minardi, Lisa. 2015. *Drawn with Spirit: Pennsylvania German Fraktur for the Joan and Victor Johnson Collection*. New Haven, CT; London: Yale University Press.

Stanley, Ted. Spring 1994. "The Fraktur: Its History and a Conservation Case Study." *Journal of the American Institute for Conservation*, 33(1): 33–45.

Weiser, Frederick. 1973. "Piety and Protocol in Folk Art: Pennsylvania German Fraktur Birth and Baptismal Certificates." *Winterthur Portfolio*, 8: 19–43.

Winner, Cherie. July 27, 2017. "Not Just the Amish: Pennsylvania Germans in American Culture." *Research/Penn State Magazine*, 37(1): 36–37.

34 Christmas Tree Ornament

INTRODUCTION

Christmas comes but once a year, but the Christmas season seems to go on forever. Whereas once upon a time the Christmas season started the day after Thanksgiving, it has now retreated into the heart of the year, skipping Thanksgiving altogether and galloping past Halloween into mid-October. Everyone complains, yet everyone still succumbs to the festivities. Better buy those gifts and decorations now; if you wait until December, they will all be gone! How has this situation developed? Is it something new? Every generation gripes about the commercialization and secularization of Christmas. But when did it begin? Was it something recent, or was it actually part of the origin story of the modern celebration of the Christmas holiday? It is a long and fascinating tale that begins before the birth of Christ himself.

DESCRIPTION

When the first Christmas trees were appearing in the United States, they were typically shown with small gifts hanging from the boughs of the tree. Sometimes gifts would be shown under the tree as well. Gifts were originally small, sweet treats and small toys for the children. As Christmas gained in popularity and, as a result of the Industrial Revolution, American factories produced more elaborate store-made products, the gifts got bigger and more expensive. Whereas the trees were originally decorated with small gifts, as the gifts got bigger, families began to decorate the tree with ornaments. One of the first types of manufactured ornament was the candy container or favor. This was made of cardboard or papier-mâché and held the sweets that were the mainstay of the children's Christmas gifts. Expensive versions of these ornaments were called Dresden ornaments. Imported from Dresden and Leipzig, Germany, between 1880 and 1910, these precious handmade cardboard ornaments were popular in wealthy households on the East Coast.

The artifact shown here is a 19th-century painted glass ornament from the collection of the Brooklyn Museum. It measures 3 ¾ inches by 2 inches by 2 inches and depicts a baby with a hood, carrying a little purse. Ornaments like this one were imported from Germany in the late 19th century. The story of these ornaments demonstrates an aspect of the commercialization of the Christmas holiday that took place at that time. Americans fell in love with their Christmas trees; they were being sold on every street corner of the major American cities by the end of the 19th century. But not everyone could afford the imported Dresden ornaments. In 1880, Frank W. Woolworth, founder of the F. W. Woolworth chain of successful dime stores, asked a Philadelphia importer to show him some cheap Christmas toys that he could sell in his first store in Lancaster, Pennsylvania. Instead, he showed Woolworth his newest import—glass ornaments from the town of Lauscha in Germany. Woolworth scoffed at these silly, inexpensive, and very fragile trinkets. He insisted that no one would know what they were for, and besides, the delicate glass baubles would certainly break on the long journey from Germany to his stores. The story goes that the importer assured Woolworth that the large return on each piece would ensure his profit despite any loss to breakage. He also guaranteed the ornaments to Woolworth, promising to return his money if he didn't sell $25 worth of the ornaments. When Woolworth reluctantly placed the small number of glass ornaments in his shop a few days before Christmas, they sold out immediately. Woolworth, anticipating the goldmine that he might have, ramped up his purchase of these ornaments every year, eventually making an estimated $25 million on imported glass Christmas ornaments.

Christians celebrate December 25 as the day that Jesus Christ was born. In late December, depictions of the Nativity scenes appear, and there are readings from the New Testament's Gospel of Luke in Christian churches throughout the world. But when did this celebration of Christ's birth at the end of December start surfacing? And why in December? Before the birth of Christianity, agrarian societies in Europe celebrated the winter solstice. The drudgery of planting, tending, and harvesting the crops was completed, and a long, cold winter was poised to begin. After the harvest, members of pre-Christian, pagan societies would thank the gods for the bounty as the gloomy melancholy of the winter loomed. With fresh grain and fresh meat from the recently slaughtered livestock, in addition to plenty of fermented libations, a winter solstice feast would be planned. All the pre-Christian cultures in northern and central Europe celebrated a big party at the time of winter solstice. The names varied, but they were all lively and boisterous. In northern Europe, a festival called Yule or Jul was celebrated by the peoples of Scandinavia, Germany, and Great Britain. Pre-Christian celebrations included gathering around a Yule log, a huge log that could burn for days, and decorating with evergreens, which, in addition to being green even in winter, were believed to ward off evil spirits with their sharp needles. Drinking of strong spirits was a component part of this festival. By the time of the Romans, a related celebration developed two centuries before the birth of Christ. This celebration honored the Roman god Saturn, and it ran from December 17 until December 23, with an abundance of feasting and carousing. Saturnalia was an important festival for the Romans. The period of Saturnalia celebrations included a number of principle attributes: eating, drinking, and debauchery. There was gambling; there were games. There was a lot of sexual licentiousness. And there was also a tradition of cross-dressing and role reversal. Men would dress as women; slaves would dress as masters, and vice versa. Following soon after Saturnalia was another holiday, celebrated on December 25, the birthday of Sol Invictus, the sun god, which was also associated with Mithraism, a secret Roman cult that was popular with the Roman army, as well as many wealthy Romans and government officials. In addition, December 25 was the winter solstice according to the contemporary Roman calendar. Following up on these holidays was another one that was universally celebrated by the Romans. It was Kalends, the New Year, which was also celebrated for several days, marking an extraordinary season of festivities. (The name Kalends is the origin of the English word "calendar.")

In the middle of the 4th century AD, there was a significant change in the Roman world. The Christian Church made the curious decision to celebrate the birth of Christ on December 25. The emperor Constantine had recently converted to Christianity, and the Church sought to promote the new religion among the pagan Romans. There was a fear in the Church that the spreading cult called Mithraism, which, like Christianity, was monotheistic, posed a serious threat. So they adopted the birthday of Sol Invictus and the Roman date of the winter solstice, December 25, to serve as the birthday of Jesus. There was no exact knowledge of the date of Jesus' birth, as it was only described in brief accounts in the Gospels of Matthew and Luke. Historians agree that the Church made a serious compromise by selecting this date. Aiming to convert as many pagans as possible to the Christian Church, they accepted the date and, with it, the rowdy celebrations that came with it. As stated by historian Stephen Nissenbaum in his book, *The Battle for Christmas*:

> [T]he decision was part of what amounted to a compromise, and a compromise for which the Church paid a high price.. . . In return for ensuring massive observance of the anniversary of the Savior's birth by assigning it to this resonant date, the Church for its part tacitly agreed to allow the holiday to be celebrated more or less the way it had always been . . . There were always people for whom Christmas was a time of pious devotion rather than carnival, but such people were always in the minority. It may be not be going too far to say that Christmas has always been an extremely difficult holiday to Christianize. (1996: 8)

The impious celebration of Christmas persisted throughout Medieval Europe. Several customs were endemic to the annual rite. The practice of "misrule" played a big part in Christmas celebrations. The term denotes the flouting of all accepted rules, and with misrule, misbehavior was rampant. At times a "Lord of Misrule" would be anointed, and this person would be in charge of all the Christmas mayhem. In 1725, an Anglican minister, Reverend Henry Bourne, of Newcastle, England, dubbed Christmas as merely "a pretense for Drunkenness, and Rioting, and Wantonness" (Nissenbaum 1996: 7). Another custom was called "mumming." This was the tradition of cross-dressing, or dressing in disguise. The mummers would go from house to house, perform for the homeowners, and then partake in food and drink. Wassailing was another type of Christmas custom that was widespread in Britain. Gangs of roving youths, usually the peasant class, would go to the homes of the gentry and sing a "wassail" or drinking song and then demand food and drink. It has been described as an aggressive or even threatening action, but it was expected at this time of year and could be compared to the modern "trick or treat" custom at Halloween. This type of behavior went on for centuries.

After the Reformation, certain Protestant sects rejected the unruliness of the Christmas celebrations and shunned the holiday altogether. When the Puritans gained power in England in the 17th century, the celebration of Christmas was briefly banned. Despite the effort, the English population roundly protested the ban, and pro-Christmas riots broke out. The seriousness of purpose of the Puritans was not taken as lightly when they relocated to the shores of Massachusetts in the early 1600s. These Puritans despised Christmas and the antics that customarily accompanied it, and they, in fact, had a profound influence on American Christmas traditions for many years. The Puritans in Massachusetts actually banned the holiday as well from 1659 to 1681, contending, not without merit, that the celebration of Christmas was merely a metamorphosis of the pagan holiday Saturnalia. Work went on, shops were open, and the concept of Christmas essentially went underground.

Christmas celebrations in the United States quietly persisted in some parts of the country. The Episcopalians, Dutch Reformed, Lutherans, and Catholics celebrated; however, many Protestant sects did not. The Congregationalists (originally the Puritans), the Baptists, the Methodists, the Presbyterians, and the Quakers, thriving sects in some areas of the United States, all de-emphasized Christmas. The areas with large German, Dutch, and Scandinavian populations cherished their Christmas celebrations, and from them, American popular culture appropriated a number of treasured Christmas symbols like the Christmas tree and Santa Claus. It was not until the mid-19th century that the various familiar Christmas traditions developed into the holiday juggernaut we know today. The constellation of Christmas customs that all came together within twenty-five years in the mid-19th century in the United States has been compared by various historians as a "big bang" or a snowball rolling down a hill (Elliott 2001; Forbes 2007). Many disparate older traditions, as well as new customs, coalesced within a few years to produce the holiday that we know today. But it was seriously helped along by three patrician men from the moneyed elite class in New York, one German American cartoonist, and one British writer and a popular ladies' magazine.

With the nation under stress as it rapidly industrialized in the 19th century, the customs of the rural agricultural society were starting to recede. Cities were growing, factories were buzzing, and workers were toiling for exceedingly long hours for little pay. Income inequality was on the rise, and poor neighborhoods in large cities like New York were teeming with the indigent. A new custom developed as members of New York's upper class began a new habit of celebrating New Year as a time for family gathering and exchanging gifts. However, relics of the centuries-old "misrule" type of raucous Christmas celebrations were reappearing, and they were infiltrating wealthy neighborhoods as well the impoverished ones. In the 1820s, roving bands of youths would dress up in disguise, similar to the mumming of previous eras, and stand outside of the homes of the well-to-do, making as much noise as they could. These gangs formed Callithumpian parades, known for their loud banging of pots and pans, whistles, and other annoyingly loud instruments. A trio of prominent New Yorkers took on this issue and facilitated the change in the way that Christmas was celebrated. These men were John Pintard, Washington Irving, and Clement Clarke Moore. Pintard, a founder of the New York Historical Society, promoted the celebration of Saint Nicholas Day. Saint Nicholas was a 3rd-century Turkish priest who was revered for his generosity and the miracles that he performed. He became a beloved figure of German and Dutch folklore. The Dutch called him Sinterklaas. Washington Irving, a friend of John Pintard and the very popular writer of "Rip Van Winkle," wrote several books that influenced the new American perception of Christmas. Diedrich Knickerbocker's *A History of New York*, written in 1809 and updated in 1821, was a satire about life in the city. In it he included descriptions of Saint Nicholas riding over the tops of trees bringing presents to children. Irving's other influential publications regarding the celebration of Christmas were his stories about life in England's fictional "Bracebridge Hall." After traveling in Britain, Irving wrote a series of nostalgic tales outlining the traditional observance of the Christmas holiday in a manor house in England. Many of these traditions were actually invented by Irving himself, but the popular stories delighted Americans who were fascinated by the charm and generosity of the so-called traditional British Christmas, however ersatz it actually was. Another promoter of a new American Christmas was the wealthy part-time professor Clement Clarke Moore, who was also a friend of John Pintard. In 1823, a poem appeared anonymously in the *Troy, New York Sentinel* newspaper. Titled "A Visit from St. Nicholas," the poem was quickly picked up and reprinted in many newspapers and gained immediate popularity. The poem, now known as "The Night Before Christmas," described in detail the visit of St. Nicholas delivering gifts to children with his "miniature sleigh and tiny reindeer." Moore did not acknowledge writing the poem until 1837. (Henry Livingston Jr. also claimed that he wrote the poem, and his family has been insisting on it ever since. Most historians, however, still attribute the poem to Moore.) The poem, one of the best-known American poems to this day, had a profound influence on the modern celebration of Christmas. Thomas Nast, a German-born American cartoonist, refined the perception of the modern St. Nick, or Santa Claus as he came to be known, in the decades after the poem's popularity spread throughout the country. His cartoons in *Harper's Weekly* magazine developed over the last half of the 19th century until the character looked very much like we expect Santa Claus to look today. A 19th-century English writer who influenced both the English and the American concept of Christmas was Charles Dickens. Like Clement Clarke Moore's poem, Dickens' novella, *A Christmas Carol*, written in 1843, is still beloved today. But the most fascinating fact about this much-loved story is that Dickens was not describing a British Christmas celebration of the mid-19th century, but he was creating it. Christmas was not universally celebrated as an intimate family gathering with a turkey dinner, a holiday from work, and charity shown to the poor. Stores were typically open on Christmas in London, as is evident when Scrooge decides to ask the boy to purchase the turkey. Dickens was a proponent of making Christmas a universally celebrated holiday, especially after he toured the United States in 1842, spending extended time with the American writer Washington Irving, who was also an advocate for a family-centered Christmas. So, in fact, both the writers who fictionalized a so-called traditional Christmas may have had influence on each other. One more interesting fact to note: the birth of Christ was not mentioned in *A Christmas Carol*. Christmas was already becoming a cultural holiday and not a particularly religious one. It was turning inward from the public hilarity of misrule to the privacy of a child-centered family gathering, with emphasis on charity and kindness.

One more factor in the big bang creation story of the modern American Christmas is the proliferation of the Christmas tree. The custom of decorating with evergreens at Christmas, or Saturnalia, or any of the various iterations of the celebration of the winter solstice, was an ancient one. But the actual Christmas tree tradition developed in Germany in the 1830s and was brought over to the United States by Germans. It was not common in the popular culture, however. Historian Stephen Nissenbaum contends that the first influential use of the Christmas tree was by a German immigrant who taught at Harvard. Charles Follen set up a Christmas tree for his young son Charley in Boston in 1835. A visiting writer named Harriet Martineau wrote about it, charmed by its gifts, ornaments, and candles, and the delight on the children's expectant faces. She predicted that the tradition would catch on in New England. To some extent it did, among the educated Unitarians in Boston who were also proponents of an innovative child-centered educational philosophy. However, although the concept of a Christmas tree did have a number of antecedents in the United States, including the one put up by Charles Follen, the proliferation and popularization of the idea came from *Godey's Lady's Book*, an exceptionally popular women's magazine of the 19th century. Sarah Josepha Hale, the editor of the magazine for forty years, was devoted to the idea of an American national culture. Although the magazine was not overtly political, Hale held personal pro-Union views during the Civil War. She felt that through the influence of the magazine, she could bring the country together with common traditions. She has been universally recognized as responsible for transforming Thanksgiving, a regional New England holiday, into a national one. She also felt that other universally celebrated holidays could bring the nation together. Christmas was one of them. When she saw an image of the young Queen Victoria celebrating Christmas with the family around a Christmas tree, she elected to reprint it, in a slightly altered image that represented an American family. Queen Victoria, newly married to Prince Albert, a German prince, adopted the German Christmas tree tradition, and an image of the family was published in 1848. Hale republished it in a Christmas edition of the magazine in 1850. She continued to promote a family Christmas celebration in every December issue of the magazine, displaying numerous images of delightful dinners and charming Christmas trees, as well as an assortment of sentimental Victorian short stories that promoted Christmas generosity, charity, and redemption.

SIGNIFICANCE

The modern American celebration of Christmas had completely taken shape by the end of the 19th century. What had arisen as a risky compromise made by the early Christian Church to appropriate a raucous Roman holiday with the aim to convert as many in the Roman Empire to Christianity as possible was transformed from a centuries-old carnival to a modern, commercial, primarily secular, family-centered holiday by 1900. And that holiday has remained the most important holiday on the American calendar, celebrated by many people of various ethnic backgrounds and even differing faiths. The modern celebration of Christmas in Japan is an example. Japanese, most of whom are not Christian, delight in the celebration of the holiday as a day of gift-giving and romance. Christmas, though still a holy day to members of the Christian religion, today shines out as a day of charity, generosity, and kindness to many others who don't necessarily celebrate the birth of Christ. Strangely enough, it was because of several influential leaders in the 19th century who helped create the modern Christmas that we continue to celebrate today. As stated by Bruce David Forbes in his book *Christmas: A Candid Story*:

> It is interesting to note that the return of Christmas was *not* the result of any concerted church-based campaign. Instead, it arose from efforts by cultural leaders and drew on broader cultural forces encouraging the general themes of generosity, family activities, and festivity in the middle of winter. In the words of commentator Tom Flynn, it is "surprising how small a role the churches played in the Victorian revival. From its inception, contemporary Christmas was primarily a secular and commercial holiday." (Forbes 2007: 66)

FURTHER INFORMATION

Elliott, Jock. 2001. *Inventing Christmas: How Our Holiday Came to Be*. New York: Harry N. Abrams.

Forbes, Bruce D. 2007. *Christmas: A Candid History*. Berkeley: University of California Press.

Forbes, Bruce D. 2015. *America's Favorite Holidays: Candid Histories*. Oakland: University of California Press.

Marling, Karal A. *Merry Christmas!* Cambridge, MA: Harvard University Press.

Moore, Tara. 2014. *Christmas: The Sacred to Santa*. London: Reaktion Books.

Nissenbaum, Stephen. 1996. *The Battle for Christmas*. New York: Vintage Books.

Schmidt, Leigh E. 1995. *Consumer Rites: The Buying and Selling of American Holidays*. Princeton, NJ: Princeton University Press.

Schnepper, Rachel N. 2012. "Yuletide's Outlaws." *New York Times*. December 14. Accessed November 6, 2019. https://www.nytimes.com/2012/12/15/opinion/the-puritan-war-on-christmas.html.

35 Shaker Chair

INTRODUCTION

In the early 19th century, the nascent United States was a vast and virtually empty nation with land to spare and few regulations. In addition, it boasted a Constitution with a mighty First Amendment that protected free speech and freedom of religion. These factors contributed to the influx of religious pilgrims fleeing persecution in Europe. Many of the first European settlers on America's shores were religious migrants, including the Pilgrims, a group of Separatist Puritans, who landed in Plymouth, Massachusetts, in 1620. By the end of the 18th century, more were on their way. One of these groups was a band of "Shaking Quakers" or Shakers who sailed across the Atlantic from Manchester, England, in 1774, and established a community near Albany, New York.

DESCRIPTION

The Shakers, officially known as the United Society of Believers of Christ's Second Appearing, was a communitarian religious group that practiced celibacy, pacifism, and gender equality. They separated themselves from what they called "the World" but had business relations with the outside society in order to sustain their communities. Though the first Shaker communities were agricultural, they soon introduced a number of industries that produced consumer products that included seeds, household items like brooms, and furniture, most commonly chairs. The artifact shown here is an example of the type of chair that was produced in the Shaker communities. The chair is made of maple with a hickory splint seat and measures 40 inches high by 16 ¼ inches wide by 16 ¼ inches deep. It is a ladder back or slat back chair, with no arms, and has three arched slats and turned posts with finials. It is very simple in style, although it has a carved label on the front of the top slat that states "Mother Ann Lee 1776" in a foliated scroll. Although the maker is unknown, it was produced at the Watervliet community, the original Shaker community located outside of Albany, New York, and founded in 1787. The date of manufacture for the chair is unknown as well, though it was most likely made between the years of 1855 and 1880. The chair is located at the Philadelphia Museum of Art. As with other Shaker furniture pieces, the chair is a simplified version of popular chair designs of the period, though the Shakers refined the designs with their attention to detail and quality. These chairs were made by hand, unlike the factory-made, mass-produced chairs that were newly appearing for sale in the United States.

The Shakers arrived on American shores in 1774, led by the prophet Ann Lee. Mother Ann, as she was called, hailed from Manchester, an industrial center in Northwest England. Mother Ann was born in 1736, the daughter of a blacksmith. Never having learned to read or write, she worked in a cotton factory and married Abraham Standerin in 1762. She proceeded to bear four children, all of whom died in childhood. Devastated by the loss, she joined a local religious group, a breakaway sect from the Quakers that had been influenced by a French group called the Camisards. This French Protestant sect had been persecuted in France and subsequently fled to England. The new group was dubbed the "Shaking Quakers" due to the frenetic trembling, quaking, singing, shouting, and walking during religious services. The name was shortened to the "Shakers." Ann Lee began seeing visions, claiming that she had a "manifestation of Divine Light," and she became leader of the group. After she had another vision, directing her to relocate to America, she organized the group, and they set off for the new world. The first Shaker settlement was in Watervliet, now known as Colonie, New York. A settlement in Mount Lebanon, New York, later became the administrative hub of the organization.

Mother Ann was convinced that the deaths of her four children were God's retribution for her carnal desires and insisted that the members of the Shaker community pursue a life of strict celibacy. This basic tenet endured throughout the lifetime of the sect, making it increasingly difficult to sustain the population. Although there were no children born into the communities, adults with children joined as did orphans who were adopted by the group. The other tenet was its communal nature. The genders lived in separate, communal quarters. All property was shared. They believed in pacifism and racial equality and the divine nature of work. Their motto was "Hands to Work, Hearts to God." Even though the Shakers were adamantly against slavery, the Shakers appealed to President Lincoln during the Civil War and received the first Conscientious Objector status for its members, so that wouldn't be drafted into the army. The Shakers also advocated for gender equality. The theology of the Shakers stressed the duality of God, which was both male and female in nature. Jesus was believed to be the male principle of God, and Ann Lee represented the female principle. And in fact, power was shared in the sect with male and female dual leadership, a radical concept during the early 19th century. The sect grew during the first half of the century, reaching its peak in the 1840s at 6,000 members in communities that spanned upstate New York, New England, Kentucky, and Ohio.

As seen in the artifact illustrated here, the Shakers advocated for simple and efficient design. Though they pursued a strict separation from "the world," they maintained a symbiotic relationship with society by producing goods that were extremely attractive and prized by the public. The teachings of the sect emphasized simplicity, utility, and craftsmanship. Their focus on efficiency led the Shakers to a number of inventions that were valued by the American people. These inventions included the flat broom, the circular saw, metal pen nibs, and a prototype of the washing machine. They were highly respected craftsmen and produced popular furniture pieces, as well as making a hugely popular line of seeds, wooden boxes, textiles, and brooms. The Shakers standardized their minimalist designs with a set of Millennial Laws that restricted the use of decorative elements in their architecture, furniture, and household products. Most of their furniture was made from maple, birch, chestnut, butternut, or pine and was most often painted or stained. The paint colors were regulated from the administration in Mount Lebanon according to the Millennial Laws. The Shakers were also known for their spare interior design. They would have plain, white painted walls with simple wooden moldings that contained pegs. On these pegs they would hang the chairs in order to clear the room.

"SIMPLE GIFTS," SHAKER DANCING SONG, WRITTEN BY ELDER JOSEPH BRACKETT, IN 1848

'Tis the gift to be simple, 'tis the gift to be free,
Tis the gift to come down where we ought to be,
And when we find ourselves in the place just right,
'Twill be in the valley of love and
Delight. When true simplicity is gain'd,
To bow and to bend we will not be asham'd,
To turn, turn will be our delight,
Till by turning, turning we come round right.

[Brackett, Joseph (attr.) 1848.]

SIGNIFICANCE

The United States of the early 19th century served as a magnet for members of radical religious and secular social movements, movements that had erupted in the aftermath of the Protestant Reformation in various regions of

Europe. The radical ideas that were endemic to many of these social movements were an anathema in rigid European societies that were ruled by the establishment church, and members of the breakaway sects were often violently persecuted. These revolutionary ideas were based on either religious or secular perfectibility of society. The religious concepts were most often millennialist in nature. These various millennialist Christian sects believed, based on references in the Book of Revelation in the Bible, that Christ would return to the earth to rule for a thousand years. At the end of the millennium, Satan would be released and the battle of the end times, Armageddon, would begin. The converse of these religious convictions was the influence of the Enlightenment with its focus on the power of reason and science. If all things could be explained and perfected by scientific experimentation, then human society could be explained and perfected as well. These various bands of iconoclasts who set out to form new communities, separate from society as a whole, endeavored to become more perfect, either through religious or secular means. Like the Shakers, these contemporaneous groups formed American utopian societies, adding to a trend that flowered in the early years of the 19th century.

The groups that fled Europe to resettle in the United States espoused a variety of beliefs. But most of them were communitarian and socialistic. The groups lived communally; they gave up all their worldly goods to join, and all property was shared among the group. Many of these groups were pioneers in pursuing social justice and equality. Most of these "intentional communities" were deliberately established far from the distracting influences of city life, and their members pursued an agrarian lifestyle. There were dozens of these communities scattered throughout the Northeast and Midwest. Some were strictly secular, like Brook Farm in Massachusetts that was founded in 1841 by the New England Transcendentalists, a group of intellectuals that included Ralph Waldo Emerson and Nathaniel Hawthorne. It only lasted for about six years, but it influenced American intellectual development, with Hawthorne satirizing the effort in his novel *The Blithedale Romance* in 1852. Another secular attempt at a utopian community was New Harmony, Indiana, founded by Robert Owen in 1825. Originally from Wales, Owen was a champion of social reform and the rights of mill workers. He also believed in a socialistic society, and his Owenite community, though unsuccessful as a utopian society, became an important center for scientific research. The attempts at launching utopian communities made by religious groups were more successful and long-lasting. The Rappites, also known as the Harmony Society, were a group that immigrated from Wurttemberg, Germany, under the leadership of George Rapp in 1803. They were Pietists and millennialists and had been persecuted by the Lutheran Church in Germany. The Rappites first settled in Pennsylvania and established a community where all property was held communally, and the members relinquished all their possessions and worked for the community without pay. They were pious and eschewed sexual relations. By 1814, there were seven hundred members, and the community was very prosperous, with a reputation for producing fine wines, spirits, and textiles. They decided to relocate to Indiana where they could expand. They established a new community that also became financially successful. In 1825, they sold the land to Robert Owen and moved back to Pennsylvania. The Rappites were a long-lasting and successful utopian community, which reached its peak in 1866, but finally dissolved in 1905, after more than a century. Another religious utopian community was founded by John Humphreys Noyes of Brattleboro, Vermont, in the 1850s. This community was called the Oneida Community, and it was located in Oneida, New York. The Oneida Community was different from many of the other religious utopian communities. Like others, they espoused beliefs in social justice. Noyes was a founder of the New Haven Anti-Slavery Society and a strict abolitionist. His followers were dubbed Perfectionists, as they believed that Jesus had already made his Second Coming and therefore the millennium had begun. Humans were already living free of sin, and a perfect society could therefore be established here on the earth. This society, begun in Oneida, with several others established in other states, was communal. What made this one different was its practice of free love, or what Noyes called "complex marriage" and "sexual communism." Members of the community could have sexual relations with any consenting adult in the group, and possessiveness was discouraged. Children were taken away from their mothers and brought up communally. However, women were given more rights than they would have had in outside society, freed from the household constraints of husband and children. The women were encouraged to eschew the corset and the heavy skirts, and instead wear bloomers, which were loose-fitting, knee-length puffy pants. The community lasted for thirty years until, due to infighting, the organization was reconstituted as a joint stock corporation. The Oneida Company, still in business, became known for production of fine silverware, dinnerware, and cookware.

The longest-lasting utopian community of the 19th century was the Shakers. Though it was founded in England in the late 18th century, it had its heyday in the United States between the 1820s and 1860s, with nineteen communities scattered throughout the Northeast, Midwest, and South. This marked the apex of the wave of utopian experimentation. The decline in the Shaker population began after the Civil War, with the Industrial Revolution and with it, the availability of mass-produced products that were less expensive than the Shakers' handmade ones. In addition, more opportunities for well-paid work led to a decrease in the number of new converts, especially men, joining the communities. Surprisingly, however, despite the restrictive rule of maintaining celibacy, the Shakers still exist, in a Shaker village called Sabbathday Lake in Maine. As of 2020, there are two members left. They had an enduring influence in American society, especially with their innovative and proto-modern spare simplicity in architecture, interior design, and furniture, presaging the "Form follows Function" motto of the modernist architects and designers of the late 19th and early 20th centuries. The Shaker songs and dances, which were standardized by the Shaker leadership during the 19th century, also had influence on American culture. The now-famous song, "Simple Gifts," written in 1848 by Elder Joseph Brackett, was memorialized in Aaron Copland's ballet *Appalachian Spring*, written in 1944. A number of former Shaker communities have been preserved as museums, introducing the iconic simplicity and spare beauty of Shaker design to modern society.

FURTHER INFORMATION

Claeys, Gregory, and Lyman T. Sargent. 2017. *The Utopia Reader*. New York: New York University Press.

Jennings, Chris. 2016. *Paradise Now: The Story of American Utopianism*. New York: Random House.

Kapur, Akash. 2016. "The Return of the Utopians." *The New Yorker*. October 3. Accessed February 21, 2020. https://www.newyorker.com /magazine/2016/10/03/the-return-of-the-utopians.

Koomler, Sharon D. 2000. *Shaker Style: Form, Function, and Furniture*. Philadelphia: Running Press Books.

Nicoletta, Julie. September 2003. "The Architecture of Control: Shaker Dwelling Houses and the Reform Movement in Early-Nineteenth-Century America." *Journal of the Society of Architectural Historians*, 62(3): 352–387.

Poppeliers, John C. January 1966. "Shaker Architecture and the Watervliet Shaker South Family." *New York History*, 47 (1): 50–60.

Russell, C. Allyn. January 1968. "The Rise and Decline of the Shakers." *New York History*, 49(1): 29–55.

Vincent, Nicholas C. March 2012. "Shaker Furniture." Heilbrunn Timeline of Art History. New York: The Metropolitan Museum of Art. Accessed February 22, 2020. http://www.metmuseum.org/toah/hd/shak/hd_shak .htm.

Slavery and Servitude

Cotton Gin

Indenture Document

Slave Ankle Shackles

Uncle Tom's Cabin Title Page

36 Cotton Gin

INTRODUCTION

The southern states formed the Confederacy and formally seceded from the Union in 1860, gravely imperiling the future of the United States as a unified nation. There were various explanations for the secession, but the major factor was the South's fear that a Republican president would attempt to abolish slavery. The newly elected president Abraham Lincoln was a Republican, and though he did not campaign on the promise to end slavery, he did advocate for limiting the number of states that permitted the practice. The South emphatically believed that abolishing or even limiting slavery would result in an existential threat to the economy and way of life that had developed in the South in the years since the American Revolution. And what did the southern economy rely on? It depended on the production of one crop in particular, and that crop was cotton. Cotton provided great wealth for most of the southern states. It was sold to mills in New England and Europe, which produced textiles that were sold throughout the United States and the world. However, cotton had not always been the cash cow that propped up the southern economy. Before the invention of the cotton gin, it was a small, niche industry, centered along the coast of Georgia and South Carolina, where a certain type of cotton, called long-staple cotton, could be grown. But after the cotton gin was introduced, the cotton industry expanded throughout the inland South and became known as "King Cotton." The profitable crop led to a continued growth in the slave trade, sustaining the institution of slavery for well into the 19th century.

DESCRIPTION

The cotton gin, a word that is a shortened from the word "engine," is a simple machine that is designed to separate the seeds from the cotton after it has been picked. The first types of cotton gins were called roller gins, and they were effective for removing the seeds from the type of cotton called long-staple or black seed cotton that could be grown in coastal areas of the South. However, the short-staple or green seed cotton, which could be grown in vast regions of the inland or "Upland" South, had many tightly clinging furry seeds that could not be removed with the roller type of gin. Eli Whitney came up with a novel design that could easily remove the seeds from the short-staple cotton variety. A replica of his design, which is shown here, is part of the Smithsonian Museum collection at the National Museum American History. This artifact is a box, open at the top, made of cherry wood, and is 14 inches long by 10 inches high. It has a narrow hand crank that turns a drum with four pulleys. This design was submitted by Eli Whitney to the U.S. Patent Office in 1794. Due to a fire in the Patent Office in 1836, the original model was destroyed, but this model was produced as a replica by Whitney to demonstrate its use in his subsequent patent infringement court cases. The Museum obtained the artifact in 1908.

Eli Whitney was born December 8, 1765, in Westborough, Massachusetts, the son of a farmer who also served as a justice of the peace. As a boy, young Eli was an inveterate tinkerer. He loved to figure out how things worked. He disassembled and then reassembled his father's watch and later built a violin from scratch. At the age of fourteen, he created a lucrative business forging nails and selling them during the Revolutionary War. He went to a private academy in Worcester, Massachusetts, and later to Yale College in New Haven, Connecticut, to prepare for a career in teaching or law. Whitney was a quick learner, and he graduated Phi Beta Kappa after only three years in 1792. Needing additional funds to continue his studies, he decided to take on work as a tutor and found a position in Georgia on the plantation of Catherine Littlefield Greene, widow of the Revolutionary War hero Nathanael Greene. At Mulberry Grove plantation, Whitney met his soon-to-be business partner Phineas Miller, another Yale graduate who would later marry Catherine Greene. Miller was employed as the plantation manager at the time. Impressed with Whitney's skill in fixing and inventing machines, Catherine Greene introduced him to some of her friends and business associates who were searching for a method of removing the sticky little seeds from short-staple cotton. Plantation owners were looking for a profitable crop that could replace tobacco, which had depleted the soil, and also faced falling market value due to Caribbean competition. Cotton was that lucrative crop that became a major player in the Industrial Revolution, first in England and subsequently in the United States. The short-staple variety of cotton could be grown in many parts of the South. But the yield was very low, as the cotton seeds had to be painstakingly removed by hand. One person, working all day, could successfully remove the seeds and end up with only 4–8 pounds of usable cotton. If only there were a machine that could mechanically remove the seeds from the cotton bolls, cotton could be a highly profitable crop. Eli Whitney decided to take on this challenge and design a machine that could separate the green seeds from the short-staple cotton.

While there were various machines that had been used for centuries to separate seeds from cotton, none of them were usable with short-staple cotton. These "gins" were called roller gins, and they effectively removed seeds from long-staple cotton. The roller gins consisted of two rods that turned against each other and pinched out the smooth black seeds from the fluffy white cotton. The roller gin was not at all effective with short-staple cotton. In order to conjure up a design that would solve this problem, Eli Whitney secreted himself in a workshop on Catherine Greene's plantation. Ten days later, he presented a new type of cotton gin that could separate the sticky green seeds. This gin used wire teeth that pulled the cotton through a metal grate, separating the seeds from the cotton and allowing the clean cotton to pass through and leaving the seeds behind. Brushes removed the fiber from the teeth. The simple machine cleaned ten times more cotton in a day than was previously attainable by the hand-removal method. Though the cotton that was produced through this method was rougher and of lower quality than the hand-cleaned cotton because the fibers had been cut in the machine, it was still usable. This cotton gin, because of its ability to increase production tenfold, could mean huge profits for the plantation owners in the Upland South, who were anxiously awaiting the new labor-saving device.

Eli Whitney knew that his novel invention would appeal to farmers in the South and would also attract copycats. He applied to the federal government for a patent on March 14, 1794. This was in the early days of the American federal government, but the concept of patents was enshrined in the Constitution, which gave Congress the authority "to promote the

---

Eli Whitney remained an inventor during his lifetime. Because of his unending litigation over patent infringements, he never made any money on his most famous invention, the cotton gin, but he did become prosperous later. In 1797, he signed a contract with the federal government to produce ten thousand muskets in two years in order to prepare for a possible war with France. To accomplish this feat, he would design machine tools that would allow unskilled workers to produce identical individual parts that would produce a musket with interchangeable parts. By doing this, each musket could be repaired with parts from other muskets. Though he was not successful in producing the ten thousand muskets in two years, he did it in ten years. He was criticized for the time it took and the cost he charged, but his records were so detailed and his accounting so pristine, the government accepted his fee. Whitney has been credited with inventing the concept of interchangeable parts, as well as with the concept of total cost accounting and economic efficiency in manufacturing. Although others have since been given the credit for inventing interchangeable parts, Whitney did popularize the concept.

progress of science and useful arts by securing for limited times to writers and inventors the exclusive right to their respective writings and inventions" (Kurin 2013: 137) in Article I. However, patents were not easily obtained at that time, and Thomas Jefferson, the secretary of state, who was given responsibility to manage the patent application process, was not a fan of the policy. He preferred the free distribution of knowledge without the constraints imposed by a patent process. Whitney submitted his application to Jefferson, which included a description, drawing, and model of his invention. Though Whitney would eventually obtain a patent for his cotton gin, it would not be established until 1807, and many copies of the products proliferated during that period. Eli Whitney would spend more than a decade filing patent infringement lawsuits. Because of the cost of the litigation, he never made much money on his most famous invention.

SIGNIFICANCE

Despite the fact that Eli Whitney did not personally profit significantly from his invention of the short-staple cotton gin, the effect of its invention on American history was significant. The plantation owners were looking for a crop that would be profitable, and cotton was extremely so. The technological advancements in textile production that took place in England, sparking the Industrial Revolution, made raw American cotton a crucial export to English mills. Because of the cotton gin, by 1810, 93 million pounds of cotton were exported, a colossal increase from the meager 500,000 pounds exported in 1793. Cotton was an exceptional product to export—it did not degrade and could easily be shipped overseas. It became the young country's biggest export; in fact, it constituted over half of all American exports. When New England constructed its first textile mills in the early 19th century, the cotton industry in the South expanded even more, reaching 2 billion pounds in 1860. Ironically, however, the invention of the cotton gin, a labor-saving device, led to an escalated demand for cheap labor as the production swelled all over the South and agricultural workers were needed to pick the cotton. These workers were African American slaves, and the elevation of the cotton crop to "King Cotton" resulted in the expansion of the slave trade in the South. The first American census reported seven hundred thousand slaves, but by 1860, there were four million. The seemingly inexhaustible thirst for new territory to plant cotton resulted in the forced removal of the Native American tribes from their land in southern states to Oklahoma in 1830 in the infamous "Trail of Tears." Southern states fought to admit new states as slave states. The demand for slave labor to pick the powerful King Cotton eventually precipitated the secession of the southern states and the Civil War.

FURTHER INFORMATION

Aikin, Charles S. April 1973. "The Evolution of Cotton Ginning in the Southeastern United States." *Geographical Review*, 63(2): 196–224.

Grove, Tim. 2014. *A Grizzly in the Mail and Other Adventures in American History*. Lincoln: University of Nebraska Press.

Kurin, Richard. 2013. *The Smithsonian's History of America in 101 Objects*. New York: Penguin Books.

Rogers, Molly. 2010. *Delia's Tears*. New Haven, CT: Yale University Press.

THIS Indenture Witnesseth, That

Edward Procter, Henry Hill, William Smith, William Phillips, Redford Webster, Thomas Perkins, Benj. Goddard, Samuel Snelling, Samuel Clap, Ozias Goodwin, William Mackay, Joseph Coolidge Jun. Esquires

Overseers of the Poor of the Town of *Boston*, in the County of *Suffolk*, and Commonwealth of *Massachusetts*, have placed, and by these Presents do place and bind out *John Adams Mann, unto Mr David Parker jun. of Reading, in the County of Middlesex, to his Wife, and their Heirs.*

and with *them* after the Manner of an Apprentice to Dwell and Serve, from the Day of the Date of these Presents, until the *Eighteenth day of May one Thousand, Eight Hundred and twenty. At which time, if the said Apprentice be living he will arrive at the age of twenty one years.*

And the said Master *doth hereby Covenant and Agree, himself, his Wife, and their Heirs, to teach the said Apprentice, or cause him to be taught, to Read, Write, & Cypher, also the art & Mistrey of a farmer.*

And also shall and will, well and truly find, allow unto and provide for the said Apprentice, sufficient and wholesome Meat and Drink, with Washing, Lodging, *Cloathing,* and other Necessaries meet and convenient for such an Apprentice, during all the Time or Term aforesaid : And at the Expiration thereof shall *dismiss the said Apprentice, with two Good Suits of wearing Apparel fitting all parts of his Body one for Sundays the other for Working Days. Suitable to his degree. and seventy Dollars in Cash.*

IN TESTIMONY WHEREOF, the said Parties have to these Indentures interchangeably set their Hands and Seals, the *Sixth* Day of *April.* in the Year of our LORD, One Thousand Eight Hundred and *four.*

Signed, Sealed and Delivered
in Presence of

Constant Freeman
Susanna Freeman

David Parker Jun.

37 Indenture Document

INTRODUCTION

During the 17th to early 19th centuries, human labor was at a premium in the vast but sparsely populated lands of North America. This shortage led to two means of providing cheap labor to American society: indentured servitude and slavery. An indentured servant was bound to his or her master through a legal contract to repay an indenture, or a loan, within a set time period. It may be surprising to learn that as many as half of the Europeans who immigrated to North America during the 17th and 18th centuries arrived as indentured servants. The system began as early as 1607 in Jamestown, Virginia, following the settlement of Jamestown by the London Company of Virginia. The company developed a system of indenture for needy European workers who were left impoverished by the Thirty Years' War. They were offered passage on a ship to the new colony in exchange for a number of years' work for a family. The contract usually lasted for between four and seven years, during which time the worker received passage to the colony and room and board. Upon termination of the contract, the indentured servant was promised certain items, which often included a parcel of land and some food and clothing in order to make a new start in the New World.

The lot of the indentured servants was never easy, as many got sick or even died on the excruciating journey across the sea. Those who made it were often subjected to harsh treatment from the masters, who were determined to squeeze every bit of manual labor out of the servant in the limited years of indenture. This system worked during the 17th and 18th centuries, as thousands of new Americans flooded into the colonies as indentured servants. Many of them had been recruited by agents, called "spirits" in Britain who induced or even kidnapped children and desperate adults with promises of a better life in the New World. In addition, a successful advertising campaign organized by the London Company and subsequently other companies ensnared despairing and impoverished Europeans to sign contracts for indenture. In the years before the Industrial Revolution in England, there were many penniless families who had been unemployed for generations. An early statistician, Gregory King, estimated that more than half the population in England in 1688 was earning less than they spent, leading to widespread poverty and diminishing the countrywide wealth. In addition to the indentured who voluntarily offered to travel to America, there were a second, smaller set, this one "undesirables" that consisted of debtors, paupers, orphans, or even political agitators. The "spirits" who convinced many of these poor Englishmen to try their luck in the colonies, many of them under totally false pretenses, were considered to be relieving the country of its surplus population. By the 18th century, similar techniques were employed in other parts of Europe, in Ireland, Germany, Holland, and Switzerland. Most of these immigrants were sent to the colonies south of New Jersey, or the British colonies in the Caribbean, where the small family farm was evolving into large tobacco, sugar, or cotton plantations, and human labor was most needed.

DESCRIPTION

The colonies of New England also utilized the indenture system, but it differed in intent and method. The indentured servants in New England were most often not indentured as a payment for passage to America. They were children and teens of residents who were too poor to care for their families. The system that was organized in Boston as well as in the other New England colonies was based on precedent of English Poor Laws, specifically the Act for the Relief of the Poor, passed in 1597. The influence of the English precedent was to codify the compulsory support of the poor, assigning civic responsibility for financial and administrative control. Although in England the Church of England played a role in poor relief, in New England the government took on the role. In Boston, the Massachusetts Township Act was passed in 1692, officially delegating responsibility for the care of the poor to a board that was called the Overseers of the Poor. They were chosen by the Town Selectmen until 1708, when the laws were amended to have the Overseers voted on during the Town Meeting. In 1735, Boston expanded to twelve wards, and therefore there were twelve Overseers. In 1772, the Overseers were incorporated, and their power within the community was immense. As the highest-ranking civic official under the Town Selectman, the Overseer had primary control over a large budget as well as over the personal distribution of all charitable donations to the poor. They patrolled the ward and looked for any family that might be in need of relief or correction, sending them to the almshouse, also known as the poorhouse, or to the punitive workhouse. If need be, the Overseer would recommend a term of indentured servitude for the children.

Children, who were identified as being at risk, either from being orphaned or being from a destitute or deviant family, could be "bound out." Binding out was a method of providing cheap labor in a perpetually tight labor market. It was also considered a moral way to provide a proper home for the child according to the religious and social standards of the community. The method of "binding out" was considered a benefit to both the children and to society in general. The term of service averaged ten years, depending on the age of the child, usually for a boy until he was twenty-one and for a girl until she was eighteen. The child served as a servant or an apprentice, and conditions varied depending on the family. However, by contract and by law, the host family was required to teach boys to read and write while teaching the girls to read only. The Overseer's task was to connect the children to appropriate families that were in need of extra hands around the house and the farm. Generally, the boys were taught a trade or animal husbandry, while the girls were taught to be domestic servants. Some of the children who were bound out became successful in their later lives. Usually, the conditions for the children were preferable to living in the almshouse, or workhouse. This method of indenture persisted for many years in Boston, and there were approximately 1,100 children bound out by the Overseers between 1734 and 1805.

The artifact shown here is an Indenture Document dating from April 6, 1804, from the town of Reading, north of Boston. The indentured servant is named John Adams Mann, and the master is David Parker Jr. The Indenture Document is shown here, and also included is the Endorsement Certificate. They are in the Rare Books Department of the Boston Public Library.

INDENTURE DOCUMENT FORM

This Indenture Witnesseth, That

Edward Proctor, Henry Hill, William Smith, William Phillips, Redford Webster, Thomas Perkins, Benjamin Goddard, Samual Snelling, Samuel Clap, Ozias Goodwin, William MacKay, Jaseph Coolidge, jed.Esquires

Overseers of the Poor of the Town of Boston, in the County of Suffolk, and Commonwealth of Massachusetts, have placed and by these Presents do place and bind out

John Adams Mann, unto Mr. David Parker jw. of Reading, in the County of Middlesex, to his wife, and their Heirs.

And with *them* after the Manner of an Apprentice to Dwell and Serve, from the Day of the Date of these Presents, until the *Eighteenth day of May, one Thousand, Eight Hundred and twenty. At which time, if the said Apprentice be living, he will arrive at the age of twenty one years.*

And the said Master _____ doth hereby Covenant and Agree, *himself, his wife, and their Heirs, to teach the said Apprentice, or cause him to be taught to Read, Write & Cypher, also the Arts & Mastery of a farmer.*

And also shall and will, well and truly find, allow unto and provide for the said Apprentice, sufficient and wholesome Meat and Drink, with Washing, Lodging, *Clothing,* _____ and other necessaries meet and convenient for such an Apprentice during all the Time or Term Aforesaid: And at the expiration shall *Dismiss the said Apprentice with two good suits of wearing apparel fitting all parts of his body, one for Sundays, the other for working days. Suitable to his degree, and seven dollars in cash.*

IN TESTIMONY WHEREOF, the said Parties have to these Indentures interchangeably set their Hands and Seals the *Sixth* day of *April* in the Year of Our Lord, Eighteen Hundred and *Four.*

Signed, Sealed and Delivered,
In Presence of
Constant Freeman
Susanna Freeman   David Parker, Jr.

ENDORSEMENT CERTIFICATE

Reading 26th March 1804—

We the Subscriber Selectmen of the town of Reading do hereby certify that David Parker of (Boston?) is a freeholder and an inhabitant of said town, and a fit and proper person to take a child or children to bring up—that he would give them good treatment, good instructions, and perform those stimulations which are required, or are customary as it respects apprentices.

James Gould
Edmon Damon
Selectmen of Reading

SIGNIFICANCE

Not all immigrants came to the United States bursting with ambition and with money in their pockets, anxious to begin again in a new, egalitarian classless society. As Nancy Isenberg so bluntly puts it in her recent book, *White Trash: The 400-Year History of Class in America*, for many years the United States served as a dumping ground for an excess population in war-ravaged Europe. These desperate people were what she calls "waste people" (Isenberg 2016: xv). Many of these folks came as indentured servants or became indentured by virtue of their poverty. Although they may have had more opportunity here that in class-bound Europe, their prospects here in the New World remained limited. The Puritans believed that poverty was ordained by the higher power and therefore inevitable. Alleviating the suffering of the poor was part of Christian charity, but eliminating it wasn't even considered. The thousands of indentured servants who arrived on our shores did gain their freedom and benefited from the fact that they were white, but many did not move up in society significantly. The majority of the indentured servants from Europe arrived at the large plantations in the southern colonies, where large crews of farm workers were necessary. After the period of indenture, the workers were freed. The height of the period indentured servants ended in the early 19th century as the demand for labor grew, especially in the South, and the cost of maintaining indentured servants proved prohibitive to southern plantation owners. The answer was to turn to African slaves, an expensive but self-perpetuating option. Slaves were never freed, and they and their progeny remained chattel for the slave owner, until the Emancipation Proclamation in 1863. All forms of indenture were banned in the Thirteenth Amendment of the Constitution, passed in 1865.

FURTHER INFORMATION

Abramitzky, Ran, and Fabio Braggion. December 2006. "Migration and Human Capital: Self-Selection of Indentured Servants to the Americas." *Journal of Economic History*, 66(4): 882–905.

Galenson, David. W. May 1980. "White Servitude and the Growth of Black Slavery in Colonial America." California Institute of Technology. Accessed June 2, 2021. https://authors.library.caltech.edu/82103/1/sswp318.pdf.

Hardesty, Jared R. 2016. *Unfreedom: Slavery and Dependence in Eighteenth Century Boston*. New York; London: New York University Press.

Hofstadter, Richard. 1971. "White Servitude." In *America at 1750: A Social Portrait*, 35–65. New York: Knopf.

"Indentured Servants in the U.S." 2003–2014. History Detectives Special Investigations. PBS. Oregon Public Broadcasting. Accessed June 2, 2021. https://www.pbs.org/opb/historydetectives/feature/indentured-servants-in-the-us/.

Isenberg, Nancy. 2016. *White Trash: The 400-Year History of Class in America*. New York: Viking.

Nellis, Eric, and Anne D. Cecere. 2006. *The Eighteenth Century Records of the Boston Overseers of the Poor*. Boston: The Colonial Society of Massachusetts.

Tomlins, Christopher L. 2010. *Freedom Bound: Law, Labor, and Civic Identity in Colonizing English America, 1580–1865*. New York: Cambridge University Press. Reviewed by Linda Sturtz. Accessed June 2, 2021. https://www.h-net.org/reviews/showrev.php?id=32263.

Wagner, D. 2005. *The Poorhouse: America's Forgotten Institution*. Lanham, MD: Rowman-Littlefield Publishers.

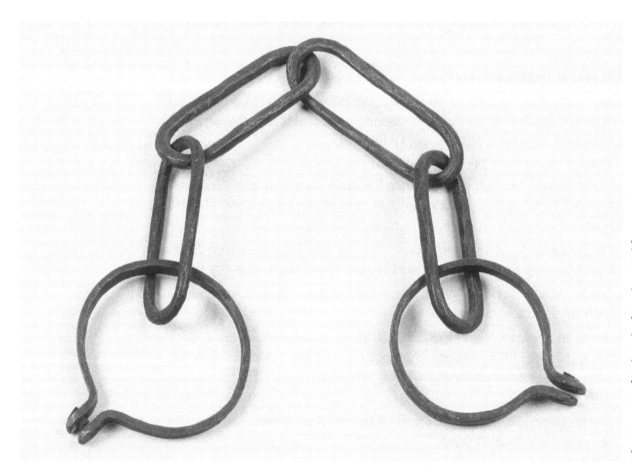

38 Slave Ankle Shackles

INTRODUCTION

The scourge of slavery, the capturing of human beings and enslaving them against their will, has been labeled the United States' original sin. Nineteenth-century South Carolina politician John C. Calhoun euphemistically called slavery America's "peculiar institution" in 1830, making it appear more paternalistic and less brutal than it actually was. But brutal it was, and continued to be, from the capturing of tribal members in Africa to the holding cells on the West African coast to the horrific journey through the so-called Middle Passage to the sale of the slaves to the lives lived by the slaves once landing at the plantation in the South. There were a variety of instruments of torture that were utilized to punish perceived infractions or merely to assert dominance. These instruments were used to physically restrain slaves for centuries, beginning with the first slave ship to arrive in Jamestown, Virginia, in 1619, up to and after the emancipation of the slaves by Abraham Lincoln in 1862. Some of the most common forms of restraint were ankle shackles.

DESCRIPTION

Ankle shackles were a type of restraining device placed around the ankles of a slave or prisoner. They were one of the instruments of bondage preferred by slave masters. The slave shackles shown in this example were used, astonishingly, in 1866, four years after the emancipation of the slaves and a year after the passage of the Thirteenth Amendment, officially freeing the slaves. The shackles are made of steel, with round cuffs and a soldered leg closure. There are four oval chain links connecting the two ankle cuffs. They were donated to the New York Historical Society in 1921. The story of these shackles is both distressing and heartwarming. In 1866, a former slave-owning legislator and judge from Americus, Georgia, disregarded the laws being put in place by Reconstruction. He placed these shackles on the ankles of a pretty, seventeen-year-old, named Mary Horn, who was still being retained, illegally, on the judge's plantation as a slave. She was in love with a man named George who lived on a nearby plantation and was hoping to marry him. In order to prevent Mary from running away to George, she was repeatedly shackled by the judge and was forced for weeks to work in the plantation cornfields with the shackles painfully cutting into her ankles. The 176th Regiment, New York Volunteers, came to town with Lieutenant Colonel William W. Badger at the lead. Badger served as the provost marshal of Sumter County, Georgia. George heard about their presence in town, and he made a request to Badger that his fiancée be released from the shackles and freed. Badger accompanied George to the plantation where Mary was being held. Seeing that her ankles were "wrapped with rags to prevent their galling the flesh" (Holzer 2013: 4), he pierced the rivets that held the shackles on with a chisel as George held Mary over the anvil. And so, the shackles were literally and figuratively removed from Mary Horn's ankles and she was freed. Colonel Badger then officiated at the marriage of George and Mary. The judge was tried in military court and jailed. When released from jail, he returned to the plantation, where a violent protest by the former slaves took place, and George killed the judge. This type of protest was not unusual after the Civil War. The Union forces assigned to the South were aware that the plantation culture was going to be hard to defeat. Many southern plantation owners still held the power over their former slaves and refused to let it go.

Ankle shackles were used on the infamous "Middle Passage" voyage that brought slaves from Africa to the plantations in North and South America and the islands of the Caribbean. In the "First Passage" of the journey, slaves were captured by African rulers who worked in concert with the European slave traders. They would procure these slaves through various methods that included trade, warfare, and kidnapping from regions of the interior of Africa. Placed in chains and ropes, the procurers would force-march the slaves in human caravans called coffles. When they arrived at the western coast of Africa, regions that are now located in parts of Ghana, Gambia, and Senegal, they were herded into pens called barracoons and imprisoned in so-called slave factories. When a slave ship would come, the representatives of the trading company could purchase them for transport across the Atlantic Ocean to the Americas. Half of the twenty million captured Africans did not survive the horrific journey to the coast. The ones who did were branded and awaited purchase for up to a year. When purchased, they would be loaded onto the specially designed slave ships for the months-long trip called the Middle Passage. These ships accommodated 450 or more slaves in lower decks with less than 5 feet of headroom. A second level of sleeping accommodation consisted of shelves along the outside of the hull that reduced the headroom even more. Shackles, also known as bilboes after their origin in Bilbao, Spain, were utilized on these slave ships, usually at the beginning and end of the journey when the slave traders feared that the sight of land would lead to insurrection. The shackles tightly bound one slave to the next in sets of two by shackling the right leg of one slave to the left leg of the next. The small openings of the shackles tore into the flesh of the slaves' legs. In addition, the lack of sanitation, fresh air, and food led to horrific epidemics onboard the ship. Upon arrival at the port in one of the slave trading centers in the Americas, the slaves would be sold again to the plantation owners and forced to travel the last leg of the journey in what is known as the Final Passage. The slave trade consisted of a system that became known as the triangular trade. The first leg of the trading system was the transport of manufactured goods like guns, cloth, ironware, and liquor from Europe to Africa. In exchange for these goods, the traders would purchase slaves and transport them to the Americas for the sale of slaves on plantations. The third leg of the triangular trade was the transport of raw materials like sugar, tobacco, and cotton from the plantations in the Americas and the Caribbean back to Europe. Another version of this triangular trade system substituted the New England states for Europe, transporting sugar to New England and rum and other manufactured goods to Africa.

LONNIE BUNCH CONTEMPLATES SLAVE SHACKLES

The secretary of the Smithsonian Institution, founding director of the Smithsonian's National Museum of African American History and Culture, and also a noted historian of African American history, Lonnie Bunch, has remarked that he makes a point of thinking about the slave ankle shackles that are on display at the museum every single day, noting that the experience "is the closest I come to understanding my slave ancestors" (Kurin 2013: 77).

SIGNIFICANCE

American slaves were forced onto slave ships and transported to this country against their will. Once here, they were considered property and compelled to perform a variety of tasks under the threat of humiliation and violent suppression. They were separated from their families and denied the right to an education. Although there were still a small number of slaves in the northern states for the first few decades of the 19th century, by 1804, all the northern states had officially abolished the practice. It was the southern states that depended on slave labor in order to fuel the economy. After the invention of the cotton gin, the number of slaves and dependence on slave labor exploded as cotton became the lifeblood of the South. The necessity of keeping slaves under control began in the infamous Middle

Passage, where torturous restraints like ankle shackles were used to control grieving slaves seeing their homeland for the last time. Plantation owners in the South continued the practice of restraining their slaves through the use of physical restraints. Even the revered general, leader, and first president of the United States and "Father of Our Country" George Washington had over three hundred slaves when he died in 1799. He called for all his slaves to be freed upon his wife Martha's death. Since he had no heirs, he could do it without incident. However, his wife did no such thing but left her slaves in her will to her grandchildren. Washington had mixed feelings about the institution of slavery. But during his life, Washington was known to agree to the use of violence in keeping his slaves under control. In 1793, his farm manager Anthony Whiting reported that he had "gave . . . a very good Whiping" to the seamstress Charlotte in order to "lower her Spirit or skin her Back." Washington replied to his manager that the treatment was "very proper" and that "if she, or any other of the Servants will not do their duty by fair means, or are impertinent, correction . . . must be administered" (George Washington to Anthony Whiting, January 20, 1793). While he was president, Washington lived in New York for the first term and Philadelphia for the second term. He opted to take a number of slaves with him while president. However, the Gradual Abolition Act of 1780 in Pennsylvania allowed slaves to be freed after six months. In order to avoid the abolition of his slaves, Washington secretly exchanged his slaves with new ones every six months. In addition, he signed the first fugitive slave act in 1793, sanctioning the seizure of escaped slaves in any state, after which they would be tried and returned to their owners. He found himself in an uncomfortable position in 1796, when one of the Washington's slaves, twenty-two-year old Ona Judge, ran away from their home in Philadelphia. Martha Washington was planning to give her away as a wedding gift to her granddaughter. Washington pursued her for three years, up until his death in 1799. The escaped slave Ona Judge, however, successfully eluded capture and lived a quiet life in Portsmouth, New Hampshire, getting married and having three children while legally still belonging to George Washington, who at the time of her escape was the president of the United States. As can be seen by the evidence of the 1866 slave shackles, the use of physical restraints as a method to control slaves did not end with the official abolition of slavery. Holding human beings as slaves was a brutal and abhorrent practice that propped up an economy that depended on it for its very survival. It was not what John C. Calhoun portrayed as a "peculiar institution" in 1830.

FURTHER INFORMATION

Dunbar, Erica A. 2015. "George Washington, Slave Catcher." *New York Times*. February 16. Accessed April 29, 2020. https://www.nytimes.com/2015/02/16/opinion/george-washington-slave-catcher.html.

Holzer, Harold. 2013. *The Civil War in 50 Objects*. New York: Viking.

Kurin, Richard. 2013. *The Smithsonian's History of America in 101 Objects*. New York: Penguin Books.

Littlefield, Daniel C. "The Varieties of Slave Labor." Freedom's Story, TeacherServe. National Humanities Center. Accessed April 26, 2020. http://nationalhumanitiescenter.org/tserve/freedom/1609-1865/essays/slavelabor.htm.

Malcolm, Corey. October, 1998. "The Iron Bilboes of the *Henrietta Marie*." *The Navigator: Newsletter of the Mel Fisher Maritime Heritage Society*, 13(10): 1.

"Slave Control." *The Digital Encyclopedia of George Washington*. Mount Vernon Ladies' Association. Accessed April 26, 2020. https://www.mountvernon.org/library/digitalhistory/digital-encyclopedia/article/slave-control/.

UNCLE TOM'S CABIN;

OR,

LIFE AMONG THE LOWLY.

BY

HARRIET BEECHER STOWE.

VOL. I.

ONE HUNDRED AND FIFTH THOUSAND.

BOSTON:
JOHN P. JEWETT & COMPANY
CLEVELAND, OHIO:
JEWETT, PROCTOR & WORTHINGTON.
1852.

39 *Uncle Tom's Cabin* Title Page

INTRODUCTION

A 2007 Pulitzer Prize–winning biography, written by historian Debby Applegate, was titled *The Most Famous Man in America: The Biography of Henry Ward Beecher*. This man, an evangelical preacher who shot to the top of the national consciousness through his forceful and appealing oratorical style, his fervent support for abolition, and his widely publicized trial for adultery, is barely remembered today despite his notoriety during the 19th century. Henry Ward Beecher was a member of the Beecher clan, a New England family that had oversized influence on American culture. In fact, it was Henry Beecher's older sister, Harriet Beecher Stowe, who has been acclaimed as the most famous woman in both the United States and the western world during the 19th century. Her total dominance throughout American society, both in the North and in Europe, where she was revered, and in the South, where she was despised, is scarcely acknowledged today. How did this mid-19th century acclaim arise? It was because Harriet, like her brother, an ardent abolitionist, wrote the book that sold more copies worldwide during the 19th century than any other book besides the Bible. This book, a passionate screed against the inhumanity of slavery, was called *Uncle Tom's Cabin*.

Harriet Beecher Stowe came from a family of Congregational preachers. Born in Litchfield, Connecticut, in 1811, Harriet moved to Cincinnati at the age of twenty-one when her father took a position as president at Lane Theological Seminary. It was during her eighteen years there that Harriet met and married a minister and faculty member at the Seminary, Calvin Stowe. Married for fifty years, Harriet and Calvin had six children. Harriet was always interested in writing and activism and, like her father and her eight siblings, despised the institution of slavery. Growing up in Connecticut, Harriet could only malign slavery hypothetically, from afar. But this was not true in the border city of Cincinnati. In Cincinnati, which was located right across the Ohio River from the slave state of Kentucky, Harriet was brutally exposed to a close-up observation of the inhumanities of the slave trade. Harriet witnessed a slave auction, where children were yanked from the arms of their mothers as families were split up and sold. Having lost her beloved eighteen-month-old son Charley to cholera, Harriet was keenly attuned to the pain of losing a child. She also confronted the chaos in the region as race riots took place and fugitive slaves hid from bounty hunters. The whole model of a slave-dependent society was right in your face in this slavery-border town. Harriet, whose husband was not wealthy, had difficulty paying the bills and caring for her growing family. As an aspiring writer, her stressful situation left little time for her to apply to her craft. It was not a happy phase of her life. She returned to New England in 1850 when her husband, Calvin, took a faculty position at Bowdoin College in Brunswick, Maine. Here she would begin her book *Uncle Tom's Cabin*, using the knowledge and understanding she obtained while living in Cincinnati.

The entire Beecher clan, even the ones in placid New England, had been enraged by the passage of the Fugitive Slave Act. This law, a part of the 1850 Missouri Compromise, required all free persons in both the North and the South to turn in fugitive slaves under penalty of law, up to $1,000 fine or six months in jail. For the first time, northern residents, who disapproved of slavery but were able to shut their eyes to it as long as it was a southern practice, were now forced to confront it head-on. Harriet's sister-in-law, Isabella Porter Beecher, begged her to use her literary skills to write about the inhumanity of slavery. Harriet, armed with the painful knowledge obtained during her years in a border state, as well as the sorrow of losing her son, began writing the book that would make her incredibly famous. A devout Christian, Harriet would later insist that God relayed the story to her through a vision.

DESCRIPTION

The image shown here is the title page of the first edition of *Uncle Tom's Cabin, or, Life Among the Lowly*, written by Harriet Beecher Stowe, published by the John P. Jewett & Company, Cleveland, Ohio, in 1852. The book, published in two volumes, was originally published as forty weekly installments in the abolitionist newspaper *The National Era* in 1851. Stowe promoted the story to the newspaper as a "word picture of slavery." The popularity of the story in the newspaper convinced the publisher to print it on March 20, 1852. The book sold three thousand copies in the first day, with the entire print run—five thousand copies—sold within the first four days. On May 3, 1852, the *Boston Morning Post* declared that "everyone has read it, or is about to read it" (Brock 2018). With seventeen printing presses running round the clock, the book sold three hundred thousand copies in the first year. In Britain, a less expensive print version sold 1.5 million copies in one year. It was a true phenomenon.

The first edition of the book was illustrated with six engraved full-page illustrations. This was an unusual expense for a first printing, but Stowe's publisher was confident that it would sell, and illustrated books were popular. The illustrator was Hammatt Billings, a trained architect who began working as a draftsman in the 1840s and then became chief illustrator of the weekly, *Gleason's Pictorial Drawing-Room Companion*. He also designed the masthead, allegedly at no cost, for the abolitionist newspaper *The Liberator*, produced by the influential abolitionist leader William Lloyd Garrison. The image on the title page depicts Aunt Chloe, Uncle Tom's long-suffering wife, in the cabin doorway. The image recalls a portrayal of a slave cabin that was depicted on Billings' already-produced *Liberator* masthead. The characters depicted in the engraving are Chloe, Tom, and their children Mose, Pete, and Baby. Billings was not given credit in the book for these engravings. The illustrations were a popular feature of the book, and some of them were reproduced over many years.

Uncle Tom's Cabin tells the parallel stories of two slaves, Tom and Eliza, who were owned by a Kentucky plantation owner, a mild-mannered but cash-starved man named Arthur Shelby. When faced with a major debt to a slave trader, George was forced to sell his best slave Tom as well as Eliza's charming young son, Harry. This is where the two plot lines diverge. Tom, a hard-working and strong man who was also a devout Christian, is sent "down the river" to be resold in the slave market in New Orleans. Being sold down the river was a desperate fate for a slave. Working in a border state like Kentucky, slaves had a modicum of freedom, as well the possible opportunity to escape. But in the Deep South, slaves were isolated on huge plantations where the idea of escaping to freedom became a mere pipe dream. But since the international slave trade had been banned, and cotton production was booming, slaves were desperately needed on the cotton plantations. More than a million slaves were shipped from the border states into the Deep South between 1790 and 1860. Tom knew this and feared the worst. However, while traveling, he serendipitously encounters a girl named Evangeline, also known as Little Eva, who takes a liking to Tom and convinces her father to buy Tom. Her father, Augustine St. Clare, though a slaveholder, is ardently anti-slavery, and he treats his slaves well. Tom was beloved by the St. Clare family and the other slaves. Sadly, Augustine is accidently killed just before he signs the manumission papers freeing Tom. When the estate is liquidated, Augustine's wife sells Tom to a cruel plantation owner named Simon Legree. Intimidated by his popularity and his devout Christian faith, Legree resolves to beat Tom to death. Arthur Shelby's son George is on his way to buy Tom's freedom, but he arrives too late. Tom, portrayed as a Christ-figure by Stowe, is dead. The story of the other slave, the young Harry, has a happier ending. Eliza, hearing that her beloved Harry would be sold, decides to run away across the frozen Ohio

River. Her husband George, working on another plantation, has already run away. They meet up and, with the help of some Quakers and the Underground Railroad, eventually make it to Canada where they can live free. In the parallel plots, and in Stowe's Christian view, both slaves achieve their freedom, though in Tom's case it is as a martyr, after death.

SIGNIFICANCE

Uncle Tom's Cabin was one of the most influential books written in the 19th century, and its popularity spanned many decades and into the 20th century. It persuaded much of American society to agree with the abolitionist cause, as readers sympathized with the slave characters depicted in the book. Stowe's activist objective was to write a book that would demonstrate the inhumanity and moral corruption of the institution of slavery. She was wildly successful in her narrative, both in the non-slave states of the Union and in Europe. In the slave-dependent South, the book hatched an anti-Tom movement and a bevy of books and articles that were written to counteract the anti-slavery message. These endeavored to establish that the lives of slaves in the South were benign, that slaves-owners were kind and benevolent, and that the tales of cruelty told by Stowe were highly exaggerated. Stowe reacted by writing another book in 1853 called *The Key to Uncle Tom's Cabin: Presenting the Original Facts and Documents upon Which the Story Is Founded, Together with Corroborative Statements Verifying the Truth of the Work*, where she defended the facts and origins of her stories. Her life in Cincinnati as an abolitionist had enlightened her to the conditions faced by African Americans, both slave and free. In addition, she based much of her story of Tom on the 1849 memoir of a slave named Josiah Henson, who Stowe credited in her 1853 book.

Uncle Tom's Cabin also spawned a whole industry of popular trinkets that depicted the characters of the book in plates, vases, cups, figurines, card games, songs, handkerchiefs, and all types of so-called tie-ins that were inspired by the book. Copyright laws did not protect a book's characters, images, or objects from reproducing them for profit until the second decade of the 20th century, so Harriet Beecher Stowe did not monetarily benefit from this plethora of Tom-related merchandise. Another outgrowth of the book was the proliferation of "Tom shows," stage adaptations that introduced the story to a whole new group of working-class white Americans. Though the adaptations performed in the 1850s were true to the book, after the Civil War, the portrayals changed. With the end of Reconstruction and the onset of the Jim Crow era, *Uncle Tom's Cabin* shows began to use racist tropes and minstrel-type performers in their popular productions. This perversion of Tom's character portrayal as a heroic and noble Christ-like figure in the book was soon reviled as a modern version of the "Uncle Tom," an African American who is a servile sellout to his race. Harriet Beecher

Stowe has taken more hits in modern criticism. Her writing has been savaged for being too melodramatic and sentimental, as has her antiquated uses of the language of race. Twentieth-century critics like James Baldwin have attacked the book as well for the passivity of Tom's suffering. However, some academics have recently given Stowe's work a re-appraisal, condemning her critics as sexist for criticizing her writing while praising other male writers of the time and defending her powerful act of persuasion. As Annette Gordon-Reed states in her article "The Art of Persuasion: Harriet Beecher's Stowe's Uncle Tom's Cabin," the book was "a cri de coeur to the American people, one that forced them to ask what kind of country they wanted their nation to be" (Gordon-Reed 2011).

FURTHER INFORMATION

Ammons, Elizabeth (ed.). 2018. *Uncle Tom's Cabin Norton Critical Edition*. New York; London: W.W. Norton and Co.

Brock, Jared. 2018. "The Story of Josiah Henson, the Real Inspiration behind 'Uncle Tom's Cabin.'" *Smithsonian Magazine*. May 16. Accessed November 20, 2020. https://www.smithsonianmag.com/history/story-josiah-henson-real-inspiration-uncle-toms-cabin-180969094/.

DeCanio, Stephen J. Fall 1990. "'Uncle Tom's Cabin': A Reappraisal." *Centennial Review*, 34(4): 587–593.

Gordon-Reed, Annette. 2011. "The Art of Persuasion: Harriet Beecher Stowe's 'Uncle Tom's Cabin.'" *The New Yorker*. June 13. Accessed November 24, 2020. https://www.newyorker.com/magazine/2011/06/13/the-persuader-annette-gordon-reed.

Harriet Beecher Stowe Center. Accessed November 16, 2020. https://www.harrietbeecherstowecenter.org/harriet-beecher-stowe/uncle-toms-cabin/.

Railton, Stephen. "Uncle Tom's Cabin and American Culture." University of Virginia. Accessed November 16, 2020. http://utc.iath.virginia.edu/uncletom/illustra/52illf.html.

Stevenson, Louise L. 2007. "Virtue Displayed: The Tie-Ins of Uncle Tom's Cabin." Uncle Tom's Cabin in the Web of Culture, Harriet Beecher Stowe Center. Accessed November 24, 2020. http://utc.iath.virginia.edu/interpret/exhibits/stevenson/stevenson.html.

Tools and Weapons

California Gold Rush Balancing Scale

Gatling Rapid Fire Gun

John Wilkes Booth's Deringer

Typewriter

Whiteley Harvester Patent Model

Division of Work and Industry, National Museum of American History, Smithsonian Institution

40 California Gold Rush Balancing Scale

INTRODUCTION

It was on January 24, 1848, in Coloma, California, that a carpenter from New Jersey named James Marshall discovered glittery golden flakes in a riverbed while building a sawmill owned by a Swiss immigrant named Johann (John) Sutter. This mill, on the banks of the American River, was the first discovery of gold in the Sierra Nevada Mountains north of San Francisco. It would become the epicenter of the Gold Rush that evolved into one of the most significant events in the 19th century in America. Historians have claimed that the Gold Rush in California transformed America, influencing the outcome of the coming Civil War and altering the American psyche. In the 1840s, the United States was still a young nation, and certain political voices agitated for the expansion of the country from the Atlantic to the Pacific. The term "Manifest Destiny" was coined in 1845 to encourage and justify the Mexican-American War and the annexation of California and the other southwestern states belonging to Mexico. Not all Americans agreed with the theory that the United States was destined by God to conquer the continent as its mission by spreading democratic values as a moral imperative. But the newly elected Jacksonian Democrat James Polk advocated for the annexation of Mexico and soon embroiled the country in the Mexican-American War in a bid to complete the expansion of the United States "from sea to shining sea." In a fundamentally unfair fight, the United States defeated Mexico and got its wish in 1848 with the signing of the Treaty of Guadalupe Hidalgo, which annexed all or parts of Arizona, California, Colorado, Nevada, New Mexico, Texas, and Utah to the United States. Mexico had ceded 55 percent of its land to the United States for the price of $15 million. The treaty was signed on February 2, 1848. The signing of the treaty took place ten days after, unbeknownst to either the Mexican or the American government, gold was discovered in the Sierra Nevada Mountains of California. The territory of California, sparsely populated by about 6,500 Californians of Spanish or Mexican descent known as

Californios; 700 foreigners, mostly Americans; and 150,000 Native Americans, now belonged to the United States.

At first the men who discovered the golden flakes in the riverbed attempted to keep mum, but soon the secret got out. The people of the city of San Francisco had heard the rumors, but most didn't believe them, until on May 12, 1848, when a wily entrepreneur named Sam Brannan paraded around town with a vial of gold nuggets declaiming "Gold from the American River!!!" It is said that the entire male population of San Francisco cleared out and headed the 100 miles east to look for that gold that was tantalizingly gleaming in the riverbeds, almost as if it was calling "come and get me!" Soon all of California was heading that way. In July, the military governor of California, Richard B. Mason, reviewed the gold fields and wrote a report for President Polk. In it he recounted tales of the astounding amounts of gold that the miners had found in the area. He also included a tea caddy containing over 200 ounces of gold and wrote that this gold would "pay the cost of the war with Mexico a hundred times over." Mason sent his report to Washington with two messengers taking alternate routes. The first one to make it arrived in the capital on November 22, 1848, after months of arduous travel. Polk, who had lobbied for the war and then took credit for winning it, was under unrelenting criticism by his opposing party, the Whigs, who accused him of creating an unjust war in the hopes of expanding slavery in the United States. Polk was thrilled to be able to claim that his new accession, California, was replete with riches, a literal goldmine. He proudly made the announcement during his yearly address to Congress on December 5, 1848, extolling the wealth that would come from the American acquisition from Mexico. He even put the gold nuggets on display at the War Office.

The rush to get to the California gold was on. The first of the gold seekers came from areas that were accessible by sea: Mexicans, Chileans, Peruvians, Hawaiians, and Tahitians. More came from Europe and even Australia. The hordes of men who hurried toward California were later called "forty-niners" because the rush began in 1849. Alternatively they were called "Argonauts" after the Jason and the Argonauts, who, according to Greek mythology, ventured off on the ship *Argo* on a quest for the Golden Fleece. After the message went out from the White House, Americans from all over the East and Midwest tried to figure out how they could make the journey west and get their hands on some of that California gold. From the East Coast, there were three methods of travel. The transcontinental railroad was another twenty years in the future. The overland route was the cheapest but the most dangerous and challenging, over the California Trail, and could take three to seven months. The longest route, which could take six to eight months, was by sea, skirting the whole South American continent around Cape Horn. The so-called short-cut was through the Isthmus of Panama. Before the completion of the Panama Canal in 1914, the trip consisted of a hot, dangerous overland journey by foot or by mule through the malaria-ridden jungles of Panama. The gold seekers would take a ship to Panama, trek across the land, and then pick up another vessel on the west coast of Panama that delivered them to San Francisco. The hordes of men, for they were almost exclusively male, permanently changed the culture of California, with a population of almost one hundred thousand non-Natives by 1849. Many American men left their families and their jobs in the hope of making a quick buck and returning home flush with cash. For most, it didn't turn out that way.

The first forty-niners to arrive in the gold country of the Sierra Nevada did find that there was accessible gold to be mined. Some fortunes were made by the earliest of the miners. However, by the time that the whole country developed gold fever, the region was overwhelmed by anxious gold seekers. Most found that the work was inordinately difficult and exhausting. Many stayed longer than they had anticipated, trying to find some gold in the next valley, desperately hoping that they wouldn't have to hobble home empty-handed. What started out as a relatively egalitarian operation at the beginning became extremely cutthroat as the region grew more crowded. Native Americans, African Americans, Mexicans and South Americans, and Anglo Americans worked alongside each other when the gold was first discovered, and there was plenty to go around. However, as the gold became less and less available, racial and ethnic tensions erupted. White miners carried out the systematic killing of California Native Americans that the Anglos dubbed "extermination" and was in fact genocide. Native Americans weren't the only victims of xenophobic violence. The thousands of foreign miners who had ventured to California to make their fortune were also targeted. Various mining districts produced so-called mining codes that barred Mexicans, Asians, or other immigrants from staking claims. The California Legislature passed a foreign miners' license tax, which was specifically aimed at Mexican miners, who were more experienced and therefore more successful at mining gold than many of the Americans. Later, the Chinese, who were barred by law from becoming naturalized American citizens, were targeted with the tax, which remained in effect until 1870 and was responsible for 25 percent of the state's revenue.

Between 1848 and 1854, three hundred thousand gold seekers rushed to California, and $300 million in gold was harvested from the region. However, whereas six thousand miners obtained $10 million in gold in 1848, by 1851, there were one hundred thousand miners competing for $80 million in gold, halving the per person output. And after the first individual miners took all the easily mined gold, companies were formed to use more sophisticated equipment to get the gold that was more difficult to extract. So the miners who didn't want to leave the area ended up working for a company earning a wage. This was not the "get rich quick" situation that they had counted on when they arrived. In fact, the people who made the most out of the California Gold Rush were the ones who "mined the miners," that is, the clever entrepreneurs who built businesses that served the mining community, like Levi Strauss, Domingo Ghirardelli, and John Studebaker. Historians have estimated that fewer than one out of twenty forty-niners went home with more money that they had when they arrived.

DESCRIPTION

The artifact in the photo shown here is a hand balance with weights, a type of portable scale that was used to weigh gold in California during the Gold Rush. This scale, housed at the National Museum of American History in Washington, DC, fits into a small metal case measuring 5 ⅝ inches long by 3 inches wide by 1 ¾₁₆ inches deep. The case is green with gold lettering that states: "MINERS' IMPROVED GOLD SCALE/Manufactured expressly for California." It also has a decorative eagle accompanying the text. Inside the case there is the hand balance that consists of two brass pans, chains, and a 5.5-inch beam. There is section in the case for the weights: three large weights for 2 ounces, 1 ounce, and ½ ounce and six disc weights: 10 DWT (pennyweight), 5 DWT, 2 DWT, 1 DWT, and ½ DWT. There is also a fractional weight and a gold nugget. The set was made in New Jersey in about 1849–1850. This type of balance scale has been in existence for thousands of years. It consists of a fulcrum, a beam, and two pans. One pan holds the item to be weighed, and the other pan holds an item with a known weight. In this case, the weights were ranged from 2 ounces to ½ pennyweight.

In the beginning, the miners who were searching for gold in California, often known as the "forty-niners," used primitive tools to find the gold. The most common tool was the flat-bottomed pan. This pan, measuring between 18 inches and 24 inches in diameter, with 3–5-inch rims, was used by most of the early miners to "pan" for gold. The gold that was found in the riverbeds and streams was called placer gold, as opposed to lode gold,

---

LAMENT OF THE UNSUCCESSFUL GOLD MINER FROM AN 1855 BALLAD

Oh, land of gold, you did me deceive,
And I intend in thee my bones to leave;
So farewell, home, now my friends grow cold,
I'm a lousy miner,
I'm a lousy miner in search of shining gold.

[John A. Stone, "The Lousy Miner," 1855.
(Rawls 1998/1999)]

which was found underground in veins between layers of rock. The placer miner would place some gold-bearing river gravel into the pan, add some water, and swirl the mixture in the pan, separating the heavier gold from the lighter gravel material. The gold would settle to the bottom of the pan. Later on, more sophisticated tools and methods were devised to extract the gold from the Sierras in California. The rocker, a type of wooden box, was invented and used by California miners. Later the technique of hydraulic gold mining was devised. High-pressure water was directed at the face of a cliff, thereby not only separating the gold but also causing severe environmental damage. The technique of hydraulic gold mining was banned in 1884.

SIGNIFICANCE

There were several significant outcomes from the discovery of gold in California. In 1848, California, newly part of the United States, had a miniscule population and little power. Most of the residents were Native American. By the time the Gold Rush had petered out, four-fifths of the Native American population had been decimated, by disease, starvation, or outright murder. Peter Hardeman Burnett, the first governor of the state of California, demanded the immediate removal of the native population and paid bounties to white residents in exchange for scalps. But, with the largest migration in American history taking place during the years of the Gold Rush, the non-native population in California grew from approximately seven thousand, most of whom were of Spanish or Mexican origin, to three hundred thousand in 1855. The economic growth brought on by the constant flow of wealth emanating from the goldmines influenced the entire nation. Businesses were built that originated as services for the miners, banks were organized, and infrastructure was constructed to serve the hundreds of thousands of new residents. The gold wealth made California an economic powerhouse. By the time of the Civil War, California played a crucial role in financing the Union army, protected the essential port of San Francisco from Confederate attacks, and provided soldiers for the Union army. The new residents of California demanded that communication services like the telegraph be installed. Powerful California businessmen, known as the "Big Four," banded together to oversee the biggest transportation project of all—the transcontinental railroad. Many unsuccessful gold seekers stayed in California, turning to the new business of agriculture. Soon California would be the leading American producer of fruits, vegetables, and wine. According to historian J.S. Holliday, "Next to the Civil War in the 19th century, no other event had a greater impact, more long-lasting reverberations, than the Gold Rush. It transformed obviously California, but more importantly, it transformed America" (J. S. Holliday, quoted in "American Experience" 2006).

FURTHER INFORMATION

"Ask the Experts: Scale Represents Transactions of the Gold Rush Era." 2016. *Antique Trader*. January 14. Accessed May 5, 2021. https://www.antiquetrader.com/collectibles/ask-the-experts-scale-represents-transactions-of-gold-rush-era.

Bethel, A. C. W. Winter 2008/2009. "The California Gold Rush and the Coming of the Civil War (Review)." *Southern California Quarterly*, 90(4): 461–463.

Brands, H. W. 2002. *The Age of Gold: The California Gold Rush and the New American Dream*. New York: Doubleday.

"The Gold Rush" (Transcript). 2006. PBS. *American Experience*. November 6. Accessed May 6, 2021. https://www.pbs.org/wgbh/americanexperience/films/goldrush/#transcript.

"The History of Weighing." Avery Weigh-Tronix. Accessed May 7, 2021. https://web.archive.org/web/20120302145347/http://www.averyweigh-tronix.com/main.aspx?p=1.1.3.4.

Holliday, J. S. Spring 1998. "Reverberations of the California Gold Rush." *California History*, 77(1): 4–15.

Maslin, Janet. 2002. "Books of the Times; How a Few Sparkling Yellow Flakes Changed History." Review of *The Age of Gold: The California Gold Rush and the New American Dream*. *New York Times*. August 19. Accessed May 5, 2021. https://www.nytimes.com/2002/08/19/books/books-of-the-times-how-a-few-sparkling-yellow-flakes-altered-history.html.

Maxwell-Long, Thomas. 2014. *Daily Life during the California Gold Rush*. Santa Barbara, CA: Greenwood.

National Park Service. 2020. "California's Role in the Civil War." May 13. Accessed May 10, 2021. https://www.nps.gov/goga/learn/historyculture/california-in-civil-war.htm.

Rawls, James J. Winter 1998/1999. "A Golden State: An Introduction." *California History*, 77(4): 1–23.

Richards, Leonard L. 2007. *The California Gold Rush and the Coming of the Civil War*. New York: Vintage Books.

Rohrbough, Malcolm J. Spring 1998. "The California Gold Rush as a National Experience." *California History*, 77(1): 16–29.

41 Gatling Rapid Fire Gun

INTRODUCTION

The 19th century in the United States was an era that featured a plethora of startling new inventions, often conjured by brilliant amateurs, autodidact generalists who conceived of something completely novel while tinkering in their backyard shop. So many American inventions, from the sewing machine, to the cotton gin, to the telegraph and telephone, to the steamboat, were dreamt up by self-educated tinkerers, who, aided by the pioneering concept of the American patent office, were encouraged to pursue their crazy dreams and profit from them. Most of these inventors were idealists who were searching for a way to improve the quality of life. However, some groundbreaking inventions that change the world can often have unintended consequences, and many of these, in fact, did. Whitney's cotton gin led to an expansion of slavery and the national crisis of the Civil War. The steamboat unintentionally carried the smallpox virus into the Missouri Valley, setting off a four-year long smallpox epidemic that killed over seventeen thousand Native Americans. Richard Jordan Gatling was another inventive genius whose most famous creation had a transformative effect on the world. Though his intentions remained benign, his most successful invention, the Gatling gun, would transform warfare and lead to a mechanization of weaponry, creating a horrifically efficient killing machine that was used throughout the world. At the end of his long life, Gatling would regret having inventing it.

The Gatling gun was invented by Richard Gatling in 1862. It was not the first repeating action machine gun, but it was the first that was effective and foolproof. The design of the gun grew out of other of Gatling's inventions. Gatling was born in Hertford County, North Carolina, in a slave-holding family that owned a 1,200-acre plantation. His parents were Mary Barnes and Jordan Gatling, both of whom descended from English colonists who settled in North Carolina. The family was chock-full of amateur inventors, including his father who invented both a cotton planter and a cotton thinner. Richard's brothers also became inventors. Richard was born on September 12, 1818, and had little formal education. He helped on his father's farm, as well as spending time teaching and working at the local country store. He was always experimenting on machinery like his father. In May 1844, he patented his first invention, a rice seed planter, inspired by the earlier machine his father invented nine years earlier. When the Albemarle agricultural region of North Carolina began to suffer from its lack of nearby waterways to transport the crops, both Richard and his brother left North Carolina to seek their fortunes out West. Richard traveled to St. Louis, where he began to work on further agricultural inventions. He later moved to Cincinnati, where he obtained a medical degree from the Ohio Medical College after a serious bout with smallpox left him eager to understand how to treat diseases in his own family. Though subsequently known as Dr. Gatling, he never practiced medicine and continued to pursue his penchant for inventing. Gatling was the inveterate inventor and received forty-three patents in his lifetime. He relocated to Indianapolis, Indiana, where he met Jemima Sanders, a member of a wealthy and politically connected Indiana family. They married in 1854.

Though a Southerner by birth, Gatling did not support slavery and freed the slaves whom he inherited from his family. When the Civil War began, Gatling was living in Indianapolis. He was saddened by the sight of the ailing and maimed soldiers who were returning from the battlefield. Though many had suffered battlefield injuries, even more had been infected with diseases like dysentery, malaria, pneumonia, and typhoid. Richard began to consider the harmful effects of war on the lives of soldiers and their families. He thought about how to reduce the human cost of war. He wanted to create something that would decrease the number of soldiers required in a wartime situation, thereby lessening the casualties as well. Always cogitating on how things work, Gatling applied the techniques that he patented for his successful seed planter to a new type of efficient rotating gun that could shoot repeating, rapid-fire bullets. By 1862, he was ready to demonstrate his new invention, which became known as the Gatling gun.

DESCRIPTION

The 1862 version of the Gatling gun shown here is a Type II .58 caliber machine gun. Colonel R. A. Maxwell suggested to Gatling that a special objectives weapon was needed for the Union army, one that was designed to defend buildings, causeways, and bridges. Though his first model, patented in 1862, was crude, Gatling continued to perfect it. The model shown here is the second version, Type II. The first Gatling gun was based on predecessors created by Ager and Ripley. Gatling combined features from both of the previous guns and attempted to correct their design issues. The Gatling gun was operated by a crank, with six revolving rifled barrels, with a bolt for each barrel. The barrels were mounted around a central shaft, which was connected to the crank. Turning the crank made the barrels rotate at the breech end. Cam action performed the cocking and firing, and the gears drove the gun. The cams were produced through a machine tool process, which insured positive action and certainty of fire. One of the persistent problems with the early Gatling guns was the gas leakage between the cylinder and the barrel, which remained an issue. The first model had paper cartridges, which were replaced by more reliable copper cartridges in the Type II model. These cartridges were mounted in a hopper, or "stick magazine," mounted above the barrels and fed into the weapon through gravity. Because of the use of gravity, the rate of shots that could be fired was limited. Steel chargers acted as firing chambers. An early model was exhibited in Indianapolis, where the governor of Indiana saw it and was duly impressed with its 350 shots per minute, writing to the assistant secretary of war, P. H. Watson, to promote its use for the military. Gatling engaged the Cincinnati firm of McWhinny, Rindge and Company to manufacture twelve prototype guns. Constantly tinkering to improve its performance, Gatling made several design changes to the gun, which ameliorated several of the issues in the Type I model. The copper cartridges made loading easier and eliminated the problem of misfiring.

The revolutionary Gatling gun made news throughout the world. President Lincoln, a 19th-century technophile, was keenly interested when he first heard about the gun. Lincoln followed the latest inventions and fell in love with the newly invented telegraph, spending hours in the telegraph room during the Civil War monitoring reports from the battlegrounds. He was also a fan of new types of weapons. Gatling wrote to Lincoln in 1864 to promote his invention, but the gun was never picked up by the Union army. General James W. Ripley, the experienced but old-school chief of ordnance for the army, was opposed to buying newly designed weapons. There had been numerous previous attempts at providing the army with new weapons, but the weapons were not effective or reliable. Ripley believed that this one would suffer the same fate. He absolutely refused to purchase this newfangled gun. Besides, Ripley, as well as a number of others in the Union army, distrusted Gatling, who was a son of the South. Gatling manufactured his guns in Cincinnati, which was located across the river from Kentucky, a Confederate state. Some of these wary Union generals feared that Gatling would sell his guns to both sides, leading to a bloodbath. However, many historians believe that the Civil War may have been shortened by years, if the Gatling gun was obtained by the Union army. Thousands of lives might have been saved. Several Union generals were impressed by the gun, and they purchased a few with their own funds. The Union navy also bought a few after Admiral John A. Dahlgren recognized its utility for defending boats and bridges. The intimidating sight of this gun made it useful in nonmilitary functions as well. During the violent Civil War draft riots in New

York City in July 1863, the guns were used to protect the *New York Times* building, which was targeted by the mob for the newspaper's support of the draft.

LEONARD JEROME SAVES THE *NEW YORK TIMES* BUILDING IN 1863

Leonard Jerome, a wealthy Wall Street trader and *New York Times* stockholder, was responsible for the placement of three Gatling guns in the windows of the *New York Times* headquarters during the Draft Riots of July 1863 in New York City. The mobs had targeted the newspaper because of its support of Lincoln's draft. The imposing sight of the guns frightened off the mob of Irish rioters, who proceeded to attack the *New York Tribune* instead. Leonard Jerome took his daughter, Jennie, to England where she would meet and later marry British lord Randolph Churchill. Jennie Jerome, the American socialite, and Randolph Churchill, the British lord, would become the parents of Winston Churchill.

SIGNIFICANCE

Gatling's gun was not used to much effect during the Civil War, but as more militaries recognized its value in the battlefield both in the United States and around the world, it eventually became one of their weapons of choice. During the Spanish-American War in 1898, Lieutenant John H. "Gatling Gun" Parker organized a unit of four Gatlings and used them broadly—against snipers, blockhouses, and into trenches, proving that the gun could be used offensively as effectively as it was used defensively. Colonel Teddy Roosevelt's Rough Riders, along with two regiments of the all-black "Buffalo Soldiers" and other American troops in the Battle of San Juan Hill in Cuba, were pinned down by Spanish fire. John "Gatling Gun" Parker brought in three Gatling guns that were used to attack the enemy in the trenches, allowing for the legendary charge up San Juan Hill. They were also used in the Battle of Kettle Hill and later halted a Spanish counterattack in Santiago, eventually winning the war for the United States. "It's the Gatlings, men! Our Gatlings!" bellowed Colonel Roosevelt at San Juan Hill. Theodore Roosevelt would soon become our 26th president after McKinley's assassination in September 1901.

One might wonder why a talented inventor and decent man would apply his talents to a killing machine. This is how the inventor of the gun, Richard Jordan Gatling, defended it in a letter written in 1877, twelve years after the end of the Civil War:

> In 1861. . . I witnessed almost daily the departure of troops to the front and the return of the wounded, sick, and dead. The most of the

latter lost their lives not in battle but by sickness and exposure. . . . It occurred to me if I could invent a machine—a gun—which could, by its rapidity of fire, enable one man to do as much battle duty as a hundred, that it would to a great extent supersede the necessity of large armies, and consequently [the] exposure to battle and disease [would] be greatly diminished. (Roark 1962: 312)

Considering the subsequent history of the invention, his defense may ring hollow in today's world. The Gatling gun was revolutionary, and it was the first effective machine gun that could shoot hundreds of shots in one minute. It was the predecessor of the Vulcan minigun, used to grim effect during the Vietnam War, which could shoot six thousand rounds per minute from a helicopter. The crank-operated Gatling gun that gave way to newer, automatic machine guns was retired and declared obsolete by the U.S. military in 1911. But the genial, mild-mannered inventor, who received forty-three patents in his lifetime, kept working on improving the gun and hoped that it would reduce the number of battle deaths. Alas, it didn't.

FURTHER INFORMATION

Baker, Kevin. 2016. *America the Ingenious: How a Nation of Dreamers, Immigrants, and Tinkerers Changed the World*. New York: Artisan.

Chinn, George M. 1951. *The Machine Gun: History, Evolution, and Development of Manual, Automatic, and Airborne Repeating Weapons*. Bureau of Ordnance, Department of the Navy. Accessed August 21, 2020. https://www.ibiblio.org/hyperwar/USN/ref/MG/I/index.html.

Keller, Julia. 2008. *Mr. Gatling's Terrible Marvel: The Gun That Changed Everything and the Misunderstood Genius Who Invented It*. New York: Viking Penguin Group.

Parramore, Thomas C. January 1964. "The North Carolina Background of Richard Jordan Gatling." *The North Carolina Historical Review*, 41(1): 54–61.

Roark, Albert E. Winter 1962. "Doctor Gatling's Gun." *Arizona and the West*, 4(4): 309–324.

Rydell, Robert W. April 2011. "Reviewed Work: *Mr. Gatling's Terrible Marvel: The Gun That Changed Everything and the Misunderstood Genius Who Invented It* by Julia Keller." *Technology and Culture*, 52(2): 397–399.

Watson, Stephanie, and Tom Harris. 2000. "How Machine Guns Work." HowStuffWorks.com. February 1. Accessed August 24, 2020. https://science.howstuffworks.com/machine-gun.htm#pt4.

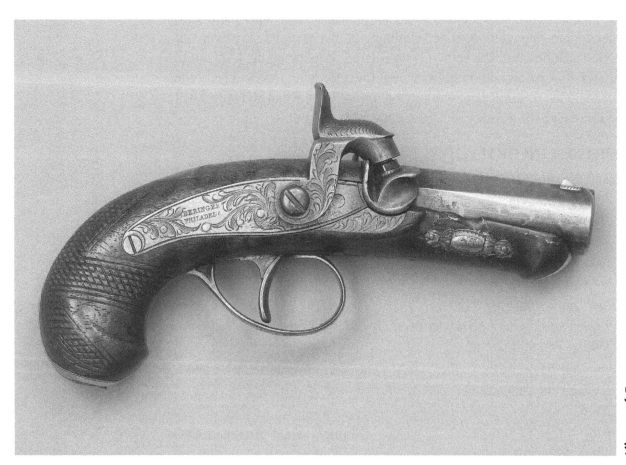

42 John Wilkes Booth's Deringer

INTRODUCTION

The brutal Civil War had finally ended. On April 9, 1865, General Robert E. Lee surrendered to General Ulysses S. Grant in Appomattox, Virginia. On April 11, Abraham Lincoln delivered his first formal public response following the surrender. On that dark and rainy evening, he emerged from the White House's second-floor north portico and greeted the excited throng of supporters. The Union had prevailed. Little did the weary president know that among the crowd were three men who were plotting against him. One of the men was an accomplished Shakespearean actor named John Wilkes Booth. President Lincoln read his written speech by candlelight. In his speech he commended the valuable service provided by black forces in the Union army and suggested that the voting rights should be conferred on the "colored man . . . on the very intelligent and on those that serve our cause as soldiers." Booth, who was a committed white supremacist, fumed when he heard these words. He detested Lincoln and had been hatching a scheme with several co-conspirators to kidnap him and demand the return of Confederate prisoners. But now he resolved that Lincoln must be assassinated. Booth was consumed with his thirst for revenge on the devastation that the Union had wrought on his beloved South.

John Wilkes Booth was born in Bel Air, Maryland, on May 10, 1838, the ninth of ten children. His parents had emigrated from England in 1821, and his father, Junius Booth, became one of the most prominent Shakespearean actors of his day. Junius, suffering from alcoholism and a touch of madness, died in 1852. His young son John desired to follow in his father's footsteps and debuted as a stage actor in 1855. In 1858, he joined the Richmond (Virginia) Theatre. While living in Richmond, Booth developed a love for the South and for southern culture. The rest of his family sympathized with the Union cause. His father and older brother had acting careers that focused on performing in northern states. Although he also performed throughout the East Coast, John wanted to distinguish himself from the other famous family members, and he settled in the Confederate capital and supported the rebel cause. He developed a national following and was earning a whopping $20,000 per year. Considered to be exceedingly handsome by his admirers, Booth also had a lively and charismatic stage presence. When the Civil War hindered his opportunities to perform in his beloved Richmond, his resentment of the north grew. He blamed the war on abolitionists. He accused Lincoln of abuse of power after Lincoln suspended the writ of habeas corpus in the border states. Booth had grandiose ideas of his power and influence and saw himself as a hero who could save the nation from Lincoln's despotic actions. Gathering a group of like-minded Southerners that he dubbed the Confederate Underground, Booth began hatching a plan to kidnap Abraham Lincoln in the late summer of 1864. Booth was concerned that the Confederate Army was losing too many soldiers to both death and imprisonment. By kidnapping the president, he mused, he could negotiate with the Union to release Confederate prisoners in exchange for the release of the president. This half-baked plan was supported by some of his co-conspirators. These accomplices included Michael O'Laughlen, Samuel Arnold, Lewis Powell, John Suratt, David Herold, and George Atzerodt. At a meeting of the group held on March 15, 1865, at Gautier's Restaurant in Washington, DC, the kidnapping of the president was discussed. Booth discovered that Lincoln was planning to attend a play at a venue just outside of the city on March 17. The group plotted to abduct Lincoln from his carriage on his way to the play. The president, however, altered his itinerary at the last minute and decided to speak to the 140th Regiment. Foiled in their plans, some members departed the group.

Booth's plans to kidnap the president were thwarted, but he was still fixated on removing Lincoln from office. After attending Lincoln's speech after Appomattox that reflected on the consequences of the South's surrender, the infuriated Booth is quoted to have threatened, "That is the last speech he will ever make!" On Friday, April 14, Good Friday, Booth stopped in at the Ford's Theatre, where he often performed, to pick up his mail. He was informed by the staff that the president and General Grant were planning to attend a performance that evening of the play called *Our American Cousin*. Booth assembled his co-conspirators to devise a plan. It was an audacious scheme. Booth would assassinate Lincoln at the theater, George Atzerodt would kill Vice President Andrew Johnson at his home at Kirkwood House, and Lewis Powell and David Herold would kill Secretary of State William Seward at his home at Lafayette Square near the White House. All these assassinations would take place at the same time, in order to generate the most political chaos. The time was to be 10:15 p.m. Booth surreptitiously entered the Ford's Theatre sometime in the afternoon on April 14 as the actors were rehearsing for the night's performance. He examined the presidential box, which had been prepared for the arrival of President Lincoln.

The box suite had two doors with locks on them, an outer door to a small corridor and an inner door to the box itself. A guard would be stationed outside the outer door to the suite to protect the president. Booth carved a notch in the plaster wall outside the box in order to accommodate a piece of wood that could secure the outer door to the box. He also drilled a small opening in the inner door where he could catch a glimpse of the rocking chair that was soon to be occupied by President Lincoln. The presidential party entered the theater at about 8:30 p.m. The group consisted of President Lincoln, his wife Mary Todd Lincoln, Major Henry Rathbone, and his fiancée Clara Harris. General Grant had decided not to attend. Booth arrived at the location about 9:30 p.m. and proceeded to go to the saloon next door to the theater for a drink. He had been drinking heavily all day. He left the saloon and entered the theatre at 10:07 p.m., climbing the stairs to the second-floor presidential box. The White House bodyguard who was assigned to guard the president, John Parker of the Metropolitan Police, was not at his post. He had wandered out of the building and into a nearby saloon called Taltavul's. Booth saw that the chair outside of the outer door was empty. He recalled seeing Parker at the saloon and realized that the president had been left unprotected. This was his chance. It was 10:15, the witching hour, the hour that he had proclaimed that he and his co-conspirators would kill Lincoln, Johnson, and Seward. Booth breezed past the first door with the empty chair and got to the second door where he espied Lincoln and his party through the peephole that he had drilled a few hours before. He opened the door, which was unlocked, and walked up to the president, lifted his gun to Lincoln's head, and shot him in the back of his head at point blank range. The wound proved to be fatal. Booth proceeded to stab Major Rathbone in the arm with a large knife and then jumped out of the presidential box onto the stage, landing awkwardly and breaking his ankle. Nonetheless, he stood on the stage, brandishing his bloody knife and proclaiming, "Sic semper tyrannis!" which translates from Latin into "Thus always to tyrants!" He also declared, "The South is avenged!" The mortally injured president was removed from the theater to the Petersen House, a boarding house across the street, where he died early the next morning. The co-conspirators all failed at their tasks, and Seward and Johnson were not assassinated. But Booth had successfully done what he had predicted. He escaped capture and was on the run twelve more days. Aided by a cadre of southern sympathizers, he was finally caught on April 26, 1865, as he and his co-conspirator David Herold slept in a tobacco barn in Port Royal, Virginia, owned by Richard H. Garrett. The Union cavalry demanded that they exit the barn. Herold did, but Booth refused, and the soldiers set the barn on fire. Booth was subsequently shot and dragged out of the burning barn. Booth died that morning on the porch of the Garrett house.

DESCRIPTION

The gun that John Wilkes Booth used to shoot Lincoln was a .44 caliber Philadelphia Deringer. The derringer pistol, originally invented by Henry Deringer of Philadelphia in 1852, was a popular handgun in the mid-19th century. The use of the term "derringer" was a misspelling of the name of the inventor. The derringer is a diminutive muzzle-loading percussion-type handgun, a single-shot pistol that contains one ball of lead. To operate the handgun, black gunpowder had to be poured down the barrel, followed by the lead ball. A percussion cap would then be placed on the nipple of the gun, and the derringer would be ready for its first and only shot. The gun was tiny and easily concealed. It was not very accurate and was most successfully used at point-blank range. A similar gun called the Remington derringer was made from 1866 to 1935. It contained an additional shot, with a second barrel of top of the first. The Philadelphia Deringer utilized by John Wilkes Booth to assassinate Abraham Lincoln was about 6 inches long with a 2 ½-inch barrel, weighing in at only 8 ounces. The mountings and trigger were of German silver. In the butt of the gun, there was a small box that contained an extra percussion cap.

The gun has had an interesting history in the aftermath of the shooting. After Booth shot Lincoln from the back near his left ear, he dropped it on the floor on his way out of Ford's Theatre to make his escape. A theater patron named William T. Kent helped remove the president to the Petersen House where he was treated. When Kent realized that he had forgotten his keys, he returned to the theater and found the gun on the floor of the presidential box. He turned it over to government investigators, and it remained in the hands of the Judge Advocate General's Corps, the prosecutors of the case against Booth's co-conspirators. The trial was a military tribunal and took place in May and June 1865. The derringer was displayed at the headquarters of the War Department (predecessor to the present-day Defense Department). In 1931, Lieutenant Colonel Ulysses S. Grant III, the grandson of the Civil War general, requested from the army's adjutant general to transfer the trial artifacts, including the weapons, to the new museum being created at the Ford's Theatre. The adjutant general adamantly denied the request, issuing this statement: "The relics should not be displayed to the public under any circumstances, on the theory that they would create interest in the criminal aspects of the great tragedy, rather than the historical features thereof, and would have more of an appeal for the morbid or weak-minded than for students of history . . . the Lincoln relics should not be placed upon exhibition anywhere" (Ford's Theatre, National Park Service). It wasn't until 1940 that the War Department demurred and transferred the trial artifacts to the National Park Service to be displayed at the Ford's Theatre National Historic Site. They went on display in 1942 and have been at the Ford's Theatre ever since.

JOHN WILKES BOOTH, ON THE INSTITUTION OF SLAVERY IN THE UNITED STATES

This country was formed for the white not for the black man. And looking upon African slavery from the same standpoint, as held by those noble framers of our Constitution, I for one, have ever considered it, one of the greatest blessings . . . that God ever bestowed upon a favored nation.

[John Wilkes Booth, in a letter to his brother-in-law, written in November 1864.

As quoted in Norton, Roger J. 1996–2019. "Abraham Lincoln's Assassination." Abraham Lincoln Research Site. Accessed April 18, 2021. https://rogerjnorton.com/Lincoln2.html.]

SIGNIFICANCE

The assassination of Abraham Lincoln has remained one of the most tragic and significant events in American history. Much of the country was convulsed in grief at Lincoln's passing as he made his heartbreaking final twelve-day journey by rail back to his hometown of Springfield, Illinois, where he was laid to rest, accompanied by the disinterred remains of his beloved son Willie, who had died of typhoid in 1862. The immediate outcome of the president's assassination was that Vice President Andrew Johnson would take the helm of the presidency. Johnson was a southern Democrat, a former slave owner and a weak leader. He was unable to follow through on Lincoln's conciliatory words, to "bind up the nation's wounds." He fought with the Republicans in Congress over allowing southern states to reinstitute laws that restricted civil rights of black citizens. The Republicans were able to push through legislation ensuring civil and voting rights for newly freed slaves, but the backlash in the South was enduring, leading to the Jim Crow laws that limited those rights. Johnson was impeached in 1868 and is considered one of the worst presidents in American history. The reconciliation between the North and the South as envisioned by Abraham Lincoln was never to be, and the resentment and bitterness engendered by the Civil War have endured ever since.

FURTHER INFORMATION

Alford, Terry. 2015. *Fortune's Fool: The Life of John Wilkes Booth*. Oxford; New York: Oxford University Press.

Greene, Elizabeth B. 2017. *Buildings and Landmarks of 19th Century America: American Society Revealed*. Santa Barbara, CA: Greenwood Press.

Jameson, W. C. 2013. *John Wilkes Booth: Beyond the Grave*. Lanham, New York: Taylor Trade Publishing.

McKenzie, David. "Booth's Deringer." Ford's Theatre. National Park Service. Accessed April 8, 2021. https://www.fords.org/lincolns-assassination/booths-deringer/.

Norton, Roger J. 1996–2019. "Abraham Lincoln's Assassination." Rogerjnorton.com. Accessed April 5, 2021. https://rogerjnorton.com/Lincoln.html.

43 Typewriter

INTRODUCTION

The concept of designing and manufacturing a machine that transcribed text in real time as if writing a letter was introduced in the early 18th century. As a matter of fact, the first known patent for such a machine was granted by Queen Anne on January 7, 1714, to an inventor named Henry Mill. The patent described "an artificial machine or method for the impressing or transcribing of letters singly or progressively one after another, as in writing, whereby all writings whatsoever may be engrossed in paper or parchment so neat and exact as not to be distinguished from print." Although the printing press had been invented centuries before in the 15th century, the idea of an individual writing each letter in order to produce one copy of a manuscript by machine was novel at the time. The 1714 patent straightforwardly described the work of the "artificial machine," but no record exists of the machine ever being built by Henry Mill. Later attempts at such a machine were made in Italy and other countries using harpsichord keyboards, which became known as "literary pianos." Some of the early inventions were intended to aid people with visual impairments, which led to Louis Braille's invention of the Braille alphabet and a machine that would emboss a page that could be "read" by the fingers instead of the eyes. William Austin Burt designed a machine in 1829, but it was never commercially produced, and it did not write any faster than the human hand. John Jonathan Pratt invented a machine that he called the "pterotype" in 1867, which appeared in *Scientific American* magazine. The promotion of this invention in the popular magazine inspired a number of other inventors, including Christopher Latham Sholes, the inventor of the machine shown here. A European device called the Hansen Writing Ball was patented in 1870 and was an early version of a typewriter that was commercially produced. The ball-shaped device did not become popular in the United States because it was never mass-produced, though some Europeans, including the writer Friedrich Nietzsche, embraced its use wholeheartedly for a period of time. However, it was the American version of the typewriter that won over the European population eventually.

With the Industrial Revolution came the expansion of the business operations as well as the explosion of telegraphy, which demanded a quick transcription of either the spoken word or a shorthand version of it. Court reporters and telegraphers were interested in obtaining a machine that could put down letters faster than a hand holding a pen. Expert pen writers could only write twenty words per minute. In addition, the burgeoning corporate and government offices that opened after the Civil War constantly generated paperwork. This flood of paper was slowed down by the clerks who had to tediously write everything down by hand. Amanuenses, assistants who take dictation, could take shorthand but then had to transcribe the shorthand by the wearisome task of handwriting the text. Businesses were realizing that they needed help producing documents both quickly and legibly. The age of the "literary piano" had arrived.

Christopher Latham Sholes, known as the "father of the typewriter," was a self-effacing man, a man who could pass as a poet, with a gentle face and a long gray beard. Sholes was not like many of the other hard-driving, self-promoting, 19th-century inventors. Born in Mooresburg, Pennsylvania, in 1819, Sholes worked for a printer as a young man. Moving to Green Bay, Wisconsin, at the age of eighteen, he began working for his older brothers who owned and published the newspaper called the *Wisconsin Democrat*. Despite his modest background, Christopher showed himself to be a quick learner and a good editor. He soon became editor of the *Madison* (Wisconsin) *Enquirer*. He founded the *Southport* (now Kenosha) *Telegraph* and published it for years. He was also associated with a number of Milwaukee newspapers. Sholes had a keen mind for many subjects. Progressive politics interested him, and he helped organize the Free-Soil Party, as well as the Republican Party in the state. Sholes served several terms in the Wisconsin state government and successfully fought to outlaw the death penalty in Wisconsin in 1853. During the Civil War, Sholes served as the Milwaukee postmaster.

Sholes liked to tinker, though because of his many interests, he did not have the extra time to indulge his creative urge for inventing for many years. It wasn't until he was forty-eight years old, when he was appointed to the less demanding position of port collector and commissioner of public works, did he feel that he had the leisure time to focus on his hobby. He had invented several devises during his career in the newspaper publishing business, which included a newspaper addressing machine and a page-numbering device. But after he read about Pratt's pterotype writing device in an issue of *Scientific American* in 1867, Sholes heartily embraced the idea of inventing a usable version. Sholes spent hours in his friend Charles Kleinsteuber's machine shop on State Street in Milwaukee. This shop not only provided machining and foundry services but also attracted a cadre of aspiring inventors like Christopher Sholes. Also in attendance was Carlos Glidden, who was working on inventing a steam-driven rotary plow. Glidden, however, noticed Sholes' work on his page-numbering device and encouraged him to try his hand on a writing machine. Sholes, Glidden, a machinist and clock-maker Mathias Schwalbach, and Samuel Soulé worked together on producing such a machine. The hulking machine they eventually produced has been called a cross between a piano and a table. It was truly in the vein of a "literary piano" because it had black-and-white piano keys, which were pressed to type the letters. It drove type bars up to press the letters into the paper through an ink ribbon. The machine received a patent on June 23, 1868. It had six white keys and five black keys, and the patent claimed that this new design provided "a better way of working type bars, of holding the paper on the carriage, of moving and regulating the movement of the carriage, of holding and applying the inking ribbon, a self-adjusting platen, and a rest or cushion for the type-bars." In a race between Sholes on his new invention and the superintendent of the Western Union Telegraph office writing by hand, Sholes won handily by typing the sentence, "Now is the time for all good men to come to the aid of the party."

DESCRIPTION

Christopher Latham Sholes thought he had completed his task: he, with the help of some of his friends, had invented a usable writing machine that was faster than the human hand. He had patented it. He was ready to get it into production. Sholes was not wealthy, and he didn't have the funding or the access to manufacturing, distribution, or marketing to get this device to the public. He and his colleagues launched a letter-writing campaign to everyone they knew who might be able to help them financially. The letters, of course, were written on the typewriting machine itself. They eventually succeeded with James Densmore, a former newspaper associate of Sholes in Pennsylvania. Densmore was impressed with the concept and bought a quarter interest in the machine, though he had never actually set eyes on it. The following year he traveled to Wisconsin where he examined the machine for the first time. He was no longer impressed. He saw many flaws in the machine's efficiency. Densmore, whose outsized, pushy personality was the antithesis of Sholes, demanded improvements before he would consent to market the device. Sholes and his colleagues proceeded to make improvements to the machine over several more years. There were various models of the machine that were produced under the browbeating of James Densmore before the successful one was finally produced in 1874.

The model shown here, dubbed Model #2, was produced in 1870. Its appearance is similar to the classic typewriter in shape. It no longer has the piano key configuration. Charles Weller, a friend of Christopher Sholes who wrote the book *The Early History of the Typewriter*, written in 1918, described it this way:

> The second machine which was sent to me in the fall of 1870 was . . . so decidedly different from the first construction that it will bear a description as to some of its parts. In the first place, the rude wooden keys contained in the first machine were replaced by metal rods with a thin brass button on which the letter or figure was cut and painted black . . . The connecting wires instead of running down to trivets near the floor ran directly from the end of the key to the type bar above, and instead of the plain slot in the brass disk . . . the type bars were set in steel bearings, very much the same as we see in the latest modern construction. (Weller 1918: 37)

In addition, there was a new rubber roller for the paper. A 5-inch diameter metal ring held the type bars, which could swing freely through the open space at the center of the ring. The typewriter, which was called a "type writer" at the time, could type only uppercase letters. It was a so-called blind typewriter, which typed letters onto the reverse side of the paper, which could not be seen until the paper was removed.

James Densmore who is quoted as saying, "I believe in the invention from the top-most corner of my hat to the bottom-most head of the nails of my boot-heels," continued to drive the typewriter inventors toward further improvements. When the others wanted to give up, Densmore kept pushing on. By 1872, after more than fifty different models were produced, the Milwaukee group had a machine that essentially resembled the modern typewriter. Sholes invented a new design for the keyboard, due to the fact that the keys got jammed when common letters were typed. The original design arranged the keyboard in alphabetical order. This design, called the "QWERTY" keyboard, a name that derives from the left top row of letters, is still used today, though it is of course no longer necessary to prevent jamming. With this revised design, a manufacturing company had to be located, one that could mass-produce this complex machine at a reasonable cost. At the suggestion of James Densmore's friend, a man named George Washington Newton Yost, the arms and sewing machine manufacturer, E. Remington & Sons, located in Ilion, New York, was given a contract to manufacture the new typewriter. This company, famed for their gun production during the Civil War, had revamped their production toward the new and popular product, the sewing machine. They assigned two of their engineers to tweak the machine for mass production, and in 1873, it was finally produced for sale. It didn't sell too well at first, but by the 1880s, it caught on with business and government offices, and by 1900, it was becoming an office requirement.

SIGNIFICANCE

Christopher Latham Sholes, the reluctant inventor, didn't make a fortune on his invention, probably netting about $20,000 all told due to the fact that he sold much of his rights to Densmore, his ever-haranguing promoter. However, he did realize that his invention had wide-ranging consequences. For the first time, women were welcomed into the workforce. Previously, men worked as clerks in the newly formed corporate and government offices. But times were changing. A larger pool of clerks was needed in the huge corporations that were formed in the late 19th century, clerks that had to handle the reams of necessary paperwork. In 1880, the Young Women's Christian Association (YWCA, the women's version of the YMCA) in New York City inaugurated a class in typing and stenography, advertising that "some firms prefer typewriting to penmanship." Soon, secretarial schools emerged, as well as high school classes in typing and stenography. For the first time, women were given the opportunity to work with men in office positions. The businesses benefited, of course. Women were paid half of what the male clerks received. Also, they remained trapped in their clerical positions—women couldn't rise through ranks like men could. But it was still an unprecedented opportunity for women to work and to be self-supporting. Even Christopher Sholes, at the end of his life, appreciated the impact of his invention on the lives of many American women when he said, "Whatever I may have felt, in the early days, of the value of the typewriter, it is obviously a blessing to mankind, and especially to womankind. I am glad I had something to do with it. I builded wiser than I knew, and the world has the benefit of it" (Snow 1982).

FURTHER INFORMATION

ASME. 2011. "Sholes and Glidden 'Type Writer': A Historic Mechanical Engineering Landmark." October 6. Accessed October 12, 2020. https://www.asme.org/wwwasmeorg/media/resourcefiles/aboutasme/who%20we%20are/engineering%20history/landmarks/249-sholes-glidden-type-writer.pdf.

Casillo, Anthony. 2017. *Typewriters: Iconic Machines from the Golden Age of Mechanical Writing*. San Francisco: Chronicle Books.

Current, Richard N. June 1949. "The Original Typewriter Enterprise 1867–1873." *Wisconsin Magazine of History*, 32(4): 391–407.

Current, Richard N. June 1951. "Technology and Promotion: The Typewriter." *Bulletin of the Business Historical Society*, 25(2): 77–83.

Heath, Frederic. March 1944. "The Typewriter in Wisconsin." *Wisconsin Magazine of History*, 27(3): 263–275.

Herkimer County Historical Society. 2019. *The Story of the Typewriter: 1873–1923*. Project Gutenberg Ebook. Accessed October 12, 2020. https://www.gutenberg.org/files/60794/60794-h/60794-h.htm#ch3.

Keep, Christopher. "The Introduction of the Sholes & Glidden Type-Writer, 1874." BRANCH: Britain, Representation and Nineteenth-Century History. Edited by Dino Franco Felluga. Extension of Romanticism and Victorianism on the Net. Accessed October 12, 2020. https://www.branchcollective.org/?ps_articles=christopher-keep-the-introduction-of-the-sholes-glidden-type-writer-1874.

Sandoval, Hannah. 2017. *The Story of the Invention of the Typewriter 150 Years Later*. Ocala, FL: Atlantic Publishing Group.

Snow, Richard F. August/September 1982. "Christopher Latham Sholes: The Seventy-sixth Inventor of the Typewriter." *American Heritage*, 33(5). https://www.americanheritage.com/christopher-latham-sholes-seventy-sixth-inventor-typewriter.

Waller, Robert A. 1986. "Women and the Typewriter during the First Fifty Years, 1873–1923." *Studies in Popular Culture*, 9(1): 39–50.

Weller, Charles E. 1918. *The Early History of the Typewriter*. La Porte, IN: Chase & Shepard, printers.

44 Whiteley Harvester Patent Model

INTRODUCTION

Some important technological improvements were lost to society during Europe's long medieval winter. For instance, concrete was commonly used by the Romans but was forgotten for centuries. Besides concrete, one of the inventions forgotten during the Middle Ages was the oxen-pulled wheat-harvesting mechanical reaper, utilized by the ancient Celts and Romans. Without the mechanical reaper, for centuries a multitude of farm workers were hired to manually cut down wheat using a tool called a scythe. It wasn't until the early 1800s that a mechanical reaper was reinvented. Once it hit the markets, scores of British and American inventors strove to come up with a version of the device, for it was a valuable tool for a developing industrial economy. Though the United States had been founded by thinkers like Thomas Jefferson, who championed the so-called self-sufficient and independent "yeoman farmer," by the 19th century, agriculture was developing into an industry. Farmers did not merely grow crops to sustain themselves and their families; they sold their crops to an ever-growing population that worked in factories and offices in the industrial economy and did not farm any crops at all. With the onset of the Industrial Revolution in the early 19th century in England and the United States, the burgeoning textile industry proceeded to pull available workers off the farms and into the factories. Willing farmhands were becoming scarce, and the farm population began to decline. The decline was precipitous. Soon after Jefferson's lifetime in 1820, 71.8 percent of the American workers were farmers, but when the 20th century dawned, the number had plunged to a jaw-dropping 37.5 percent. (By 1960, the number had decreased to 6.1 percent.)

In 1833, a device was patented by Obed Hussey, a one-eyed ex-whaler from Maine. It was the first mechanical reaper patented in the United States. It wasn't the only one, however, and Hussey spent many subsequent years in a patent fight with Cyrus McCormick, who invented an improved version of the device in 1834. Though McCormick officially lost the patent war with Hussey in court, which was nicknamed the "War of the Reapers,"

McCormick was infinitely better as a business and self-promoter, and he ended up winning the long-term public relations battle. Cyrus McCormick was born on a farm in Virginia's Shenandoah Valley. His father, a tough Scots-Irish farmer, owned a 1,200-acre farm, whiskey distillery, and farm-implement shop. He was an inveterate tinkerer and loved the idea of being an inventor, though he was never a successful one. His son Cyrus, however, also enjoyed tinkering in the shop. His aspiration was to design a usable reaping machine. In 1834, he took out a patent on his new device and began to manufacture it himself. McCormick was not successful at marketing his mechanical reaper at first, and it took ten years before he sold a single one. But Cyrus was adept at self-promotion and spent years traveling the world promoting his "mechanical man." He entered competitions and won a number of them, taking home the Gold Medal at the London Crystal Palace Exhibition in 1851. McCormick was even elected to the French Academy of Sciences for "having done more for agriculture than any other living man." By 1846, after continually improving the design, McCormick's reaper began to sell due to the new international demand for American wheat after the British wheat crops failed. McCormick, though a Southerner born and bred, saw opportunity in the grassy, verdant plains of the Midwest. There, huge crops of wheat could be grown with the aid of a mechanical device that significantly reduced the demand for manual labor. McCormick made the brilliant and consequential decision to relocate his factory to Chicago, which was a tiny backwater when he settled there in 1847. However, its access to the Great Lakes, the Erie Canal, and the soon-to-be-built railroads meant that it would soon become the transportation hub for the Midwest, connecting to the East Coast, and eventually the entire western region.

McCormick built a large factory in Chicago and sold five hundred reapers in the first year, increasing his sales threefold by year number two. He paid fair wages in the early years and kept improving his production techniques as well as his product. One of his most successful sales innovations was his policy of offering a deferred payment plan, which delighted his farmer customers who were perennially short of cash. He demanded only $30 down for the $130 reaper and accepted monthly payments, adding on only as much interest as would have been charged by a bank. He also gave a money-back guarantee. Located in the Midwest, McCormick sent sales representatives to farms around the region that demonstrated the machines and taught the local farmers how to use them. McCormick became hugely successful and sold his company to International Harvester in 1902.

DESCRIPTION

There were many improvements made to the horse-drawn mechanical reaper over the decades after the first ones were produced by McCormick and Hussey in the 1830s. They all chopped off the wheat stalks with a large blade. However, the early reapers required that the wheat be raked off the machine by hand. Improvements in the later designs added "self-raking" models, introduced by Jearum Atkins, which pushed the wheat off the platform onto the ground, forming bunches that would be manually tied into bundles called "sheaves." The farmworkers would then stack the sheaves into piles that were called "stooks." For the last step the farmer would thresh and winnow the wheat to remove the inedible chaff and preserve the edible grains of wheat. One of the most successful innovators in mechanical reapers during the 19th century was William N. Whiteley. Born in 1835 in Springfield, Ohio, Whiteley began working in his father's farm-implement manufacturing company, the Whiteley and Fassler Company. In 1852, the teenaged William Whiteley attended an exhibition of reapers at a local farm and began tinkering with ideas for harvester innovations. His first successful machine was produced in 1856. Eventually William took control of the organization and renamed the company the Champion Machine Company. Located in Springfield, Ohio, the city became known as "the Champion City." Whiteley received forty-two patents for his inventions. One of the patents is for the machine shown here, the Whiteley Harvester from 1877. This harvester, patent number 197,192, was issued on November 13, 1877. It was a combination reaper and mower with removable attachments that could be used separately to either reap or mow. This machine contained attachments that were able to reap, rake, or mow. There was a large wheel next to the driver's seat from which the farmer could steer the horses and control the attachments. The brand name of this harvester was Champion. The Champion Company became the largest producer of farming implements in the world by the 1800s, during which time it was able to produce more than twelve thousand reapers per year. When Whiteley opened up his new plant in 1882, it was the largest factory of its kind in the entire world, employing over two thousand workers. Whiteley sold the Champion line to the firm of Warder, Bushnell & Glessner in 1887. In 1902, five firms, including Whiteley's and McCormick's, banded together to form the famous firm of International Harvester Company.

THE HAYMARKET RIOTS IN 1886

It was a strike in the McCormick plant in Chicago that led to one of the first industrial riots in American history. Workers at the McCormick Harvesting Machine Company, incensed by the persistent low wages and demanding an 8-hour day, struck and were locked out as tensions flared. Violence erupted, and a protest was called for May 4, 1886, at Haymarket Square. At the protest a bomb was thrown, killing one police officer. The police fired at the protesters, killing eight.

SIGNIFICANCE

The various iterations of the mechanical reaper, and its descendants, the reaper/mower, reaper/raker, harvester, or eventually, the harvester combine, which was able to reap, thresh, and winnow a variety of grain crops, altered the agricultural business in the United States. Before the invention of the mechanical reaper, many farm hands were necessary to harvest wheat. In the South where cotton and tobacco were kings, farm hands were needed throughout the growing season. This made it expedient to keep a group of farm hands at the farm, usually slaves, to tend to the crops on a regular basis. However, wheat was different. Sowing, that is, planting wheat, didn't require a large number of laborers. And during the growing season, wheat could be left to grow without much fuss. But harvesting it had to be done quickly at the end of the growing season and required many laborers for a short period of time. This labor shortage prevented even prosperous farmers from growing much wheat. The United States had a unique problem with its vast size and limited population. Whereas in Europe, farms were small and labor was cheap, mechanization of farming was not as essential. But in the United States, especially as the country expanded west, the cost of labor was prohibitive. The labor demand was intense but intermittent. This meant that the introduction of a machine to do the reaping could replace the expense of hiring temporary labor. And it certainly did reduce the necessity of hiring temporary labor. It took four people, two oxen, and ten hours to harvest two hundred bushels of wheat in 1830. It took the same amount of time, with the aid of harvesting combines and thirty-six horses, to harvest twenty thousand bushels of wheat sixty-five years later, by the end of the 19th century. The reaping machine was the catalyst that opened up the vast expanses of the Midwest to grow wheat, which brought down the price of bread and made the United States the "bread basket of the world."

FURTHER INFORMATION

Baker, Kevin. 2016. *America the Ingenious: How a Nation of Dreamers, Immigrants, and Tinkerers Changed the World.* New York: Artisan.

Brookover, Charles. Spring 2013. "The Champion No. 4 Combined Mower and Self-Raking Reaper." *Small Farmer's Journal*, 37(2). Accessed June 1, 2022. https://smallfarmersjournal.com/the-champion-no-4-com bined-mower-and-self-raking-reaper/

"MBA Cases: Cyrus McCormick—The Business of Agriculture and the Reaper Invention." IBiz. Accessed September 21, 2020. https://www .youtube.com/watch?v=HHIlFuj1yZI.

McNamara, Robert. 2020. "Invention of the McCormick Reaper." August 26. Accessed August 31, 2020. https://www.thoughtco.com /mccormick-reaper-1773393.

Olmstead, Alan L. June 1975. "The Mechanization of Reaping and Mowing in American Agriculture, 1833–1870." *Journal of Economic History*, 35(2): 327–352.

Smith, Scott S. 2016. "Cyrus McCormick Revolutionized Framing Worldwide with the Reaper." *Investor's Business Daily*. April 14. Accessed September 18, 2020. https://www.investors.com/news/management/leaders-and-success/cyrus-mccormick-revolutionized-farming-worldwide-with-the-reaper/

Transportation and Travel

Bicycle Pin

Covered Wagon

Steamboat Sketch

Transcontinental Railroad Gold Spike

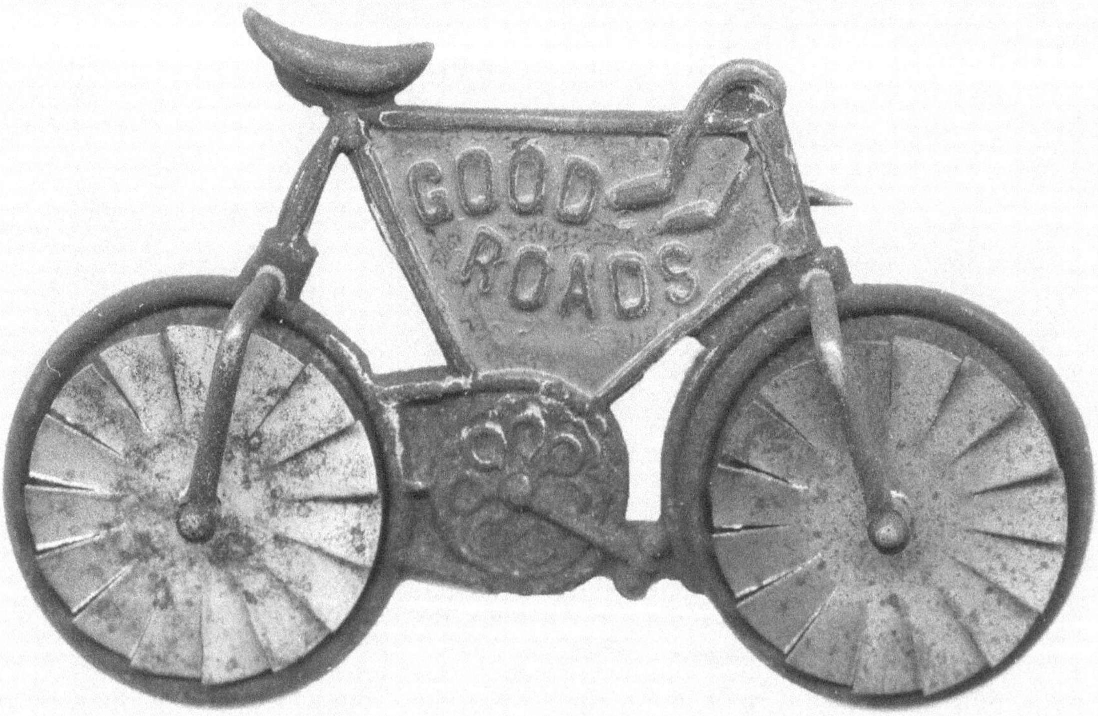

Historic Richmond Town

45 Bicycle Pin

INTRODUCTION

The narrative of 19th-century American civilization boasts a succession of transportation innovations, kicked off by the invention of the steamboat at the dawn of the century and carried on with the completion of the transcontinental railroad in the 1860s. These technological advances transformed American society and encouraged development of the west. But it wasn't until the last decades of the 19th century that a new mode of transport was invented, one that encouraged the personal freedom to travel wherever and whenever on one's own personal schedule. This allowance for individual mobility, so beloved by Americans to this day, was not, however, led by the invention of the motorcar at the turn of the twentieth century. It was pioneered by another newfangled contraption, which was invented in France in the 1860s and dubbed the "velocipede." A version of this unwieldy machine, an early example of the bicycle that Americans called the "high-wheeler," became popular in the United States in the 1880s, with a total of one hundred thousand sold by 1886. Though dangerous and difficult to maneuver, the high-wheeler developed a following among the emergent professional class that had the time and the discretionary income to purchase the pricey machines.

In 1884, the British inventor John Kemp Starling produced the first "safety bicycle," which had two identical-sized wheels and closely resembled the bicycles sold today. The first safety bicycle sold in the United States was produced by A. H. Overman in 1887. The introduction of the safety bicycle led to a fad that would sweep through America's high society and last for the next twenty-five years. Bicycles were "the next big thing" as Americans hit the open road and rode for miles out of the city and into the country. By 1896, there were 2.5 million bicycles on the road. Everyone tried the new contraption, including Mark Twain, who wrote, "Get a bicycle. You won't regret it, if you live" (Angier 2015). William McKinley exploited the national bicycle enthusiasm to deliver his progressive Republican message in his 1896 campaign against populist Democrat William Jennings Bryan.

313

He used bicycle imagery and depicted himself on a bicycle on his campaign literature and buttons, with the caption "To the White House." The bicycle craze also influenced women's mobility, freedom, and even clothing. Though men were the consumers of the dangerous high-wheelers, after the introduction of the safety bicycles, women jumped on the bandwagon as well. For the first time, an individual woman could get on a bike and ride anywhere she wished, without the responsibility of getting horses and wagons involved. Clothing, in addition to behavior, was transformed. A movement to loosen up the uncompromising corset and encourage the wearing of "bloomers," which were a ladies' version of pants, was part of the "rational clothing" movement that accompanied the invention of the safety bicycle. In response to the bicycle craze, a new national organization that called itself the League of American Wheelmen, or the LAW, was formed in 1880 by an influential group of riders from the cities of the Northeast and Midwest.

DESCRIPTION

The influence of the LAW was central to the eventual improvement of American roads. The organization founded a campaign for safe roads that they called the Good Roads Movement. The artifact shown here, from the collection of the Staten Island Historical Society, is a metal pin produced by the LAW that depicts a safety bicycle with the motto "Good Roads" stamped in the blue enameled section between the handlebars and the seat. The wheels on the pin actually spin. On the back of the pin is a pin clasp. Though not dated, the pin is estimated to have been produced between 1887 and 1905. The dimensions of the pin are 1 inch high by 1 ¾ inches wide.

In addition to campaign pins, brochures, and other ephemera, the LAW published a magazine called *Good Roads*, beginning in 1892. It also produced local maps of various locales for the cyclists' use. The LAW had power because of the wealth and influence of its high-profile members. But they were up against a century of political muscle that was adamantly against using taxpayers' funds to build roads. No federal funding had been used to build or improve American roads since the Jefferson administration, and by the end of the 19th century, the condition of the nation's roads was disgraceful. The administrations of the 19th-century presidents, Madison, Monroe, and Jackson, all vetoed proposed legislation to build or maintain roads. The maintenance of roads was deemed a state responsibility. The states as a rule relegated the responsibility down to the individual communities. Therefore, wealthy cities could build paved roads, but once out of the city, the roads were nothing but muddy, dusty, and unpaved paths. There was a reason for this. Once out of the city, small, family-run farms blanketed the nearby rural countryside. At the edge of the farm was a road that the farmer considered an extension of his property. He would use the road to transport his produce to the local market. The local communities accepted what was called a "cuvee" system of tax payment from the farmers, who were responsible for maintaining the roads that abutted their farms. The cuvee system meant that the farmers paid their taxes in labor rather than cash. They maintained the roads abutting their property in lieu of paying taxes. However, the maintenance of the roads was not high-priority for these overworked, cash-strapped farmers. They postponed the roadwork until all the farm work was completed and, even then, accepted the poor conditions of the road from freeze/thaw cycles and ruts, mud, and dust as merely another example of the natural order of things, over which the farmers had no control. This type of maintenance was certainly not a scientific pursuit, even though engineering research done at the country's finest universities had already attained the knowledge and capacity to design and build fine roads. But, alas, these roads were only built in the cities, where road maintenance was a high priority and engineers were hired to design and maintain them.

So along comes the recreational cyclist, typically a wealthy, professional man (or sometimes a woman) who rides out of town for miles, enjoying the freedom of the bicycle as well as the beauty and fresh air of the countryside. Once out of the city limits, the roads deteriorate and the ride is no longer enjoyable. Bicycles of this time period were not made to navigate bumpy dirt roads. The local bicycling organizations, soon joined by the powerful national organization, the LAW, pushed the national, state, and local governments to take charge of improving the roads. This set up a direct conflict between the farmers and the cyclists. The farmers resented the intrusion of these machines that frightened their horses, as well as the city slickers that rode them, who spoiled their land for Sunday picnics, in a classic early example of the rural-urban divide. In 1893, an Iowa farmers' convention averred that "[w]e don't want any eastern bicycle fellers or one-hoss lawyers with patent leather boots, to tell us how to fix the roads that we use" (Wells 2006: 150). The LAW, utilizing its influence on the national scene, resolved to appeal to the farmers' own interests in order to coax them to relinquish their long-standing claim on rural road maintenance. With their plethora of pamphlets and other publications, the LAW made a direct appeal to the farming community using a two-pronged approach. First, they affirmed that better roads would lessen the isolation of the farmers, with muddy roads hampering easy travel, calling it a "mud tax." Improved roads increased the profit of the farmers by as much as 60 percent, using fewer horses and providing easier transportation, according to the LAW. Maybe the farmers didn't want to pay the government a tax to build and maintain the roads, but the poor quality of the roads actually cost the farmers in lost time, lower property values, and higher transportation expenses. The second point of the LAW's two-pronged approach was to appeal to the social opportunities that could arise with the improvement of the rural roads. Farmers could travel much more easily, visit town, go to church, and entice their children to stay home and not escape to the city. This would raise the economic prospects of the region in general. Eventually, many members of the farming community were persuaded by the arguments of the LAW. The cyclists were on their way to transforming the national policy of road construction and maintenance in the United States.

MARSHALL "MAJOR" TAYLOR

Marshall "Major" Taylor was the fastest cyclist in the United States from 1897 to 1900. Bicycle racing was extremely popular at the time. Taylor was only the second African American to win a world championship in sports.

SIGNIFICANCE

The LAW, formed in 1880 at the Gilded Age resort of Newport, Rhode Island, stated in its constitution that it must "promote the general interests of cycling." In 1888, it amended it constitution to add this pledge: "to secure improvement in the condition of the public roads and highways" (Reid 2015: 148). The organization published a textbook, titled *Making and Mending Good Roads & Nature and Use of Asphalt for Paving*, and distributed it to legislators and city and county officials. Not only did they want to encourage government officials to assume the role of road builder but they also intended to show them how to do it. This, from a bicycle association. And soon the LAW's influence and zeal would bear fruit. The LAW argued that improved rural roads would benefit the country at large, as well as the interests of the farmers, economically, socially, and by introducing a national Rural Free Delivery (RFD) postal system. The farmers accepted the arguments put forth by the city-slickers of the LAW, and the two interest groups formed a united front. The appeal was made to the state and federal governments to address road construction and maintenance. A clause to a federal agriculture bill created the Office of Road Inquiry (ORI) in 1893, with $10,000 granted for the purpose of road research. Behind the scenes, the cyclists of the LAW subsidized and managed the ORI. The ORI would eventually be transformed into the Federal Highway Administration. The role of the federal government in the building of roads in the United States was now set in stone. However, the influence of the bicycle movement didn't last. Bicycle mechanics would soon turn their efforts to the newest "next big thing"—the horseless carriage, also known as the automobile. The importance of good-quality roads became even more critical to the automobile manufacturers. Roads were built, culminating in President Eisenhower's National Interstate and Defense Highways Act of 1956. Few people remember the essential role played by a scrappy and influential group of cyclists who were determined to improve their experiences cycling out into the countryside through their campaign for "Good Roads."

FURTHER INFORMATION

Alvey, Noelle. 2014. "Marshall 'Major' Taylor: The Incredible Story of the First African-American World Champion." *National Museum of American History*. March 19. Accessed June 2, 2022. https://american history.si.edu/blog/2014/03/marshall-major-taylor-the-incredible-story -of-the-first-african-american-world-champion.html

Angier, Natalie. 2015. "The Bicycle and the Ride to Modern America." *New York Times*. July 13. Accessed August 20, 2021 https://www.nytimes .com/2015/07/14/science/the-bicycle-and-the-ride-to-modern-america .html.

"The First Freedom Rider?" National Museum of American History. Accessed June 2, 2022. https://americanhistory.si.edu/object-project /bicycles/bicycle-medals.

Grant, Jesse. 2021. "Whites on Bikes: Race and Exclusivity of Early Bicycling, 1869–1900." U.S. History Scene. Accessed August 20, 2021. https://ushistoryscene.com/article/early-bicycling/.

Hugill, Peter J. July 1982. "Good Roads and the Automobile in the United States 1880–1929." *Geographical Review*, 72(3): 327–349.

Reid, Carlton. 2015. *Roads Were Not Built for Cars: How Cyclists Were the First to Push for Good Roads & Became the Pioneers of Motoring*. Washington, DC: Island Press.

Vogel, Andrew. Winter 2010. "Hamlin Garland's Roads, the Good Roads Movement, and the Ambivalent Reform of America's Geographic Imagination." *Studies in American Naturalism*, 5(2): 111–132.

Wells, Christopher W. Spring 2006. "The Changing Nature of Country Roads: Farmers, Reformers, and the Shifting Uses of Rural Space, 1880–1905." *Agricultural History*, 80(2): 143–166.

46 Covered Wagon

INTRODUCTION

An iconic part of the American frontier myth is the wagon train laboriously hauling families of pioneers on their journeys west. Scores of American westerns have been made for film as well as television that depicted the wagon trains among the cowboys and Indians. A popular early computer game called "The Oregon Trail" taught kids about the adventure of out-fitting the wagon and navigating the trails on the way out west as fictional pioneers in 1848. The "covered wagon" was the vehicle of choice for these pioneers before the transcontinental railroad was completed in 1869. There were two popular types of wagons that made the trip out west. These were used on the Oregon and Santa Fe Trails, as well as the Great Wagon Road in the southeast and the Mormon Trail that took Mormons from their home in Illinois to their new settlement in Utah. The two types of wagons were the Conestoga Wagon and the Prairie Schooner Wagon.

DESCRIPTION

The beautiful example shown here is a Conestoga wagon from the National Museum of American History. It was acquired from a Pennsylvania collector, and its exact provenance is unknown, though the museum estimates that it was in service between 1840 and 1850. It is a very large wagon, one of the largest ever made, at 18 feet long and almost 8 feet wide. The Conestoga wagon became popular in the mid-1700s in southeastern Pennsylvania, though its first known mention was by Ben Garcia in 1717. The name is derived from the Conestoga River near Lancaster, where there were a number of Swiss and German settlements. The Conestoga River got its name from the Conestoga tribe, a part of the Susquehanna tribe. The term "Conestoga" is a corruption of the French term *Grandastogues*. The wagon was typically used to haul freight, and it was heavy and durable. The frame and suspension were made of wood, typically white oak, with the wooden wheels rimmed with iron for greater strength. The original German wagon makers, or wainwrights, were fine craftsmen, and they typically added decorative German folk art in the ironwork. This wagon is painted bright blue, with bright red running gear, which was typical. The wagon has a white canvas cover, which is also called a bonnet. The unique curved shape of the Conestoga adds to its beauty. The side panels of the Conestoga had a curved profile, sweeping up at the front and the rear. This design was a practical as well as beautiful one—the cargo would not shift as much going up and down hills. The craftsmen who designed and constructed these wagons were concerned with its looks as well as its practicality. This may be the reason that the Conestoga wagon is the one that is most often depicted in western movies about wagon trains. Though the Conestoga is a visual standout, in reality it was the smaller and more accommodating prairie schooner wagon that most often made the trip out west on the Oregon Trail.

The Conestoga wagon, hardy and heavy, was the tractor-trailer of its day and was used primarily to haul freight. Though originally a type of farm wagon, its size and muscle made it a perfect vehicle to carry heavy loads to distant locations. It could carry upward of 12,000 pounds in freight. The typical Conestoga required six horses, although some of the smaller ones utilized four. The horses that were often used by these big wagons were called Conestoga horses. They were long-legged, tall, and heavy. They most likely originated in Chester County, Pennsylvania, and they were a product of selective breeding. When the Conestoga wagon was no longer used by the second half of the 19th century, the Conestoga horse was no longer bred. The wagon always had bells attached to the elaborate harnesses. The lead horse would have five bells, the second pair would have four, and the horse nearest the wagon had three. The bells on the Conestoga wagon were a trademark of this type of wagon and symbolized the success of the wagoner. The expression "I'll be there with bells on," meaning that you are joyously anticipating coming to the event, originated with the bells of the Conestoga wagon. All Conestoga wagons included a tool box, which was fastened to the left side of the wagon, many of which were handsomely decorated. A feed box, stored at the rear, was hung in front of the horses when the wagon was stopped so the horses could eat. Each wagon also had an axe, a tar pot that was hung on a hook and staple. The tar pot contained pine tar and was used to lubricate the wheels. The running gear of the Conestoga wagon was typically painted red. The rear wheels were between 54 and 72 inches in diameter and 3 ½ to 4 inches wide. The front wheels of the wagon were smaller. The driver of the wagon was called the "wagoner," and he typically sat on the last horse on the left, closest to the wagon, although sometimes he walked alongside or sat on the "lazy board," which extended from the wagon. The wagoners took pride in their vehicles. On their trips carrying freight, they often stopped at taverns along the road that catered to them like truck stops do today. They would eat and drink and sleep on the floor in their bedrolls. The overnight stay would cost about $1.75, including lodging, meals, and care for the horses.

THE ORIGIN OF THE TERM "STOGIES"

Wagoners, the truck drivers of the Conestoga hauler wagons, were a tough and sturdy breed. They wore flannel shirts and smoked a certain type of long, thin cigar called the "Stogie," named after the Conestoga wagon. The term now refers to a thin, cheap cigar, though it sometimes is used to describe any cigar.

SIGNIFICANCE

The Conestoga wagon was the freight hauler of the second half of the 18th century and the first half of the 19th century. It started out as a farm wagon but soon grew into the premier transporter of America's early years. The wagon plied the Great Wagon Road, an ancient pathway that was called "Jonontore" by the local tribes. This road went from Philadelphia through the Shenandoah Valley of Virginia to Augusta, Georgia, and carried goods for the one hundred thousand German and Scots-Irish immigrants who settled Appalachia. The Conestoga was also used to bring goods back and forth from the Northwest Territory, the huge land mass of the present-day Midwest that was ceded to the United States from Britain in the Treaty of Paris after the Revolutionary War. The first federally funded road, called the National Road, was built between 1811 and 1838. It stretched from Cumberland, Maryland, to Wheeling, Virginia (now West Virginia) to Ohio, Indiana, and Illinois. This upgraded road was able to handle the Conestoga wagons that carried finished goods and supplies west for the settlers and returned with loads of products that could be sold on the East Coast, like flour, whiskey, tobacco, furs, and coal. The lumbering trains of Conestoga wagons were able to travel only 10–15 miles per day.

The Santa Fe and Oregon Trails opened up the far west to American settlers. At first, the popular Conestoga wagon was the preferred vehicle for the early settlers and traders. However, the longer distance, tougher travel conditions, and the dearth of water made it difficult for the team of horses to make the trip, so the wagoners decided to use teams of oxen. But the Conestoga wagon was big and heavy and overstressed the oxen, many of whom died before the trip was completed. Settlers liked the idea of taking oxen or mules out west where they would be useful on the farm. But another type of wagon was needed. So a new variation on the wagon design was introduced, the prairie schooner. These wagons were adopted from smaller farm wagons and could be pulled by a team of six to ten mules or four to six oxen. They were typically only 4 feet wide and 10 or 12 feet long. They did not have the large bonnet, or cover, that the Conestoga had, but they did have a canvas cover, which looked like a sail from a distance, hence the term "schooner." These wagons became popular for the trip out West, and many were produced by the Studebaker Brothers wainwrights in South Bend, Indiana. Although the more picturesque and stately Conestoga wagon is depicted in most movies and television shows that portray wagon trains moving along the Oregon or Santa Fe Trail, it was most likely the little, sturdy, and flexible prairie schooner that carried most settlers out west during the middle of the 19th century. However, once the transcontinental railroad was completed in 1869, and the railroads were able to transport both settlers and freight, the era of the classic wagon trains was dead.

FURTHER INFORMATION

Haney, Leighton. April 1984. "The Conestoga Wagon." *Tredyffrin Easttown Historical Society History Quarterly Digital Archives*. 22(2): 43–50.

Harris, Karen. "Real-Life Covered Wagons: 8 Facts You Didn't Know." *History Daily*. Accessed July 15, 2020. https://historydaily.org/covered-wagons-facts-trivia-didnt-know.

Kurin, Richard. 2013. *The Smithsonian's History of America in 101 Objects*. New York: Penguin Books.

Kurin, Richard. 2016. "The Conestoga Wagon: The Road Westward." *The Great Courses Daily*. September 26. Accessed July 15, 2020. https://www.thegreatcoursesdaily.com/the-conestoga-wagon-pushing-westward/.

National Park Service. "Conestoga Wagon Replica." Scotts Bluff National Monument. Accessed June 2, 2022. https://www.nps.gov/places/conestoga-wagon.htm.

National Park Service. "Scotts Bluff: Traveling the Emigrant Trails." Scotts Bluff National Monument. Accessed June 2, 2022. http://npshistory.com/brochures/scbl/traveling-the-emigrant-trails.pdf

National Park Service. "Scotts Bluff: Wagons on the Emigrant Trails." Scotts Bluff National Monument. Accessed June 2, 2022. http://npshistory.com/brochures/scbl/wagons-on-the-emigrant-trails.pdf

Richards, William N. October 1967. "Review: Conestoga Wagon 1750–1850: Carrier for 100 Years of America's Westward Expansion." *Pennsylvania Magazine of History and Biography*, 91(4): 477–479.

Stewart, George R. February 1962. "The Prairie Schooner Got Them There." *American Heritage*, 13(2). Accessed June 2, 2022. https://www.americanheritage.com/prairie-schooner-got-them-there

White, Roger B. October 23, 2012. "Covered Wagons and the American Frontier." *National Museum of American History Blog*. Accessed July 15, 2020. https://americanhistory.si.edu/blog/2012/10/conestoga-wagons-and-the-american-frontier.html.

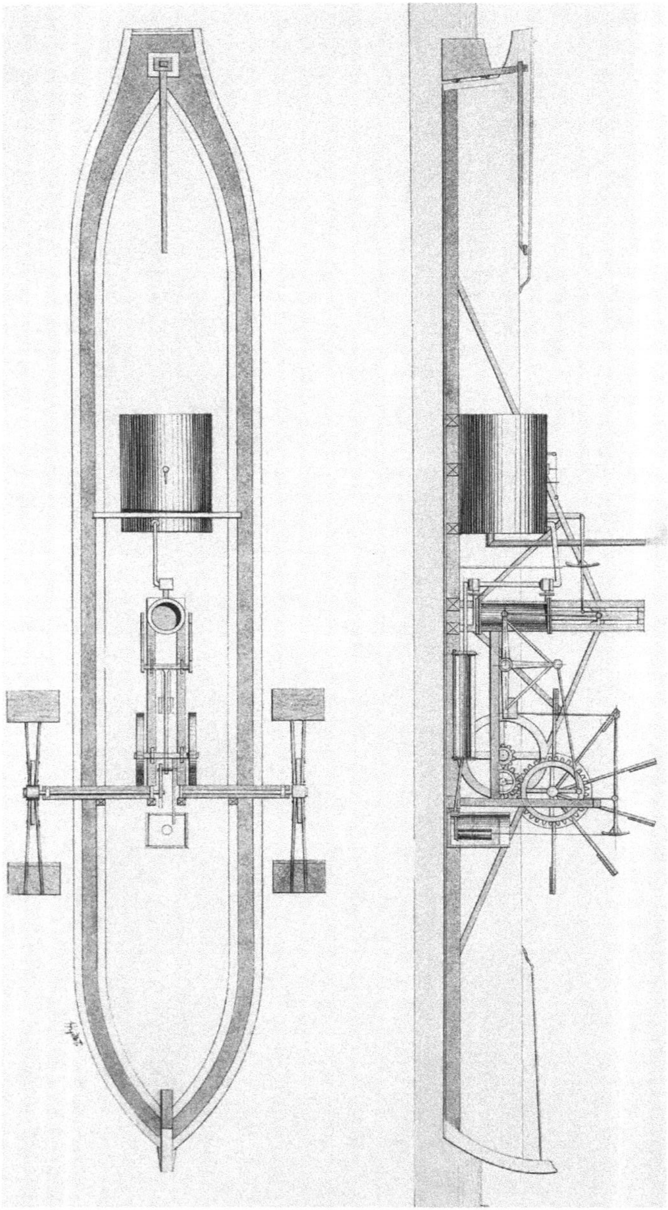
DeA Picture Library/Bridgeman Images

47 Steamboat Sketch

INTRODUCTION

Before the railroad revolutionized both travel and industry in the mid-19th century, the most efficient method of traveling or shipping goods was over water. Overland travel was laborious and risky, over unpaved roads. Boats could carry more cargo than any carriage could. By the end of the 18th century, inventors were looking into building canals where there was no existing waterway or where it was impassable because of treacherous currents or waterfalls. An innovative system of man-made canals was built in England after the nascent Industrial Revolution demanded increased shipping to and from the newly built factories. In the United States, the concept of canal building was on the minds of several of the founding fathers, most notably Thomas Jefferson. Another idea that was floating around in the United States and Europe was the concept of a faster boat that was not dependent on the current or the winds. Riverboats were safe, and there were efficient methods for transporting people and goods in cargo boats. Unpowered boats, called keelboats, were similar to barges, and they plied the great rivers and canals carrying cargo. They were operated by men using oars or poles, which pushed the boat along and were extremely slow. Propelling a keelboat against the current was so difficult that it often wasn't even attempted. The great Mississippi River flowed south from a tiny lake in northern Minnesota all the way down to its mouth at the Gulf of Mexico, so most of the commerce took place in a southward direction. The small riverboats would meet larger sailing vessels in New Orleans where the cargo would be transferred. The sailing ships would sail all the way around Florida and up the East Coast to New York and Boston. It was a long, expensive, and arduous journey. Providing power from engines to navigate the Mississippi and other rivers was not possible. In 1769, the Scotsman James Watt invented the first powerful and efficient steam engine. After a number of fits and starts, he teamed up with Matthew Boulton and formed the engine manufacturing company Boulton and Watt, which became very successful and had an enduring influence on steam engine technology in both Britain and the United States.

Soon inventors were thinking about using steam to power a boat. Experiments were performed, using the technology invented by Watt's steam engine. William Symington built a number of pleasure steamboats in the late 18th century in Scotland. Joseph Bramah of Piccadilly, England, patented a paddle wheel to be used with a steam engine. James Rumsey invented a system of hydraulic jet propulsion that drew water into the bow and out the stern of the boat, propelling it forward. He utilized this technique in the 1780s in the Potomac River in the United States. The most prominent test of steamboat technology in the United States took place on a summer route on the Delaware River. The inventor was a Connecticut man named John Fitch. After building the 45-feet-long prototype, Fitch demonstrated it to delegates to the Constitutional Convention in 1787. He then built a larger 60-feet boat with stern-mounted oars and used it to carry passengers between Philadelphia and Burlington, New Jersey, during the summer of 1790. Fitch entered into a patent fight with James Rumsey but eventually secured the first American steamboat patent in 1791. His success was fleeting, however, and he lost financial backing because his patent did not include allowing him a monopoly on the use of the product. Fitch, though an ingenious inventor, was not a good businessman in any sense. He continued his attempt to secure more funding, traveling to France and then to England to convince backers to invest in his invention. He was unsuccessful and returned to the United States with no funding in hand. Fitch died in 1798 at age fifty-five and was never able to complete his mission to invent a viable steamboat business.

The first financially successful steamboat was launched by Robert Fulton in 1807 in New York City. Fulton's story differed from Fitch's in several ways. Fulton was a handsome and charismatic figure, who made the right connections with powerful and wealthy investors. Robert Fulton was born in Lancaster County, Pennsylvania, on November 14, 1765. After being homeschooled by his mother, he was sent to a Quaker school at the age of eight. Fulton showed talent in painting, and in 1782, he left for Philadelphia to pursue a career in art. He was particularly good at painting miniatures, which were tiny portraits that were popular with the well-to-do before the advent of photography. His contacts were beneficial to his career; he even painted a portrait of Benjamin Franklin and carried a letter of introduction with him when he traveled to England in 1786. Fulton opted to change his concentration to civil engineering design. In 1787, he crossed the channel to France where he stayed for seven years, studying canals and taking out several patents. England and France were at war, and Fulton developed an interest in warfare during that period of time. He researched a type of torpedo that would explode under water and with it a vessel that could remain underwater, a submarine, or, in Fulton's words, a "plunging machine." He called the machine the *Nautilus* and attempted to convince the French authorities to sponsor its construction. Finally, in 1800, the French minister of marine granted him permission to build it. He tested the remarkable machine in the Seine River where it was able to stay underwater for 20 minutes. When used against British ships, however, it proved too slow and clumsy to catch the quicker British ships. Fulton tried to convince Napoleon to sponsor the construction of more submarines, but soon a peace accord was signed between the two nations, and Fulton's devious and dangerous new invention was no longer necessary to the French.

Fulton turned to another project, designing a boat powered by steam. He met a man in Paris named Robert Livingston, who was the chancellor to France under President Thomas Jefferson. Livingston was a man of significant influence, power, and prestige. Fascinated by the concept of a steam-powered boat, Livingston had been given the monopoly rights to operate a boat powered by steam or fire on all waters of New York State for a twenty-year period. Livingston and Fulton formed a partnership that would turn out to be lucrative to both men and transformational to the transportation history of the young United States. Fulton set about to design a boat that would be able to carry sixty passengers and travel between New York City and Albany at a speed of 8 miles an hour. He contacted the Boulton and Watt Company in England and signed a contract to build a steam engine that would be shipped over to New York. At the same time that this negotiation was taking place, Livingston was involved in another transformational contract, the Louisiana Purchase. After Napoleon secretly acquired the Louisiana Territory from Spain in 1800, President Jefferson sent Livingston and James Monroe to Paris to negotiate with Napoleon to sell the huge territory to the United States. In 1803, the territory was sold at a price of $15 million. Livingston knew that the control of the Mississippi River and the port of New Orleans was crucial to the economic growth of the United States. So too was the addition of the new steam-powered boat that could navigate the Mississippi in both directions quickly and efficiently. This was the steamboat that he was developing with his partner Robert Fulton.

DESCRIPTION

The artifact shown here is the sketch drawn by Robert Fulton for the French prototype of the new steamboat he was designing for use in New York. This watercolor sketch is located at the Musee de la Marine in Paris. The first boat tested in Paris was encouraging, though it sank when the engine broke the hull. Fulton built a larger version. This boat, 75 feet long and 8 feet wide, was launched on the Seine in Paris on August 9, 1803. A large group of dignitaries was present early that evening to view the newfangled machine. The boat was propelled by side paddle wheels. Livingston was thrilled with the potential of this new steamboat and had his monopoly of navigation rights in New York waters extended.

After another stint in England, Fulton headed back to the United States in 1806 to build his New York City steamboat. He contacted the best craftsmen in the city to fashion this revolutionary boat. Shipwright Charles Brownne of Corlear's Hook on the East River in Manhattan built the flat-bottomed, straight-sided wooden vessel. Robert McQueen was the millwright who built the ironwork paddle mechanism. The boiler was built by a local coppersmith, and, of course, the all-important engine was a 24-horsepower Boulton and Watt design built from Fulton's own specifications and shipped over from England. The boat looked like a skiff, a type of shallow, flat-bottomed open boat. It had a small cabin, which contained the boiler, had two tall masts for auxiliary power, and a 30-feet-high smokestack in the center of the boat. There were wheels on either side, each with twelve huge paddles. The rudder was operated with a tiller like those on sailing vessels. Although known commonly as the *Clermont*, the original name for the boat was the *North River Boat*. The name *Clermont*, after Robert Livingston's Hudson River estate, was a later renaming of the vessel. These were the specifications of the groundbreaking *North River Boat*:

> Built: 1807
> Hull: wood, built by Charles Brown
> Length: 133 feet
> Breadth of beam: 18 feet
> Depth of hold: 7.1 feet
> Engine: Built in England by Boulton and Watt
>   Diameter of cylinder: 24 inches
>   Length of piston stroke: 4 feet
> Boiler: Copper, low pressure
>   Length: 20 feet
>   Height: 7 feet
>   Width: 8 feet
> Wheels: 15 inches in diameter, 8 paddles to each wheel
>   Length: 4 feet
>   Dip: 2 feet
>
> (Kotar and Gessler 2009: 11)

On August 17, 1807, the vessel made its maiden voyage, cheered on from the Christopher Street dock in Greenwich Village by an excited group of New Yorkers, many of whom expected a mishap like an exploding boiler. Known as "Fulton's Folly," this boat was derided as much as it was respected. However, the forty passengers on the boat were relieved that it left the dock without incident and chugged up the Hudson River toward Albany, passing all the other various boats on the river. It stopped at Clermont where it picked up Robert Fulton and continued on its way to Albany, averaging 4.5 miles per hour. The trip back was even faster, making the 150-mile voyage in a record 32 hours. This was a groundbreaking trip and foresaw the influence of the boat powered by steam that could navigate American's mighty rivers.

SIGNIFICANCE

The effect of the trailblazing *North River Boat*, aka *Clermont*, on the history of the United States was immediate and enduring. Fulton went ahead and refitted the steamboat to make it more comfortable for passengers. He promoted the vessel to prominent New Yorkers as a luxurious way to travel, and they jumped at the chance. The investment was phenomenally successful, and Fulton benefited wildly from his 50/50 contract with Livingston. He married Livingston's cousin, bought a mansion in the city, and continued his quest to expand steamboat service throughout the nation. The Mississippi was his next venture, and it was even more successful. For the first time, steam-powered boats could travel both upriver and downriver. Though he and Livingston did not get a monopoly for the Mississippi River service, the service grew exponentially in the next half-century. By 1830, there were two hundred steamboats plying the Mississippi River, and by 1840, there were five hundred. The riverboats were outfitted ever more luxuriously for its wealthy passengers. In addition, a different type of steamboat, the western steamboat, was designed to carry freight in both directions upriver and downriver, reordering the flow of commerce. This advantage gave New Orleans an even more prominent place in the American economy. Now goods could travel up to the newly settled Midwest from the South. This opened up the Midwest to more settlement. With the completion of the Erie Canal in 1825, the Midwest was available to a new population. The steamboat altered the flow of commerce and revolutionized transportation in the United States. Although Robert Fulton spent many of the subsequent years in patent litigation, he did finally succeed in making the fortune he had been seeking. He died in 1815 from consumption at the age of forty-nine and is buried with other prominent New Yorkers in the Trinity Church Cemetery on Wall Street.

FURTHER INFORMATION

Burrows, Edwin G., and Mike Wallace. 1999. *Gotham: A History of New York City to 1898*. New York; Oxford: Oxford University Press.

Kotar, S. L., and J. E. Gessler. 2009. *The Steamboat Era*. Jefferson, NC; London: McFarland & Company, Inc.

Longley, Robert. 2021. "Biography of Robert Fulton, Inventor of the Steamboat." ThoughtCo. February 16. Accessed April 19, 2021. thoughtco.com/robert-fulton-steamboat-4075444.

Sutcliffe, Andrea. 2004. *Steam: The Untold Story of American's First Great Invention*. London: Palgrave McMillan.

U.S. Army Corps of Engineers. "A History of Steamboats." Accessed April 22, 2021. https://www.sam.usace.army.mil/Portals/46/docs/recreation/OP-CO/montgomery/pdfs/10thand11th/ahistoryofsteamboats.pdf.

1869. **May 10th.** 1869.

GREAT EVENT

Rail Road from the Atlantic to the Pacific

GRAND OPENING
— OF THE —

Union Pacific

RAIL ROAD,

PLATTE VALLEY ROUTE.

PASSENGER TRAINS LEAVE

OMAHA

ON THE ARRIVAL OF TRAINS FROM THE EAST.

THROUGH TO SAN FRANCISCO

In less than Four Days, avoiding the Dangers of the Sea!

Travelers for Pleasure, Health or Business

Will find a Trip over The Rocky Mountains Healthy and Pleasant.

LUXURIOUS CARS & EATING HOUSES

ON THE UNION PACIFIC RAIL ROAD.

PULLMAN'S PALACE SLEEPING CARS

RUN WITH ALL THROUGH PASSENGER TRAINS.

GOLD, SILVER AND OTHER MINERS!

Now is the time to seek your Fortunes in Nebraska, Wyoming, Arizona, Washington, Dakotah Colorado, Utah, Oregon, Montana, New Mexico, Idaho, Nevada or California.

CONNECTIONS MADE AT

CHEYENNE for DENVER, CENTRAL CITY & SANTA FE

AT OGDEN AND CORINNE FOR HELENA, BOISE CITY, VIRGINIA CITY, SALT LAKE CITY AND ARIZONA

THROUGH TICKETS FOR SALE AT ALL PRINCIPAL RAILROAD OFFICES!

Be Sure they Read via Platte Valley or Omaha

Company's Office 72 La Salle St., opposite City Hall and Court House Square, Chicago.
CHARLES E. NICHOLS, Ticket Agent.

G. P. GILMAN,   JOHN P. HART,   J. BUDD,   W. SNYDER,

48 Transcontinental Railroad Gold Spike

INTRODUCTION

Manifest Destiny, the widespread belief during the 19th century that the expansion of the United States from "sea to shining sea" was not only justified but also inevitable, was coined in 1845 by influential journalist John L. O'Sullivan while advocating for the annexation of Oregon and Texas. The relief valve that the opening of the West represented lured thousands of eager settlers to pack up their prairie schooner wagons and make the treacherous journey on wagon trains that lumbered along the Oregon or Santa Fe Trail. The perilous trip took six months and had to be started in the spring, so it could be completed before the onset of the winter. Such risk didn't deter these hardy souls from venturing out, but the situation would soon be transformed when the transcontinental railroad opened in 1869. Railroad lines had already been built along the East Coast beginning in the 1830s, and the South and Midwest were connected by networks of railroads by the 1840s. California was annexed in 1848 after the Mexican-American War, the same year that gold was discovered there. The region soon became a magnet for fortune-seekers and settlers. In 1850, California joined the union as the 31st state. Congress began investigating the possibility of building a railroad to California. In 1853, Congress appropriated funding for the Army Topographic Corps "to ascertain the most practicable and economical route for a railroad from the Mississippi River to the Pacific Ocean." Surveyors were sent out to investigate four separate routes, and debates took place regarding the advantages of a northern or southern route. No matter which route they opted for, any transcontinental railroad would require risky and dangerous construction over an intimidating landscape of mountains and deserts. The task was daunting, but despite the Civil War that was raging, President Abraham Lincoln advocated for the railroad to be built, and on July 1, 1862, he signed the Pacific Railway Act. This legislation authorized land grants and government bonds to two companies, the Central Pacific Railroad and the Union Pacific Railroad, to lay the track for the country's

333

first transcontinental railroad, with the Central Pacific Railroad coming from the west and the Union Pacific Railroad coming from the east. They would meet at the middle.

DESCRIPTION

This 1869 official poster announced the grand opening of the first transcontinental railroad. The ceremony took place on May 10, 1869, at Promontory Summit near Ogden, Utah. The poster, printed by the Union Pacific Railroad, was more of an advertisement for the rail service than an invitation to the ceremony. The text of the poster, loaded with rapturous promotion of the service and the ceremony, states the following:

> May 10th, 1869. Great Event. Rail Road from the Atlantic to the Pacific. Grand Opening of the Union Pacific Rail Road. Platte Valley Route. Passenger Trains Leaves Omaha on the Arrival of Trains from the East Through to San Francisco In less than Four Days, Avoiding the Dangers of the Sea. Travelers for Pleasure, Health or Business. Will Find a Trip over the Rocky Mountains Healthy and Pleasant Luxurious Cars & Eating Houses on the Union Pacific Rail Road. Pullman's Palace Sleeping Cars Run with all Through Passenger Trains. Gold, Silver and other Miners. Now is the Time to Seek your Fortunes in Nebraska, Wyoming, Arkansas, Washington, Dakota, Colorado, Utah, Oregon, Montana, New Mexico, Idaho, Nevada or California. Connections Made at Cheyenne for Denver, Central City and Santa Fe, at Ogden and Cheyenne for Helena, Boise City, Virginia City, Salt Lake City and Arizona. Through Tickets for Sale at all Principal Railroad Offices. Be Sure They Read Via Platte Valley or Omaha. Company's Office is 72 LaSalle St., Opposite City Hall and Court House Square, Chicago. Charles E. Nichols, Ticket Agent. G. P. Gilman, John P. Hart, J. Budd, W. Snyder.

The Grand Opening ceremony celebrated the meeting of the two locomotives, one traveling west-to-east and one traveling east-to-west at Promontory Point, north of the Great Salt Lake. At exactly 12:57 p.m. local time, railroad dignitaries hammered in ceremonial golden spikes. The telegraph system that had been set up allowed for this great event to be announced throughout the nation, and, in fact the whole country celebrated. There were cannons in San Francisco and Washington, DC, and whistles were blown and bells were chimed in American cities and towns. This amazing engineering accomplishment impressed the public, who understood the significance of turning a six-month journey into a two-week one. This was not only a literal connection but also a symbolic one, at once knitting together the East to the West, across a 3,000-mile span.

The story of this remarkable feat was an improbable one, filled with risk and requiring courage, vision, and government investment. As with many ambitious projects, this one featured a dollop of greed and avarice. Congress knew the importance of bringing rail lines out to the West, both for settlement and for industrial development. It began making land grants in 1850 to the Illinois Central and Mobile and Ohio railroads and continued the practice until 1871 when it granted land to the Texas and Pacific railroads. In total, the U.S. government granted over 170 million acres to more than eighty different private railroad companies. The companies had rights of way of 200 feet on each side of the track. They also received $16,000–$48,000 for each mile of track laid, depending on the terrain. Much of this land did not end up being used for railroads, however. Some of the companies sold the land at bargain prices to farmers, ensuring settlement as well as business for the railroad. The visionary engineer who sparked the idea of actually constructing this seemingly impossible feat was a man named Theodore Dehone Judah. Known as "Crazy Judah" for his obsessive attachment to the idea, he indefatigably lobbied both the western influencers and the Washington bureaucrats to sign on. When he was able to devise a workable route through the mountains, he set out to found a company to actually build it. Needing political support, Judah approached Leland Stanford, wholesale grocer and soon-to-be governor of California, who was ultimately convinced. Additionally, Judah invited three other men to be initial backers: Collis P. Huntington and his partner Mark Hopkins, who were hardware wholesalers, and Charles Crocker, a dry goods merchant. This group became known as the "Big Four."

The construction of the western portion of the railroad, the Central Pacific, began in January 1863, but at first the going was tough. In fact, only 18 miles of track were laid in that year and only 12 miles more in the following year. The terrain was rough, and the route went through the Sierra Nevada mountain range. The company was having trouble hiring laborers to do the strenuous work. Charles Crocker, working as the construction manager, was struggling to hire even a fraction of the four thousand laborers needed to pursue the work. He often had only eight hundred on the job at one time. The workers Crocker hired in the early years were mostly Irish immigrants, shipped in at great expense from the East Coast. Many Irish laborers disliked the strenuous work and abandoned the project, preferring to take their chances at making a fortune in the Nevada silver mines. Crocker then attempted to hire freed slaves, Mexican immigrants, and even Confederate war prisoners. None of these worked out. Thinking outside of the box, in 1865, Crocker suggested an absurd notion: hiring immigrant Chinese laborers. Since 1850, Chinese peasants from the Canton province had been fleeing destitute poverty in their homeland and immigrating to the United States, envisaging the Gum Shan, or "Mountain of Gold," rumored to be in the American West. The Chinese workers found work in the mines as well as in other laboring positions. Soon prejudice against the Chinese developed in California that would continue for years to come and lead to a variety of restrictive laws against the Chinese that culminated in the federal Chinese Exclusion Act, enacted in 1882. So even though Charles Crocker had a brilliant idea to hire Chinese workers for the railroad construction, the idea did not sit well with his labor supervisor, James Strobridge. In addition to being prejudiced against Chinese, Strobridge also felt that the slight stature of the Chinese would prevent them from being able to undertake the demanding work. However, he was desperate, and he agreed to hire a small contingent of fifty men on a trial basis. He was soon impressed with the quality and quantity of the work done by the Chinese laborers. He was also impressed with their temperament: sober, punctual, clean, and well-behaved, the Chinese soon became the preferred laborers on the work gangs. They ate healthier food; they bathed regularly and even washed their clothes. They didn't drink whiskey but subsisted daily on lukewarm tea, which was helpful in keeping the horrendous scourge of dysentery at bay. By 1868, the Chinese made up 80 percent of the Central Pacific workforce. The Chinese workers were admired by the management, called "Celestials" because of their spiritual beliefs. However, the management took advantage of their status, and they received less pay than the other workers, receiving $27 per month, minus room and board. The Irish workers received $35 per month, board provided.

After two years of excruciatingly slow progress, by the third year, the Central Pacific had completed the punishing construction of the railroad over the Sierra Nevada Mountains, and the pace picked up. The track was completed through Nevada, reaching the Utah border by 1868. The Union Pacific, the eastern portion of the railroad, encountered different complications in their quest to complete the transcontinental railroad. Hiring enough workers was a struggle just as much for the Union Pacific as for the Central Pacific. It wasn't until the Civil War ended in 1865 that Thomas Durant, the railroad executive for the Union Pacific, was able to hire out-of-work Civil War veterans to work on the project, as well as a bevy of newly arrived Irish laborers. Major issues for the construction crews were attacks from Native Americans that dogged them at every turn. The Sioux, Cheyenne, and Arapaho tribes did not appreciate the usurping of their land for the white man's railroad. And the American military did not cut them any slack, as the U.S. Cavalry often accompanied the armed railroad workers. Civil War general William Tecumseh Sherman wrote in 1867: "The more we can kill this year, the less will have to be killed the next year, for the more I see of these Indians the more convinced I am that they all have to be killed or be maintained as a species of paupers" (Mintz 2016). The tracks for the Union Pacific were laid nonetheless, as the inexorable construction of the railroad prevailed. Once the engineers devised a workable strategy, the construction persevered with military-like precision. As the crew reached a new section of track, they would construct temporary housing for the workers. Soon a contingent of ancillary businesses would join the fray, creating a spectacle that became known as "Hell on Wheels." This group of hangers-on provided entertainment of all stripes, including saloons, gambling houses, and brothels that amused the laboring crews, setting up shop at the end of the track section and moving on each time a new section was opened up.

The building of the transcontinental railroad also led to one of the most heinous political scandals of the 19th century. Thomas Durant, vice president of Union Pacific, and a group of his friends, purchased a Pennsylvania loan company called Credit Mobilier. They used this fund-raising vehicle to fraudulently set up dummy corporations, which could raise funds for the construction of the railroad, some of which were illegally diverted into the greedy hands of the investors. In addition, because of the government's role in funding and regulation, investors in Credit Mobilier bribed members of Congress, ensnaring them in a scandal that damaged the Grant administration when the scandal was exposed in 1872.

THE CHINESE EXCLUSION ACT

In 1882, Congress passed the Chinese Exclusion Act, which barred future Chinese immigration into the United States and denied naturalization for those already in the country. This law was not repealed until 1943, when Franklin Roosevelt repealed it during World War II. It prevented immigration from China and citizenship for Chinese Americans for over sixty years.

SIGNIFICANCE

The culmination of this engineering feat was the driving of the golden spike, the symbolic completion of the Union Pacific and Central Pacific railroads as they finally met at Promontory Point in Utah on May 10, 1869. Photographers were present for the event, and one of the most famous photos of 19th-century America displays a vast array of workers, politicians, engineers, and, of course, the two locomotives face-to-face, to celebrate the momentous event. Though Irish laborers who had been part of the construction crew were shown in the photo, no Chinese workers were included. The first transcontinental railroad served as not only an incredible engineering accomplishment but it also succeeded in connecting the nation in significant ways. After the first route was completed in 1869, the Northern Pacific was completed in 1883, the Atchison, Topeka and Santa Fe was completed in 1883, and the Great Northern was completed in 1893. These railroads served as arteries to a widespread and disparate land, delivering goods to all regions in efficient and rapid fashion for the first time in the nation's history. Coal, agricultural products, manufactured goods, and even prepared foods could travel from west to east and east to west in a few days, transforming the American industrial economy. Citizens could also make the trip, a dangerous trip that once cost $1,000 and took months now cost $150 and took two weeks in comfort and safety.

Other factors that resulted from the construction of the transcontinental railroad are less obvious but just as noteworthy. This vast land, 3,000 miles across, had no standard timing system. When riding the earliest trains, no clocks were set to a standard setting, and in fact, most trains just traveled on their own schedule and were very unreliable. They also used the local time of the stations that they stopped at, confusing all passengers who were planning a trip. William F. Allen, secretary of the General Time Convention, came up with a nationwide standard timing plan, with four time zones across the country: Eastern, Central, Mountain, and Pacific. When the railroads agreed to accept the plan, the nation put the plan into effect at noon on Sunday, November 18, 1883. Another railroad-related improvement was the standardization of the gauge of the track. While the northeast and Midwest adopted a gauge of 4 feet 8 ½ inches, the contrary South adopted a wider 5-feet gauge, in the vain hope that the North could not invade the South, or at least it would deter invasion. In the West, a narrower gauge was used because of the steep mountains. This differentiation hampered travel and commerce, and by 1890, the nation had all adopted a uniform gauge, using the original gauge originating in the East and Midwest.

FURTHER INFORMATION

Ambrose, Stephen. 2000. *Nothing Like It in the World: The Men Who Built the Transcontinental Railroad 1863–1869*. New York: Touchstone Books.

American Experience. "Workers of the Central and Union Pacific Railroad." PBS. Accessed July 20, 2020. https://www.pbs.org/wgbh/americanexperience/features/tcrr-workers-central-union-pacific-railroad/.

Andrist, Ralph K. 1987. *The American Heritage History of the Confident Years*. New York: Bonanza Books.

Bain, David H. 1999. *Empire Express: Building the First Transcontinental Railroad*. New York: Penguin Books.

Cashman, Sean D. 1993. *America in the Gilded Age: From the Death of Lincoln to the Rise of Theodore Roosevelt*. New York; London: New York University Press.

Hansen, Peter A. Spring–Summer 2013. "Still Controversial: The Pacific Railroad at 150." *Railroad History*, 208: 8–35.

Library of Congress. "The Transcontinental Railroad." Accessed July 20, 2020. https://www.loc.gov/collections/railroad-maps-1828-to-1900/articles-and-essays/history-of-railroads-and-maps/the-transcontinental-railroad/.

Mintz, S., and S. McNeil. 2018. "Building the Transcontinental Railroad." *Digital History*. Accessed July 20, 2020. http://www.digitalhistory.uh.edu/disp_textbook_print.cfm?smtid=2&psid=3147.

PBS American Experience. Accessed July 27, 2020. https://www.pbs.org/wgbh/americanexperience/features/tcrr-workers-central-union-pacific-railroad/.

Swischer, Donna. 2012. "The Transcontinental Railroad." Linda Hall Library. Accessed July 20, 2020. https://railroad.lindahall.org/index.html.

Work and Education

LOWELL OFFERING

December, 1845.

" Is Saul also among the prophets."

A REPOSITORY
OF ORIGINAL ARTICLES, WRITTEN BY
"FACTORY GIRLS."

LOWELL: MISSES CURTIS & FARLEY.
BOSTON: JORDAN & WILEY, 121
Washington street.
1845.

Entered according to Act of Congress, in the year 1845, in the Clerk's Office of the District Court of the District of Massachusetts.

49 *Lowell Offering* Title Page

INTRODUCTION

The birth of the Industrial Revolution in the United States has been attributed to some innovative textile mills located in New England that used a revolutionary integrated manufacturing system. These mills were built by Francis Cabot Lowell and featured a manufacturing process called the "Lowell System" or the "Waltham-Lowell System." The city of East Chelmsford, a farming community located along the Merrimack River, 25 miles northwest of Boston, was later named Lowell after the famous industrial pioneer. The city of Lowell built a series of mills that used power from a system of canals that were built in the early 19th century. In 1796, merchants from coastal Newburyport built the 1.5-mile-long Pawtucket Canal in order to circumvent the Pawtucket Falls in East Chelmsford and transport lumber from New Hampshire to their local shipbuilding industry. The longer Middlesex Canal was constructed in 1804. With the new ease of transport along these canals, manufacturing industries began to develop in the East Chelmsford area. These industries included glassworks and sawmills. Soon a mill was built that prepared raw wool for spinning and weaving, a task that was completed in the homes of local farm families. The American textile industry had originated in Pawtucket, Rhode Island, along the banks of the Blackstone River, where English immigrant Samuel Slater built the first fully power-driven machine for spinning yarn, using designs based on a British technology that he pilfered from an English textile factory where he had been employed. The use of this revolutionary technique soon spread through newly built mills in the region.

The United States had depended on British imported textiles, but political interruptions like the Napoleonic Wars and the Embargo of 1807 prevented the importation of British goods and spurred on the American textile industry. Enter Francis Cabot Lowell. Lowell was a scion of a prominent Newburyport family, one of the famous "Boston Brahmin" caste of elite New Englanders and son of a member of the Continental Congress and federal judge. He owned a business that imported cloth from England, and in 1810, Lowell spent two years there with his family to study the British textile industry. Lowell was aware that the Industrial Revolution in Britain had produced an underclass of poor and desperate factory workers, toiling in alarmingly dreadful conditions. Lowell imagined an upgraded American version of the English textile mill, using the British power loom and providing improved working conditions for the factory workers.

Upon his return from England, Lowell solicited a coterie of investors from his Brahmin class, and in 1813, they launched a company that they called the Boston Manufacturing Company. Their initial mill was built in 1814, in Waltham, just outside of Boston. Lowell was able to utilize the technology that he remembered from his British mill visits, and he introduced the revolutionary integrated manufacturing process that he called the "Waltham-Lowell System." This technique combined all the aspects of the complicated textile manufacturing process, from raw cotton to finished cloth, with the aid of a water-driven power loom, all under one roof. Soon his company took advantage of the water power along the Merrimack River in the town of East Chelmsford. He built several mills, bought up property, and took over control of the water rights and canal construction in the surrounding area. The revolutionary new manufacturing system combined all the steps in cloth manufacturing in one gigantic building.

Now the issue was how to provide the labor for these mills. In the 1820s and 1830s, the United States, unlike Europe, had plenty of land but not many people. Labor was expensive here, whereas in Europe unlanded peasants had limited opportunities and were often obliged to work in factories for low wages. Children were forced into working alongside their parents in dirty and dangerous mills and manufacturing facilities. Francis Cabot Lowell aspired to invent a better system. His notion was to create an industrial utopia that avoided the evils of the British system. He planned to hire local farmgirls to work in the mill, to pay them in cash, to provide a decent place to live and an educational atmosphere, and to limit their employment to a year or two so they could go back to their homes, get married, and live a middle-class American life, thus preventing the doomed formation of a permanent underclass. This was a revolutionary concept. Lowell was a devout Christian and vowed to appeal to the Protestant values that were prevalent in early New England society. He realized that there was a cohort of young girls in nearby farm families that were underutilized on the family farms. However, these families often needed cash to help out the family, possibly to send the boys (unhappily not the girls) to college or to help out financially in other ways. He sent out emissaries to recruit workers for the mills. These families needed persuading to permit their young daughters to go out into the working world while keeping their precious reputations intact. At that time, women did not work, except on the farm, so this was groundbreaking. In order to assuage the family's concerns, Lowell promised to maintain a strictly paternalistic culture. He built company-owned female-only dormitories where the girls would live, *in loco parentis*, under the watchful eye of matrons. He encouraged the girls to use lending libraries and utilize the educational opportunities provided by the company. In Lowell's view, giving the girls the opportunity to be independent and further their education while toiling at the mill was a mutually advantageous situation. This situation held true for the first decades of the Lowell mills.

DESCRIPTION

The artifact shown here is the title page of a publication produced by the mill girls of Lowell. Encouraged by the mill owners to spend their limited free time in educational pursuits, in the 1840s, the girls formed seven Mutual Self-Improvement Clubs. In addition to patronizing the very well-stocked circulating libraries, the girls attended frequent lectures from contemporary cultural and political icons like Horace Greeley, John Quincy Adams, Robert Owen, and Ralph Waldo Emerson. The intellectual ferment induced by these lectures led a number of the girls to get together, form the self-improvement societies, and write. These clubs were actually literary clubs, the first women-run literary clubs in the United States. In 1840, initially with the help of Reverend Abel Charles Thomas of the Second Universalist Church, they produced a literary magazine that they called *The Lowell Offering*, a publication that was dubbed "A Repository of Original Articles Written by 'Factory Girls.'" A thirty-page magazine, *The Lowell Offering* sold for six and a quarter cents per issue. The mill owners, the Boston Associates, recognized the benefit of supporting these efforts and provided bulk subscriptions that underwrote the production of the publication. This made excellent public relations for the company, as well as providing a creative outlet for the workers.

This title page, shown here from the January 1845 edition, was standard for all *The Lowell Offering* editions from 1840 to 1845. It shows a young girl standing in a garden, holding an opened book in her right hand. A decorative floral design frames the picture. On the right-hand side is the edge of a rural farmhouse, while on the left-hand side is a large beehive. In the background is a depiction of the giant mill building, a school house, and a church steeple. According to an editorial published in the magazine, the beehive is included as an emblem of industry and intelligence. Beneath the image of the girl is a saying, chosen carefully by the writers: "The worm on the earth may look up to the star." The editorial states that the sentiment expressed *aspiration*, "that their situation was lowly but their aims high." At the bottom of the page is the publication information: "Lowell: Misses Curtis & Farley. Boston: Jordan, Swift & Wiley, 121 Washington Street, 1845."

FROM *THE LOWELL OFFERING*, DECEMBER 1840

Not all contemporary critics were champions of the Lowell mill girls. An article from the *Boston Quarterly Review*, written by Orestes Brownson in 1840, disparaged the girls this way: "[F]ew of them ever marry; fewer still ever return to their native places with reputations unimpaired."

This was the response from *The Lowell Offering*: "Whom has Mr. Brownson slandered . . . girls who generally come from quiet country homes, where their minds and manners have been formed under the eyes of the worthy sons of the Pilgrims, and their virtuous partners, and who return again to become the wives of the free intelligent yeomanry of New England and the mothers of quite a proportion of our future republicans. Think, for a moment how many of the next generation are to spring from mothers doomed to infamy!"

[Gilder Lehrman Institute of American History, 2013.]

SIGNIFICANCE

The monthly publication of *The Lowell Offering* lasted from 1840 to 1845. It grew in popularity over the years, gaining supporters throughout the region and nationally. The girls wrote a variety of content, much of which was typical of teenage girls of any era—romantic poems and stories that appealed to the other girls. But soon the girls would write more pointed essays, describing their difficult lives in detail. This led to a new movement, a labor movement, demanding higher wages and a shorter workday. After the unfortunate early death of Francis Cabot Lowell, the new owners of the mills had less altruistic considerations. The cash payments for the girls, though fairly low, were higher than any female would get anywhere else. But when the economy slowed, the mill owners cut wages by 15 percent and increased their hours. The girls protested their treatment and went on several strikes, which they called "turnouts." They formed the Lowell Female Labor Reform Association in 1845, with the mission to "labor actively for reform in the present system of labor." The organization petitioned the state legislature to institute a 10-hour day, a battle that would continue until a law was finally passed in 1874. The mill girls eventually quit the mills as the conditions continued to deteriorate. After the Civil War, poorer, more desperate immigrants from Ireland had begun to arrive, and they were willing to accept the lower wages and more draconian work conditions. The dormitories of the mill girls were converted into tenements for the newly arrived immigrant families. The era of the Yankee "mill girls" had ended.

FURTHER INFORMATION

Brooks, Rebecca B. January 25, 2017. "What Was the Lowell System?" *History of Massachusetts Blog*. Accessed February 14, 2021. https://historyofmassachusetts.org/lowell-mills-factory-system/.

Green, Amy. "Francis Cabot Lowell and the Boston Manufacturing Company." The Charles River Museum. Accessed February 18, 2021. https://www.charlesrivermuseum.org/fcl-bmc.

Levinson, Jeff. 2007. *Mill Girls of Lowell*. Boston: History Compass.

"Lowell Mill Girls and the Factory System, 1840." 2013. The Gilder Lehrman Institute of American History. Accessed February 14, 2021. https://www.gilderlehrman.org/history-resources/spotlight-primary-source/lowell-mill-girls-and-factory-system-1840.

The Lowell Offering. Vol. 5. Accessed February 9, 2021. https://babel.hathitrust.org/cgi/pt?id=hvd.32044019620822&view=1up&seq=85.

Robinson, H. Jane Hanson, Carroll Davidson Wright, Massachusetts Bureau of Statistics of Labor. 1889. *Early Factory Labor in New England (from the Fourteenth Annual Report of the Massachusetts Bureau of Statistics of Labor for 1883)*. Reprint ed. Boston: Wright & Potter Print. Co.

Tyler, Gus. September 1978. "Review: Putting Girls through the Mill." *Change*, 10(8): 54–56.

U.S. Department of the Interior. 1996. *Lowell: The Story of an Industrial City*. Washington, DC: Division of Publications, National Park Service.

The
"Father of his Country"
INDEPENDENCE!
Liberty
Freedom

50 Indian Boarding School Drawing of George Washington

INTRODUCTION

By the 1880s, the United States had expanded westward from coast to coast. The inconvenient fact that the land was already occupied by Indigenous peoples was becoming more and more of an issue as the influx of new immigrants surged into the western half of the country in search of new places to settle. The Native Americans had been relentlessly driven out of their ancestral lands since the nation's inception. Now the clarion call of Manifest Destiny to conquer the continent had virtually run out of territory to conquer. The last gasp of the Native American battle to retain land took place on the Great Plains in the territories of Montana and the Dakotas. The Battle of Little Bighorn in 1876 was the beginning of the Indian Wars in the western territory that ended with the Massacre at Wounded Knee in 1890 and a desperate attempt to conserve Indian culture with the ill-fated spiritual movement called the "Ghost Dance."

"Kill the Indian, save the man." This motto originated from Army Brigadier General Richard Henry Pratt, the founder of the Carlisle Industrial Indian School. It was a metaphor, of course. Pratt did not want to actually kill Indians; his desire was to save them from certain annihilation. His belief was that by teaching the Indian to embrace the white culture and values, he could save the Indian race from the extermination that was demanded by the majority of the American people and their elected representatives who had embraced the alternate motto "the only good Indian is a dead Indian." If, by forcing them to assimilate into white culture he had to forcibly annihilate all aspects of their own culture and values, so be it. Assimilation was the only way that he and his supporters saw to protect the lives of America's Indigenous peoples. Some critics have claimed that Pratt didn't see the Indians as human beings; in fact the opposite was true. As an experienced veteran of the Indian campaigns out West, Pratt had developed a respect for the tribes as human beings. In Pratt's belief, they were certainly uncivilized and inferior to whites, but he believed that they could be educated and trained to be productive members of white society.

Richard Henry Pratt had spent from 1867 to 1875 in Indian Territory as an officer of the 10th Cavalry, commanding a unit of African American "Buffalo Soldiers" and Indian Scouts. Pratt's task during this time was to make sure that the Kiowa, Cheyenne, and Arapaho tribes stayed on their reservations in the Red River areas of Texas and Oklahoma. But as more new settlers came into the area, some members of the tribes continued to raid the settlements. The government decided that these so-called hostiles had to be arrested and jailed. In 1875, seventy-two warriors from the Cheyenne, Kiowa, Comanche, and Caddo tribes were rounded up and sent into exile by train, thousands of miles away in St. Augustine, Florida. This tropical region was alien to these men, and taking them into a completely unfamiliar environment was part of the plan. Pratt, who was chosen by the government to supervise the prisoners, had his own ideas, and as soon as they arrived in Florida, he cut off their shackles, cut their hair short, and clothed them in American military uniforms. They were treated as recruits, trained in keeping their uniforms clean and pressed, and introduced to military drills. Local women taught them to read in exchange for archery lessons. Some prisoners were trusted enough to be hired as guards. In 1878, at the end of their sentence, Pratt persuaded seventeen of the prisoners to continue their education at the newly opened school for African American youth in Virginia, the Hampton Institute. This was the only school available to them, for these were Indians, and no other school would accept them. Hampton Institute would continue to educate Native Americans until the 1920s.

At this point Pratt saw an opportunity to open a school dedicated solely to Indians. His philosophy was developing: Native American children should be removed from their homes, away from influential family and customs, and magically transformed into productive Americans. He lobbied his friends, both in Congress and his wealthy progressive supporters on the East Coast, for funding. In 1879, Secretary of the Interior Carl Schurz agreed to allow him to use an abandoned military base in Carlisle, Pennsylvania, to set up his school. His plan was to induce some of the tribal leaders to send their children to the school, thereby encouraging the rest of the tribe to follow. He was somewhat disingenuous in explaining that learning English would help the tribes in their negotiations with the government. Although this was true, his real aim was to remove the children from their tribal influences permanently, so their English knowledge couldn't actually help the tribes in the end. Pratt was successful, however, and in October 1879, eighty-two children were placed on trains for the long trip to Pennsylvania.

As soon as the children arrived, the staff cut their long hair on the boys and issued military uniforms, a traumatic experience for these children. Then they were brought into a classroom and asked to pick English names, first and last, for themselves. They were prohibited from speaking their own native languages and forced to learn English. For the first time in their lives, they were compelled to follow a strict schedule, with bells ringing all day for breakfast, class, lunch, dinner, and bedtime. They were also sent to church and encouraged to convert to Christianity. Their school day consisted of two parts; they were taught half a day of academics and half a day of trades. The boys were instructed in carpentry, tinsmithing, and blacksmithing, and the girls in the domestic arts like cooking and sewing. Music and art were also part of the curriculum. A band was formed that consistently played at Presidential Inaugural Parades. Sports were also a big part of the program at the Carlisle School. Part of Pratt's vision for the school was to keep the Native American children far away from their families' influences. He arranged for them to be sent to local non-Indian families for the summer in an immersion program that Pratt called the "outing system." The children worked on the farm helping out the family and accompanied them to the shops, church, and so forth. The summer program was the most popular, but other programs included a two- to three-year program where the children lived with the family for the entire time and attended local schools. A third program consisted of sending the children to urban families where they could learn nonfarm skills. The outing system was popular with local families, many of whom were Quakers and supported Pratt's vision for the assimilation of the Indians.

DESCRIPTION

The artifact shown here is an example of artwork produced by a student at the Carlisle Indian Industrial School from the class of 1891. The artist is a student named Charles Dagenett. It is a portrait of George Washington done in colored pencil and depicts Washington's head and shoulders. Above Washington's head in colorful pencil, it states, "The 'Father of his Country,' Independence!" On the either side of Washington's head are written the words "Liberty" and "Freedom." The portrait is part of a booklet of drawings completed by Dagenett. The title page of the booklet states, "Presented to Susan Longstreth by Charlie Dagenett. Drawn by Charlie Dagenett. From Peoria Indian Quapaw Agency, Ind. Ter."

The other drawings in the booklet are mostly maps drawn by Dagenett depicting battles from U.S. war history, like the Siege of Yorktown and the Capture of Ticonderoga. Charles E. Dagenett entered the Carlisle School on November 15, 1887, and graduated in 1891. After graduation, Dagenett attended Dickinson College in Carlisle and proceeded to graduate from Eastman Business College in Poughkeepsie, New York. He became the supervisor of Indian Employment in Denver, Colorado, in 1910; executive committee chairman of the American Indian Association in 1911; and the supervisor of Indian Employment at the Indian Office in Washington, DC, in 1915. He married a fellow Carlisle student, Esther Miller.

THE STORY OF JIM THORPE

James Francis Thorpe, known as Jim, was a student at the Carlisle Indian Industrial School in the early 1900s. His mother was a member of the Sac and Fox Indian tribe from an Indian reservation in Oklahoma. His supreme athletic abilities were recognized at the Carlisle School by the famous coach Pop Warner who trained him in football. He continued his career in track and field and won two gold medals in the pentathlon and decathlon in the 1912 Olympics. The medals were revoked in 1913 after charges of professionalism in his early years were made. The stripping of the medals from Thorpe has been recognized as an example of racism, and they were reinstated in 1983. Thorpe had a sterling athletic career, eventually becoming a professional baseball player, but he was never able to make much money due to the endemic racism that plagued him throughout his post-athletic career.

SIGNIFICANCE

In recent years, there has been a painful reckoning regarding the legacy of the Indian boarding schools, now known as residential schools. Pratt's vision became a reality in the years following the founding of the Carlisle Indian Industrial School and a model for the twenty-five residential schools opened by the Bureau of Indian Affairs. Residential schools were opened all across the country with the mission to assimilate Indian children and destroy the Native American culture, to, in fact, "kill the Indian, save the man." But the initial good intentions of General Pratt turned into a national system with many harmful consequences. Government parsimony in funding these ubiquitous schools led to poor nutrition, poorly maintained schools, and generally harsh conditions. Crowding and poor sanitation resulted in many children dying of diseases such as tuberculosis, measles, trachoma, and other bacterial diseases that were not yet controllable by antibiotics. All the schools had cemeteries on site that were the final resting places for many children who never returned home. Although the teachers hired by Pratt and his fellow reformers in the early years were highly trained, as the system grew, many Indian children were cruelly treated by poorly trained teachers in both government and religiously run schools. In 1891, a compulsory attendance law was passed, requiring parents on reservations send their children to boarding schools outside of their homes. The reaction to these punitive regulations was intense; although some parents and children, considering their economic circumstances, appreciated the opportunity to be housed, fed, and taught in residential schools, many others resented it. Children like Charlie Dagenett who led successful lives in the white world were the exception to the rule. Many children ran away from the schools, resulting in harsh punishment. Some even set fire to the school or attempted to undermine the institution in as many ways as possible. Many took pains to keep their language alive through secretive means. Pratt's concept of replacing one culture with another, like changing your clothes, was never a legitimate one despite the reformers' aspirations for it. The children who were educated at these boarding schools often returned to their homes on the reservations. They were suddenly a cultural amalgam; not accepted in the white world, they didn't feel comfortable in the Indian culture that had been so fiercely denigrated during their school years. The consequences of building these schools have not been pretty: generations of children being snatched away from their homes, with parents never allowed to bring up their kids, have led to a damaged population with a lack of parenting skills and an epidemic of depression and addiction. The legacy of these boarding schools has been complex, but overall it has been a depressing chapter in the continuing tragic story of the unconscionable treatment of the Indigenous population by the white invaders.

FURTHER INFORMATION

Adams, David W. 1995 [2020]. *Education for Extinction: American Indians and the Boarding School Experience, 1875–1928.* Lawrence: University Press of Kansas.

Carlisle Indian School Resource Center. Archives and Special Collections. Dickinson College. Accessed June 6, 2022. https://carlisleindian.dickinson.edu/.

Carlisle Indian School Project. 2020. Accessed July 3, 2021. https://carlisleindianschoolproject.com/.

Davis, Julie. Winter 2001. "American Indian Boarding School Experiences: Recent Studies from Native Perspectives." *OAH Magazine of History*, 15(2): 20–22.

Fear-Segal, Jacqueline, and Susan D. Rose. 2016. *Carlisle Indian Industrial School.* Lincoln: University of Nebraska Press.

"History and Culture: Boarding Schools." 2021. Northern Plains Reservation Aid. Accessed July 3, 2021. http://www.nativepartnership.org/site/PageServer?pagename=airc_hist_boardingschools.

"Interior Department to Investigate Abuse of Indigenous Children at American Boarding Schools." July 14, 2021. Equal Justice Initiative. Accessed July 18, 2021. https://eji.org/news/interior-department-to-investigate-abuse-of-indigenous-children-at-american-boarding-schools/.

Landis, Barb. 2017. "History of the Carlisle Indian School." Cumberland County Historical Society. Accessed July 3, 2021. https://carlisleindian.historicalsociety.com/history-of-the-carlisle-indian-school/.

National Park Service. 1961. "Carlisle Indian Industrial School National Historic Landmark Inventory—Nomination Form." National Register of Historic Places. Accessed July 3, 2021. https://npgallery.nps.gov /GetAsset?assetID=5f1603a1-d20b-41a3-8158-bd65ebdca54e.

Pember, Mary A. 2019. "Death by Civilization: The Traumatic Legacy of Indian Boarding Schools." *The Atlantic*. March 8. Accessed July 3, 2021. https://www.theatlantic.com/education/archive/2019/03/traumatic-legacy -indian-boarding-schools/584293/.

Petersen, Rebecca. "The Impact of Historical Boarding Schools on Native American Families and Parenting Roles." Accessed July 18, 2021. https:// minds.wisconsin.edu/bitstream/handle/1793/66821/Peterson.pdf.

51 Scrimshaw Sperm Whale Tooth

INTRODUCTION

One of the most vital and lucrative American industries in the first half of the 19th century was whaling. The products provided through whaling served as crucial components in many of the country's most essential products—products like lamp oil, candles, corsets, perfumes, soap, and industrial lubricants. New Bedford, Massachusetts, on Buzzard's Bay just west of Cape Cod was the nation's whaling capital in the mid-19th century and also was the wealthiest city per capita in the United States at the time. The whaling industry teetered on the precipice of the nascent Industrial Revolution in the United States but was eventually extinguished as the revolution passed it by in favor of other, more modern technology. But while it flourished, the industry was at the forefront of America's industrial development. Its whaling ships contained state-of-the-art equipment at the time. They roamed the earth searching for whales, from the Arctic to the South Pacific. The great American novel, *Moby Dick* by Herman Melville, is a paean to the allure of the whale hunt, as described by Melville, who was a man who had plenty of personal experience in the trade.

Whaling was introduced to the English settlers by the Native American tribes. Nantucket, named "far away land" or "sandy, sterile soil tempting no one" by the Wampanoag tribe who inhabited the sand-swept island, served as the center of the industry for over a century. When the ships grew larger and required a deeper port, New Bedford took its place. The founders of Nantucket, a small group of families who purchased it in 1659, were a variety of Protestant sects. However, in 1703, a proselytizing Quaker John Richardson converted one of Nantucket's most prominent citizens, Mary Coffin Starbuck. Soon, due to her influence on the community, the entire island practiced the Quaker faith. The influence of the Quaker religion was crucial to the success of the whaling industry going forward. The first settlers attempted to be farmers, but the "sandy, sterile soil" on this 14-mile-long island did not promote it, so they switched to the whaling trade. At first, whaling was done at the shore because there were so many

357

whales that they could be easily spotted from viewing platforms built on the land. During the months of November to April, right whales would migrate from the North Atlantic to the Massachusetts coast seeking warmer water. The whalers would board small boats out to the whale, where they would harpoon it, chase it if necessary, and then drag it back on the beach and flense or butcher it. The blubber, which is the whale's thick layer of fat, and the baleen, the brown, hard flexible material from the whale's mouth, also known as whalebone, would be removed. It would be transported to try-houses, also called tryworks, which were brick oven furnaces used to render the oil from the whale blubber. The oil would be poured into casks and, with the whalebone, would be sold in East Coast markets. The whalebone, another useful part of the whale, was used as a stiffener for women's corsets.

It wasn't too long before the waters off the East Coast of Massachusetts were overfished and the Nantucket whalers began searching for an improved whaling technique. By the mid-18th century, a technological advance allowed for longer and more far-reaching whale hunts. Instead of removing the blubber at a nearby tryworks on land, the new larger whaling vessels were outfitted with the furnaces on the ships themselves. This freed up the ship to travel on long whale-hunting voyages. Now the ships could search far and wide for the whales, and the voyages extended to two, three, or even four years at sea. In 1789, the first whaling ship sailed around Cape Horn to the Pacific Ocean. For the next half century, many whaling ships plied the waters of the Pacific in pursuit of whales. So many whaling ships originated in Massachusetts that in 1846, with 640 ships, there were three times as many American whalers out to sea as the rest of the world's whaling ships combined. The life of a whaler was a tough one, arduous, interminable journeys in cramped, roach-infested quarters. However, the opportunities were unusual for this era in the United States. The Quakers of Nantucket believed in equal opportunities, and they were the first to hire African Americans to work alongside whites. In addition, there were often Native Americans, Portuguese immigrants, Hawaiians, or other Pacific Islanders, as well as convicts or homeless street kids. Depending on your assigned job on the ship, you took home a certain fraction of the ship's profit.

DESCRIPTION

The men on a whaling ship would endure hours of struggle at the sighting and subsequent killing of a whale. However, on these grueling voyages, there would be many more hours of tedium when the whale hunt was completed, in anticipation of another whale sighting. These hours would be taken up with a variety of activities. Rules were extremely strict on the ships, so that order was maintained. And the physical space was severely limited. However, some leisure activities took little space and added interest to their humdrum lives. Many of the men wrote journals, not the official journal that the captain wrote but personal ones, often accompanied by lively drawings. Other projects included needlework, ropework, or fishing. If a whaler caught a fish, it was presented to the cook who would prepare it and share it with the crew. Sharks and dolphins were favorites, although turtles and flying fish were also enjoyed. The most celebrated project that the whalers enjoyed was the art of scrimshaw. The term describes the carving on ivory or bone that was done on the leftover teeth and bones from the whales that had already been dismembered. Whalers who took up this craft were called "scrimshanders." The origin of the term is unknown, but it has been used to describe this type of handicraft since the early 19th century. Scrimshaw is considered the only truly American folk art.

The scrimshaw shown here is a sperm whale tooth from the Pennsylvania Museum of Art. It dates from between 1825 and 1835 and measures 5 ⅛ inches tall by 2 ½ inches wide by 1 ¾ inches deep. The artist is unknown. The tooth shows a typical theme for scrimshaw, a beautiful whaling ship with sails unfurled on a black sea with an American flag blowing in the wind. In order to prepare the tooth for carving, the artist would scrape with a knife and sand the tooth with a shark skin until it was smooth. A chamois would be used to polish the tooth. Often, the artist would pin a picture or print onto the tooth and prick the outline with a needle. Then he would take off the print and connect the dots of the needle pricks. Some artists were competent enough to do the etching freehand. Once etched, the artist would then fill in the etching with lamp black, a combination of carbon and whale oil. For other colors, tea, vinegar, berries, or octopus dye could be used. The most common themes were nautical ones, though some artists etched portraits of other sailors, family members, or fashionable young women. It was totally up to the artist to choose a subject. Other parts of the whale were also used for scrimshaw, including the baleen, used for corset stays. Sometimes artists would carve useful items out of the whalebone, items like napkin rings, or pie crimpers. Most scrimshaw artists whiled away their leisure time making these small gems to give to their families or sweethearts, although some sold them when back in port. Scrimshaw artists were often anonymous, though there were several known artists. Edward Burdett of Nantucket began his whaling career in 1822, and Frederick Myrick, also of Nantucket, actually signed and dated his works. As the golden age of whaling came to an end in the 1850s, an artist named Nathaniel Sylvester Finney, of Plymouth, Massachusetts, made a name for himself as a scrimshaw specialist. After his whaling career ended, he opened up a studio in San Francisco and sold his products, making him the first scrimshaw artist to make a living selling his work.

MOBY DICK

Herman Melville's masterpiece *Moby Dick, or The Whale* is considered by many to be the great American novel. Published in 1851, it was panned by the critics and sold only three thousand copies in Melville's lifetime. The plot was inspired by Melville's own adventures on a whaling expedition, as well as the tragic true story of the sinking of the *Essex* whaling ship, which took place in 1820 off the coast of South America. The *Essex* was rammed by a huge, irate whale. The crew evacuated into three small boats. Thousands of miles from land and starving at sea, eight men survived by cannibalizing the others, drawing lots to decide the men's fates. *Moby Dick* is loosely based on the story as told by the *Essex*'s surviving crew members. Melville's portrayal of Captain Ahab, obsessed by a thirst for revenge on a whale that bit off his leg on a previous expedition, is also an allegory for man's search for meaning in life. Moby Dick, the whale, represented the knowledge that Ahab was searching for, a search that was ultimately futile, as Ahab lost his sanity and died without ever acquiring the knowledge that he craved.

SIGNIFICANCE

Though the whaling industry was crucial to a newly industrializing nation, it started a long decline after the discovery of petroleum in Titusville, Pennsylvania, in 1859. The popularity of whale oil for oil lamps decreased as the availability of kerosene, made from petroleum, grew. Eventually, as women's fashions changed, corset stays made from whale baleen were no longer in demand. The disruption of the Civil War where many whaling vessels were destroyed by Confederate raiders also contributed to the decline of an already-distressed industry. The whaling industry did soldier on into the 20th century, with new steam-powered whalers taking the place of the old sailing vessels. Gun-loaded harpoons made the killing of whales a quick and efficient slaughter. Happily, the collapse of the whaling industry is credited for saving the whales from extinction. The United States officially outlawed whaling in 1971, although limited whaling is permitted to certain Indigenous cultures. In 1986, the International Whaling Commission banned commercial whaling because of the extreme depletion of most of the whale stocks, though Japan, Norway, and Iceland have registered objections to the ban and still allow some commercial whaling.

FURTHER INFORMATION

Boyall, Jessica. 2021. "The Beautiful, Brutal World of Whaleship Art." Atlas Obscura. January 25. Accessed March 23, 2021. https://www.atlasobscura.com/articles/whaling-logs/.

Hoare, Philip. 2010. *The Whale: In Search of the Giants of the Sea.* New York: Harper Collins.

Marrero, Meagan E., and Stuart Thornton. 2011. "Big Fish: A Brief History of Whaling." *National Geographic.* November 1. Accessed March 25, 2021. https://www.nationalgeographic.org/article/big-fish-history-whaling/.

McGuane, James. 2013. *The Hunted Whale.* New York, London: W.W. Norton & Co.

Melville, Herman. 1851. *Moby Dick.* New York: Dover Publications (Reprint).

PBS. American Experience. 2010. "Into the Deep: America, Whaling and the World." Accessed March 24, 2021. https://www.pbs.org/wgbh /americanexperience/films/whaling/.

"What Is Scrimshaw? The Whaler's Art." 2020. *Yankee Magazine.* January 23. Accessed March 23, 2021. https://newengland.com/today/today /what-is-scrimshaw/.

Division of Work and Industry, National Museum of American History, Smithsonian Institution

52 Student's Writing Slate

INTRODUCTION

The earliest schools in the American colonies were church-sponsored, and the purpose of the schools was to teach the children how to read the Bible. The first law that required public education was the Old Deluder Act of 1647 in the Massachusetts Bay Colony, which ordered that every township with fifty or more households appoint someone to teach all children to read and write. Not all townships complied with this edict, but the schools that were set up focused on producing an elite class of future leaders. The responsibility for the education of the general populace was still left to the families. The ethnically and religiously homogenous nature of the Puritan colonies made it possible for Massachusetts to have the first state-run public schools. The other colonies, however, with their more ethnically and religiously diverse and geographically spread out populations, did not favor a state-run school system. They preferred their own church-run, locally based schools. The new nation passed laws ordering each new western territory to set aside a property to build a public school in the Land Ordinance of 1785. However, it was not fully implemented. George Washington recognized the power of a well-informed populace in a democracy, admonishing American leaders in his 1796 Farewell address to "promote . . . institutions for the general diffusion of knowledge." Thomas Jefferson was the first American politician to advocate for public education in the United States through legislation. Jefferson's belief was that a functional democracy could survive only with a well-educated citizenry. He submitted a bill to the Virginia House of Delegates twice, in 1778 and 1780, which he called the Bill for the More General Diffusion of Knowledge. In the 1780s, James Madison tried to pass it once again. This legislation called for state-run public schools. In order not to infringe on the rights of local communities or parents to educate their children, the law allowed for some local schools and home schooling, but in the end, all children had to pass a national examination. Unfortunately, the bill was never passed. From the very beginning of nationhood, the United States faced a battle between local and state control of public schools.

By the early-mid-19th century, educational reformers introduced the "Common School Movement." The concept behind the so-called common school was an egalitarian one—since there were so many immigrants entering the United States at the time, from so many diverse backgrounds, the common-school advocates sought to bring the immigrant children into the public schools. Here they would interact with children from other backgrounds and be educated in American values. Calvin Ellis Stowe, educator and husband of Harriet Beecher Stowe and a common school promoter, warned, "Unless we educate our immigrants they will be our ruin. It is no longer a question of benevolence, of duty, or of enlightened self-interest . . . we are prompted to it by the instinct of self-preservation." The most influential activist for the common school movement was Horace Mann, a state senator from Massachusetts who became the first secretary of the Massachusetts Board of Education. In his capacity as board chair, he fought for state funding for public schools, paid for through state taxes. He argued to separate religious and public education. He also founded teacher-training colleges, originally called "normal schools," because they set standards or norms for teacher training. Horace Mann, in concert with feminist leaders like Susan B. Anthony, Elizabeth Cady Stanton, and Catherine Beecher, encouraged women to enter the teaching field for the first time. Whereas men were the schoolmasters in the early years of the republic, the number of new schools being built and the increase in population led to a dearth of qualified male teachers. The reformers advocated for women to be trained as teachers. Their pay was significantly lower, and they were not likely to leave for a more lucrative profession, as the men were. Women didn't have many other professional options. Mann traveled to Europe, where he was impressed by the Prussian system of public schools. Those common schools emphasized that all children, no matter the background or economic level, should be able to attain the same level of education through publicly funded schools. Another German idea that improved the American school organization was the new concept of separating students based on their age and ability, called age grading. Most early schools put all age and ability ranges in one classroom.

Mann's influence extended beyond Massachusetts to many other states. However, the resistance to some of his reforms was persistent. Although he instituted a law in 1852 that made education compulsory in Massachusetts, some states in the West didn't follow suit until the 20th century had begun. The resistance to the common school movement came from a number of factions. In rural areas, farmers resisted compulsory schooling. They often denied that farmers' children needed an education and, in addition, that the children were essential to attend to farming duties. Another faction that opposed the idea of common schools comprised the many newly immigrated Catholic families that were concentrated in certain regions of the country. In New York City, the powerful Catholic Church was so resistant to local public schools that it set up a parallel parochial school system that still exists today. Despite the resistance, most of Mann's reformist recommendations for public education eventually took hold.

DESCRIPTION

The artifact shown here is a combined slate with numeral frame that dates from circa 1890. It is made of slate, with a wood frame, metal wires, and wood beads. It measures 8 ¾ inches wide by 8 ¾ inches high by ½₂ inches thick. Above the slate is the numeral frame or abacus. There are two rows of beads with ten beads in each row. They are colored red, orange, yellow, green, and blue. Although the origin of this slate is unknown, several American inventors received patents for similar devices in the 1870s and 1880s. These inventors include Freeman D'Ossone of Philadelphia in 1871; Henry Stewart of Erie, Pennsylvania, in 1883; and Charlotte Francis Roddey of New York City in 1886. Slates have been used for centuries and were the most important classroom equipment in the early American classrooms. Each student would have his or her own slate that was brought to class. Slate pencils were used to scratch on the slate until chalk became available. Students would write their lessons on the slate, and the teacher would have to check each student's work before moving on to the next lesson. The slate would be wiped clean with a rag. By 1890, slates were still used in American classrooms, though the introduction of mass-produced paper had made the student's personal slate less necessary.

One of the most important innovations in the American classroom was the blackboard. Basically a large slate that was hung at the front of the classroom, the blackboard allowed the teacher to write lessons on the board and teach a large class the same lesson at the same time. The first application of a blackboard for the whole classroom's use was in 1800 by James Pillans, geography teacher in Edinburgh, Scotland, at the Old High School. He connected a number of smaller slates in order to draw maps for the class. In 1801, in the United States, George Baron utilized a large wall-mounted blackboard consisting of smaller connected slates in order to teach mathematics to his class at West Point. The concept of connecting the slates to create a large board caught on quickly, and by 1840, larger boards were mass-produced and transported by railroad to classrooms all over the country. An influential educational method of instruction, which was called the Lancasterian or monitorial system of public education, also made use of the newly available blackboard. In 1803, Joseph Lancaster, a British schoolmaster, published an educational plan that recommended using the best students as "monitors" or assistant teachers. The Lancasterian method of teaching used a systematic approach, with detailed instructions for classroom organization, teaching of certain subject matters, and teaching to large groups. By utilizing these monitors, one teacher could educate as many as three hundred students. Because of the paucity of qualified teachers, this method was popular for a period of time in the 19th century because it was an inexpensive and effective method to teach a large number of students. An essential piece of equipment with the Lancasterian method was the blackboard, which was hung at the front of the large classroom. Eventually, after the introduction of normal schools that prepared a professional teaching class, the Lancasterian method faded from popularity. Though the Lancasterian method did not survive, its legacy can be seen in present-day American universities, where freshman introductory classes are often given in eight-hundred-seat lecture halls, and graduate students assist the professor.

SIGNIFICANCE

Public education in the United States was, and still is, a political hot potato in many ways. Who has the control—the local township, the state government, or the federal government? Since the dawn of the republic, local control of schools has been a uniquely American feature of the public school system in the United States. Even the venerable Thomas Jefferson couldn't initiate a state-run public school system in Virginia, though he tried mightily. The trend has been toward more centralized control as the federal government makes attempts to standardize certain aspects of education. The system remains, however, mostly funded locally and mostly through property taxes, which exacerbates the inequalities of the system. But the little combination slate and abacus shown in this artifact is an example of how public education has fundamentally changed since the 19th century. The little one-room schoolhouse, with a teacher attempting to teach all ages and all abilities at the same time, while the students write their lessons on their individual slates, has gone the way of the horse and carriage due to influential reformers such as Horace Mann and Joseph Lancaster.

FURTHER INFORMATION

Brackemyre, Ted. 2021. "Education to the Masses: The Rise of Public Education in Early America." U.S. History Scene. Accessed March 30, 2021. https://ushistoryscene.com/article/rise-of-public-education/.

Buzbee, Lewis. 2014. "The Simple Genius of the Blackboard." *Slate*. October 15. Accessed April 1, 2021. https://slate.com/human-interest/2014/10/a-history-of-the-blackboard-how-the-blackboard-became-an-effective-and-ubiquitous-teaching-tool.html.

Cremin, Lawrence A. 1988. *American Education: The Metropolitan Experience, 1876–1980*. New York: Harper & Row.

Herbst, Jurgen. Autumn 2002. "Nineteenth-Century Schools between Community and State: The Cases of Prussia and the United States." *History of Education Quarterly*, 42 (3): 317–341.

Komline, David. 2020. *The Common School Awakening: Religion and the Transatlantic Roots of American Public Education*. New York: Oxford University Press.

Krause, Steven D. Spring 2000. " 'Among the Greatest Benefactors of Mankind': What the Success of Chalkboards Tells Us about the Future of Computers in the Classroom." *Journal of the Midwest Modern Language Association*, 33(2): 6–16.

GLOSSARY

Abacus   The abacus, also called a counting frame or numeral frame, is a calculating tool that has been in use since ancient times.

Amalgamation   A term used during the antebellum period to describe racial mixing of African Americans with whites.

Amanuensis   A literary assistant, in particular one who takes dictation or copies manuscripts.

Andiron   Also known as a firedog, andirons are generally found in pairs at either side of a fireplace. It is a decorative bracket that holds the logs above the floor of the hearth so that air can circulate around the logs and provide cleaner burning with less smoke.

Baleen   Made out of keratin, the same protein that makes up human fingernails and hair, baleen is found in the jaws of large whales. It is often called whalebone, but it is not actually bone.

Barracoon   An enclosure in which black slaves were confined while awaiting being picked up by the slave ships.

Bilboes   Shackles with an iron bar, which slides across to enclose the ankles.

Bivalve   A type of mollusk that is inside a hinged shell. Examples of bivalves are oysters, clams, mussels, and scallops.

Bobbin   A cylinder or cone holding thread, yarn, or wire, used especially in weaving, machine sewing, and lacemaking. Also used in Victorian hairwork.

Bonnet   The canvas cover on a Conestoga wagon.

Breech end   The back part of a firearm. Guns or rifles can either be loaded from the breech end or muzzle, which is the front part.

Breeches   Short trousers that are fastened just below the knee. They were popular in the 17th, 18th, and early 19th centuries but now are worn primarily for horseback riding.

Buckram   Stiff cotton cloth soaked in wheat starch paste and dried, to produce a stiff fabric used for undergarments like corsets.

Busk   A rigid element that is at the center front of a corset.

Callithumpian   A noisy parade of loud instruments, or a noisy, cacophonous group.

Cam   A cam is a rotating or sliding piece in a mechanical linkage used to transform rotary motion into linear motion.

Camisards   Huguenots (French Protestants) from a remote region of southern France. In the early 1700s, they protested against Louis XIV's Revocation of the Edict of Nantes, which made Protestantism illegal, for which they were violently persecuted. Eventually, they fled to England.

Canton   The top inner quarter of a flag.

Cartel   An association of manufacturers or suppliers with the purpose of restricting competition and maintaining prices at a high level.

Charivari   A noisy mock serenade performed by a group of people to celebrate a marriage or mock an unpopular person.

Clavichord   A Clavichord is a keyboard instrument dating from the late Middle Ages until the Classical period in music. It is a precursor to the piano.

Coffle   A line of slaves shackled together.

Cossacks   Cossacks are a group of people predominantly located in the steppes of Russia. They were semiautonomous and semi-military.

Cotton gin   A machine that could be used to separate the seeds from the cotton bolls in order to produce cotton. The cotton gin designed by Eli Whitney was used with short-staple cotton, the type that made cotton into "King Cotton," the major crop in the South before the Civil War.

Cravat   A decorative fabric worn around the neck, it was the predecessor to the necktie.

Crepe   A silk, wool, or synthetic fiber fabric with a crimped appearance. The term "crape (crepe)" typically refers to a form of the fabric associated specifically with mourning.

Daguerreotype   A photograph taken by an early photographic process employing an iodine-sensitized silvered plate and mercury vapor.

Damper   In a cookstove, a damper regulates the flow of heat within the stove toward the chimney. This can make the oven hotter or direct the heat to the burners on the top.

Dandy   A man who is extremely concerned with fashion and appearance.

Dynamo   A dynamo is a type of electrical generator that creates direct current, now obsolete.

Dysentery   Infection of the intestines resulting in severe and bloody diarrhea.

Electromagnetism   The interaction of electric currents or fields and magnetic fields.

Evangelicalism   A worldwide trans-denominational movement within Protestant Christianity that maintains the belief that the essence of the Gospel consists of the doctrine of salvation by grace alone, solely through faith in Jesus's atonement.

Fancywork   Ornamental needlework, a popular hobby for women in 19th-century American households.

Firkin   A small wooden vessel or cask, it was used to store butter.

Flensing   The butchering of a whale.

Fraktur   A Gothic typeface, also known as a blackletter typeface, used in Germany and brought over to the United States by Pennsylvania Germans. The term *fraktur* is also used to describe the illuminated manuscripts created by Pennsylvania Germans that celebrated milestones and events in the lives of the German families.

Free-Soil Party   An American political party that opposed the expansion of slavery into the western territories. It existed from 1848 to 1854, when it merged with the Republican Party.

Gauchos   Gauchos are the nomadic horsemen of the Argentine and Uruguayan Pampas (grasslands), who thrived from the mid-18th to the mid-19th century.

Guilloche   Architectural ornamentation resembling braided or interlaced ribbons.

Hagiography   A biography of a saint or a fawning biography that idealizes its subject.

Harpsichord   A harpsichord is a keyboard instrument, dating from the 15th century. The strings are plucked, not struck, as a piano's is.

Husbandry   The care, cultivation, and breeding of crops and animals.

Hydrotherapy   A 19th-century water therapy.

In loco parentis   Acting or done in the place of a parent.

Jumbo   A type of generator used by Edison, named after Jumbo the elephant, a 19th-century circus star.

Lobotomy   A surgical operation involving incision into the prefrontal lobe of the brain. It was formerly used to treat mental illness.

Manumission   Release from slavery.

Memento mori   A Latin phrase that translates to "remember you must die." A memento mori is something that serves as a reminder of death and mortality.

Metrazol therapy   A treatment of schizophrenia used in the 1930s, it induced convulsions.

Millennialism   From *millennium*, Latin for "a thousand years," it is a belief expressed in the Book of Revelation that Christ will establish a one-thousand-year reign of the saints on the earth (the millennium) before the Last Judgment.

Miscegenation   Marriage or cohabitation by persons of different races.

Mollusk   An invertebrate that includes oysters, snails, mussels, and octopuses. They live in aquatic habitats and most have an external shell.

Normal schools   A normal school is an institution created during the 19th century to train high school graduates to be teachers by educating them in the norms of pedagogy and curriculum.

Pancheon   A shallow dish used to store milk while waiting for the cream to rise to the top, also called a setting dish.

Patent   A license issued by the government that confers a right or title for a set period, excluding others from making, using, or selling an invention.

Pennyweight   A pennyweight (dwt) is a unit of mass equal to 24 grains, $\frac{1}{20}$ of a troy ounce, $\frac{1}{240}$ of a troy pound, approximately 0.054857 avoirdupois ounce and exactly 1.55517384 grams.

Percussion   A percussion instrument is a musical instrument that makes sound through being struck or shaken.

Percussion cap   The percussion cap is a type of single-use ignition device for muzzle loading firearms, which allow them to be fired in any weather condition.

Phrenology   The pseudoscience that contends that one's character and intelligence can be deduced from the shape of the head and the bumps on the head.

Physiology   The branch of biology that deals with the normal functions of living organisms and their parts.

Pine tar   Pine tar is a dark, tacky substance produced when heat and pressure are applied to pine wood to decompose it. It has a long history as a wood preservative. It is also used in baseball to enhance the grip of a hitter's bat.

Placer mining   The mining of gold or other minerals in stream bed of alluvial deposits, which are the deposits that are left by the water of rivers or floods.

Platen   The cylindrical roller in a typewriter against which the paper is held, or, on earlier typewriters, the flat plate on which the paper was held.

Polymath   A person of broad knowledge or learning, a "Renaissance man."

Pony beads   Pony beads are plastic or glass beads similar to seed beads but much larger in size.

Populist   A politician who strives to appeal to ordinary people who feel that their concerns are disregarded by established elite groups. The word "Populism" comes from Latin for "the People."

Prohibitionists   People who advocate for the complete banning of all alcoholic drinks. A nationwide constitutional ban on all sale and consumption of alcohol was enforced in the United States from 1920 to 1933.

Propaganda   Information, especially of a biased or misleading nature, used to promote or publicize a particular political cause or point of view.

Proprietary   Used, made, or marketed by one having the exclusive legal right to make the product.

Putti   A representation of naked children, especially cherubs or cupids in Renaissance art. Putti is the plural form; putto is the singular.

Reserve clause   The right of a baseball team owner to maintain control of a player's contract even after their contract had expired, binding that player to a team indefinitely.

Rounders   A game originating in Britain that is considered the antecedent to the American game of baseball.

Sabbatarians   Christians who advocated for keeping Sunday as the Lord's Day, as a day of worship and rest. Sunday blue laws, which are local laws that enforce the closure of all commercial businesses on Sunday, are a modern manifestation of the influence of Puritan Sabbatarians.

Scythe   A tool used for cutting crops such as grass or wheat, with a long curved blade at the end of a long pole attached to which are one or two short handles.

Semaphore   A system of sending messages by holding the arms or two flags or poles in certain positions. It is used today for maritime purposes.

Sitz bath   A small bathtub where a person sits, submerging only the lower part of the body.

Skiff   A shallow, flat-bottomed open boat.

Slanting Gobelin stitch   A common slanted stitch used in embroidery.

Staple   A U-shaped piece of wire or metal with pointed ends for driving into a surface to hold a hook, pin, bolt, wire, or the like. A staple was used on the side of the Conestoga wagon to hold a hook.

Stay   A rigid strip used for stiffening a garment, such as a shirt collar, girdle, or corset.

Strigil   A tool with a curved blade that was used by Ancient Greeks and Romans to scrape off oil and dirt after a bath or after exercise.

Tabloid   A newspaper having pages half the size of those of a standard newspaper and dominated by headlines, photographs, and sensational stories.

Technophile   A lover of technology.

Telegraph   A system for transmitting messages from a distance along a wire, also known as electrical telegraph.

Thresh   To separate grain from the plant.

Tondo   A circular painting or relief.

Tonsorial   Describing the cutting, clipping or trimming hair, or shaving with razors.

Tourniquet   A device (such as a band of rubber) that prevents bleeding or blood flow by compressing blood vessels.

Trachoma   A disease of the eye caused by infection with the bacterium *Chlamydia trachomatis*. It can lead to blindness.

Trammel   An adjustable hook used to vary the height of a pot or kettle, which is cooked over fire. It allows for controlling the heat of the fire and the rate of cooking.

Trepanning   Also known as trepanation, trephination, trephining, or making a burr hole, it is a surgical intervention in which a hole is drilled into the human skull. Often used for relief of bleeding on the brain.

Tryworks   Brick oven furnaces that render oil from whale blubber.

Unitarian   A liberal sect of the Christian Church that believes in one God, not the Trinity.

Velocipede   An early version of the bicycle.

Whatnot   A popular piece of furniture in 19th-century Victorian homes, a whatnot was a version of the French étagère, with multiple shelves used to display a variety of items.

Whelk   Sea snail.

Wove paper   A writing paper with a uniform surface, which is created with wires woven together so that no specific pattern is visible. This new papermaking technique was invented by James Whatman in England in the 18th century. It is still used as the standard papermaking technique today.

SELECTED BIBLIOGRAPHY

For a thorough and complete discussion on the how-tos of researching arti-facts, see the "Selected Bibliography" introduction in Helen Scheumaker's excellent *Artifacts from Modern America* (Greenwood, 2018).

Museum and Library Websites

Museums and libraries are useful sources for research about historical artifacts. Despite restricted budgets, staffs at museums and libraries are increasingly finding the resources to digitize their collections, often add-ing pertinent historical information to accompany the image. Libraries also serve as valuable resources for both their collections and for digitized documents.

Brooklyn Museum
https://www.brooklynmuseum.org/
Carlisle Indian Historical Society
https://carlisleindian.historicalsociety.com/
Chicago History Museum
https://www.chicagohistory.org/
The Cleveland Museum of Art
https://www.clevelandart.org/
Ford's Theatre
https://www.fords.org/
The Henry Ford
https://www.thehenryford.org/
Historic Richmond Town
https://www.historicrichmondtown.org/
Library of Congress
https://www.loc.gov/
Metropolitan Museum of Art
https://www.metmuseum.org/
Minnesota Historical Society
https://www.mnhs.org/

Library of Congress Digital Collections
https://www.loc.gov/collections/
National Archives
https://www.archives.gov/
National Museum of African American History and Culture
https://nmaahc.si.edu/
National Museum of American History
https://americanhistory.si.edu/
National Museum of the American Indian
https://americanindian.si.edu/
New York Historical Society
https://www.nyhistory.org/
New York Public Library
https://www.nypl.org/
Philadelphia Museum of Art
https://philamuseum.org/
Winterthur Museum, Garden, and Library
https://www.winterthur.org/

Useful Online Resources

The 1619 Project
https://www.nytimes.com/interactive/2019/08/14/magazine/1619-america
-slavery.html
Abraham Lincoln Research Site
https://rogerjnorton.com/
American History Research Guide
https://library.si.edu/research/american-history
American Social History Project • Center for Media and Learning
https://ashp.cuny.edu/
Digital History
http://www.digitalhistory.uh.edu/
Documenting the American South
https://docsouth.unc.edu/index.html
Gilder Lehrman Institute of American History
https://www.gilderlehrman.org/
History Matters
http://historymatters.gmu.edu/
Virginia Center for Digital History
http://www.vcdh.virginia.edu/index.php?page=VCDH
UShistory.org
https://www.ushistory.org/

Historical Scholarship

Adams, David Wallace. 1995 [2020]. *Education for Extinction: American Indians and the Boarding School Experience, 1875–1928.* Lawrence: University Press of Kansas.

Adams, Russell B. 1978. *King C. Gillette, the Man and His Wonderful Shaving Device.* Boston: Little, Brown and Co.

Ahlstrom, Sydney E. 2004. *A Religious History of the American People.* New Haven, CT: Yale University Press.

Aikin, Charles S. April 1973. "The Evolution of Cotton Ginning in the Southeastern United States." *Geographical Review*, 63(2): 196–224.

Alford, Terry. 2015. *Fortune's Fool: The Life of John Wilkes Booth.* Oxford; New York: Oxford University Press.

Ambrose, Stephen. 2000. *Nothing Like It in the World: The Men Who Built the Transcontinental Railroad 1863–1869.* New York: Touchstone Books.

Ames, Kenneth L. 1992. *Death in the Dining Room & Other Tales of Victorian Culture.* Philadelphia: Temple University Press.

Ammons, Elizabeth (ed.). 2018. *Uncle Tom's Cabin Norton Critical Edition.* New York; London: W.W. Norton and Co.

Angier, Natalie. 2015. "The Bicycle and the Ride to Modern America." *New York Times.* July 13. Accessed August 20, 2021. https://www.nytimes.com/2015/07/14/science/the-bicycle-and-the-ride-to-modern-america.html.

Ashenburg, Katherine. 2007. *The Dirt on Clean: An Unsanitized History.* New York: North Point Press.

Bain, David H. 1999. *Empire Express: Building the First Transcontinental Railroad.* New York: Penguin Books.

Baker, Kevin. 2016. *America the Ingenious: How a Nation of Dreamers, Immigrants, and Tinkerers Changed the World.* New York: Artisan.

Barth, Edna. *Hearts, Cupids, and Red Roses: The Story of the Valentine Symbols.* New York: Clarion Books.

Blum, Deborah. 2018. *The Poison Squad.* London: Penguin Books.

Bollet, Alfred J. 2002. *Civil War Medicine: Challenges and Triumphs.* Somerville, NJ: Galen.

Brands, H. W. 2002. *The Age of Gold: The California Gold Rush and the New American Dream.* New York: Doubleday.

Burrows, Edwin G., and Mike Wallace. 1999. *Gotham: A History of New York City to 1898.* New York; Oxford: Oxford University Press.

Butler, Jon, Grant Wacker, and Randall Balmer. 2000. *Religion in American Life: A Short History*. Oxford; New York: Oxford University Press.

Carter, Robert A. 2000. *Buffalo Bill Cody: The Man behind the Legend*. New York: John Wiley & Sons.

Cashman, Sean D. 1993. *America in the Gilded Age: From the Death of Lincoln to the Rise of the Theodore Roosevelt*. New York; London: New York University Press.

Casillo, Anthony. 2017. *Typewriters: Iconic Machines from the Golden Age of Mechanical Writing*. San Francisco: Chronicle Books.

Claeys, Gregory, and Lyman T. Sargent. 2017. *The Utopia Reader*. New York: New York University Press.

Clark, Clifford E., Jr. 1986. *The American Family Home: 1800–1960*. Chapel Hill: University of North Carolina Press.

Coates, Ta-Nehisi. 2015. "What This Cruel War Was Over." *The Atlantic*. June 22. https://www.theatlantic.com/politics/archive/2015/06/what-this-cruel-war-was-over/396482/.

Cooper, Grace R. 1976. *The Sewing Machine: Its Invention and Development*. Washington, DC: The Smithsonian Institution Press.

Coski, John M. 2005. *The Confederate Battle Flag: America's Most Embattled Emblem*. Cambridge: Belknap Press of Harvard University.

Cowan, Ruth S. 1983. *More Work for Mother: The Ironies of Household Technology from the Open Hearth to the Microwave*. New York: Basic Books.

Cremin, Lawrence A. 1988. *American Education: The Metropolitan Experience, 1876–1980*. New York: Harper & Row.

Current, Richard N. June 1949. "The Original Typewriter Enterprise 1867–1873." *Wisconsin Magazine of History*, 32(4): 391–407.

Devine, Shauna. 2014. *Learning from the Wounded: The Civil War and the Rise of American Medical Science*. Chapel Hill: University of North Carolina Press.

Dolin, Eric J. 2010. *Fur, Fortune, and Empire: The Epic Story of the Fur Trade in America*. New York: W.W. Norton & Company, Inc.

Douglass, Frederick. 1855. *My Bondage and My Freedom*. New York; Auburn, AL: Miller, Orton and Mulligan.

Elliott, Jock. 2001. *Inventing Christmas: How Our Holiday Came to Be*. New York: Harry N. Abrams.

Fear-Segal, Jacqueline, and Susan D. Rose. 2016. *Carlisle Indian Industrial School*. Lincoln: University of Nebraska Press.

Feder, Norman. 1965. *American Indian Art before 1850*. Denver: Denver Art Museum.

Finnegan, Margaret. 1999. *Selling Suffrage: Consumer Culture and Votes for Women*. New York: Columbia University Press.

Fischer, Claude. 1992. *America Calling: A Social History of the Telephone to 1940*. Berkeley: University of California Press.

Fleming, Candace. 2016. *Presenting Buffalo Bill: The Man Who Invented the Wild West*. New York: Roaring Brook Press.

Florey, Kenneth. 2013. *Women's Suffrage Memorabilia: An Illustrated Historical Study*. Jefferson, NC; London: McFarland & Company, Inc.

Forbes, Bruce D. 2007. *Christmas: A Candid History*. Berkeley: University of California Press.

Forbes, Bruce D. 2015. *America's Favorite Holidays: Candid Histories*. Oakland: University of California Press.

Goldstein, Warren. 1989. *Playing for Keeps: A History of Early Baseball, 20th Anniversary Edition*. Ithaca, NY; London: Cornell University Press.

Gordon-Reed, Annette. 2011. "The Art of Persuasion: Harriet Beecher Stowe's 'Uncle Tom's Cabin.'" *The New Yorker*. June 13. Accessed November 24, 2020. https://www.newyorker.com/magazine/2011/06/13/the-persuader-annette-gordon-reed.

Gray, Charlotte. 2006. *Reluctant Genius: Alexander Graham Bell and the Passion for Invention*. New York: Arcade Publishing.

Greene, Elizabeth B. 2017. *Buildings and Landmarks of 19th Century America: American Society Revealed*. Santa Barbara, CA: Greenwood.

Griffin, Brett. 2019. *Yellow Journalism, Sensationalism, and Circulation Wars*. New York: Cavendish Square.

Grove, Tim. 2014. *A Grizzly in the Mail and Other Adventures in American History*. Lincoln: University of Nebraska Press.

Gura, Philip F. 2017. *Man's Better Angels: Romantic Reformers and the Coming of the Civil War*. Cambridge; London: The Belknap Press of Harvard University Press.

Hardesty, Jared R. 2016. *Unfreedom: Slavery and Dependence in Eighteenth Century Boston*. New York; London: New York University Press.

Harris, Leslie M. 2003. *In the Shadow of Slavery: African Americans in New York City, 1626–1863*. Chicago: University of Chicago Press.

Herkimer County Historical Society. 2019. *The Story of the Typewriter: 1873–1923*. Project Gutenberg Ebook. Accessed October 12, 2020. https://www.gutenberg.org/files/60794/60794-h/60794-h.htm#ch3.

Hess, Stephen, and Sandy Northrop. 1996. *Drawn & Quartered: The History of American Political Cartoons*. Montgomery, AL: Elliott & Clark Publishing.

Hoare, Philip. 2010. *The Whale: In Search of the Giants of the Sea.* New York: Harper Collins.

Hochfelder, David. 2012. *The Telegraph in America, 1832–1920.* Baltimore: Johns Hopkins University Press.

Hofstadter, Richard. 1971. "White Servitude." In *America at 1750: A Social Portrait*, 35–65. New York: Knopf.

Holzer, Harold. 2013. *The Civil War in 50 Objects.* New York: Viking.

Horse Capture, Joseph D., and George P. Horse Capture. 2001. *Beauty, Honor, and Tradition: The Legacy of Plains Indian Shirts.* Minneapolis: Minneapolis Institute of Art.

Isenberg, Nancy. 2016. *White Trash: The 400-Year History of Class in America.* New York: Viking.

Jennings, Chris. 2016. *Paradise Now: The Story of American Utopianism.* New York: Random House.

Keller, Julia. 2008. *Mr. Gatling's Terrible Marvel: The Gun That Changed Everything and the Misunderstood Genius Who Invented It.* New York: Viking Penguin Group.

Khosrova, Elaine. 2016. *Butter: A Rich History.* Chapel Hill, NC: Algonquin Books.

Komline, David. 2020. *The Common School Awakening: Religion and the Transatlantic Roots of American Public Education.* New York: Oxford University Press.

Koomler, Sharon D. 2000. *Shaker Style: Form, Function, and Furniture.* Philadelphia: Running Press Books.

Kotar, S. L., and J. E. Gessler. 2009. *The Steamboat Era.* Jefferson, NC; London: McFarland & Company, Inc.

Krueger, Glee F. 1978. *A Gallery of American Samplers: The Theodore H. Kapnek Collection.* New York: E. P. Dutton, in association with the Museum of American Folk Art.

Kurin, Richard. 2013. *The Smithsonian's History of America in 101 Objects.* New York: Penguin Books.

Kurlansky, Mark. 2007. *The Big Oyster: History on the Half Shell.* New York: Random House Trade Paperbacks.

Levinson, Jeff. 2007. *Mill Girls of Lowell.* Boston: History Compass.

Lobel, Cindy R. 2014. *Urban Appetites: Food and Culture in Nineteenth Century New York.* Chicago: University of Chicago Press.

Loesser, Arthur. 1954. *Men, Women and Pianos: A Social History.* New York: Dover Publications, Inc.

Lord, W. B. 1868 [2007]. *The Corset and the Crinoline: An Illustrated History.* Mineola, NY: Dover Publications.

Manseau, Peter. 2017. *Objects of Devotion: Religion in Early America.* Washington, DC: Smithsonian Books.

Marling, Karal A. *Merry Christmas!* Cambridge, MA: Harvard University Press.

Maxwell-Long, Thomas. 2014. *Daily Life during the California Gold Rush.* Santa Barbara, CA: Greenwood.

McGuane, James. 2013. *The Hunted Whale.* New York; London: W.W. Norton & Co.

McLean, Alice L. 2006. *Cooking in America, 1840–1945.* Westport, CT: Greenwood Press.

McMillen, Sally G. 2008. *Seneca Falls and the Origins of the Women's Rights Movement.* New York: Oxford University Press.

Melville, Herman. 1851. *Moby Dick.* New York: Dover Publications (Reprint).

Minardi, Lisa. 2015. *Drawn with Spirit: Pennsylvania German Fraktur for the Joan and Victor Johnson Collection.* New Haven, CT; London: Yale University Press.

Moore, Tara. 2014. *Christmas: The Sacred to Santa.* London: Reaktion Books.

Nasaw, David. 2000. *The Chief: The Life of William Randolph Hearst.* New York: Houghton Mifflin Harcourt.

Nelson, Elizabeth W. 2004. *Market Sentiments: Middle-Class Market Culture in 19th Century America.* Washington, DC: Smithsonian Books.

Nissenbaum, Stephen. 1996. *The Battle for Christmas.* New York: Vintage Books.

Norton, Roger J. 1996–2019. "Abraham Lincoln's Assassination." Rogerjnorton.com. Accessed April 5, 2021. https://rogerjnorton.com/Lincoln.html.

Oldstone-Moore, Christopher. 2016. *Of Beards and Men: The Revealing History of Facial Hair.* Chicago; London: University of Chicago Press.

Op Den Kamp, Claudy, and Dan Hunter. 2019. *A History of Intellectual Property in 50 Objects.* Cambridge: Cambridge University Press.

Ormsbee, Thomas H. 1952. *Field Guide to American Victorian Furniture.* New York: Bonanza Books.

PBS. American Experience. 2006. "The Gold Rush" (Transcript). November 6. Accessed May 6, 2021. https://www.pbs.org/wgbh/americanexperience/films/goldrush/#transcript.

PBS. American Experience. 2010. "Into the Deep: America, Whaling and the World." Accessed March 24, 2021. https://www.pbs.org/wgbh/americanexperience/films/whaling/.

Peterkin, Allan. 2001. *One Thousand Beards: A Cultural History of Facial Hair*. Vancouver: Arsenal Pulp Press.

Poskett, James. 2019. *Materials of the Mind: Phrenology, Race, and the Global History of Science, 1815–1920*. Chicago; London: University of Chicago Press.

Reid, Carlton. 2015. *Roads Were Not Built for Cars: How Cyclists Were the First to Push for Good Roads & Became the Pioneers of Motoring*. Washington, DC: Island Press.

Richards, Leonard L. 2007. *The California Gold Rush and the Coming of the Civil War*. New York: Vintage Books.

Ring, Betty. 1993. *Girlhood Embroidery: American Samplers& Pictorial Needlework, 1650–1850*. New York: Alfred A. Knopf.

Ritter, Lawrence. 2010. *The Glory of Their Times: The Story of the Early Days of Baseball Told by the Men Who Played It*. New York: Harper Perennial Modern Classics.

Roell, Craig H. 1989. *The Piano in America, 1890–1940*. Chapel Hill: University of North Carolina Press.

Rogers, Molly. 2010. *Delia's Tears*. New Haven, CT: Yale University Press.

Rybczynski, Witold. 1986. *Home: A Short History of an Idea*. New York: Penguin Books.

Sandoval, Hannah. 2017. *The Story of the Invention of the Typewriter 150 Years Later*. Ocala, FL: Atlantic Publishing Group.

Scheumaker, Helen. 2008. *Love Entwined: The Curious History of Hairwork in America*. Philadelphia: University of Pennsylvania Press.

Schlereth, Thomas J. 1991. *Victorian America: Transformations in Everyday Life, 1876–1915*. New York: Harper Perennial.

Schmidt, Leigh E. 1995. *Consumer Rites: The Buying and Selling of American Holidays*. Princeton, NJ: Princeton University Press.

Scull, Andrew. 2015. *Madhouses, Mad-Doctors, and Madmen*. Philadelphia: University of Pennsylvania Press.

Shepard, Barnett. 2008. *Tottenville: The Town the Oyster Built*. New York: Preservation League of Staten Island and Tottenville Historical Society.

Shrimpton, Jayne. 2016. *Victorian Fashion*. Oxford: Shire Publications.

Silverman, Kenneth. 2003. *Lightning Man: The Accursed Life of Samuel F. B. Morse*. New York: Knopf.

Smeins, Linda E. 1999. *Building an American Identity: Pattern Book Homes and Communities, 1870–1900*. Walnut Creek, CA: AltaMira Press.

Smith, Virginia. 2007. *Clean: A History of Personal Hygiene and Purity*. Oxford: Oxford University Press.

Steele, Valerie. 2001. *The Corset: A Cultural History*. New Haven, CT; London: Yale University Press.

Stern, Ellen, and Emily Gwathmey. 1994. *Once Upon a Telephone: An Illustrated Social History*. New York: Harcourt Brace.

Strasser, Susan. 1982. *Never Done: A History of American Housework*. New York: Henry Holt and Company.

Stross, Randall. 2007. *The Wizard of Menlo Park: How Thomas Alva Edison Invented the Modern World*. New York: Crown Publishers.

U.S. Army Corps of Engineers. "A History of Steamboats." Accessed April 22, 2021. https://www.sam.usace.army.mil/Portals/46/docs/recreation/OP-CO/montgomery/pdfs/10thand11th/ahistoryofsteamboats.pdf.

U.S. Department of the Interior. 1996. *Lowell: The Story of an Industrial City*. Washington, DC: Division of Publications, National Park Service.

Warren, Louis S. 2006. *Buffalo Bill's America: William Cody and the Wild West Show*. New York: Alfred A. Knopf.

White, Roger B. 2012. "Covered Wagons and the American Frontier." *National Museum of American History Blog*. October 23. Accessed July 15, 2020. https://americanhistory.si.edu/blog/2012/10/conestoga-wagons-and-the-american-frontier.html.

Williams, Susan. 2006. *Food in the United States, 1820s to 1890*. Westport, CT; London: Greenwood Press.

Wills, Garry. 2006. *Lincoln at Gettysburg: The Words That Remade America*. New York: Simon & Schuster.

Winchell, Mike. 2019. *The Electric War: Edison, Tesla, Westinghouse and the Race to Light the World*. New York: Henry Holt and Company.

Yanni, Carla. 2007. *The Architecture of Madness*. Minneapolis: University of Minnesota Press.

Zinn, Howard. 2005. *A People's History of the United States*. New York: Harper Perennial Modern Classics.

INDEX

ABOUT THE AUTHOR

Elizabeth B. Greene is a freelance writer and former interior designer at the College of Staten Island. She received a bachelor's degree in art history from McGill University in Montreal, where her specialization was modern art and architecture. She attended the Columbia University Historic Preservation Program at the Columbia Graduate School of Architecture, Planning and Preservation. Greene is the author of "Homes in the Gilded Era, 1881–1900" in *The Greenwood Encyclopedia of Homes through American History*, a title that received excellent reviews from a variety of reviewers, including a Booklist Starred Review, and was selected for the 2008 Booklist Editor's Choice List. She is also the author of Greenwood's *Buildings and Landmarks of 19th-Century America: American Society Revealed*, published in 2017, which was rated "Highly Recommended" by *Choice*. In addition, she is the author, with Edward Salo, of Greenwood's *Buildings and Landmarks of 20th- and 21st-Century America: American Society Revealed*, published in 2018.

Lightning Source UK Ltd.
Milton Keynes UK
UKHW032237021222
413231UK00009B/202